The Ultimate Retirement Planning Guide

Retire Like You're On Apollo 13

Brian Keith Moon

This book uses the Apollo 13 mission, which turned a disaster into a success, to illustrate the challenges you face in retirement and how you can succeed even if things go wrong.

Independently published
Publication date: July 21, 2026
ISBN-13: 979-8-3483-3891-6

Here's What's Inside...

Apollo 13

This book is dedicated to the men and women of the Apollo 13 program.

Jim Lovell, John Swigert, and Fred Haise of the Apollo 13 crew,

and those who gave the ultimate sacrifice:

Gus Grissom, Roger Chaffee, and Ed White of Apollo 1.

Acknowledgments

I want to thank my wife, Nery, for her encouragement and support.

My son, Masyn, and my daughter, Xeanne.

I would like to thank my office manager, Mandi Rios, who keeps me in line, and my business partner and partner-in-crime, Mubashir Subhani, RICP, RSSA, and CF2.

I want to thank my long-time friends Keith and Amy Speicher for their encouragement.

I would also like to thank the following people who helped me greatly:

Norman Haug, RSSA

Martha Shedden, CRPC, RSSA

Dwight Rich, CFP, RSSA

David Scranton, CFP

Patrick Walsh, Product Coach

Brett Saddler, Compliance Officer

Peggy Alexander, Medicare Insurance Agent

James Brose

Rick Bates

Marina Watts, Mortgage Loan Officer

Slyvia Suarez

Ed Slott, CPA

Darrel Paulson, CEO

Introduction

"Every community needs a Brian Moon. In fact, we need many of them. These are the people who see a problem and find a solution. They don't give up. They don't accept no." -Lubbock Online Editorial 06/05/2010

"That's the kind of person I am looking for: Someone who is comfortable and believes in who they are, regardless of what people may think. "—Marcus Lemonis, CEO of Camping World and Reality TV personality of The Profit.

If you have $10,000.00 or $10,000,000 dollars, how do you invest that for retirement? There are numerous opinions on the approach you should take. Who should you hire to objectively advise and provide the investments your family needs to save for a stable retirement income? I want to help you wade through all the noise, conflicts of interest, and confusion of investing. I approach this book with two goals:

"To Entertain and Educate!"

I promise not to get into the weeds with complex jargon and philosophical rhetoric to 'prove' to you how smart I am. (Now, you know I am totally going to do that.) I hope to make you laugh and show you how to make the right decisions for you and your family when planning your retirement. But first, allow me to introduce myself and my business partner.

Who We Are

Our firm is Toro Bravo Investment Advisors, LLC, a Texas State Registered Investment Advisor (RIA). My name is Brian Keith Moon, and my business partner is Mubashir Subhani. (He goes by just Subhani since that seems easier for our clients to pronounce.) I have been in the business of selling and advising securities since 2000, when I went to work for a firm named Edward Jones. I received the Ed Jones Prospecting Award for opening 110+ new accounts in my first year. Before that, I was an insurance agent (starting in 1997), selling life, health, long-term care, and annuities. Before that, I was a business owner and participated in ministry in my 20s. (That kept me out of trouble, child support, and jail.) The first company I started was a janitorial service called Moonlite Services.

My experience (Curriculum Vitae or CV for the smart people) is as follows:

- Registered Representative series 24, 7, and 63 (Inactive since 2024). These registrations are your standard stock and bond broker transaction-based providers, allowing me to manage investments on a commission-based compensation.
- Investment Advisor Representative –IAR series 66 Fiduciary fee-based compensation model. (2004)
- Insurance (Life, Health, Disability, & Annuity) licensed since 1997.
- Rang the closing Bell at the NASDAQ on September 20, 2013
- My first Life Insurance job was American General (Captive Life Insurance Company)
- My first DBA as an insurance agent was Astrea Financial Services in 1998
- My first job as a stockbroker was with Edward Jones in 2000
    - Received the Ted Jones Prospecting Award 2001 (110 new accounts in my first year)
- Worked for AIG (Valic Financial Advisors) in 2003
    - Received the Excellent Advisor award in 2004 (Top 10% of the sales force)
- In 2006 I became an independent financial advisor under Institutional Securities Corp-Broker/Dealer & RIA
- Started with BrokersXpress/BXadvisors in 2008 -Independent B/D & RIA
    - No awards just Lucky to be Alive 2008 & 2009
- Moved to SCF Securities -Independent B/D & RIA in 2012
    - Received the Diamond Advisor award from SCF in 2013, 2014, 2015, 2016, and 2017
- Moved to Crown Capital Securities -Independent B/D & RIA in 2018 and served as Office of Supervisory Jurisdiction Principal (OSJ Principal)
    - Received Crown Capital's Diamond Level Advisor award in 2019
- Finalist for Advisor of the Year (Southwest Region) 'Investment News Awards.'[1]

---

[1]The InvestmentNews Awards provide a national platform to recognize the standout work of financial advisors, RIAs, wealth managers, broker-dealers, asset managers, and the service partners who support them. The annual award, Celebrating Excellence in Wealth Management. Finalists and winners will be featured across InvestmentNews and its digital channels, with coverage that reaches one of the most influential audiences in financial advice.

"That's all I have to say about that." —Forrest Gump

The Year the Tech Bubble Popped

Unlike the advisors who came into the 'business' during the 11-year bull market (2009 - 2020), my start was more chaotic. My entry into the securities business was a baptism in fire! After receiving my securities registrations (Series 7 and 63)[2] and completing Edward Jones's new advisor training program, I watched the Dot.Com bubble burst. The NASDAQ lost 76% of its value ($5 Trillion dollars lost!), then I watched in horror as terrorists attacked NYC on 9/11/2001, destroying the Twin Towers. Followed came the telecom crash in 2002. I remember calling an old friend from my hometown in Ohio. I never forget what he said, "Brian, maybe selling stocks isn't a good idea."

I had a slow start at Edward Jones despite being the only one in my class of 100 to take an order for a $100,000 GTE bond paying 7.2% interest. It took me almost 3 years to graduate from Segment 1 to Segment 2. So, in 2003, I moved to AIG/Valic, a company specializing in employer-sponsored retirement plans offered primarily in Universities and K-12. I spent three years there, then started my practice as an Independent Financial Advisor in 2006. In 2007, I completed the coursework and testing for a Certificate in Financial Planning from Boston University.

My goal in becoming an Independent Financial Advisor was to control my business and serve my clients without the conflicts of interest prevalent at the Big Wall Street firms. No more being 'encouraged' or cajoled into offering certain financial products or investments that 'maybe' best for the clients but were, in fact, more profitable to the firm. I was tired of the Big Firms shoving products down clients' throats rather than focusing on customized financial planning to help them reach their specific goals. At one firm where I worked, my income was directly tied to how much I sold of the company's proprietary annuity product. I did not like that conflict of interest.

[2] Disclaimer: My Series 7 and 24 securities licenses have been inactive since January 2024.

I officed for six years on my ranch outside Hale Center, Texas (population 2,200). I traded risky stock and ETF options during that time. I used complex Technical Analysis and Fibonacci ratios to execute buy and sells. I had a very mixed track record with amazing, breathtaking gains (100% average return in 2009 and 45% return in 2010) with incredible volatility. No matter what I did, I could not control the losses that inevitably happened, and I was always one bad trade away from disaster.

These experiences have helped shape my objectivity in managing clients' retirement plans. I have seen the good and bad that the markets have to offer.

"I know both how to be abased, and I know how to abound: everywhere and in all things I am instructed both to be full and to be hungry, both to abound and to suffer need."
—Philippians 4:12 KJV I

In Hale Center, Texas, we built a small (800 sq ft) office nestled between a barn and the horse corral on our 70-acre ranch. We raised a horse, some cattle, and chickens (because fresh eggs are better). We enjoyed the simple country/farm life. My clients who came to see me traveled down a Farm to Market Road to a 1500-foot gravel turn row, passing a cotton crop, to reach my office. This farm community was similar to where I grew up.

I grew up in a farming community in Ohio. My father was a truck driver, and my mother a beautician (it sounds like a country song, but Daddy never went to the pen). As a teenager, I raised pigs, goats, horses, ducks, and chickens on that farm. We sold the pigs when they reached the ideal slaughter weight. We sold chicken and duck eggs, and I actually hand-dug a duck pond on our property! I was raised on hard work and a modest standard of living. We never had a new car, and my first driving lesson was on a tractor. When I sold the pigs, my parents insisted that one was for the family freezer; I repaid my parents for any costs, and the rest was my profit. Hard work and entrepreneurism are the values I carry with me to this day. (I remember calculating my wage per hour for raising the pigs at 25¢.)

In addition to managing money, I have worked in prison ministry and philanthropy. When we moved to our Hale Center ranch in 2006, the local EMS closed. In a small farm community, an ambulance is critical. The nearest hospital was 15 minutes away. Let's do the math. You hurt yourself and call the ambulance. At a minimum, it arrives 18 minutes later. They load you up, taking another 5-20 minutes, then drive 15 minutes to the hospital.

You could be literally dead in that time. In the month that the Hale Center EMS closed, a farmer had a heart attack. The Plainview Ambulance arrived 1 hour later. He arrived at the hospital deceased. This ambulance closure was the only 3rd time in 5 years that Hale Center EMS had shut its doors.

I decided to get involved. The Hale Center EMS had already reopened. I approached the director (Joe Soliz) and asked what was needed to help the organization. They were financially solvent and adequately staffed but needed equipment and a new ambulance. They also needed radios. They still used pagers to be called out in an emergency. Pagers! It was 2007, and they were still using pagers! Why? I asked.

Additionally, their heart monitor was comparable to a Commodore 64 computer. (It was one of the first consumer computers offered in the 1980s.) It had a green screen and three sensors. The heart monitor is a key piece of equipment for an ambulance. Today's heart monitors have color screens alongside 12 sensors+ and can feed information en route to the emergency room.

I decided to run a fundraiser. First, understand that outsiders are NOT trusted in a small Texas town like Hale Center. I had no kinfolk in Hale Center or Texas, for that matter. It was an uphill road as far as people trusting me were concerned. I remember shopping with my wife at the Walmart in Plainview, and an old farmer came up to me and said I wouldn't raise any money in Hale Center. No one liked the EMS because of its history. Now "that" is encouragement!

A further challenge was that Hale Center had 800 families and a population of 2000. Not exactly a deep pool. I presented my ideas to the EMS board of directors. I set a goal of raising $25,000 by reaching out to businesses and individuals. The money would be used to improve the equipment and training, and provide a down payment for an ambulance. After we raise the money, I would apply to FEMA[3] for a grant to buy a new ambulance (because FEMA requires the community to match 5% of the cost). I asked for their blessing to run an official fundraiser, volunteering my time. They voted yes and thanked me for being willing to help.

I learned later that after I left, the entire board started laughing and, yes, laughing. What an idiot this guy was. One of the board members, the elementary school principal, Jackie King, said, "The people of Hale Center are going to eat him alive!" Jackie was the first to congratulate me and say he was wrong!

---

[3] The Federal Emergency Management Agency.

First, I made a fundraising plan. I was not going to have a hot dog cookout or a bake sale. I did the math. I might make a few hundred dollars at most, and it would take a lot of time and work. Most people approach fundraising thinking too small. I remembered this quote:

***"As long as you're going to be thinking anyway, think big." —President Donald Trump*[4]**

I instead leveraged the power of businesses. I sent letters to businesses across the South Plains and Hale Center. (My area was about 50-70 miles around Hale Center.) I proposed that each donation be recognized with an ad in a magazine (that I would produce) and distributed to Hale Center and its neighboring city, Cotton Center. Additionally, a billboard would be erected to recognize contributors further.

I set up contribution levels: Supporter ($199 or less), Silver ($200-$499), Gold ($500 - $999), Platinum ($1,000 - $1,499), and Diamond ($1,500 and over). I saw many $500 and $1,500 checks.

My offer to businesses was to promote and advertise their generosity to the EMS. The contributions slowly came in at first (yes, people were criticizing my efforts). I remember walking into a gift shop in Hale Center. While I spoke to the owner, his wife flew out of the back room like an angry bobcat and told me, "It would be a cold day in hell before she would contribute to my fundraiser!" Yeah, it was that brutal.

The EMS Fundraiser Brochures

As part of the fundraiser, I published 2 40-page brochures (over 2 years) to promote Hale Center and the businesses/individuals that contributed to the Hale Center EMS fundraiser.

These brochures had articles I wrote about people in Hale Center, the local city government, the schools, the police department, and local businesses.

This brochure went to every post office box and was inserted in the Sunday edition of the Plainview Herald newspaper.

There was a local newspaper in town. I wrote an article describing my plan and listed the contributors by order of support level. Some people, like Mayor Gene Carter and the town pharmacists Bob and Tany Brown, were early contributors. So, it was a short list at first. People started seeing friends listed as contributors. That was powerful. Some who openly criticized the

[4] Whether you like or hate him he always followed his own advice.

effort sent funds, I believe, just to be listed in the newspaper each week. Many businesses also sent me checks. Walmart alone gave us $3,000.00 that year and $4,500.00 the next. We received funds from McDonald's, Burger King, State Farm, Vista Bank, Cactus Feeders, Covenant Hospital, and Centennial Bank,[5] with numerous others.

I raised $38,000.00 that year, exceeding the $25,000.00 goal. In the second year, we brought in $47,000.00. I was recognized in 2009 at the Hale Center Chamber of Commerce Annual Banquet for my efforts. The long-time Hale Center resident doctor said,

"Anyone could have told Brian that a fundraiser would not work in Hale Center. Fortunately, he didn't know that." —Doctor Ray Freeman, MD, retired,

After two years of fundraisers, I applied for a FEMA grant and received $118,000.00 to purchase a new state-of-the-art ambulance for a small farm community in Texas. With the help of my ex-wife and staff, I raised $215,000.00 for the Hale Center EMS in total. I did all of this without experience in fundraising, grant writing, or connections in the community. But despite that, we accomplished a lot. After the first fundraiser, I was asked to join the EMS board of directors. I accepted, and I worked on the organization's business plan and other operational issues. The EMS received a monthly operational budget from Hale County. I was asked to give the monthly report to the Commissioners Court for several years, and worked hard to set the processes that helped make the EMS successful for years to come.

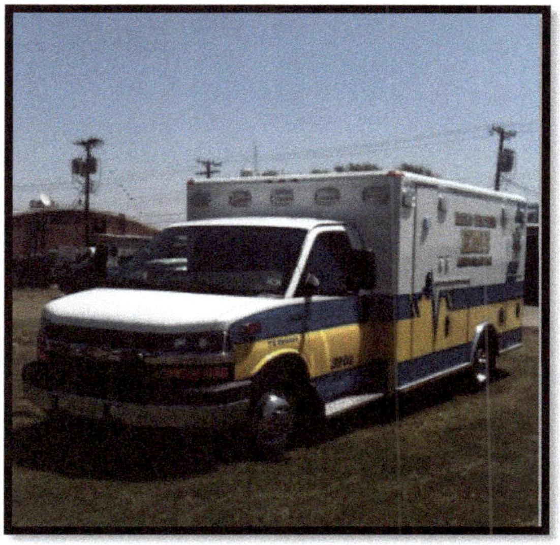

(Pictured here is the ambulance purchased with the grant from FEMA that I applied for with matching funds from the fundraiser I ran.)

I was featured in local News reporting and interviewed by local television. One writer wrote the following:

[5] It was Hale County State Bank at that time.

"Every community needs a Brian Moon. In fact, we need many of them. These are the people who see a problem and find a solution. They don't give up. They don't accept no." -Lubbock Online Editorial.[6]

I know I am tooting my horn here, but I never give up. In 2013, the 'Invest in Others Foundation' nominated me for its Community Service award, which provided the Hale Center EMS with a $5,000 grant check. I traveled to New York City with my wife and son for the gala, and I got to ring the closing bell on the NASDAQ exchange on September 20, 2013. (It was supposed to be the opening bell, but was changed at the last minute.)

---

[6] Lubbockonline.com 2010-06-05 Hale center supporters bring shut down EMS back to life.

The 'Invest in Others' Charitable Foundation made the following statement concerning choosing me as a finalist for the community service award:

"We received hundreds of impressive nominations this year, and narrowing our decision to only three finalists per category proved extremely challenging. Your dedication and leadership inspired us all, and we are moved by your generosity and commitment to improving the lives of others in your community. Finalists were determined by a diverse panel of industry leaders and were selected based on their level of involvement, contributions, and the impact of their efforts."

ward
ith the

Those who donated to my fundraiser felt they got something in return for their support. Here are some letters I received due to my volunteer fundraising efforts:

Ruth Robillard
Owner/Operator
5201 4th St.
Lubbock, TX 79416

i'm lovin' it™ 806.441.6736

December 1, 2008

Mr. Moon,

I would like to tell you what a pleasure it was to work with you on the Hale Center EMS project. It is always important to us to be involved with the surrounding communities and you provided us that opportunity. When I read the letter you sent on the Hale Center EMS project I did not know how you would be able to accomplish so much but you were very impressive. The way you took the time to ask me how I wanted my coupons placed in the brochure. The information you gave me on the location of the billboard and where our logo would be featured. The time you spent afterward to make sure I got a copy of the brochure and asked me my thoughts on the event. It truly was a fabulous event that resulted in heavy return of the coupons that we placed in the brochure. I believe it was a win/win situation for both of us. I will gladly participate in this event again and I would highly recommend participation in the Hale Center EMS event to everyone. Please do not hesitate to call if you ever need anything from your local McDonald's. We are here to help!

Sincerely,

Ruth Robillard

Ruth Robillard
McDonald's Plainview

COUNTY OF HALE

806 839-2142 Office
806 292-5852 Mobile

PLAINVIEW, TEXAS

June 1, 2009

To Whom It May Concern,

I am honored to write a reference letter for Mr. Brian Moon. His character is very outstanding and Hale Center is very fortunate to have him as citizen of the community.

In addition to working and making a living for his own family, Brian finds time to get involved in life around him. He works very hard for community projects. He has a servants' heart. I have admired Brian in his work ethics to raise money for the Hale Center EMS project. He took the task with passion.

Brian is an optimist, and a problem solver. He puts real thought into the task at large, Brian see things that other people would not see. He is meticulous in his work as well as enthusiastic.

I have known Brian for about three years; he has helped me with my income tax the last two years. I really want to express what an unselfish and diligent person he is.

I would highly recommend Brian for any task where integrity, enthusiasm, hard work and trustworthiness are valued.

Sincerely,

Gary Koelder

Gary Koelder
Hale County Commissioner
Precinct 3

June 8, 2009
To Whom It May Concern:

It is my pleasure to introduce Brian Moon to you.

I first met Mr. Moon at the elementary school, where I work as principal. He and his wife were willing volunteers, which is unusual in these times. Later, the city council appointed me to serve on the EMS board. Mr. Moon offered to conduct a fundraiser for the Hale Center EMS. As a new member of our community, he was concerned for the future and stability of our ambulance service. The service had been forced to close two years earlier due to a lack of funds. I was appreciative of his concerns, and made the motion to allow Mr. Moon to proceed with his efforts. After he left our meeting, we all laughed. Fundraisers just do not usually work in Hale Center. People can be rude about the whole process. As a newcomer to the community, he did not know what he was facing.

Obviously, we did not recognize the skills Mr. Moon possesses. Each month, he brought the committee a report on funds committed to the fundraiser. At the end of the fundraising period, Brian Moon had single handedly raised over $35,000 for the Hale Center EMS. Did I mention we live in a very poor rural community? Brian repeated the process this year and raised over $47,000. Our EMS is not only surviving, but also completing desperately needed upgrades. Is Brian Moon an effective fundraiser? In two years, he has proven himself in the small community of Hale Center. What can he accomplish for you?

Sincerely,
Jackie King
806-292-2335
jking@hale-center.k12.tx.us

During this time, I ran my Financial Services firm from my Hale Center ranch. In 2013, my ex-wife and I moved our residence and office to Plainview to be closer to Walmart. (Ok, I think that's funny) So yeah, I had had enough farm life. My epiphany came when I was on a ladder 10ft off the ground, screwing in a piece of tin that was coming loose from the barn. I started thinking, "Hey, don't I make money managing money? Why am I doing this?"

Years later, after my unfortunate divorce, I relocated to Amarillo, Texas, in 2021. (We had already relocated the office to Amarillo in 2019) And in 2022, I married a woman living in the Philippines. Due to the lockdowns and quarantines, I couldn't enter the Philippines, so we flew to Costa Rica to get married, during which we zoomed[7] in for family and friends. Over 100 people watched the wedding remotely. A few months after our wedding, we had a reception in my wife's hometown of Lucena in the Philippines. See the pictures below:

I applied for a marriage visa, and we waited three years for the approval. On August 10th of 2025, my wife and daughter legally immigrated to the USA. In this marriage, I am also adopting a daughter named Xeanne.

Welcome to Amarillo, Texas, my wife and daughter, Nery and Xeanne.

My daughter Xeanne (17) and I at our reception in the Philippines in 2022.

---

[7] Zoom is a video conferencing software that allows large numbers of people to attend meetings remotely via the internet.

Amarillo Police Gift Bags

During COVID, my office put together a gift bag for 150 police officers in Amarillo as a demonstration of support and appreciation. The event was covered by the local news channels 7 and 10. In the picture below, we are presenting the gift bags for the local police. (Which just happened to be the day after police academy graduation.) It was August of 2020, so everyone was still masked up.

Designations RICP, RSSA, & CF2

In addition to my Certificate for Financial Planning from Boston University,[8] I earned the Retirement Income Certified Professional (RICP) designation in April 2026, the Registered Social Security Analyst (RSSA) designation in 2020, and the Certified Financial Fiduciary (CF2) designation in 2021.

I was selected as a finalist for the InvestmentNews Advisor of the Year Award in 2026.

In my professional career, I have sold or advised most of the investments that retail clients use. This includes IPOs, Secondary Offerings, Stocks, Bonds, Mutual Funds, Private Equity, ETFs, Variable Annuities, Options, and other investments. I have much real-life experience and knowledge, which I hope to use to help you.

---

[8] Boston University's certificate program for Financial Planning is not a designation but a university distance learning program. The program is also a qualified prerequisite for the educational requirement of the Certified Financial Planner (CFP) designation.

My Hobbies

I love to cook as an amateur chef. In 2021, I competed in an Iron Chef contest with my country club. I adopted the moniker 'Chef Big Tasty.' (My wife is Tigress) I came in third in that contest. I pulled the salmon as my protein against a ribeye and a filet mignon. In Amarillo, Texas, I had no chance against steak. But the judges liked my crepes and grilled salmon with asparagus.

Several of my clients came to the competition. I enjoy cooking and sharing my creations with family, friends, and clients. This is a hobby since restaurants are awful investments. I have a YouTube channel called, you guessed it, 'Chef Big Tasty'.

I competed in an 'Iron Chef' competition. I placed 3rd. I pulled the salmon against Filet and Ribeye. In Amarillo Texas 3rd place was a miracle!

When we visit the Philippines, my wife, daughter, and I will cook food to give to our neighbors on the street. I once made Biscuits and Gray for over 100 people. The bible says there is more happiness in giving than receiving. The next pictures show this. I also have a video on YouTube, @Chef Big Tasty, of me making egg fried rice in front of my wife's house in Lucena, Philippines. Many times we made food and gave it away on the street. Once I baked a turkey with stuffing, mash potatoes and fresh bread to give away.

How I Met the Kid with the Weird Name

In 2015, I received a call from Dr. Subhani, a client and a neonatologist for the Children's Hospital at Texas Tech. He asked me to intern his son, who was interested in entering the world of finance. The last thing I wanted to do was intern an entitled millennial college kid. So, I told Doctor Subhani, yes, I would love to intern your son!

Doctor Subhani's son, Mubashir, showed up in my office on a Sunday evening in a suit and tie. I had not seen him in casual clothes for almost two years after that. I learned that Mubashir was not an entitled millennial college kid.

He worked as an intern for me while he completed his degrees at Texas Tech in Economics and Political Science (Honors College, Summa Cum Laude). He also did internships in Pakistan for Citibank (derivatives, bonds, foreign exchange trading), data analysis for Jobin (a technology startup in Spain), and agricultural strategy consulting for Bancolombia in Colombia. This helped develop a broad base of knowledge and experience in business. He has also completed the coursework and three exams to earn the Retirement Income Certified Professional (RICP) designation. Did I mention he speaks four languages? Typical overachiever and an excellent Wealth Manager! He is like the smart grandson our clients need.

Large companies like Goldman Sachs and JP Morgan hire this kind of talent straight out of university. I could see his drive and desire to be the best in his field. Mubashir was not interested in working for the big firms as an entry-level newbie. I offered him a job, and he declined. He countered that he would like to be an equal partner. I laughed and laughed and said, "Do you have any money?" Mubashir had money, nearly no debt (or student loans), and a good credit report.

"Are you really in your 20s?" I asked. So, we started a new corporation and a new registered investment advisor firm in the State of Texas. Toro Bravo Investment Advisors, LLC was born.

Mubashir Subhani (everyone calls him by his last name, Subhani, because it is easier to say) was born in Brooklyn, NY, to legal immigrant parents from India and Pakistan, who both became naturalized citizens of the USA. He was eight when his parents moved the family to Amarillo, Texas. Where he was from worried me. I told him, *"Subhani, in Texas, you keep this business of being born in New York City to yourself."*

Subhani was inspired to work in finance through his own family's experiences. His great-grandfather owned one of the largest, most successful printing press companies in Aligarh,

India. What happened to it? From a lack of legacy estate planning measures, those closest to the owner took advantage of him to snatch all of it away from the family when he passed away. That wealth and legacy were gone forever! This story deeply affected Subhani. He decided he wanted to help others manage their wealth smartly and avoid this kind of disaster.

Subhani's father immigrated to the US to finish his medical training and become a Physician Assistant Professor at Texas Tech and the Northwest Texas Hospital NICU. His mother loves cooking, gardening, feeding ducks, and knitting blankets for babies at the hospital.

I like to say that certain people have an 'immigrant attitude.' What do I mean? Per capita, immigrants are most likely to become millionaires and work hard to get there. Likewise, being successful was drilled into Subhani from a young age. He was taught to use all the opportunities that the USA offers. He graduated with an International Baccalaureate degree from Amarillo High School and graduated from Texas Tech Honors College Summa Cum Laude.[9] Subhani is passionate about planning and investing in his clients' best interests. He understands why you should plan now and for the next generation.

Subhani has been a great partner and an intelligent analyst. He is the Head of Research and a Wealth Manager for Toro Bravo. After working with him for 10 years, I feel truly blessed to be partnered with this guy. Working together, we are trying to make a difference for our clients who want unconflicted advice for retirement.

Executive Office Manager - Mandi Rios

I hired Mandi in 2012, a few months before I relocated the office to Plainview Texas from Hale Center. We worked together for 6 years until she quit to move to Canyon, Texas, for family reasons. I stayed in touch, and in 2022, when I lost my office manager in the Amarillo office, I asked her if she wanted to come back.

I always say Mandi is Donna from the series Suits or (depending on the day) Cary from King of Queens. I would characterize our relationship as brother and sister.

[9] With distinction (with reference to college degrees and diplomas). For Texas Tech a grade point average of 3.5 – 3.69 earns the honor of Cum Laude.

We had an argument one time, and I fired her. She responded, “No, I am not fired.” “Really?” I responded, “I just said you are.” “Well, I am not.” Then she went back to work, and I went back to my office to figure out just what happened. I am pretty sure we all work for her.

Her strong suit is taking care of our clients. She is in charge of all the administrative tasks at Toro Bravo, which she does extremely well. She once drove 20 miles in a rare Texas snowstorm to deliver paperwork that a client needed to sign. I was out of town, and though I appreciated the dedication, I told her, “Let’s not risk your life in the future.” After all, she has kids!

I am blessed to have an office manager like Mandi to work for.

Toro Bravo Investment Advisors, LLC & the BBB Torch for Ethics award.

Why the name Toro Bravo for our company? In Spain, it means 'Fighting Bull'. The idea that we are fighting to find bull markets (or to make money) for our clients was the message. We market-tested the name and found some interesting comments. To Texan Hispanic/Mexican folks, they heard 'Mean Bull.' For example, an expression in Spanish says, "Be careful that dog is bravo" or mean. It seemed to resonate positively with everyone of Hispanic heritage we asked. Non-Spanish speaking, on the other hand, heard 'Brave Bull.' So, we had a business name and a bull's head logo. Welcome to Texas!

In 2026, we were privileged to win **the Better Business Bureau Torch for Ethics award.** The award committee liked our approach to business investment advice. Our focus on retirement income, risks, cost, and lifestyle first, with a retirement planning approach before investments are discussed.

I was nominated as a Finalist for the 2026 Advisor of the Year by the Investment News Awards.

Updated Version

This book is the 2026 version that has been updated for the Social Security Fairness Act, the One Big Beautiful Bill, and other tax updates. I made a few other minor changes as well. (ok, a I was nominated as a Finalist for the 2026 Advisor of the Year by the Investment News Awards.

Conclusion

So, here is our short history. Let me tell you what you'll get out of this book. We will talk about retirement planning—the process and the point! The point is to know where you're going before you start investing all willy-nilly. The most important part of the plan is Social Security. As a registered social security analyst, I am qualified to speak on this topic.

Why Apollo 13? They accomplished an amazing feat in recovering from what should have been a fatal accident. Can we engineer success in your retirement? This story inspires what is possible. I wanted a story that relates to retirement planning, and I saw parallels in the Apollo 13 story.

I hope you enjoy it and the practical lessons that will help you successfully retire, even if things go wrong.

My goal is that your planning makes retirement go right! We will discuss retirement plans, developing a checklist, Social Security income, lowering taxes, financial advisors, investments, and everything necessary for retirement. Remember, my goal is to entertain and educate. I aim to make this an easy, fun read that helps you learn how to save and invest more effectively through a Financial Advisor.

Most importantly, this book is written specifically for those <u>nearing and in retirement</u>!

I hope my illustrations help you understand what you must do for a successful retirement launch and mission. If you are looking for stock picks, you got the wrong guy! If you are over 50 and looking to get ready for and to launch your retirement mission, this book will help you do that. Now that you have my background, I know your going to enjoy this book.

I hope to have a positive impact on your retirement mission. So, Retire Like You're on Apollo 13.

Sources in the footnotes

I used readable and available articles as the sources of my research. If you decide to look up more information, I want you to access it easily. I could have referenced academic white papers and research; unfortunately, those sources are gibberish to the average person and may require subscriptions to access. I chose Investopedia as a primary source of information because it is accessible to ordinary people, is free, and is accurate. Investopedia is a reliable guide if you want to know more about investing. They, however, lack opinion and advice. I give that in loads!

The economic and market information has been obtained from published sources. While I believe such sources to be reliable, I do not assume responsibility for the accuracy of such information. You should consult with a financial professional, attorney, or tax professional before acting on any information provided here.

This information is not intended to be used as the primary basis for investment decisions, nor should it be considered as advice designed to meet the specific needs of an individual investor. Some of the information here is my views and opinions, and may conflict with other established sources.

Chapter 1
Preliminary Brief

This book uses the Apollo 13 mission, which turned a disaster into a success, to illustrate the challenges you face in retirement and how you can succeed even if things go wrong.[10]

I started my professional career in finance in 1992 when I completed the H&R Block tax preparation course and worked the tax season, filing tax returns. (I'll never forget the old, retired lawyer handing me a shoebox of receipts and his previous year's tax return. That was fun, and I didn't know I could charge him extra for all the research I had to do.) Then, in 1997, I became an insurance agent for American General Life. I sold life, accident, cancer, and disability insurance. The company sent me out to collect cash from policyholders—yes, you heard correctly, cash. I remember one family leaving the money for their policy under a rock on the front porch next to a wooden rocking chair. I would punch the amount on a portable tablet and print a receipt.

I moved into independent life insurance sales for a year, and then I got hired by Edward Jones. I was baptized in fire as I started my career as a security registered professional in the worst market in 30 years. I saw the 2nd plane crash into the Twin Towers from my Edward Jones office in Lubbock, Texas. That memory is still vivid after over two decades. After three years with Jones, I accepted a financial advisor position with AIG/Valic. They introduced me to group retirement 403b plans at Texas Tech and West Texas A&M University. In 2006, I became an independent financial advisor.

If you can't explain it simply, you don't understand it well enough. —Albert Einstein

[10] My objective in using these stories as an educational device is not intended to criticize or dishonor the great men and women who sacrificed for this history-making accomplishment.

This is Not Your Normal, Boring Financial Planning Book.

This is different from your usual investment financial planning guide. First, no pictures of laughing old people, golden eggs, or DaVinci code graphics. So, let me explain how I got this crazy idea for a book. The year 2008 was challenging for a financial advisor. (The flashback begins) I started my independent firm less than two years after breaking away from the Big Wall Street culture and control to start my own business. I wanted to build something client-centric without the significant Big Wall Street conflicts of interest I was sick of.

I started my independent securities business in 2006; as Murphy's law would have it less than two years later, we saw a massive stock market decline of over 50%, with a blood bath extending to the bond markets. The prevailing attitude among investors was one of no general confidence in the economy or investments. My business was literally on the floor. I didn't lose any clients, but struggled to bring in new clients or new money. Investors were scared to invest or even change their investments, fearing they would miss the recovery after suffering heavy losses.

As a family, we made some difficult financial choices. We stopped eating out, reduced our frivolous expenses, took no vacations, and got very lean financially. My eight-year-old son complained that we didn't go to McDonald's anymore and wanted to call my company to tell them to pay me. It was both funny and sad.

One of my cost-cutting personal finance efforts was to get rid of Direct TV. At the time, we lived on a 70-acre ranch in rural Hale Center, Texas. One of my morning rituals at the time was to watch the morning stock market shows. Since I sent the DirecTV equipment back and didn't have a fancy Apple smartphone yet, I only had an under-the-counter 7" TV/DVD player in my kitchen. (Remember those? I had to fight for mine at a black Friday sale.)

I had 2 DVDs, Apollo 13 starring Tom Hanks and Devil Wears Prada. (We had other DVDs, so don't ask me why I watched those two over and over) Money was tight, and we tightened the belt. I took four paragraphs to tell you I was broke and watched Apollo 13 repeatedly. I am a space buff and found the Apollo 13 story a tremendous American accomplishment. When I felt anxious, I watched Meryl Streep being mean to the cutie pie, Anne Hathaway. Then, back to Apollo 13. (Reading this, I sound like a weirdo.)

But Apollo 13 Blew Up?

Wait, you say, didn't the Apollo 13 blow up? You're right; they barely survived and never landed on the moon. Yes, Apollo 13 has been called "A Successful Failure." The explosion that crippled the spacecraft and ended the dreams of Jim Lovell and Fred Haise to walk on the moon, and also threatened to leave them (plus Jack Seigert) dead in space. The Apollo 13 spacecraft would have been a tomb and a floating remembrance of America's failure for thousands of years.

What NASA's men and women accomplished was a marvel of ingenuity, smart risk-taking, and making decisions on the fly. Remember, they couldn't just turn around and abort when the explosion occurred. They weren't even sure what went wrong until long after landing in the South Pacific Ocean.

They engineered a safe return, landing under enormous uncertainty, time pressure, and risks.

If you want to learn more about Apollo 13, I recommend the movie (you don't have to watch it 30 times, as I did) or Jim Lovell's book Lost Moon. (The movie did take a few liberties with facts for the story.)

In 2019, I started conducting a seminar called "Social Security Questions You Have and Answers You Need. How the Lessons of Apollo 13 Can Help Your Retirement." In that seminar, I compared what was done to save the lives of those brave NASA astronauts to illustrate the challenges you face in retirement. We learn by stories, and I couldn't imagine a more powerful story than Apollo 13. Apollo 13 bounced back from disaster, and this was no easy challenge and could have had a different ending. If you plan to retire in the next 10 - 15 years or are already retired, this book will be worth reading.

"If you are looking for stock-picking tips, you got the wrong guy!"

This book is for pre-retirees and retired persons who have hit the launch button or are preparing to "go for launch" on retirement.

I will discuss the following:

- What is the effectiveness of conventional retirement planning advice?
- The effect of volatility on your retirement accounts.
- We will discuss your stage of life for retirement.
- How to effectively plan for retirement using a checklist.
- The importance of Social Security in your retirement planning.

- Tax Strategies you can employ to add income in retirement.
- How to protect your widow from higher taxes.
- The right investments and philosophy for a successful retirement.
- Understanding your Money Objectives.
- Does it matter if your advisor is a fiduciary?
- How do you not run out of money in retirement?
- How to identify conflicts of interest in your advisor and (more importantly) his firm?
- Choosing the advisor with the right stuff.
- Avoid guest-starring on American Greed.

I hope to help you make the right decisions for a successful retirement. My goal is to make all of this entertaining and educational. I hope to open your eyes to realities in the business of investment advice and planning. Frankly, this book may change how you see retirement and investing. I will tell many jokes and wrap financial planning concepts into the Apollo 13 story. I hope that you enjoy this 'read' while you learn about retirement planning.

Go for Launch' on Your Retirement.

The Apollo 13 astronauts were commander James Lovell (42), lunar module pilot Fred Haise (36), and command module pilot John "Jack" Swigert (38). Swigert was a last-minute addition for Ken Mattingly, who had been exposed to German measles and was bumped from the mission.

APOLLO 13 PORTRAIT

From Left to Right Jim Lovell, John Swigert, Fred Haise. Image credit: NASA

I want to explain a few things about the Apollo 13 mission and spaceship. This will help you to understand the analogies and illustrations in this book. Don't worry; I won't get bogged down in the technical details.

Technical Details

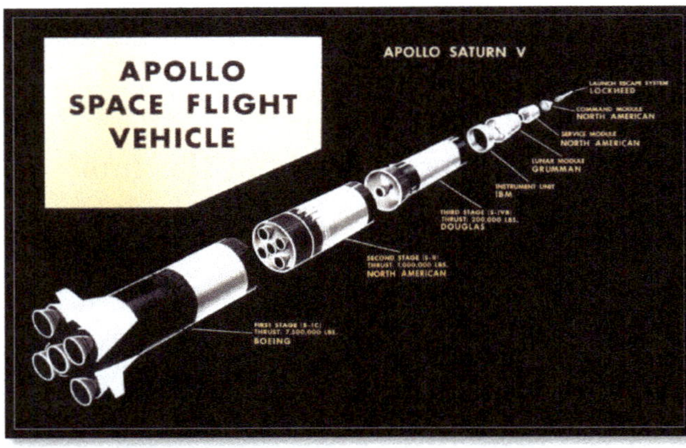

https://www.nasa.gov/history/

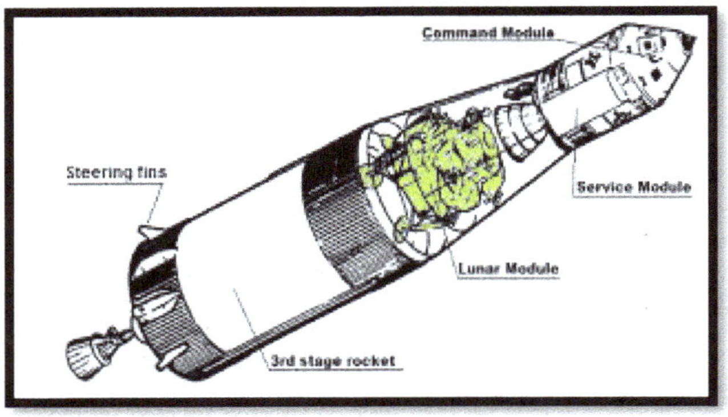

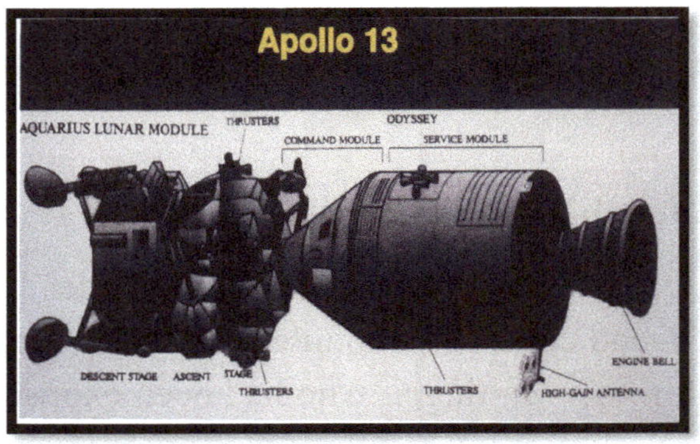

The Apollo 13 spaceship was a long rocket that launched in stages. Each piece broke away as its usefulness ended. Once in space, all that was left were the Service Module (SM), Lunar Excursion Module (LM), and Command Module (CM). They separated the Lunar Module from the Command/Service module and reconnected nose to nose. These maneuvers were practiced in a simulator in Houston for years before the launch.

Once in space, there were three modules left: the Service Module (SM), the Command Module (CM), and the Lunar Exploratory Module (LM or LEM). While joined, the Service and Command modules were called CSM.

The LM (named Aquarius) would have been piloted by Fred Haise and Jim Lovell to land on the Moon, as Apollo 11 did (Edwin "Buzz" Aldrin and Neil Armstrong) or Apollo 12 (Charles "Pete" Conrad and Alan Bean) had done. Lovell and Haise would have climbed into the LM (Lunar Excursion Module, the spider-looking craft), disconnected from the command/service module (named Odyssey), and piloted the LM to land on the moon. After conducting some planned science projects and moonwalking, they would have blasted off the moon's surface to rendezvous with Jack Swigert on Odyssey (Command /Service module or CSM), which was keeping the station in orbit around the moon.

The next part of the mission was to travel back to Earth, separated from the LM, and later disconnect from the service module (letting it float off into space as they did with the Lunar module). Lastly, they would pilot the command module to re-enter Earth's atmosphere and parachute into the Pacific Ocean.

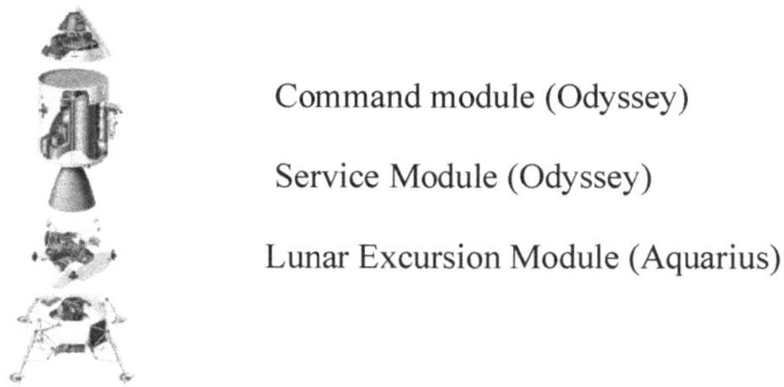

Now, let's talk about the Service Module. Located under the Command Module, it contained the oxygen tanks, main engine rocket motor, fuel, most of the electronics, and other items needed for flight in space. When the oxygen tank exploded, that entire module became unreliable and unusable. They didn't know what was damaged and couldn't take a chance on firing the main engine, as it could explode. To make matters worse, they couldn't see the problem inside the ship. They could see what was damaged only after separating and taking the pictures below.

Odyssey's damaged service module, as seen from the Apollo Lunar Module Aquarius, hours before reentry. -Source NASA

The Command Module (sitting above the service module and equipped with oxygen and batteries) had to be completely shut down to conserve power and oxygen for re-entry. They used the spider-looking LM as a lifeboat until re-entry, when they jettisoned it into space. On April

17th, they splashed down in just the command module. The LM was built for two astronauts, not three, so it was definitely tight quarters.

> **Flight controllers** work at computer consoles and use telemetry to monitor various technical aspects of a space mission in real-time. Each controller is an expert in a specific area and constantly communicates with additional experts in the "back room." The flight director, who leads the flight controllers, monitors the activities of a team of flight controllers and has overall responsibility for success and safety.
> -Wikipedia Flight Controller 2024

Flight control in Houston wanted to do a 'direct abort,' turn around, and go back after the accident, but there had been an explosion in the SM, and they had no idea if starting the engines in the service module would end the mission in a big boom. Not good, obviously. So, they did a 'free return trajectory' by allowing their momentum plus using the Aquarius engines (LM) for course adjustments to go around the moon and back to Earth again. This added five days to the mission.

They were using this equipment in ways that were never intended. You don't go to space and say, "Hey, y'all, hold my beer." But they made 'hold my beer' decisions as they used the LM's engine to make course corrections by aligning the Earth in the side window. It is a definite "Hey y'all, watch what my Ford truck can do!" type of plan. *But it worked because they simulated their plans at Houston's mission control before trying it in space.*

Aquarius (LM) was now a lifeboat whose engine was intended to land on the moon. It was now being used to do course corrections. The command module (which had batteries and oxygen supplies) had to be completely turned off to conserve its resources for reentry. (Remember, turning off means there is no heat or oxygen. The Aquarius, which was built for 2, was doing that now.)

The crew of Apollo 13 had so many issues to resolve. They previously developed procedures to deal with all crises that could happen so they could respond quickly. But new problems that weren't once considered were cropping up. Like the cloud of debris that blocked their view and made it difficult to navigate. Why was this a problem? They needed to hit a tiny Earth re-entry window, or they would bounce right out of the atmosphere. Because it was space, the explosion's debris was traveling with them. Mission control tested re-entry procedures to ensure they would work. They weren't just 'holding on' until the ship returned to Earth.

The Tiger team at mission control had to work out every problem on Apollo 13 and tested it in the simulators in Houston.

This story has a happy ending, as Apollo 13 returned to Earth with no crew losses. No matter what the market throws at you, I want the same result for your retirement. Can we develop and build a ship and mission that sees you through retirement, no matter what happens? We will talk about developing your own 'procedures' for a successful retirement mission.

So, if you're ready, this preliminary brief is over; it's time to proceed to "*Pre-Launch—The 120-Page Plan.*"

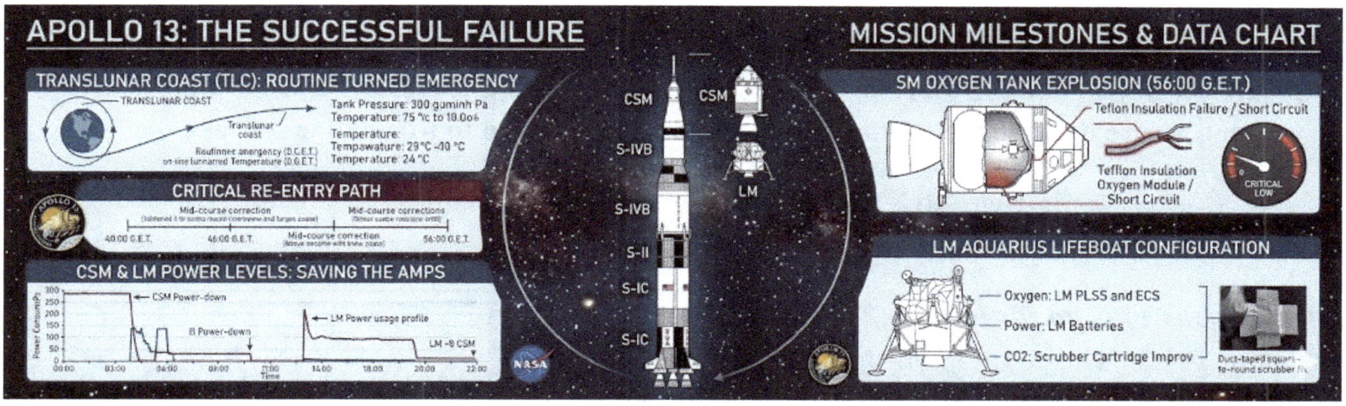

Chapter 2
Pre-Launch 'The 120-page Plan'

"We choose to go to the Moon. We go to the Moon in this decade and do other things, NOT BECAUSE THEY ARE EASY BUT BECAUSE THEY ARE HARD because that goal will serve to organize and measure the best of our energies and skills because that challenge is the one we are willing to accept, one we are unwilling to postpone, and one which we intend to win, and the others, too."

- JF Kennedy's address at Rice University September 12, 1962.

Source: NASA

Mission control is go for launch," said the flight in Houston, Texas. The countdown started, and years of preparation hinged on this moment. The rockets ignited, and the giant Saturn 5 rocket exploded in a controlled fury, pushing the Apollo 13 spacecraft into space. One engine glitched during launch, but it was a beauty to see otherwise, and a successful launch.

Think about it: your retirement is the same! You are so ready to hit "go for launch!" You have worked and saved for years and are now prepared to do this. Sometimes, you are over the office drama or have become burned out on the job or business. Maybe you have a retirement party at work, and everyone says they will miss you. Your boss jokes that you weren't doing anything anyway, so why leave? (You are thinking, why indeed).

Before you hit go for launch, you need to run through the retirement launch checklist (see Chapter 3).

"Retirement is essential to get right. And you get one chance to get it right!"

The Apollo program ran simulations on every conceivable problem they could encounter and a procedure to handle it. (I will speak of what procedures you have for risks in retirement, often in this book).

Some economic or investment risks could delay or cancel 'retirement launch day.'

I have seen folks delay retirement due to market crashes, income shortfalls, penalized Social Security benefits, or having to re-enter the workforce after retirement.

Don't let this happen to you!

Running simulations and retirement stress test scenarios will help you to make measured and reasoned retirement decisions. Improving your retirement mission success.

Remember, Apollo 1

"Apollo 1 caught on fire during a plugs-out test on February 21, 1967. The astronauts were incinerated in minutes. The fire cost the lives of **Gus Grissom, Roger Chaffee, and Ed White (heroes pictured here)** because of the incorrect design and engineering of the spacecraft.

The review board identified the following factors as contributing to the accident:[11]

- An ignition source most probably related to "vulnerable wiring carrying spacecraft power" and "vulnerable plumbing carrying a combustible and corrosive coolant."
- A pure oxygen atmosphere at higher than atmospheric pressure
- A cabin sealed with a hatch cover that could not be quickly removed at high-pressure
- An extensive distribution of combustible materials in the cabin
- Inadequate emergency preparedness (rescue or medical assistance and crew escape)

Very smart people designed and built the Apollo 1 spacecraft. But it took this tragic accident to see the inadequacy of the designs. A legendary NASA astronaut (Apollo 1 backup pilot) said before the tragedy,

"There's nothing wrong with this ship that I can point to, but it just makes me uncomfortable. Something about it just doesn't ring right."[12]
—Command Pilot Wally Schirra describing Apollo 1.

Have you had an uncomfortable feeling about your investments? When you voice your concerns, what do you hear from the Big Wall Street community, i.e., your financial broker? Buy and hold long-term because the market always performs best over time. It's the Warren Buffett way. Time in the market is opposed to timing the market. But like Wally Schirra, who

---

[11] Quoted from Wikipedia.org Apollo 1; reference Apollo 1 -The Fire January 27, 1967, Apollo by the numbers a Statistical Reference.
[12] Lost Moon -Jim Lovell & Jeffery Kluger

felt that Apollo 1 was off somehow, you might feel the same about the investments that will provide your retirement lifestyle.

It took three brave astronaut deaths to change the Apollo program's engineering approach to spaceship design. Why am I talking about this disaster? The financial planning world has its share of Apollo 1-style research that is promoted to assure you that their offerings will have a high probability of success. We have had two market crashes (2000-2003, 2008-2009) that have been the equivalent of Apollo 1.

This is the purpose of a retirement plan: to assure you that your retirement is adequately thought out and based on facts, data, and investment recommendations, that withdrawals will be sustainable for the risk level you are comfortable with, and that they will last for your entire retirement mission.

I contend that many retirement plans are Apollo 1 designs.

"Nearly two-thirds (63%) of non-retirees said they fear running out of money more than death, versus less than half (46%) of retired respondents.[13]

Your mission success goal is <u>not to run out of money</u> in retirement.

You hire a Financial Planner (a Fiduciary, no less) with an impressive designation[14] and a graduate from an impressive university to help you 'plan.' retirement. He/she does an exhaustive review of your finances and assets and hands you a comb-bound 120-page Plan.[15] Ka Boom! As it hits the conference table. Your planner reviews it with you and your wife. Page after page of boring data and statistics. But you're hungry and want to get out of there. So, you say, "OK, Uncle,[16] invest my money." You feel that you have planned and planned well. You scored 90 and have a 30-year average return of 6.5% with a 4% withdrawal rate. It makes sense. You are assured growth in your distributions means you will get inflation increases. That's good. You

[13] Source: "New 2022 Retirement Risk Readiness Study from Allianz Life Insurance Company of North America (Allianz Life)."

[14] Investopedia.com -Financial certifications, aka financial designations, are credentials that investment and financial industry professionals' use. Represented by a trio or duo of letters after a name, they indicate a degree of education/training and specialization on the part of the individual

[15] The 120 Plan is an exaggeration intended for humor. Most financial plans I used to produce were indeed many, many pages.

[16] When we were kids, we would pin each other to the ground until he said, Uncle! Not sure where this came from.

are not falling for a random salesman of financial products. You have a Fiduciary Financial Planner, just like the financial website said.

Every broker/Advisor touts a 'Plan.' Informed clients have a planner rather than a broker. As I will explain,

The words 'fiduciary and plan' do not assure anything.

"Everybody has a plan until they get punched in the mouth," Mike Tyson said before his fight with Evander Holyfield.

I ask you, were Apollo 1 engineers uneducated idiots? No, they were very smart from the best universities. Did the contractor who built the spacecraft cut corners? No, quality of workmanship was not an issue. Did the astronauts have faulty procedures? Again, no. (Lack of emergency preparedness was cited as an issue, but no emergency procedure would have saved the astronauts.) Later, spacecraft designs corrected all these issues and learned how to better foresee future mistakes. They learned how to view risk. Apollo 13 was almost a disaster as well. Still, American on-the-fly ingenuity and engineering saved the lives of the astronauts.

There is plenty of poor engineering in the Financial Planning industry. Nowadays, nearly everyone is a Fiduciary, but it doesn't mean your retirement will succeed. Most investors worry (as they should) about conflicts of interest and bias in securities advice and offers. The word is out that a fiduciary is legally obligated to operate in your best interest at all times. I want to ask you, do you think by saying the words 'I am a Fiduciary' you are guaranteed not to get bad advice that helps the advisor more than you?

Most financial planning is intended to instill confidence in investment recommendations. The riskier the plan, the higher the advisory fee (this is where the 'Fiduciary' makes money). If the retirement plan 'proves' a successful retirement with ponies, rock candy, and rainbows then a 1.5% fee with a 1% sub manager fee is worth it![17]

Let's discuss some data sets commonly used to provide misleading or risky advice. Is this really a problem, you ask?

A recent Dalbar study (20 years ending on December 31, 2019) showed that US stock market return came in at an annualized 6.06%, and investor returns at 4.25%[18]

---

[17] Yes sarcasm. I wish I didn't have to footnote my jokes.

[18] Source: Dalbar, Inc. "2020 QAIB Report." Since 1994, DALBAR's Quantitative Analysis of Investor Behavior (QAIB) has measured the effects of investor decisions to buy, sell, and switch into and out of mutual funds over short and long-term timeframes. These effects are measured from the perspective of the investor and do not represent the

Why are investors performing so badly compared to the averages in the stock market? Did the 120-page Fiduciary Plan fail? According to the Dalbar study, "To the extent that it exists at all, most of it (all of it?) is created by poor decisions via the majority of investors."[19]

Who is this person that Dalbar is referring to? You? Being part of the vast unwashed rubes[20] that are messing up the stock markets? Wait, the last I saw, most investors depended on the advice of Financial Advisors to invest, and they typically hold their investments even when there are losses, listening to the advice of said Advisors. The 'poor decisions' made by investors are often based on the professional financial industry of advisors, planners, and brokers. It is said that the Hedge Funds and Big Wall Street Institutions set the direction for the markets. These are sharp and savvy guys. Are these ones making poor decisions? Let us look at some of the advice from the 120-page 'Plan' and then talk about how you can better learn from these bad Apollo 1 designs. First, I ask you, does a financial plan increase your retirement success?

The Conflicts of Interest

Many advisors and their firm's <u>entire revenue may depend</u> on their clients investing in the stock markets, certain proprietary products[21], or mutual funds. An economist and former Goldman Sachs strategist, Abby Cohen, once said, "Goldman Sachs gets paid 3x more on equity mutual funds over bond mutual funds. Big Wall Street has numerous conflicts of interest regarding the advice it offers. Advisors may use 'financial data' that supports the investments or strategies they recommend. This is not always a conspiracy plot against you. Your advisor may *believe* that growth investments will be in your best interest in the long term. He may view statistics as data-based 'proof' of this advice. Let us consider some elements of the financial plan.

"Lies, damned lies, and statistics" —Mark Twain

Monte Carlo Simulations/Analysis

We ran a TV commercial on Super Bowl LV in 2021. (It didn't run nationwide, just in the local Amarillo, Texas market) The graphics we used in the commercial was based on Monte

---

performance of the investments themselves. The results consistently show that the average investor earns less – in many cases, much less – than mutual fund performance reports would suggest."
www.dalbar.com/productsAndServices/QAIB

[19] Capitalspectator.com/investor-returns-vs-market-returns-the-failure-endures/

[20] Rube -a country bumpkin: Source Oxford Languages

[21] A proprietary product could be a mutual fund, ETF, annuity or another type of investment that is designed by the institution or broker who offers or advices your accounts. Since they generate or share in the revenue of the product, it can be a conflict of interest and other issues that work against your interest. See Mutual Funds: Brand Names Vs. House Brands at Investopedia.com

Carlo simulation. (Go to our webpage to see it.) This is common and often focused on as key data in your planning. The academics love Monti Carlo because it is hard to explain. You know, I am not going to say nice things about Monte Carlo, but I have to admit that I used it for over 20 years of my professional retirement plans. We have discarded these statistics that do little to give you actual retirement success and recommend you disregard them as well.

"I'm not a fan of financial plans that use straight-line projections or Monte Carlo risk analysis to support investment proposals. Here's why: They can lull people into a false sense of security or lead them to believe that the stock market is the answer for all of life's potential calamities."
—Timothy Barrett Trust Counsel August 14, 2019[22] Kiplinger.com

The name "Monte Carlo" is based on a gambling city in Monaco. (Lovely, right?) The calculation uses hundreds of market scenarios to calculate your probability of success. The way it is used (by most planners/advisors) is like this;

Your Financial Planner says, "Your current portfolio has a 29% chance of success; however, make the changes we recommend, and the probability of success will increase to 90%, or you can run out of money and move in with your kids, penniless and poor. Investing with us will reduce the chance, to only 10% chance, that you will have to live in a box on the street or with your kids, annoying them until you die."

"Well, sign us up then! I like increasing my chances of not being homeless!" you say.

Are we supposed to be impressed with a 1 out of 10 failed mission potential?

Doesn't that *actually* suck? But wait, there is more. Monte Carlo is assuming or not accounting for a lot of variables that may change (over a 20 to 40-year retirement), like the following: when you die, taxes, technology changes, natural, geo-political, health, healthcare, rise of AI enslaving all of us in salt mines, and so on.

But there is a Black Swan

---

[22] Kiplinger.com/article/retirement/t064-c032-s014-why-financial-adviser-hates-monte-carlo-analysis Timothy Barrett Educational and Professional description- Kiplinger.com/author/timothy-barrett-trust-counsel

This scoring, called Monte Carlo, assumes a perfectly efficient market. As Black Swans have proven (Black Swans are events that aren't supposed to happen and do anyway), a formula cannot possibly be relied on. Monte Carlo is in every financial planning software I have seen. (Read the disclosures accompanying the Monte Carlo page in the plan. It pretty much warns you not to trust it.)

Consider that, if you have $1 in your account at the end of your life, Monte Carlo sees that as a success. We are guessing how long you will live. If we projected you would live to 90, what would happen if you lived to be 95? The formula didn't account for that, so you better ring up the Kevorkian Center after your 90th birthday.

"If you can tell me the <u>date of your death</u>, I can build a bulletproof retirement plan,"
— Bob Powell, CFP & Financial Journalist.

> Let's go back to the 90% probability.
>
> ***"Would you board an airplane if 1 out of 10 crashed?"***
>
> Convincing you that this batch of investments has 'better' probabilities is asking for a Black Swan party in your retirement. By the way, NASA would never launch with a 10% failure potential! Entering a portfolio with those odds doesn't make any sense.

NASA's unmanned Antares rocket explodes on launch (2014)

It is Stating the Obvious.

If I were to look at a plan with a low Monte Carlo score, the problems would be obvious, and I wouldn't need Monte to tell me. For example, guess what happens if you distribute 10% per year from your retirement?

Depending on your investment performance, you'll run out of money in 11-14 years, which is less time if you have a losing stock market year. That is simple math. Thank you, 120-page Plan; I couldn't possibly figure that out.

"If an advisor uses Monte Carlo to analyze your retirement, don't walk but run from him"
—David Scranton, CFA, CFP, CLU, ChFC,
best-selling author and founder of 'Sound Income Strategies'

Pfau /Young Study - The Dangers of Monte Carlo Simulations

"In reality, no rational person spends their last dollar and then declares bankruptcy."

In 2023, Ph.D. economist Wade Pfau and Massimo Young CFA* did a study entitled "The Dangers of Monte Carlo Simulations." Allow me to quote Laurence Kotlikoff, Ph.D. (Boston University), describing Monte Carlo simulations of portfolio survival rates:

"These survival rates determine whether a proposed investment strategy is viewed as safe. Safe, in this context, means having an 80 percent or higher probability of a client sustaining their retirement-spending target. The residual 20 percent potential failure rate? That's the probability the client goes broke, whether in the near term, mid-retirement, or closer to the end of life. No economists would view a one-in-five chance of insolvency as "safe," but this is conventional planning's "fiduciary" standard."—Advisorpedia.com

Kotlikoff concludes his devastating critique of financial planning this way. "The Wade Pfau and Massimo Young (or PY) study doesn't directly object to conventional planning's methodology. Instead, it shows that conventional planning, as implemented in practice, is dangerous. It entails massive extra risk that no one had previously recognized. In clarifying this risk, PY reinforces the view of mainstream economics: Conventional Financial Planning is Unsafe at any Speed."

Wade Pfau said the following on using Monti Carlo in Retirement Planning:

"Monte Carlo simulations create a false sense of security... they produce vastly differing results depending upon the firm a client may be meeting with. Exposing Monte Carlo as unscientific and arbitrary will lead to more investors enjoying better financial outcomes."

"It is virtually malpractice to fail to protect [constrained] retirees against risks that can reduce or even wipe out their incomes... nothing in a Monte Carlo simulation guarantees the continuation of any retiree's income."

"Probability-based retirement income strategies are highly sensitive to the capital market assumptions used... Seemingly small changes in those assumptions can mean the difference between projecting a comfortable lifestyle and financial ruin."

*CFA – Chartered Financial Analyst, a globally recognized designation provided through the CFA Institute. "Candidates are required to pass three levels of exams covering areas such as accounting, economics, ethics, money management, and security analysis." —Investopedia.com

There is a lot of criticism for Monte Carlo analysis, but did you notice the quote I started with? To quote the quote about Monte Carlo,

"They can lull people into a false sense of security or lead them to believe that the stock market is the answer for all of life's potential calamities."[23]

"Monte Carlo does not plan for Armageddon or even Covid... they should not be the final judge of strategies." —Harold Evensky[24]

Monte Carlo cannot, and does not, prove the Advisor's recommendations (usually in the stock market) are safe or sustainable. Many things can happen that Monte Carlo can't account for. Here are some examples:

- Did you ever think terrorists would destroy our largest buildings in NYC?
- Did you think that real estate would crash and nearly take the whole US banking system with it?
- Did you think a virus would kill millions of people worldwide and force you to stay home for almost a year?

Monte Carlo analysis is guessing on a gamble.

Monte Carlo is based on Math, so it has to be true.[25]

Average Returns?

Are returns ever average? The S&P 500 index 'averaged' 6.09% from 2000-2019. Let's say you need 4% income from your account. Everything thing is fine, right? 6.09% (average annual return) - 4% (distribution) leaves you with 2.09% of the excess return in your account, which is good because that gives you a rising income to keep up with inflation, but hold on.

Have you ever gotten an average market return? The markets are volatile; you're up, then you're down. It's often called a roller coaster. Look at the Market History chart (illustration 2.2). Do you see consistent average market returns? You don't get an 'average rate of return ever!' You instead get messy ups and downs. You are told that the solution is to buy and hold. Buy quality investments and ride through all the volatility. Let me destroy that non-logic.

---

23 Kiplinger.com/article/retirement/t064-c032-s014-why-financial-adviser-hates-monte-carlo-analysis.

24 The "Wealth Management" Pioneer: He is credited with popularizing the term "Wealth Management"

25 This and similar statements following are sarcasm.

The Effect of Volatility on Your Retirement

Let's say you lost 30% in a bad market year. (For context, the S&P 500 suffered a 37% loss in 2008.) You need to gain +43% to get back to where you were, provided you do not take withdrawals! Remember, this loss could be 2 or 3 years in the making.

Illustration 2.1

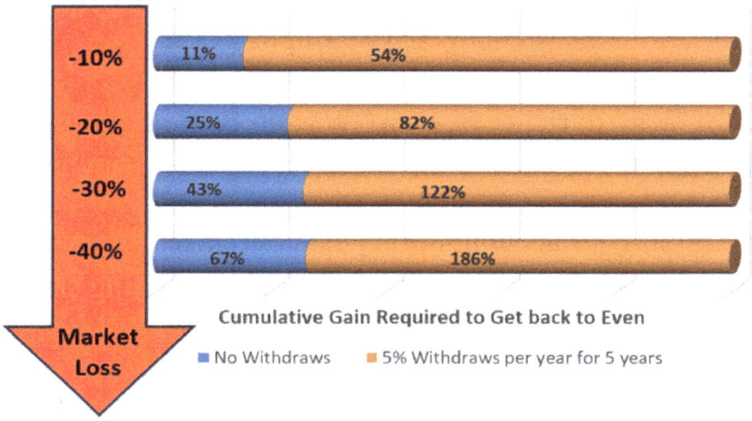

Since all down markets recover every time, simply wait, right? The recovery could be another 2-4 years. But what if you took a 5% withdrawal from your account each year (for retirement income because you're retired) while you wait? What happens then? Consider this:

☆ ***After a 30% loss, if you continue to withdraw 5% annually, you will need 122% total return or an average 24% annual return over five years to get back to even!***

Wow, let that sink in. Earning 122% in 5 years is Ponzi scheme money. This is why so many retirees reduce their income and lifestyle during retirement! Instead of spending their retirement savings after account losses, they reduce their spending. So, you stop eating out or disengage from friends and family because you don't have the money.

Ladies' lunch and golf time are also canceled, which is sad. Have you seen this happen to someone retired? Did you assume they were getting old? It may have been for financial reasons. Then there are medical bills. The fear of not having enough money for doctors and prescriptions causes money concerns and induces sacrifices.

It's like you're on Apollo 13. After the explosion, the astronauts on Apollo 13 (Lovell, Hayes, and Seigert) sat in a cold and dark spacecraft. They couldn't use the power because they were unsure how much energy they had to re-enter the earth's atmosphere. They ate frozen food and rationed water.

That is no way to retire! Go back to illustration 2.1 for a moment. Do you understand that *+24% annual returns* (122% total) for five years are not likely to happen? Now, notice the following chart. Let us assume you take 4% out and no fees on 1 million dollars (Imagine I said that like Dr. Evil[26]).

The Faith-Based Church of Buy and Hold

"Holy Congregation, join me in prayer. May buy and hold, bless you all of your days. Thank you, Lord, Amen."

"Buy and Hold is the highway to riches heaven. Warren Buffett, our prophet and savior, has shown us the way.[27] If the Market goes down, all you need is faith in buy and hold."

Buy and Hold works well in your accumulation years but differs from your distribution years. If you're taking income, how do you hold it? Surely not by selling shares! That's the opposite of hold. Too often, *this is the Plan* when markets fall. You call your broker, and he says, "Follow the wisdom of buy and hold, and you will beat the market." What? Losing money is not a plan that makes any sense; if you are taking withdrawals, that is *not* holding. See illustration 2.1 for what happens when you take withdrawals after a market crash.

"I think buy and hold is a crock of s." —Mark Cuban[28]***

The 4% Rule

In 1994, a financial advisor (William Bengen) published a paper called 'Determining Withdraw Rates Using Historical Data' in the Journal of Financial Planning. He found that retirees could spend 4% of their retirement and adjust that for inflation in the following years. Bergen assumed a portfolio of 50% stock market and 50% bonds. His study revealed that all portfolios lasted at least 35 years. (at a 3% withdrawal rate, the portfolio lasted 50 years)[29] There is much discussion on whether this rule is valid. It is not.

This popularized research justified retirees to consider growth investments in their portfolios for the first time. Before, it was a foregone conclusion that you would use bonds for retirement income. Now, 'research' said that equities (stocks) were safe for retirement planning. The 90's saw the rise of retail investors entering the stock market.

---

[26] Dr. Evil is a fictional character from the Austin Powers movies, played by Mike Myers.
[27] Yes, more sarcasm.
[28] YahooFinance.com 'Diversification? That's For Idiots' Mark Cuban Slams Warren Buffett's Investment Strategy: 'I Think Buy And Hold Is A Crock' — Who's Right? By Jeannine Mancini June 17, 2024
[29] "What Is The 4% Rule For Retirement Withdrawals?" By Rob Berger Forbes Advisor

The bull market that spanned 2009 -2020 had high growth rates and low bond yields. In this period, a growth stock portfolio was great! But not in most other time periods. If your retirement is 20-40 years, the 'other' time periods where you see significant declines matter.

Sequence of Returns Risk

Then there is the issue of the Sequence of Returns risk. Here is how this works: If you have two or three years of negative returns while taking withdrawals, it can cause a death spiral in your portfolio that you can't recover from. 'Experts have recommended a 60/40 portfolio (with 60% stocks and 40% bonds). Still, some have challenged the validity of this long-term strategy if growth rates drop.

And there is the rub. We don't know what the future looks like for stocks and bonds. I would have never predicted we would have over 13 years of nearly 0% fed rates before it happened. Risking your future on an arbitrary percentage (4% rule) doesn't make sense. Do you want proof? Again, look at illustration 2.1. There is your 4% rule.

Suzi Orman*[30] said, *"Do not use the 4% rule on any level." While promoting 3% as safe.

"The 4% rule is blind to the new reality of what you experience as a retiree."
—Dr. Michael Fink, PhD, CFP

And More Research is being published on the 4% Rule.

"Three Morningstar researchers found that the 4% rule may "no longer be feasible."

Christine Benz, Jeff Ptak, and John Rekenthaler are the authors of "The State of Retirement Income: Safe Withdrawal Rates."[31] They further stated, "Morningstar estimates that the standard rule of thumb should be lowered to 3.3% from 4%," they say in the paper." Again, see illustration 2.2 (below) on how well the 4% worked in 2000 -2013.

"For wisdom is a protection just as money is a protection, but the advantage of knowledge is this: Wisdom preserves the life of its owner." -Ecclesiastes 7:12 NWT

---

[30] Source: Suze Orman slams the 4% retirement rule as 'very dangerous' — while its creator Bill Bengen now says it's too conservative. What's the new golden number for your golden years? -by Bethan Moorcraft.
[31] Think Advisor November 16, 2021: "4% rule is dead."

Your Oxygen Tank Explosion

When Jack Swigert hit the switch to stir the oxygen tanks, a fault caused them to explode, damaging the spacecraft and changing the mission. The Moon landing was canceled. Making history was canceled. Now the mission was safe recovery of Jim Lovell, Fred Haise, and Jack Swigert. The mission went from historic exploration of the Moon to survival. Is there an event in your retirement that could cause you to cancel golf outings, ladies' lunches, gifts to the grandchildren, or travel plans in your retirement? The oxygen tank explosion changed the Apollo 13 mission.

What oxygen tank explosion event could change yours?

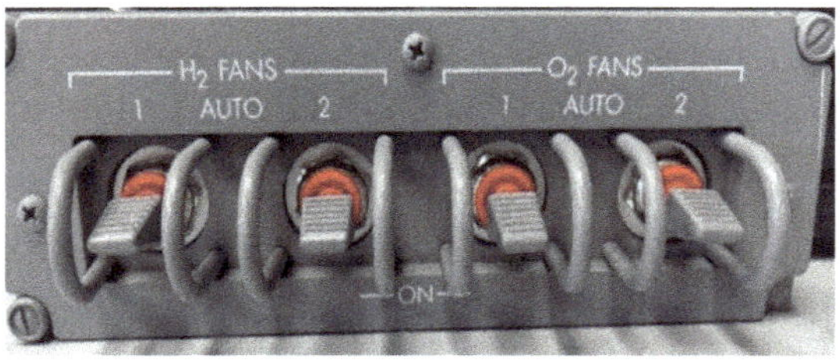

(A replica of the fan switches on the Command Module that started the oxygen tank explosion on Apollo 13.)

Market History

DATE	BEG. CAS	S&P 500 Total Return	WITHDRAWAL	END CASH
1/2000	$1,000,000	-9.10%	40,000	**$871,496**
1/2001	$871,496	-11.89%	40,000	**$728,734**
1/2002	$728,734	-22.10%	40,000	**$531,372**
1/2003	$531,372	28.68%	40,000	**$637,080**
1/2004	$637,080	10.88%	40,000	**$663,272**
1/2005	$663,272	4.91%	40,000	**$654,123**
1/2006	$654,123	15.79%	40,000	**$713,949**
1/2007	$713,949	5.49%	40,000	**$713,041**
1/2008	$713,041	-37.00%	40,000	**$418,385**
1/2009	$418,385	26.46%	40,000	**$480,779**
1/2010	$480,779	15.06%	40,000	**$508,140**
1/2011	$508,140	2.11%	40,000	**$479,099**
1/2012	$479,099	16.00%	40,000	**$514,132**

Illustration 2.2

"My biggest concern is buy-and-hold advisors who don't modify their allocation in response to market risk." – William Bengen, Think Advisor Bengen revises 4 rules.

The last point I will make here is that Bengen seems to indicate that you would have to adjust allocations for market risk. Does that include the safe 4%? Will you need to reduce or eliminate it during market downturns?

"Sequence risk is the danger that the timing of withdrawals from a retirement account will have a negative impact on the overall rate of return available to the investor. This can have a significant impact on a retiree who depends on the Income from a lifetime of investing and is no longer contributing new capital that could offset losses." -Investopedia.

Sequence Risk Avoidance is a matter of Luck

"***Sequence risk is, for the most part, <u>a matter of luck</u>. If you retire in a bull market, your account may grow large enough to sustain a subsequent downturn. If you retire in a bear market, your account balance may <u>never recover</u>." -Investopedia 'Sequence Risk: Meaning, Retirement, Protection'***

Sequence of Returns risk is hard to plan for in a growth portfolio. Investopedia says, "Sequence risk is a matter of luck." <u>Luck</u>! Are you kidding me?

Your Big Wall Street Retirement Plan

Is Retirement planning supposed to be based on luck, rainbows, or unicorns?

But here is the problem: if you get three years of negative return in your accounts at the beginning of retirement, you are circling the drain after that! Your options are to look for a unicorn riding a rainbow.
Wait, is this in the 120-page Plan? Yes, if you read the fine print. (Ok, they don't say unicorns, but they say not to trust the assumptions.)

WTW? (What the World?) Where is Monti Carlo now? Someone call Mr. Bengen. Did the 4% rule account for sequence of returns risk? Do you mean to tell me that if I retire in a recession, I might *destroy* my retirement if my timing is bad? (If you just die, everything is solved.) Yes, that is exactly what they are saying. Sequence risk is your exploding oxygen tank. This can end your retirement mission, leaving you in the cold and dark, conserving what is left of your money. Can you survive the retirement mission? Where is the procedure for that in the 120-page Plan?

But if nothing terrible happens in the first three years of retirement, is everything fine? If you take increasing amounts of income (to match inflation), then the answer is no. This risk stays with you.

Three Crummy Options for Sequence Risk

According to Investopedia, they give three options to protect against the sequence of returns risk;

1) Go back to work. (Walmart may be hiring greeters)
2) "Keep saving and investing even after you retire." (*Essentially, stop taking Income*, italics mine)
3) Diversify into high-quality bonds and government bonds.

The first option sucks and may not be possible for you. (Only half of people who retire can go back to work, usually due to health reasons) The second option sucks too. Find more money to put into retirement? That means giving up your monthly withdrawal from your retirement and taking some from your social security benefits. The third option falls into investing for Income, which we will discuss later.

Where are your withdrawals for income in these options? It could be a retirement failure if you get hit with a sequence of returns problem; however, the Big Wall Street firms are unconcerned and recommend you continue investing in growth. What is your 'procedure' for this risk? Preferably, it is a procedure that doesn't involve you being forced back to work or giving back your income to save your retirement accounts. Let me put that statement another way: ***stop all Income from your retirement plans until it becomes sustainable again. Oh, it sucks to be you.***

When I completed the Retirement Income Certified Professional (RICP) program, I was amazed at the number of income strategies that require you to reduce your income in difficult markets. Again, a 'crummy' option.

Bucket Planning to Avoid Sequence Risk

OK, do you want to bet on what I think of bucket investing? I'll wait. Now, let us start with what bucketing is. The concept is simple and very visual. You take the funds you need for years 1-5 in bucket #1 and invest very conservatively. (Short-term investments like CDs or cash equivalents) Next, you put medium-risk investments in bucket #2 for a 5-year hold, then you make even more aggressive investments in bucket #3 for a 10-year hold, and you can do a fourth bucket of aggressive growth investments for a 15-year hold. This process will 'theoretically' allow you to invest in aggressive growth investments while allowing you not to sell shares for Income. At the same time, you take Income from bucket #1. Does it work?

"First impressions can be deceiving. Notwithstanding its initial appeal, there are both theoretical and practical problems with the Bucket Strategy." —Forbes, 'The Bucket Strategy, Is Flawed-Here's A Better Way'

A major bucket strategy problem is that it depends on growth investments and low-yielding income investments. As bucket #1 drains to zero, you hope and pray that bucket #2 has grown enough to replace bucket #1. From 2000 to 2012, there was a period of no growth in the market. That is 13 years. So, buckets #2 & #3 are toast. But if you look at 2009 -2021, you're pretty good, except your cash investments pay less than 1%. This means bucket #1 has an extremely low growth rate (below inflation) and is essentially dead money. In bucketing, you have the same problem as other styles; you invest in an uncertain future, hoping everything turns out if you just give it enough time. Investopedia says this about the psychological effect of bucketing;

"Unfortunately, some clients have a hard time with these strategies when the market experiences a sharp downturn or correction. They may see the aggregate value of their retirement account trend lower and become worried, which could lead to risk aversion and poor decision-making.[32] "

Investopedia says that the systematic withdrawal strategy is similar in theory. (This strategy involves selling shares for income, which I will discuss in depth in Chapter 3.) This is yet another way to convince you to take risks by investing in growth in retirement.

"...<u>thanks to the effects of local fallacies and investors' cognitive biases</u>. A bucket strategy often makes clients more comfortable with market declines and appropriate risk-taking than traditional systematic strategies do."—Investopedia[17]

Are they saying this strategy is all psychological? Are you investing in the Matrix or the real world? The bucket strategy is not a guarantee or even a reliable long-term strategy. Its success will require a certain level of market timing, good management, and solid market performance, just like the other strategies.

---

[32] Quote from Investopedia.com 'Bucket Strategy vs. Systematic Withdrawals: Knowing the Difference'

"The pretty buckets made me feel better about my risky investments."

Now refer back to Illustration 2.2, and then continue.

Starting With a Million Dollars

Remember illustration 2.2? After 13 years, your $1 million dollars (again, Dr. Evil's voice) is now $514,132.[33] (Let's say that in Scooby Doo voice, "Ruh Roh Shaggy") If your retirement journey started when you were 65 and you are now 78, do you feel like *staying* in the market? By the way, you haven't had a raise in your income in 13 years!

You are no longer taking 4%, but you are now in an unsustainable 8%.

(Wow, sucks to be you.) You will probably start to consider dropping your income and invest in 'safer' investments, and why wouldn't you? You are on a path to zero! It is a matter of how long you will live. Does the 4% rule still see success because you still have money? You have half of the money you started with, but let's see what happens in 22 years. According to research, ***you 'should be' OK.*** Retirement planning based on hopes, wishes, and butterfly kisses.

With $514,132 left of your million dollars and 78 years old, are you staying in the Market?

But the greatest Bull market is ahead of you, and it will save the day! (If you are invested right) If you buy and hold, "you will be fine," they say. Here's the problem: ***you don't know that!*** After all, the US lost its AAA credit rating in 2011. Europe has serious debt problems, and growth is slowing in China. OMG! These were serious worries in 2012. They said you need a 10-year time horizon, but it is now a 20-year horizon, and next, you will need *30 years*, so buy and hold faith in Buffett works.

Who is cool with losing half of their money, saying the research says it will return?

The next crash could be coming (there have been two big ones in the last 25 years that lasted a total of 13 years). Think about it: you are 78, and 50% of your money is gone! With a 8% withdraw rate, you can't take any more risks. Your kids are going to intervene and take power of attorney over you. "Dad, you're down 50%," your daughter says. "You need help!" To make

---

[33] Chart in illustration 2.2 is provided by Sound Income Strategies

things worse for many people, the constant stress of the markets can lower their quality of life and life spans! (Dying fixes running out of money. Yeah, that is dark.)

I know many 78-year-olds in excellent health who look good to live into their 90s! But if you pull back on the risk, your return drops, your income drops, and you miss the great rally 2013 - 2019—assuming you are invested correctly for it. Human nature does not sit still with faith in the 4% rule. Action is needed.

"You will never be happy in retirement if you are constantly worried about your assets, the markets and interest rates." —Tom Hegna The Psychonomics of Retirement

This Kind of Drop Might Kill You.

Many elderly folks stay home, withdrawing from friends and family due to financial instability, like the Apollo 13 astronauts who spent days in a cold and dark spaceship due to having to conserve power after the explosion. You are now doing the same. Jim, Fred, and John only had to wait five days; you have the rest of your life. So, you decline golf invitations or ladies' lunch dates. You draw back, watch Wheel of Fortune in a dark house (conserving electricity), and pay bills instead of living your best retirement days. The astronauts on Apollo 13 didn't have the Wheel of Fortune to watch, so there's that.

Chronic stress has far-reaching implications for our health and longevity.

"Research shows that overreacting, constantly worrying, and living in a state of perpetual anxiety can reduce life expectancy." —Mark Stibich, PhD

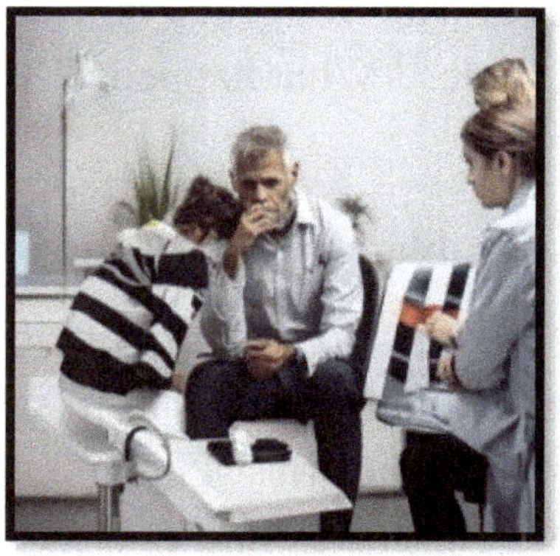

Stress not only impairs our immune system, leaving us susceptible to diseases, but also increases the risk of developing cardiovascular problems and accelerates telomere shortening, **contributing to the development of age-related diseases and reduced lifespan**.

"By recognizing the profound impacts of stress on our longevity and taking proactive measures to manage stress, we can pave the way for more vibrant and fulfilling lives." [34] — **Chelsea Hetherington, PhD**

[34] How Stress Can Shorten Your Lifespan by Chelsea Hetherington, PhD

My point is that no one lets their retirement savings shrink by 50% without pushing the panic button. You might reallocate to 'safer' investments (locking in your losses permanently and losing your potential for recovery) or stop taking withdrawals and reduce your lifestyle to a subsistence level for years. The stress can erode your health and take the fun out of retirement.

Market declines may cause you to grow old and die.

"Retirees who are surrounded by their family and friends — and who also have a substantial check coming in every month for the rest of their lives — are much happier, according to an article published in Time and The Big Wall Street Journal. Studies show that they also live longer."[35] -Kiplinger

Multiple high-quality studies show that retirees with lifetime income—annuities or pensions—tend to live longer.[36] Not because they are magical, but because guaranteed income reduces financial stress, increases consumption of health-preserving goods, and stabilizes behavior. More in Chapter 6.

13 years of No Growth

The S&P 500 dividend average for 2000 - 2012 is about 1.84%. That is not much to live on. $18,400 roughly. The total return paints a bleaker picture. Looking at the chart (illustration 2.2), you're thinking, "If I add back the withdrawals ($40,000 per year x 12 years = $480,000 and not based on income but selling shares), I am still down $5,868."

Thirteen years with an ending balance of $514,132.00. Think about that: 13 years of no growth <u>with</u> dividends reinvested. If you paid an advisor fee of 1.5%, take off another 12% off the value.[37] What happened, you ask?

The problem with withdrawals; this goes against the <u>hold of the buy-and-hold</u> strategy.

Go back to the volatility chart above (illustration 2.1). Do you see that taking Income from retirement after a downturn sets you up for an eroding retirement account? By the way, that is your sequence risk. I have seen this happen. The people who say Buy and Hold see no problem with you **<u>selling shares</u>** to get Income.

---

[35] Retirees with a Guaranteed Income Are Happier, Live Longer Kiplinger Ken Nuss December 24, 2020
[36] www.aleprevitero.com/wp-content/uploads/2025/05/Previtero_annuity_longevity.pdf
[37] Source Stock Return Calculator for S&P 500 at buyupside.com (Start January 1, 2000 – January 1, 2013)

If you have to sell shares of a stock or mutual fund during downturns in the Market, you will have two problems. 1) You have to sell more shares to get the income you desire, and 2) those shares will be gone when the market does recover. Your account will have a difficult time coming back.

New retirees have come to my office, showing me their account statements and saying:

"I am running out of money."
"What did your advisor say," I ask.
"He said I am spending it," the new client responds.
"So, it's your fault," I ask. <Uncomfortable stare>.
"Um, yes, that is the implication," the client says <Uncomfortable stare>.

Now, sometimes, a client withdraws too much from retirement accounts. (I have seen this often, with the client testifying that the broker said nothing. Sometimes, that is a selective memory, but I don't judge.) But often, it's the market volatility that is wrecking your retirement. How did you get to this point?

The 120-page 'plan' told you (in addition to the Monte Carlo analysis score) that your average performance of the recommended portfolio is higher than your income needs and will grow to provide inflation adjustment. Years later, it is not the 120-page Plan that will be blamed for the wheels coming off your retirement. Do you want to guess whose fault it is? Dalbar says it's you, you unsophisticated, unwashed rube. To quote Dalbar, "Investors so often cost themselves money because the behaviors elicited by short-term focus are almost always irrational." In other words, 'take your medicine like a man.'

The 120-page Plan is based on Math, so it has to be true.[38]

Modern Portfolio Theory Statistics (MPTS)

I took a financial planning course at Boston University in 2009 and earned a certificate in financial planning. In the investments section, I learned how to calculate the standard Deviation

---

38 More sarcasm. Do you get how this works?

on a portfolio. (It's Algebra) It was then that I had an epiphany—a *major epiphany about Standard Deviation.*

Many financial advisors flash the modern portfolio theory statics as *'proof'* that your portfolio has less risk and more return. Low betas with high alpha and lower standard deviation will prove you can trust the market with all your retirement. The problem is that unless you are an advanced math person, none of these terms make sense to even college graduates. Most people don't say huh? What does that mean? Because they don't want to appear stupid. So, they nod along with the exhaustive analysis the 120-page Plan provides.

Standard Deviation is based on Math, so it has to be true.

Before I took my financial planning courses, I studied and experimented with portfolio construction using MPTS (Modern Portfolio Theory Statics). I was part of a study group using Morningstar portfolio software to design proper portfolios using mutual funds. I never saw any measurable results from our efforts. I think we sounded smart.

MPTS is used to test a portfolio's risk and performance. According to the website Investopedia,[39] It says, "Standard Deviation (a Modern Portfolio Theory Statistics) measures the dispersion of a dataset relative to its mean and is calculated as the square root of the variance by determining each data point's deviation relative to the mean.[40]" Clear as mud, right?

SNAP BACK TO COHERENCE!

That last paragraph likely put your brain into shutdown mode. Sorry, stand up and get the blood into your brain. MPTS is an effort to make you feel that 'math' has proven your investment strategy will work and how darn smart your financial advisor is. Because we know math is the answer. But does it?

So, what was my epiphany? When I learned how to calculate standard deviation, I discovered it is based on past performance! Um, why is that a problem, you ask? Let me share some words our regulators require us to put on every marketing piece produced by advisors and financial firms.

"Past Performance is not a guarantee of future results."

---

[39] A great free investor resource that I find factual and reliable.
[40] Investopedia.com quote from the article "Standard Deviation Formula and Uses vs. Variance"

Just because a stock, mutual fund, money manager, or any other investment made money in the past does not mean it/he/she/non-binary will make money in the future, or worse, you could lose what you made. The standard deviation calculation uses past performance. Understand that the stock market, like businesses, goes through cycles. A low standard deviation (especially when calculated under five years) can be counterintuitive and might indicate the portfolio has more risk.

Let's say you are looking at a portfolio of investments that have been performing well for the last three years. What does the standard deviation indicate regarding the riskiness of the portfolio? It says it is low, especially if compared to a terrible portfolio. If you look at any Ibbotson chart (a chart that tracks asset classes and/or sectors), you will notice that rising asset classes, most of the time, will have 3-5 years of positive growth followed by a cyclical downturn. Of course, there will be exceptions, but using MPTSs like standard deviation as scientific 'proof' of lower risk is often misleading or lacks predictive power that you will make any money. (Again, read the fine print in the 120-page Plan.)

For another example, if your portfolio is a high-performing mutual fund, a change in the fund managers often (very often) leads to the fund's declining performance. However, the standard deviation on said fund says it is less risky. That is past performance, baby, and ***past performance guarantees nothing!***

Like Monte Carlo analysis, Standard Deviation, and other Modern Portfolio Theory Statistics are not reliable measures for risks and are used to, as I quoted previously, "…lull people into a false sense of security or lead them to believe that the stock market is the answer for all of life's potential calamities."[41] These measures are often the focus of many financial plans and coincide with Big Wall Street's desire for you to invest in its growth investments.

Remember, Apollo 1 was also based on math and engineering.

"Figures don't Lie, but liars figure." —Mark Twain

DIY Financial Calculators

You already know where I am going with this one. But these Do-It-Yourself calculators often do the same thing as professional financial planning software. Hence, we are back to unicorns and rainbows in retirement

[41] Timothy Barrett Trust Counsel August 14, 2019 Kiplingers.com

planning. Also, if you enter the information wrong, what do you get? There is a saying, "Garbage in, Garbage out."

The book "Get What's Yours Social Security" calls out many Social Security calculators as worthless.

Social Security -The Gateway to Retirement

Social Security calculations are an essential retirement plan section that can easily be muffed up. Getting Social Security right couldn't be more critical. Often, the software used in financial planning programs is inadequate for correctly estimating your social security benefits or the advisor needs training on how social security works. Many advisors depend on the SS statement for benefit amounts. The social security benefit amounts on the statements can be off by 10% or more.[42] Depending on your situation, your *entire* social security benefit could be wiped out.[43]

If this part of the planning is not done right, it could drastically change your retirement. Understand this:

96% of people get less than they should from Social Security

$111,000 is lost by the average American household[23]

I earned my RSSA designation in 2020.[44] Initially, I thought it would be an excellent designation to encourage people to attend my Social Security seminars. What I learned in the coursework and recommended reading floored me. I was also ashamed that I hadn't been helping my clients with this planning previously. Even my Social Security seminars back then were more about the future of Social Security and changes in the program than the practical advice and planning I now give. The average person receives $300,000 from SS over their lifetime, and some couples receive as much as $2,000,000.00[45] This is a serious retirement asset and must be planned carefully and competently.

Social Security is the Gateway to Retirement.

---

[42] Source: Get what's yours Social Security by Laurence J. Kotlikoff, Philip Moeller, and Paul Solman

[43] Every situation is different and depends on being subject to GPO -Government Pension Offset can reduce benefits to zero or WEP, Windfall Elimination Provision that can lower benefits up to -49%

[44] Registered Social Security Analyst or RSSA administered by the National Association of Registered Social Security Analysts.

[45] Source: National Association of Registered Social Security Analysts

For some retirees, what you get from social security might be more than the value of your retirement accounts. I recreated our educational seminar after getting my RSSA designation. I named it "Social Security Questions You Have Answers You Need, How the Lessons of Apollo 13 Can Help Your Retirement." That seminar became the inspiration for this book.

Suppose your Advisor doesn't understand how social security works (assuming the financial planning software has good SS analysis) or doesn't know the right questions to ask you and how to enter the information correctly. In that case, you will get incorrect income estimates, which could cause you to take more risks in your retirement account and investments or get less out of Social Security.

I took a financial planning course at Boston University.[46] I remember it being very light on Social Security information. Most advisors, from my experience, do not understand how Social Security works, and even if the retirement planning software is good at Social Security calculations[47], the Advisor's lack of competency may cost you. (More on this in Chapter 4.)

Understanding the incentives of waiting to file for Social Security can also mean using your retirement assets to fund retirement. At the same time, you wait for your 'Optimal Social Security Filing date.' Which could mean a much higher and potentially more secure retirement income. This is real planning.

Overpayments are always Your Fault

Finally, if Social Security *overpays* you, they will take it back even if it is their mistake, and years later. I helped one client who had her Social Security suspended by the SSA until she paid back an overpayment of $18,000. I tell this story in Chapter 4 on Social Security. Obviously, having Social Security reverse benefits will affect your retirement.

Conclusion on Financial Planning

Years ago, I read a great book called "The Number" by Lee Eisenberg. He talked about how many. Advisors have clients fill out a questionnaire, which is then sent to someone in New York, and the 120-page Plan is returned.

---

[46] I completed my coursework and earned a certificate in Financial Planning in 2007. My view may not reflect the current curriculum.
[47] We discuss this in depth in Chapter 4.

The point is that financial plans are often mindlessly produced to support the Advisors/Firm recommendations. Yes, especially Fiduciary or Fee-only planners.

I have brought in many new clients over the years, and no one brought me the 120-page Plan prepared by another advisor to review. No one ever asked me, "What happened? The 120-page Plan said this would work. Do you see the Monte Carlo Analysis, the Modern Portfolio theory stats, and the average return calculations? Why am I running out of money? Did we not follow the 120-page Plan?

"Analysis by LIMRA, a financial services trade association, shows that 87% of people with a written retirement plan feel confident in achieving their desired retirement lifestyle, in contrast to 70% with an informal plan.[48]***"***

The above quote is why financial advisors will provide you with a retirement plan just before recommending you invest in a growth portfolio, where you sell shares for income. I have made fun of the 120-page Plan. It makes perfect sense to plan retirement in writing. The advice industry has used these seemingly high-level fiduciary-inspired plans to sell services or products, thus misleading retirees to believe high-level planning has been completed and they have a strong likelihood of retirement income success. If the planner is a Fiduciary then it is legally obligated to be in your best interest!

I submit that the 120-page Plan is either fluff or intended to steer you where the firm makes the most money, has a conflict of interest, or is a sales pitch. In most cases it lacks income strategies to rely on selling shares for income in retirement.

"You admitted to using these plans in your practice," you say. Yes, I presented hundreds of retirement plans, but my clients' success or lack thereof depended *on what I did after the plan was constructed*. No investor in their right mind has a 30-year static portfolio. There will be changes made.

Summing Up

There is a better way of planning for retirement. Ultimately, the '120-page plan' may be more about marketing and recommending risky stock market investments wrapped up in 'planning.' Yes even from or especially from a Fiduciary. As I described, the very premise of many of the assumptions is flawed. Since you read articles in the media that say 'only use a fiduciary planner,' then you assume they must be right.

---

[48] These Four Traits Lead to More Retirement Savings -Kiplingers by Jacob Schroeder published December 26, 2023

I do believe in Retirement Planning. However, I contend that today's standard financial planning tools turn into pages and pages of incomprehensible data with assumptions based on Monte Carlo simulations, MPTs, shoddy Social Security analysis & average market performance numbers:

"MPT's, Monte Carlo's, Average Returns, buy-and-hold philosophy, and 4% rule are intended to support stock market investing, mutual funds, third-party managers, or proprietary products."

The Job Interview

Before I became a security-registered financial advisor, I started in the insurance business (this was the 90s). It didn't take me long to decide that I also wanted to offer investments. I started interviewing with different Big Wall Street firms for a job. One Big Wall Street company invited me to what I thought was a job interview. It was not an interview. Instead, I walked into a room of people who had just gotten off work from the factory. I was the only one in a suit and tie. The speaker did his routine. If we pass the life insurance, securities, property & causality, and mortgage broker exams, we could do comprehensive financial (full color; they mention this more than once) plans with clients and cover all their financial needs. (Would the guy who manages your investments also write your auto insurance and mortgage?)

The full-color Plan sold life, car, long-term care, and homeowner's insurance, refinanced your mortgage, invested your money, and planned retirement! (It also had a recipe for julienne fries.) Yes in the 1990s it became clear that investors respond to planning. So, make it pretty and look smart.

I looked around the room and I didn't see a crowd of financial over-achievers. I saw people with average jobs looking for a side hustle. I pointed out that these licenses/registrations would take months or years to prepare for each and thousands of dollars in fees (that was in the 90s; they are harder and more expensive now). I left that seminar ticked off that I put on my good suit for this. And so was my introduction to the 120-page Plan. The message this Big Wallstreet company gave its new recruits couldn't be clearer:

"If we throw a giant full-color plan in front of a prospect, then they will buy anything."

Yes, I am a Fiduciary

I carry the Certified Financial Fiduciary designation or CF2.[49] Fiduciaries, by definition, must always act in their client's best interests. The implication is you will always get good advice from a 'fiduciary' since it's the law! This is a false view.

[49] See nationalcffassociation.org for more on a Certified Financial Fiduciary

It doesn't mean you are getting the best advice. I will discuss this in Chapter 6, but for now, consider if the 'fiduciary' only offers mutual funds in a fee-based managed account. Do you think they will promote that as the best investment method? If the 'Fiduciary' is limited by what his firm offers, is it still unconflicted advice? The term 'fiduciary' is overused and abused. The result is you being enticed to invest based on the idea of a 'fiduciary.'

But consider the Dalbar study I referenced at the start. **A Dalbar study showed that US stock market return came in at an annualized 6.95% and investor returns at 3.95%**[50] (Oh, that is lower than 4% of the so-called 'safe' return). Why are average investor returns so low? Are the 120-page plans failing? According to Dalbar, it said, "To the extent that it exists at all, most of it (all of it?) is created by poor decisions via the majority of investors." If this is true, are you supposed to trust your 20 to 40-year retirement to the markets promoted by Big Wall Street firms?

The 'Plan' may be for the Firm to make money.

Any advisor worth his salt helps his clients plan to some degree. How much income will you receive, how much risk of loss are you taking, and other issues need to be considered when planning retirement. **The Big Box Big Wall Street financial firms want you to invest in what makes <u>them</u> the most *long-term money*.** That may be a diversified portfolio of stocks and bonds they make markets in or a list of recommended mutual funds, money managers, or proprietary funds that have monetary influence on the advisor.

Thanks to the 14-year Bull Market[51]

But what did we say about past performance? Not a guarantee of future results? The conditions that gave us the massive bull market that started in 2009 and ended in 2022 have changed. As an example, stock buybacks. One research report indicated that 40% of the 2009-2020 returns where due to stock buy-backs.[52] Due to extraordinarily low interest rates, companies borrowed money and bought back their stock. This greatly affected earnings, which helped fuel increasing share prices. The Jobs Act penalizes corporations from borrowing money, and the Inflation Reduction Act adds a tax to stock buybacks. So, you say? These are some

---

[50] 30-year performances for Average Investor returns vs. S&P 500 total return. Source: Dalbar

[51] 2009 – 2022 is considered the longest bull market.

[52] Goldman published multiple notes showing that share repurchases accounted for roughly 40% of total U.S. equity returns since 2011. A share repurchase is when a company buys its own stock in order to shrink the amount available in the market.

examples of component changes that fueled the long bull market. Counting on what happened in 2009 – 2020 to repeat itself is rolling loaded dice on your retirement.

The Retirement Casino

But since the math changes when you start drawing Income, your risk of a bear market eroding your retirement is significant. Then you have a sequence of returns risk; do you feel lucky? You don't take your retirement accounts to a craps table, for goodness' sake! If you're looking for repeatable cycles, consider how successful the 90's was for the stock market. A crash and a 13-year period of no growth followed that. Where the future of markets is precarious. We have a national debt of 38 trillion and many other concerns. It is time to approach your retirement with what actually works long-term.

"My contention is most retirement planning is not leading to better retirement outcomes and requires faith that markets will be alright."[53]

Monte Carlo, Average Returns, 4% Rule, Modern Portfolio Statistics, Sequence of Returns risk, and Bad Social Security planning, oh, my.[54] I believe that Big Wall Street has been building Apollo 1 spaceships for retirees as part of its business. They explode, and then everyone forgets what happened. Except for retirees who change their lifestyle so their retirement account can recover over the next 10 years or more.

Many planners and firms use retirement planning software to promote their proprietary products, mutual funds, third-party managers, or market-based investments (i.e., stock market) to encourage <u>you to feel confident in taking more stock market risk</u> because the data and plan support your risk-taking.

"Conventional Financial Planning is Unsafe at any Speed."
—Laurence Kotlikoff, PhD (Boston University)

This also applies to the so-called Fiduciary planners who are said to operate <u>only</u> in your best interest but make their 'best' fees by investing <u>all</u> your money in the stock market. (More on this in Chapter 6.) These advisors may use the statistical data we discussed here as the basis for careful management in a growth equity portfolio.

---

53 This is the opinion of the author and may conflict with other established sources.
54 Wizard of Oz reference. Remember looking forward to the spring viewing on TV? That was awesome.

"I was there when the strength of men failed… It should have ended that day, but evil was allowed to endure." —Elrond the Elf Ruler from Lord of the Rings.

I was trained and retrained to use average market performance to convince *you* that growth investments are safe for long-term retirement funds! This is a misapplied buy-and-hold philosophy, and it can have a devastating effect on your long-term retirement. Bad advice on social security can cost you thousands or even over $100,000[55] in lifetime benefits.

The 120-page Retirement plan is often a pitch for products, services, or growth investments disguised as an unbiased plan.

Harsh Truth: ***A Fiduciary may not always act in your best interest.***[56]

---

[55] Source: "The Retirement Solutions Hiding in Plain Sight. "Capital One United Income June 28, 2019
[56] More on this topic in Chapter 6 'Your Spaceship Awaits You.'

What is your Retirement Compensation Plan?

Don't allow the Fiduciary label to exert undue influence on your decisions. There is a better way to plan for retirement. This chapter outlined some of the problems in the financial industry. Financial columnists tell you to go to a 'fee only' fiduciary advisor, get your 120-page plan, put your money in a fee-based managed account, and everything will work out fine. It's a label, my friend because advice is conflicted. You need a '**retirement compensation plan**.' Did you not spend your career negotiating for an employment compensation plan? You need to enter retirement with the same goal!

"Enter the planning process with the right Philosophy. The rest will fall into place."

If you approach your planning with the right investment philosophy, I believe you can secure a reliable retirement compensation plan with less stress for a happier retirement. What is that? It's the same question you ask every time you interview for a job: "How much does it pay?"

Yes, I want to put income first, above all else. It is the only method that has long-term sustainability. I said it already: selling shares for income puts your future in the hands of the stock market with the hope that it will continue to rise and rise. We know from history that this is a dangerous plan. Income is the key.

Apollo 13 needed power for the entire mission. The last thing to happen was parachutes. Running out of power before they deployed would have been a disaster. Running out of money in the last ten years of retirement would be your parachute failure.

"Show me the money!" —Tom Cruise as Jerry Maguire.

The next chapter is developing your checklist for a successful retirement launch, followed by chapters outlining Social Security and Taxes you need to plan for. Then, we can finally discuss building the retirement ship and the investments you need to consider. I want to provide some basic principles based on our knowledge of the markets and human nature so you can make the best choices for you and your family.

Now, let's consider planning from which you can actually benefit. I aim to help you develop a plan that can last you the 20 to 40 years that your retirement will last. I will discuss this in depth later in this book, but let me give you a hint now.

Retirement planning needs to be based on Income!

Chapter 3 will discuss the reason for a successful retirement launch, The Checklist.

The 120-page Plan Review

- Very smart people built Apollo 1, but it was still a disaster. The same could be true of your retirement plan.
- Your plan's purpose should be to not run out of money in retirement.
- Could you have an Oxygen Tank Explosion event in your retirement?
- Market declines or crashes can *change your retirement lifestyle*. Canceled Gold, ladies' lunches, no gifts for the grandchildren, or no traveling.
- You should not walk but run from anyone using the Monti Carlo simulation for retirement planning.
- Average market return data is misleading and inaccurate for planning retirement.
- The 4% rule may require massive drawdowns of your retirement, requiring your faith and time for it to come back.
- Buy and Hold works when accumulating your retirement but fails during distribution.
- Have faith in God, not buy and hold.
- Volatility can kill your retirement. (Illustration 2.1)
- Selling shares for income is very risky.
- Sequence risk is, for the most part, a matter of luck. Can we plan retirement without depending on luck?
- If we had two major market crashes with a 13-year no-growth market, could it happen again?
- Bucket planning is more conceptual than anything else and has a high potential to fail.
- Chronic stress has far-reaching implications for our health and longevity.
- The 120-page Plan is based on Math, so it has to be true. (Sarcasm)
- "Past Performance is not a guarantee to future results." (Not Sarcasm)
- The point is that financial plans are often mindlessly produced to support the Advisors/Firm recommendations.
- The implication is you will <u>always</u> get good advice from a 'fiduciary.' This is a false.
- Conventional Financial Planning is Unsafe at any Speed." -Laurence Kotlikoff, PhD (Boston University)
- Enter the planning process with the right Philosophy. The rest will fall into place.

- What is your Retirement Compensation Plan?
- Put income first above all else. It is the only method that has long-term sustainability.
- The 120-page Retirement plan is often a pitch for products, services, or growth investments disguised as an unbiased plan.
- Enter the planning process with the right Philosophy. The rest will fall into place.
- Retirement planning needs to be based on Income!

Chapter 3
Pre-Launch 'The Checklist'

"I watch a lot of astronaut movies... Mostly Star Wars. And even Han and Chewie use a checklist."
—Jon Stewart (former Daily Show host)

NATIONAL AERONAUTICS AND SPACE ADMINISTRATION

APOLLO XIII
CSM 109

CSM LAUNCH
CHECKLIST

PREPARED BY
FLIGHT CREW SUPPORT DIVISION
SPACECRAFT SYSTEMS BRANCH

JANUARY 5, 1970

Retirement Planning You Can Benefit From: Prepare for Launch.

Okay, in the last chapter, I destroyed conventional financial planning. Sorry about that, but it had to be done. Your retirement is too important to worry about Big Wall Street's feelings. We understand Apollo 1 design is a disaster. This checklist, which I am about to share with you, took me years to develop and design. It is simple to understand and focuses on what will make your retirement launch and mission successful. But first, let's talk more about Apollo 13.

Apollo 13 launched on April 11, 1970, from Cape Canaveral (called Cape Kennedy at the time). It took nearly a decade to get ready for this moment. Primary and backup crews tirelessly practiced scenarios in large simulators replicating the Apollo 13 spaceships before the launch day. (See Illustration 3.2)

Before launching, NASA simulated every scenario and contingency it might encounter and prepared procedures to deal with them.

Pilots likewise have backup plans or contingency plans when flying an airplane. NASA calls them procedures. One procedure they developed involved using the moon landing craft (the Aquarius or LM) as a lifeboat in case of a CSM[57] catastrophic failure. This part is essential; they

---

[57] CSM -Command Service Module

never thought for a minute that the landing craft part of Apollo 13 would be used this way. But they never thought the main part of the ship (Service Module) would blow up, either.

I refer to developing _procedures_ pretty frequently in this book. *NASA's _Procedures_ allowed them to respond quickly to problems/crises and reduce risks.* You have a procedure whether or not you planned it. The procedure may be to crash and burn; that is a terrible procedure.

Is your unplanned retirement procedure to stop taking income from your retirement accounts and wait for the markets to recover, or risk running out of money?

Checklist Origins

Practical retirement planning should involve a checklist of actions and calculations that is based on Income. Checklists dated back to the 1930s and were first used in aviation. After the Boeing Model 299 crashed in 1935, killing two pilots, checklists were introduced into aviation safety. The crash was due to the pilot's failure to disengage the gust locks, which were used to keep the control surfaces stationary while the plane was parked. After that, the checklist ensured that pilots would take all necessary steps before takeoff. Since then, checklists have become an essential tool for ensuring safety and efficiency in a variety of fields, such as medicine, manufacturing, construction, and retirement.

Like the Apollo program, you spent decades saving for your retirement launch. Your retirement should be done with a planning approach, not a buy these investments 'sales pitch' based on 4% rule average returns or Monti Carlo simulations. Every pilot uses a checklist before the flight. Unsurprisingly, the Apollo program lived by the checklist and saved lives by the checklist. You may start this planning a few months before you want to retire, but it is better to begin it at the start of the transition stage, 5 – 10 years before retirement.

Before the Transition stage, you are in the Accumulation stage. (The goals of accumulation are saving, investing, and, of course, accumulating retirement assets). Transition is reducing risk, increasing income investments, and aligning your finances to prepare for your retirement launch date.

"No pilot, no matter how great his talent and experience, fails to use his checklist."
—Charlie Munger (Legendary Co-manager with Warren Buffett)

The Checklist to prepare for your retirement launch:

✓ Social Security Income estimates and optimal filing dates
✓ Income sources for retirement
✓ Retirement Asset Inventory
✓ Retirement Objectives
✓ Expense/Debt review
✓ Your ideal retirement life
✓ Retirement Income Needs and Wants
✓ Tax Strategies to employ now and later
✓ Investment Strategy (Moving from the G to the I)
✓ Review of your Advisor(s)

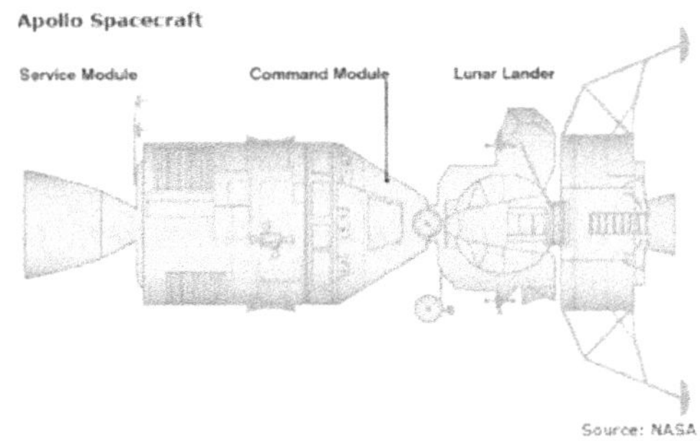

The Stages of Retirement

'Most accidents happen on the way down the mountain.' While many in our industry focus on the climb—the accumulation of assets—earning the RICP® is about mastering the descent.' —Dr. Wade Phau PhD, CFA, RICP® American College of Financial Services professor of practice.

This quote from Wade Phau, a researcher in retirement planning, should be a warning against accumulation investing in retirement. Too many advisors are focused on the accumulation of retirement assets and in most cases are paid for exactly that!

Now, notice illustration 3.1 below. If you start in the accumulation stage, using a diversified buy-and-hold strategy to accumulate your retirement savings. You are taking huge equity risks, knowing you have time in the markets to smooth out the ups and downs. Approaching retirement (i.e., ten years of retirement), it is time to jettison the accumulation stage for the transition stage. Taking less risk means less return, but the alternative is delayed retirement or a considerably lower lifestyle in retirement.

Wanting more turns causes many people to get stuck in the accumulation stage. After all, ***it's a big rocket with lots of power!*** You made your money with a disciplined or even a random investment strategy. As Wade Phau indicated in the quote above, many pre-retirees had to cancel their planned retirement in 2000 or 2008 due to the extraordinary drops in the stock market[58] or had to make complex, drastic lifestyle changes because they had much less to retire

[58] When referring to 'Stock Market' returns I am referencing the S&P 500 index as the measure unless noted otherwise.

on. Money fuels your retirement; if it gets burned up in a stock market decline or a failed aggressive investment, this is quite serious. Since knowing the future of the economy or markets is impossible, continuing to ride the rocket that got you to retirement is dangerous.

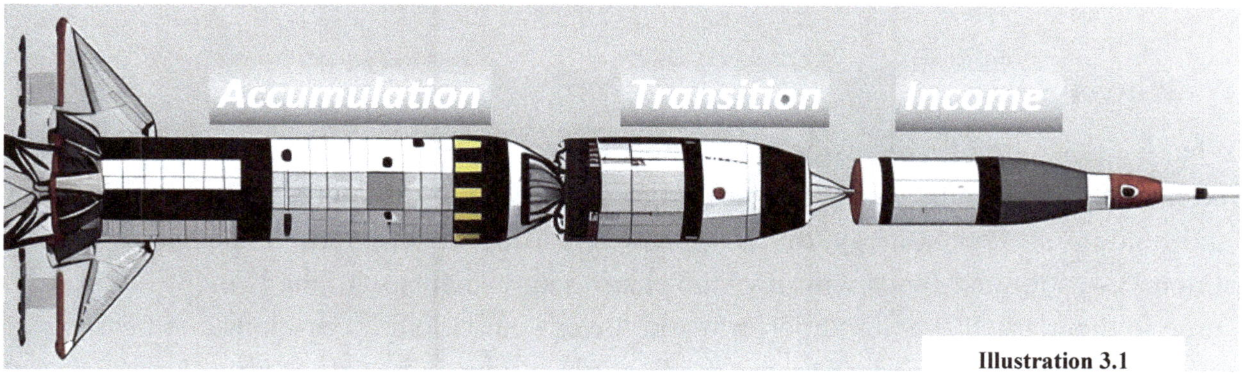

Illustration 3.1

At what age should you begin the Transition Stage? It depends on when you plan to retire, but 10 years before retirement is an excellent time to start adjusting risk and identifying what could cause you to delay retirement.

"… as you approach retirement — say you've got 10 to 15 years until you plan to call it quits your mindset should shift to a more consistently conservative approach." [59]

This means avoiding the Oxygen Tank Explosion in your retirement. Before you label me a perma-bear or anti-market guy, I am not against investing in stocks or market-based investments for retirement. We manage accounts invested in CDs, private equity, stocks, bonds, and ETFs. There are risks with all investments; how we deal with them and plan for them is the question. Faith in the 4% rule is not how we operate. The Apollo team recognized the big-time risks of going into space but to space and the moon, they did. Likewise, we will plan for your launch into retirement.

Will a glitch or outright market explosion change your retirement launch date or anticipated retirement income? We prepare procedures for this in the transition stage.

After the accumulation stage rocket gets you to high orbit, the transition stage positions your retirement ship for the next part of the mission. We will discuss approaching the transition stage in your savings, investments, taxes, and social security benefits planning. Your income stage of the retirement mission could last 20 to 40 years! Preparing your ship with the necessary provisions is critical. Does it matter if the 50% crash in the value of your investments doesn't

---

[59] See Kiplinger.com "10 to 15 Years From Retirement? Time to Scale Back Risk" by Kevin Wade

occur until mission year 19? You need to prepare the launch date and the longevity of your supplies on this mission.

Now, let's crawl into the SIM (simulator) and plan this retirement mission together.

Big Wall Street Advice

What is the length of a recession? Investopedia says the average is 9 months. When I entered the investment business at Edward Jones, I was told to sell quality investments, follow a buy-and-hold investment strategy, diversify, and invest for the long term. (The list of 'quality investments' was mutual funds with revenue-sharing agreements with the firm.[60]) I was also told that 'time in the market' would outperform and lower your risks in recessions and bear markets.[61] This advice is standard across the financial advice industry. At my sales training class in St Louis, a grizzled grey-haired veteran in an awesome suit stood in front of my class and told us to say to clients, "If your account drops and you're really mad, come down to my office and throw a brick through the window. But first, wrap a check around the brick. Because you will want to add to your account."

So, we had a special list of mutual fund investments with 10-year investment performance that the firm recommended, an analyst-recommended stock list, and a bond inventory to sell to clients. Be like Warren Buffett was our motto to buy and hold for the long run!

When I entered the business in 2000, it was the end of the fantastic 1990s bull market. I saw technology stocks go down first as the tech bubble burst, (-76% loss) and then rest of the market followed. When we thought the markets had bottomed, 9/11 happened. Interest rates started being cut, which caused bonds and CDs to pay extremely low interest. This lasted 3 years, and the recovery lasted another 4 years, for a total of 7 years from top to full recovery! Technology stocks took considerably longer to recover at 16 – 17 years!

Everything had a great track record until it didn't. We would also talk about 'dollar cost averaging' being your friend. What is dollar cost averaging? To quote from Investopedia;

"Dollar-cost averaging involves investing the same amount of money in a target security at regular intervals over a certain period of time, regardless of price. By using [DCA], investors may lower their average cost per share and reduce the impact of volatility on their portfolios."
—Investopedia.com

---

60 www.wealthmanagement.com/news/ed-jones-agrees-pay-75-million-revenue-sharing-case

61 Bear Market is when investments are losing money. The markets are being slapped down by the bear's paws. Bull Markets are when investments are going up. The bull's horns are thrusting the markets up.

That certainly sounds good, but it is an '*accumulation stage*' strategy (see illustration 3.1). While conventional wisdom has shown the soundness of investing consistently, after all, you don't need the money now. Many advisors love Dollar Cost Averaging because research has shown that you don't need to 'time' the market if you DCA. If you miss the opportunity to buy low, dollar cost averaging usually averages you out. You can buy more and prepare for the next bull market when the market declines. This stage gets you to high orbit, but remember it's an 'accumulation stage' strategy.

Do you agree that now is the time to prepare for your Mission (Income) Stage?

Dollar Cost Averaging is Limited.

That is what we try to accomplish in the transition stage. If you have more than a decade before retirement, dollar cost-averaging[62] helps you flatten the volatility of the markets. This *could* improve your performance.

Dollar Cost Averaging will not protect your large accumulated retirement savings from losing money.

Consider that if you have a $500,000 401(k) account balance and add $15,000 a year, dollar-cost averaging only helps your recent investments. We need a risk reduction strategy or risk massive losses just when you are preparing to retire from your job.

Reverse Dollar Cost Averaging is No Bueno[63]

However, when someone says 'however,' it's rarely good what is said next. Doing withdrawals is Reverse Dollar Cost Averaging and has the opposite effect on the value of your accounts in retirement. (I refer you to Chapter 2, illustration 2.1) When you begin taking income for retirement, you are no longer buying and holding if you are selling shares for income. This is reverse dollar cost averaging and has a powerful negative effect on your retirement savings. How do you fix this? Don't sell shares for income. Instead, have your retirement *cash flow* (say that like a late-night DJ) income. That way, you never sell shares for retirement income. (*Cash Flow* = Interest or Dividends)

"I have a little Charlie Munger on my shoulder every day when I look at a deal, and he's just saying two words, "Cash flow, cash flow," Kevin O'Leary Shark Tank.

---

62 Dollar Cost Averaging does not guarantee investment results.
63 No Bueno is Spanish for 'No Good'. Hey, I am in Texas, that's why.

Buy and hold is an accumulation stage strategy. The transition stage is a time to prepare for the distribution stage (retirement). If too much market fuel (i.e., money) gets burned in a downturn, it can change your retirement mission. Working longer, retiring later, or retiring on a reduced lifestyle. (i.e., smaller retirement check)

You need to ask yourself, "What scenarios would be '<u>mission failure</u>' in Retirement?"

For example, let's say you plan to retire in 10 years. That is a fairly long time. You must take your retirement account balances, savings rate, pensions, and other assets you intend to use for retirement and factor in your after-tax income goal with a projected Social Security income number.

If you were in an Apollo simulator (training for the mission), an engineer would throw something bad at you. What happens to the ship? Can you respond in a way that eliminates the problem? You might have to engineer a solution (they called them 'Procedures'), develop a process to deal with it, or identify the problem quickly and respond quickly. These simulations prepared the astronauts to react quickly and correctly to problems to prevent mission failure.

"If you are retiring in 5 years or less, you're not going to save or invest your way out of this."
-Robert Powell, CFP and financial Journalist, from a Podcast interview.

Making it Up

Why do investors keep a growth or aggressive stance in their 401k/IRA accounts up to and into retirement, thus skipping the transition stage? Sometimes, it's a misapplied buy-and-hold strategy, or they may not comprehend the retirement-altering risks they are taking. Some hope a few years of 10%+ returns will get them to the target retirement goal. Past performance may entice them to keep going. Robert Powell commented on this in a podcast interview. Powell stated that studies have shown that you won't significantly change your retirement by aggressively investing. Studies have shown that your last few years are more likely to hurt you than help by pursuing an aggressive investment strategy. You should be looking to reduce risk or switching to income-producing investments.

What happens if your retirement savings lose 25% - 50%? Are you safe to retire? *Or will you be forced to delay retirement so your retirement account can recover*? According to studies, only 50% of retirees who <u>want</u> to keep working are unable to do so.[64] A major loss in your accounts and poor health may mean a lower lifestyle than you planned for retirement.

---

[64] According to Robert Powell, CFP and financial Journalist, from a Podcast interview.

The 2000 and 2008 downturns took 7 and 6 years to recover fully. That was 13 years of no growth.

If you didn't retire in 2007 and exited stocks, you missed the top of the market and suffered a 40-50% downturn in value. It took six years to recover from that fall. What was your procedure? Work longer or until you die? The transition stage is vital to retiring on your launch schedule.

The Purpose of the Transition Stage

This is where you reduce portfolio risk, reduce or eliminate unsecured debt,[65] and increase your income-producing investments so that nothing stops you from quitting. What if you are already retired? Under the same 25%—50% account decline risk, will you be able to continue withdrawing, or will you have to reduce your income to protect the long-term sustainability of your retirement savings? Is that your procedure? Spend less? Stay home in a dark house, sit on the couch, pay bills, and watch Wheel of Fortune?

Not only is investing in growth in retirement dangerous, but your retirement will also depend on the market or the economy. Downturns will force changes to your retirement standard of living.

One approach to risk is known by the acronym **T.E.A.M.**

- **Transfer it**
- **Eliminate the risk**
- **Accept it**
- **Mitigate it**

Pilots use this all the time when deciding how to handle risk. In my experience, however, many advisors are too cavalier regarding risk. After all, the idea is that you only need to Buy and Hold with time in the market for long-term investment success. Many Big Wall Street firms encourage this thinking since it relies on investing your money in the growth markets for which *their* revenue is best. This relies on '*time in the market*' to mitigate *your* risk.

"The greatest untold story of the Apollo 13 mission is that of the spacecraft simulators." —Gerald Griffin, Apollo Program Mission Control Flight Director.

[65] See Chapter 5, Taxes, for more on debt.

What letter from TEAM are you taking to handle risk in retirement?

Illustration 3.2 Apollo Simulators
Image courtesy of NASA

What was the SIM?

SIM, short for Simulator, was an exact replica of the spaceships to be used in the mission and was used to practice the many maneuvers the pilot and crew would need to perform when on the mission.

During these practice sessions, engineers would challenge the astronauts with potential problems and errors, some of which could be catastrophic. This prepared the astronauts to be ready for anything and to develop procedures to handle problems they may encounter.

When engineering the rescue of Apollo 13, flight directors had backup crews run their plans through a SIM. The operators were to ensure the procedure would work and to understand any risks or problems before sending it to the Apollo 13 crew for implementation. This was too important to get wrong! Likewise, your retirement is too important to get wrong.

SIM your accounts

When evaluating your investment portfolio (or a proposed portfolio), there is software that can '**stress test**' your investments. This would simulate the effects of a downturn on your investments. Further, an analysis of how much income is being generated from dividends or interest, and your total costs. This is where we normally start in our planning process, and it helps you understand you're your retirement beyond hopes and wishes and butterfly kisses.

Many investors are encouraged to be riskier than they are to make sure they qualify for the investments the advisor is recommending (pushing). If you skip the transition stage and stay an accumulator until retirement, that is not good. Imagine if you are strapped into one of the Apollo ships and the countdown is running, then the flight controller (called flight) cancels the launch due to a sudden change in fuel. The launch is scrapped as they figure out what happened.

Riding into 2000, 2008, or 2020 as an accumulator with the plan to switch to Income later ends badly if you're a day late and a dollar short. Apollo 1 never made it to the mission. It blew up on the launch pad. This was a sad tragedy that could have been avoided. The same is true of planning the investments that carry you through retirement. Timing the perfect exit from the market is statistically more luck than planning.

Let's go back to the 20-year retirement plan. I will be a NASA sim operator for the Apollo program. You are at the controls of a mock space capsule, pretending to fly through space (retirement) to prepare for the real thing. I throw a massive drop in the markets at you. What do you do? Accept the risk by waiting for markets to turn around? How long does that take? Oops, it's too late. Your retirement is dead, and the mission fails. Do you get along with your son and daughter-in-law? Maybe you can move in with them? Ok, that is dramatic, but you see the point.

Do you remember when I stated the average time for a recession? Nine months, according to the smart people. But how long can your account go down and stay down? If you look at the chart below, you will see that previous market crashes have taken 7 to 6 years to recover. Did you cash out in 2007? That is unlikely. Few people saw 2008 and the Great Recession coming. How many investors massively reduced their market risk before it rolled back down? Very few did. Wow, that is amazing when you think about it. The future of the markets is nearly unknowable, and being out before it tanks rarely happens.

"Only liars manage to always be out [of the market[66]] during bad times and in during good times." —Bernard Baruch, Market Spectator, Statesmen[67]

66 I added the bracketed [the Market] to the quote for clarity.
67 see Wikipeda.com -Bernard Baruch 1870 – 1965

The previous quote is from the turn of the last century!

Not much has changed. I have found that people who say they can perfectly time the market, going from growth to stable, are either lying or have terrible overall performance due to being out when the markets are going up.

Illustration 3.3 source SIS

This quote from Benard encapsulates what happens when rmance. ***Everyone invested in 2000 that lacked the clairvoyance to 'time the market'*** in 2007 (and get out), we saw 13 years before finally returning to even! 13 years of no growth! (Provided you did not take income, then it's worse)

The Best Way to Avoid a Train is to Get Off the Tracks.

Large drops in the stock market can change retirement. I know many who delayed retirement for years or accepted a lower income in retirement. The years following were phenomenal for the markets. At the time of this book's publication, there are cracks in the wall. Are we getting ready for the big one? There have already been two - 20% declines in 2020 and 2022. We spent $6 trillion financed by US debt in 2020 and 2021 to escape the COVID disaster.[68] Can our nation afford to do it again? As we continue to test severe market volatility, we must ask ourselves: Is it safe to continue with an accumulation-style investing approach so close to the retirement launch date?

"It's like flying with a dead elephant on our back." —Jim Lovell, Apollo 13 Commander.

Are You Still Holding on to the Accumulation Stage Rockets?

So, the market is down. Why is that a big deal? Doesn't it always come back? Yes, it does, but you are thinking like an accumulator again. When you retire, the game and math changes when you approach or are in retirement. Adjusting risks is crucial. Your accounts might not have time to come back before the big day. Then, you are faced with delaying retirement, changing your standard of living in retirement, or risking running out of money by trusting in

---

68 Source: CNN "$6 trillion stimulus: Here's who got relief money so far"

the Bob Marley financial planning anthem. (See below and remember Bob Marley[69] smoked a lot of pot)

"Baby, don't worry about a thing; every little thing is going to be alright," -said a Broker channeling Bob Marley's song 'Everything's Gonna Be Alright.'

[69] a Jamaican singer, musician, and songwriter. Considered one of the pioneers of reggae… born in Jamaica. - Wilkipedia

Market Volatility Steals Time

Financial Planner Michael K. Stein, a Certified Financial Planner (CFP) wrote about the stages a retiree goes through in retirement in his 1998 book, The Prosperous Retirement: Guide to the New Reality. When you retire you have the energy, time, and health to do a lot. The question is, will you have the money? These stages can be illustrated as ***Go-Go years, Slow Go years, and the No Go years***.

As you age, there is a decline. It happens to everyone. If you don't plan retirement correctly, you may miss the Golden (Go-Go) years due to a lack of income.

Getting your retirement right is important for happiness and precious time!

Now, let us review the checklist I detailed earlier in this chapter. When we meet with our clients, we draw most of these questions out on a glass wall in our conference room. It helps everyone to visualize the issues they are facing. We do not consider these appointments to be 'Sales Meetings.' We call it our new client onboarding. We don't even consider investment recommendations until we have been hired. This typically takes three meetings to accomplish. Our clients have high confidence in their approach to retirement and their investments.

The Math Changes when you take Income in Retirement[70]

Now the Checklist (Checklist items are marked with a ✓)

✓ Social Security Income estimates and optimal filing dates

When you retire, you do not need to file for Social Security benefits immediately. Early claiming is at 62, and your benefits top out at 70[71]. The longer you wait to file, the more lifetime inflation-adjusted benefits you receive. Spending some of your retirement accounts may be wise to allow your Social Security benefits to grow. You do, however, want to run a Social Security

[70] Not sarcasm.

[71] On average waiting until age 70 to collect Social Security retirement benefits adds 76% more. Other factors can affect benefits.

Analysis report. You might be thinking I will download a statement from SSA. That statement will not give you accurate information unless you plan to file for benefits in the next few months. I can project the effects of your future earnings and inflation on your benefits. I will cover more in Chapter 3, Pre-Launch Planning Social Security.

✓ Income Sources for Retirement

Here is where you list your income and how long that income will last. This helps define how much income you need from your retirement plans. Most retirees have savings and Social Security. But you may also have a pension, cash value life insurance, or royalties, to name a few. Remember, some royalties fluctuate in income or can end completely. You may need to research this. Pensions likewise may not offer increases in the cost of living. Some pensions may give you a partial or full lump sum at retirement. It would be best if you evaluated the IRR[72]. For example, if the IRR is 2%, could you get a better rate through an annuity or a stock and bond account? Another way to consider this is to calculate the payments over 10 or 20 years and compare them to what you could get in an investment account with the lump sum offer.

Pension Tips

Some pensions offer a reduced benefit if you want your spouse to receive checks after you die. Consider whether a life insurance policy could be a cost-effective option for a reduced benefit to provide for a spouse. For example, pension option (1) may be a $3,000 lifetime pension, and option (2) is a $2,000 Lifetime Pension with spousal continuance.[73]

If a permanent life insurance policy would replace the lost pension for a $500-a-month premium, then going with option 1 and buying life insurance would net you an extra $ 500-a-month income.

Liquidity sometimes becomes an issue. Meaning there is no cash you can access in an emergency. Pension plans only offer a benefit (i.e., a monthly check), and you lose the check when you die. (There is usually a spousal continuance, but at a reduced benefit.) This needs to be thoroughly evaluated before you retire to choose the best options.

We also need to factor in taxes. Taxes are often overestimated using tax brackets and marginal rates, but that is not your effective tax rate. Overestimating taxes could cause you to

---

[72] Internal Rate of Return

[73] Spousal continuance -the pension payments are continued by your spouse in case of your death.

miss planning opportunities because you are misled about taxes, like Roth Conversions—more on this in Chapter 5.

Real Estate Investments

We list real estate under Income due to the capital generally being illiquid. (We always exclude your primary home from net worth and income inventory lists.) Income from Rental real estate can be difficult. The cash flow is often positive, and depending on the time you have owned it, the depreciation can leave you with no taxes to pay. (Income becomes taxable when full depreciation is realized[74]) However, rental real estate involves work and management. evictions, squatters, tenants moving, maintenance, and town ordinances can all make rental real estate a full-time job with stress and liability. Toilets that need to be fixed dealing with renters, planning for unexpected expenses, property taxes, income taxes (after it's been fully depreciated), and so on. There is also liability from lawsuits, renter theft, and renter damages. If you own many properties, you must decide how many to hold post-retirement. This affects your income.

Your rental real estate income will be fully taxable after the depreciation is fully realized.

Hiring a management company often significantly reduces your income. Now, you need to decide if all this risk and hassle is worth it and whether the net income on your capital is greater than the passive investment yield.

For example, you own $500,000 of real estate value, and the net income after expenses = $15,000 or 3% of your capital. Can you make more on a passive investment? If you add the cost of your personal aggravation and involvement, is it still worth it? "But you say I pay 0% taxes on that 3%." Nay, nay, I say. When you sell the property, if it is fully depreciated, you pay a capital gains tax on the proceeds and potentially a depreciation tax of 25%. Also, the income will be taxable once the depreciation is fully written off. So the real question is: after adjusting for taxes, time, stress, and opportunity cost, is the return still worth it? Consider these questions.

Who will manage your real estate as you age, and will it still be profitable?

When you die, will your spouse and children be able to continue your property holdings as you did?

Often, it makes sense to sell the properties and invest in assets that will be easier to manage and pass to heirs (when you die) after retirement. This will depend on your income need and the type of rental real estate you own. There is a powerful step up in basis upon death to consider as

[74] Rental Real Estate Taxes -Investopedia.com

well. Developing procedures on how real estate is managed is important to consider in retirement.

Wait, I made my wealth from Real Estate! And some made their wealth working at a job or in a business. Life changes when you retire. Be careful spending your Go-Go years working on real estate or a business.

Post Retirement Employment

Part-time work is also a tricky endeavor. You want to project this on the low side. Finding work after retirement is not so easy. Many highly paid executives find that no one wants to be seen with them after retirement and are not interested in paying enormous amounts of money for a part-time executive. This seems strange but is unfortunate. So, be careful when counting on a consulting gig after you retire. You usually have to develop this while in the business, not after. Developing relationships and contracts with solid offers before you retire will improve your chances of being a consultant after retirement.

Without solid concrete contracts and employment offers, your post-retirement consultancy could be a dream.

> One of my clients retired from Texas Tech University as a Pharmacist. She immediately wrote a policies and procedures manual that Texas Pharmacies are required to have. It kept her in the Profession, and she made a considerable retirement income selling this manual, which she directly marketed to independent pharmacies. No publisher was needed. She died a few years ago. Her husband told me he still gets calls for the policy and procedures manual.

Post Retirement Businesses - Where Everyone Knows Your Name

If you dream of retiring to a bar where 'everyone knows your name,'[75] you want to be careful. Small businesses are tricky and risky. If you watch shows like Kitchen Nightmares, the Profit, or Bar Rescue, you can see the mess very successful people get into. A small business can quickly go from net income to a money-eating beast. (see picture) Your retirement should not be more stressful than your career was. The other issue you must consider is what happens to the business if you fall ill or die.

---

[75] Quote from the 80's sit-com theme song named Cheers

Finally, do you have it in you to start another company? This can make retirement a non-retirement. Business is hard and often takes more than just capital and an idea to make it work.

Will your spouse or heirs be able to handle the responsibility and decisions needed to continue its successful operation if you die or become ill?

Big Tom's Burgers Fries and Pizza Pies

A small business is not always easy to sell, especially if the business is in trouble. Here is a personal story. I decided to build a restaurant in 2009. The name was 'Big Tom's Burgers Fries and Pizza Pies.' It was a cool 50's restaurant. How did it go, you ask? Not too good, I say. It was an unmitigated disaster. My restaurant manager (Tom), whom I thought I knew well, was not up to the task. (Had I investigated his past employers before entering the partnership, I would have discovered a history of poor employment and bad management decisions. Beware of putting friendship or family above business.) After nine months and losing $120,000, we closed the restaurant. The experience strained the relationship between my wife, son-in-law, stepdaughter, and other family. Business is hard and has a high chance of failure, even among experienced businesspeople. Eight restaurants out of ten will fail within five years, with 60% failing the first year.[76]

Here is a Headline That Reiterates Our Experience.

Garth Brooks' relationship with Trisha Yearwood was put to the test when they opened his Friends in Low Places honky-tonk bar in Nashville. 'I don't think God could invent anything that would make me and Miss Yearwood want to be apart' -Garth Brooks from Fox News article, March 8, 2024.

Reduce Stress and Risk in Retirement, Not Increase It.

---

[76] Source: https://atonce.com/blog/what-percentage-of-restaurants-fail-in-the-first-year

I do not recommend pursuing small businesses, restaurants, or real estate in retirement. This stress can affect your marriage and health. These ventures require long-term commitments, operational stress, and a high risk of losing your capital. If you move forward with starting or buying a business, get a CPA to craft a business plan and a lawyer to work out the contracts and legal aspects, like incorporating the business to shield your personal assets from lawsuits or business failure. Consider the succession planning aspect. Your spouse or heirs may not have the business or negotiating chops that you do. This may be a problem when you die. Buy/Sell agreements with life insurance might be an option.

Also, consider *borrowing* the start-up cost instead of liquidating your retirement accounts. Look at businesses where you have previous experience. Consider a partnership group instead of being the sole owner. (More on this in Chapter 5 on taxes.) Don't risk your retirement in a high-risk venture. Protect your Capital!

Creating a Job for Your Kid

Sometimes, retirees invest in a business to 'help' a child or grandchild. This often goes bad, so please be careful. No one is going to tell you that your kid is an idiot. If your capital burns up in this business, no one wins. Please don't ask my opinion about your family; I am too nice.

When the Apollo program built its spaceships, it constantly had to decide between risks, costs, and objectives related to fuel, weight, and design. Tradeoffs were constant. Ultimately, they wanted to land on the moon and return home safely. Look at your checklist items, Retirement Objectives, and Your Ideal Retirement Life, and ask where a small business fits.

When asked by reporters about what it was like to be sitting on top of the rocket for his Mercury mission, Alan Shepard answered, "The fact that every part of [the] ship was built by the lowest bidder."

✓ Retirement Asset Inventory

Like listing your income sources, your retirement assets will be your bank accounts and other assets like 401k, 403b, 457, and other IRAs. How are these assets invested, and what is the current strategy employed? It would be best to stress test the risk and investment strategy used. It is essential to evaluate the income level (interest and dividends) produced and whether you can improve it. You need to be aware of growth strategy investments in retirement for the reasons I previously outlined.

✓ Identify Retirement Objectives and Risks

Your objectives should determine your investments. We look at the top three. Many advisors ask these questions only *after* they have pitched a product or investment to you; your objectives didn't actually matter. They often encourage you to accept higher risk categories because of buy and hold. I remember calling compliance departments at former firms I was with to ask what the difference between conservative, moderately conservative, moderate, or aggressive was. No one wanted to answer that. But this is one of the most important data points to understand.

It would be best if you ranked what is most important to you:

Generating income to meet or exceed your retirement goals.

Make sure your risk is appropriate for you.

Maximize growth for a large purchase or leave a legacy.

"Know Thyself" -inscribed on the Temple of Apollo, Delphi, Greece.

Know Yourself, Risk Capacity vs Risk Tolerance

*"**Risk Tolerance** refers to an individual's psychological willingness to take on risk. It is about your emotional and psychological comfort with risk."*

*"**Risk Capacity*** relates more to the *financial ability* to endure potential losses."[77]

Knowing yourself about this is essential. An advisor might recognize that you can take the risk from a purely financial standpoint. For example, if you lost 50% of your retirement portfolio, you might still be able to cover your desired income. Using the retirement plan data discussed in Chapter 2, an advisor may try to convince you to accept a higher risk than you are emotionally cut out for. It would be best to stand firm on the level of risk you can take. (You likely need to find an advisor philosophically aligned with you.) If you get a statement on your accounts that says you are down $250,000, will this ruin your day or month? Who cares if you can afford it? Constant worry is a terrible way to live; this stress has been proven to shorten one's life.

[77] Quoted from Investopedia.com "What Is the Difference Between Risk Tolerance and Risk Capacity?"

In addition to determining objectives, we must seriously discuss how much risk of loss you can tolerate. (Review illustration 2.1 from Chapter 2.) Next, we will write out the following:

0%	$1,000,000
-12%	$850,000
-25%	$750,000
-37%	$630,000
-50%	$500,000

To the left column is the percentage loss.
The right column is the effect on an account starting at $1,000,000.00
We use this to visualize what the losses look and feel like.

Illustration 3.4

- ***At what loss amount are you losing your mind?***
- ***At what loss percentage are you searching for the panic button?***
- ***How would the loss affect your spouse?***
- ***What loss % would cause changes to your retirement lifestyle or your mental peace?***

We had a prospective client in our office who lost it because she was down -12% on her IRA with another advisor. Then, she said that a -25% downside was acceptable. We pointed out why she was there. She smiled and said maybe not -25%. Remember, there is a difference between being able to afford losses and how losses will affect your mental health.

Please review illustration 2.1 in Chapter 2 again. Do you remember how volatility can affect your retirement and how it magnifies your losses when taking income? Illustration 2.2 demonstrates a 4% hypothetical withdrawal with S&P 500 performance between 2000 and 2013. Now, think about your risk tolerance above. Too many ‘advisors’ want you to trust the market with no procedure for losses except to hold.

Is your procedure for a market crash to suspend your income until your account value returns?

Apollo 13 Had Procedures.

Thinking out procedures for what can go wrong is so important. The lifeboat procedure of Apollo 13 saved the lives of the astronauts. They did not have time to come up with it on the fly, and any mistakes could have ended the mission then. If you have significant losses in retirement, that will be a stressful lifestyle change. Finally, losing money and switching to ‘safe’ investments locks in your losses. This option is often necessary, but could have been avoided with accurate risk analysis in the beginning, with a procedure for losses.

"I am fond of telling people when they create their plan to make sure they are doing some scenario planning around what is the best case, probable case, & worse case outcomes …" Robert Powell, CFP & Financial Journalist, in a podcast interview "How Do I Generate Income."

The Risk Quiz

The advisor gives you a page of questions. You answer the questions, and your answers generate a score that correlates to your risk level. The purpose of the 20 questions is for you to score a higher risk tolerance than you might typically accept. If you mess up one question, you might do better on the next. Also, the advisor has proof (to the regulators at the next audit) that he probed your risk tolerance.

The standard risk tolerance options are Conservative, Moderately Conservative, Moderate, Aggressive, and Speculation. I have asked compliance principals at different affiliated companies I have worked with to define these words, but they were always reluctant to do so.

Understanding the primary objectives and risk tolerance, or, more precisely, how much you can stand to lose, helps you focus on the correct investments or strategy to pursue. If your objective is income, do you continue to withdraw 4% of $1,000,000? What happens if you lose 50% of the value? Now, you are at an 8% draw. You will need to reduce your income (or eliminate it) to protect the value of your account(s) or risk running out of money.

We use software that ***stress tests*** your portfolio against previous market declines. If you are comfortable with -12% but the stress test reveals your portfolio has a -37% or -60% downside potential, then you have a problem to solve.[78] We do this instead of Monti Carlo's analysis, which considers massive losses and $1 remaining in your account before you die a win.[79] The 4% rule does the same by looking at your portfolio over 35 years and seeing success. But will you need to have a lot of faith in the 4% rule if your account loses 50-70%?

Don't worry, your money will come back, your advisor says—time in the market vs timing the market, he says. Don't worry about burning up your Go-Go years with lower or no income and health-eroding stress.

[78] No software can guarantee your loss target won't be exceeded. Past Performance is not a guarantee to future results.

[79] Most Monti Carlo simulations will accept $1 remaining before death as a success.

✓ Retirement Expense/Debt Review

What are your monthly/yearly expenses? After retirement, how will those change? How much revolving debt do you have, and what is your plan to pay that down? One way to do this is to do a Top-Down analysis. Look at your household's annual income and subtract the taxes, retirement savings, and other non-retirement expenses. This becomes your retirement base income. This can be a truer income in retirement. You can add up all your expenses and approach it bottoms up, but most people tend to understate their base income needs.

In the transition stage, it is important to pay off credit card debt and other obligations you have taken on. Some folks we meet are paying their kids' college debt. One caution, however, is that many want to pay off the home mortgage. This may be the lowest interest you pay in most cases. The other debt should come first, followed by building up uninvested cash reserves and then paying down the mortgage. In Chapter 5, I will talk about options for large purchases in retirement.

Come to Terms with Your Spending.

Occasionally, someone comes into our office whom we can't or don't want to help. Let me explain with a story. After attending one of our educational events, a woman and her son scheduled an appointment. At first, we were excited because she had $2 million in liquid assets. Further, we discovered that her accounts had negative returns over the last decade. During the great bull market! How was that even possible?

I asked some questions, and we realized her accounts had been nearly $5 million 10 years ago. I asked her 40-something son what his career was. He was very shifty about that question. I also found out he golfed nearly every day. He wore an expensive golf polo shirt, designer shoes, and had no job. He got an allowance from his dearest mommy. Finally, we could determine that the amount she was taking from her savings was enormous and unsustainable.

My partner, Subhani, broke the ice on the underlying problem we were seeing.

"At this rate of spending, you're going to be out of money in 5 years," he said, looking up from his time value of money calculations.

I knew what was happening, but I couldn't give them the answers they wanted. They need to cut spending drastically, meaning her son needed to get a job. On the other hand, they would need an enormous investment return to sustain their accounts and spending. We gave them some options, from aggressive to safer, with a reasonable withdrawal rate. (I did not tell the son to be a man, get a job, and stop sucking your mom dry because, apparently, I am nice) The conversation drifted, and they said they would call us for another appointment, which we both knew wouldn't happen.

The moral of the story is that there is a limit to how much you can take from your accounts before they run dry. Children can be a drag on parents in retirement if they do not support themselves. You may need tough love to get your adult children to make better decisions about employment and spending. You may not want to do this, but it will happen someday. It may be after you die. The piper will need to be paid. You may need to apply financial discipline to yourself. Dave Ramsey has courses that may assist you.

The Financial 'Day of Reckoning' *will come for your children. If it is after your funeral, you won't be able to guide them through it. Better, the tough love comes from you. Cutting off a child financially is difficult. Remember, we learn through adversity and hard times. If your child loses a house or has to live in a low-rent district, they will learn and be better for the lesson.*

"Experience: that most brutal of teachers. But you learn, my God do you learn." -C.S Lewis

I can't make the numbers do something impossible. Uncontrolled spending will have consequences. Please act before you run out of money. Dave Ramsey's money management courses have helped many people control their spending. He points out that new spending habits take 90 days to implement.

As for me, I stopped being nice. I tell it like it is. One client came in with an unsustainable number of withdrawals from his accounts. I explained that this would result in going to zero. Subhani (my business partner) showed him the numbers. Next came the uncomfortable stare from him and his wife. Finally, he said, "Why didn't my (Big Wall Street firm) advisor tell me this?" He transferred his accounts to us, and we got him on a sustainable income plan at the risk level he was comfortable with. We are close friends, and he is my unpaid Sous Chef at my client dinners.

"Being a smart shopper is the first step to getting rich." – Mark Cuban.

✓ Your Ideal Retirement Life

- ➢ What is your plan after you and your spouse retire?
- ➢ Will you spend more time with your grandchildren? (School events, athletics, band.)
- ➢ Will you buy an RV and travel?
- ➢ Will you book as many cruises as possible?
- ➢ Will you do charity work?
- ➢ Will you volunteer at your church?
- ➢ Will you pursue hobbies?
- ➢ Can you mentor?
- ➢ Will you golf more?
- ➢ Do you want to do more than sit in a chair, pay the bills, and watch Jeopardy?

I want to____ in retirement (me)

I want to____ in retirement (your spouse)

Do something great in retirement!

I once read an article about a guy who took his grandson to every baseball stadium in the US. Now, that is a memory that was impossible when he had a 9-5 job!

Also, it's important to talk this over with your spouse. We have had onboarding meetings that exploded with differences between spouses. We have had couples who discovered they wanted different things out of retirement. Suddenly, I was a marriage counselor instead of an advisor.

Next, how much do these dreams cost? This is an important step and avoid the whole we are simple people routine. Everyone has dreams. Can we make them happen? Retirement can be much more interesting if you understand your 'want' income from your 'need' income.

Do you want to do more in retirement than sit in a chair watching Jeopardy and paying bills?

✓ Retirement Income Needs and Wants

How much will you need to fund your needs and wants in retirement? Let us say you are deciding on retiring in a few months, but you realize you have been planning to pay the bills when you retire and are not thinking about your wants in retirement. Now you have to decide:

Do I work longer? Plan to work part-time after retirement? Find a way to reduce some expenses to allow for the wants.

The net income you are currently living on is a good start. However, it is essential to consider the cost of your ideal retirement life. Once we arrive at a number (high and low), we can see how to achieve it. Then plan for the things you want to do if the money was available. Needs and Wants.

✓ Tax Strategies to employ now and later

The biggest tax preparation you need to look at is your IRA/401k/403b accounts. These become massive tax bombs in retirement. First, you need to start a Roth IRA if you haven't already. In order to access the money in a Roth tax-free, you need 5 years in any Roth IRA (Roth in your 401k does not count towards the 5-year clock) and be over 59.5 years old. A tax review is also needed to see what can be employed to lower future taxes and improve tax efficiency—more on this in Chapter 5, Taxes.

✓ Investment Strategy (Moving from the G to the I)

"The four most dangerous words in investing are, it's different this time." — Sir John Templeton.

Now, we consider the investments that align with your risk and objectives. Once you have cleared your checklist, the choices become apparent, and the work of clearing out the toxic investments in your portfolio and moving ahead with the risk and investments that are in your best interest.

Investment Strategy is a high-level view and not a product or service pitch. There is more than one way to skin a cat. I'm not sure why we want to skin a cat, but the point I am making is that there are several ways to get you where you want to be. But first, we need to know where we are going.

The Formula for a More Successful Retirement

Here is where you need a philosophy change. This is not a new thing. It is so basic you may wonder why you didn't think of this before. Here it is:

TR = I + G

Total Return = Income (Interest/Dividends) + Growth (Capital Gain/Loss)

Illustration 3.5

"If you want retirement to be stress-free, invest for the I, not the G."[80]

According to a recent survey, death is not America's #1 fear, but rather running out of money.[81]

Too many retirees are depending on *growth* to fund retirement, not *income*. This is like jumping on an alligator. How long before he snaps you in half?

For a successful retirement, income should be first, and growth should be second. Look at Illustration 2.2. Do you see the 13-year zero-growth market? Drawing from growth investments during that time would cause you to lose 50% or more of your account's value.

Understanding the risks that the markets contain has been particularly challenging since 2008 for two reasons. The lowest interest rates on fixed income like government bonds, corporate bonds, and CDs. This has caused investors to look to the equity markets. The greatest and longest bull market (especially for growth stocks) we have ever seen.[82]

---

[80] We are not implying any investment is without risks or considerations. All investments have varying risks of loss that should be explained and understood before investing. I credit this quote to public speaking trainer Patrick Peason.

[81] Survey done by Allianz Life 2023 "Americans Facing a New Retirement Reality"

[82] The S&P 500 went up 401% from March 9, 2009 – February 19, 2020. Returns are cumulative and based on the S&P 500 index price movement only, and don't include dividends. You can't invest directly in an index.

When 2008 came along, we were facing a massive recession, possibly a depression, from an overheated real estate market collapsing and taking the banking system with it. Big Wall Street overborrowed, overleveraged, and over-risked its balance sheets. In response, the Federal Reserve Bank lowered its overnight rate to nearly zero, and it remained for over a decade. With bonds offering low yields, investors began relying on the equity markets for their retirement savings.

Interest Rates Have Stayed Low for Over a Decade. This has pushed Investors into Growth Stocks!

After they (the Fed Bank) dropped rates to nearly zero, they went out and bought trillions of dollars of bonds out of the market (called Quantitative Easing) three times! Now with the rise of the machines, Artificial Intelligence where do we go from here. The riskier the markets get, the higher they go. Folks, this never ends well!

Imagine you went to a farmers' market to buy some watermelons. Then, someone came in and started buying the watermelons, driving the prices up. The Feds did the same thing, changing fixed-income investing for a decade! The investors moved towards stocks and out of bonds, giving us the longest bull market in our history.

Yes, interest rates bottomed out. Unless you like 1% on a CD or less than .10% on a money market, you might have no other choice but to invest in the stock market. Low interest rates caused a new phenomenon. Corporations started borrowing money at really low rates and bought back their stock. This caused their earnings to rise. Huh, you ask? Why does a company buying its own stock cause its earnings to rise? Don't you have to sell more products or services over the previous quarter and make more money, you ask?

Let me break it down for you, Barney[83] style.

A closely watched number when investing in stocks is called EPS or Earnings Per Share. Allow me to illustrate. Let us say you have 100 teddy bears, and they collectively receive 100 dollars per year, which is $1 per bear. If I repurchase ten bears and take them out of circulation, there will be 90 bears, but there is more. Now, if the 90 bears still receive $100, the EPB (earnings per bear) is no longer $1 but $1.11 per bear. There are fewer bears, but the same amount of revenue. Fewer bears to share earnings with. (Barney disapproves of not sharing. Now let's hug.)

83 You know Barney the dinosaur, the Kids TV show. I am simplifying the Price to Earnings ratio. I suggest going to Investopedia for a more substantial read on this topic. Don't search for Barney style.

When a company's profitability increases (more E or earnings), the stock price generally increases.[84] But wait, you ask; everyone can see this, right? It isn't a secret that the company, I mean, Bears, didn't make more money; they just manipulated the bear/stock value. (It's called financial engineering, you rube) And yes, stock analysts could see this happening and were good with it. (Especially for corporation executives who get paid in stock options. Higher stock prices mean more cha-ching in the option exercise!)

Consider that the US GDP[85] from 2010 to 2019 averaged +2.21%. Folks, that is low economic growth. But wait, the stock market went up *401%!* Is it any wonder that everyone's retirement went into stocks? But not any stocks, *Growth Stocks!*[86] We even made a new name for the highest-growth performers. They are called FANG and the Magnificent 7.[87]

"The market can stay irrational longer than you can stay solvent."
—John Maynard Keynes, English Economist and Philosopher.

In recent years, technology stocks (now called the AI trade) have exploded. With higher prices come high Price to Earnings ratios. The most concerning statistic at this point is the market's overvaluation, especially in technology.

Using P/E (PE is Price to Earnings), how much you are paying for a stock with respect to how much the company earns. Imagine a business is for sale for $100,000. You find out it makes $10,000 a year. The PE = 10 or 10 times earnings. What if the owner instead wants $300,000 with the same earnings? You are paying a PE =30 or 30 times earnings. How much the business can grow its earnings will be your primary question. Deciding the right price to pay for a business is hard, and if the business revenue drops, so does its value.

To make matters worse, the S&P 500, which is supposed to be 500 US stocks, is 42% Technology with 22 stocks making up 45% of the index.[88] This is very concentrated and now depends on a few companies.

---

[84] There are other factors that influence stock prices but earnings (current & future) are accepted as the primary factor.
[85] Gross domestic product (GDP) is the total monetary or market value of all the finished goods and services produced within a country's borders in a specific time period. -Investopedia.com
[86] According to the S&P 500 Guide to the Markets Fact Set, Standard and Poor's, JP Morgan – U.S. Data are as of 09-30-2023
[87] This is not a recommendation to purchase any security. FAANG -Facebook, Apple, Amazon, Netflix and Google. Magnificent 7 -Meta, Amazon, Nvidia, Microsoft, Apple, Alphabet and Tesla.
[88] State Street Global Advisors (SPDR): Look at the "Sector Breakdown" for the SPY ETF, which tracks the index directly.
Goldman Sachs Investment Research in March of 2026 stated 22 companies make over 40% of the S&P 500.

Blah, Blah, Blah. Why do I care?

Ok, this may seem in the weeds here, but the powerful US stock market is overvalued! If we look at the PE or price-to-earnings on the S&P 500, it is very rich.[89] Richer than it was before the 2000-2002 and 2008-2009 market crashes.

S&P 500	**10 yr avg**	**25.9 PE**	**2026**	**PE**	**31**	**??**
	50 yr avg	**19 PE**	**2000**	**PE**	**30**	**market lost 47% by 2002**
			2008	**PE**	**23**	**market lost 57% by 2009**

People are falling over themselves to invest. I remember people taking cash advances on their credit cards in 1998 and 1999 to invest in the markets. That ended badly. The danger to their retirement is serious. Market conditions are changing as they always do. Past winners may not continue to grow at the same rate they did once everyone has their product. A disappointing earnings growth number (notice I didn't say negative earnings, we don't need negative earnings to produce a market crash).

In 2026, a lower growth number for key businesses could result in a *27% – 30% market decline if the PE pulls back to just 20*! Notice that the 50-year average listed above is 19.[90] Makes you think.

Déjà-vu de 2000?

The markets look to me very similar to 2000. The internet was expanding, and every company was purchasing desktop computers like they were going out of style in order to replace mainframes and mini-computers in preparation for Y2K!

Y2K came and went. The lights stayed on, and electronic Armageddon was avoided. The Dot-coms and Hardware companies, however, saw a massive drop in earnings! (We didn't need so many computers.) The Tech bubble popped, and the NASDAQ loss 78%, and the dot coms went to zero. It took ***17 years*** for Technology to recover its 2000 peak stock prices.

Could the same thing happen once the data centers are built? History repeats itself. The market always comes back from crashes and drops. For you its about time. Another 13 year no growth market at 65 years old means you are 78 years old when it recovers. A major oxygen tank explosion!

---

[89] These PE numbers are based on where they were in January 2026.

[90] 2. Taken from Think Tank Warning: 7 Threats to the US Stock Market & Economy 02/10/2026

That is a lot of life to miss trying to time the markets.

- *"How would you feel if a market downturn caused you and your wife to reduce your spending significantly and caused you to stop traveling, dining out, and buying gifts for children or grandchildren?*
- *How would you feel if your lifestyle changed because the market crashed again and your account with it?*
- *Would you share this news with friends and family?*
- *Does running out of money in retirement concern you? It should.*

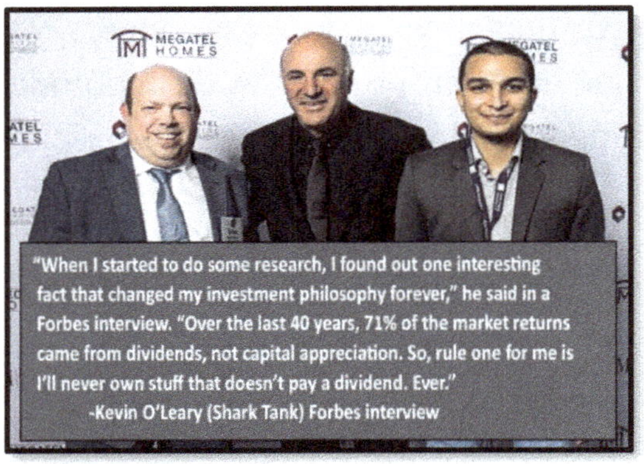

Photo of with Kevin O'Leary in 2020.

(This is not photoshopped! I would have picked a picture of me skinner)

Refocusing Your Formula for a More Secure Retirement

If you look at the past, every bull market ends. Stressing about whether the market is ready to decline is not any way to retire. Focusing on income in retirement is a better way. Let us consider how dividends play a significant role in long-term performance.

$100,000 invested in the S&P 500 in 1980:

Without dividends reinvested, it would have grown to <u>$1,790,000,</u> or 17.9 times its value in 2019.

With dividends reinvested, it would have grown to <u>$5,285,290</u> or over 52 times its value in 2019.

In retirement, you are no longer able to buy and hold. You need to access this money; you need *cash flow*. ***(Say that like a late-night DJ)***

One year or 20 years, does it matter?

The last thing to happen on Apollo 13 was the deployment of the parachutes. Running out of power then would have sucked. Whether a severe market decline happens in one year from now or in twenty, it doesn't matter. This will significantly affect your retirement income for you and your family. If you are 65 and retired and depending on growth investments, I can't tell you enough that selling shares for income is dangerous. The market history is clear, and good times end. What is your procedure for that? I hope it isn't cutting your income and waiting it out. It was cold and dark on Apollo 13 when they cut the power to 12 amps, meaning nearly everything was off. They only had to wait four days. You will have to wait to die. Not exactly a great plan.

Or maybe you think you can time the market and be out when the proverbial 'crap hits the fan.' Basing your future on 2009 – 2020 market history is dangerous. Retirement should not be messing around in the market; you need reliable income for you and your spouse. You may not be able to recoup next time.

Again, with Reverse Dollar Cost Averaging

No one can predict where the market is going. When you are an accumulator, consistent investments in your portfolio during the stock market's ups and downs will make you money over the long term and smooth out volatility. We call it dollar cost averaging. But as I have repeatedly said, when you retire and begin withdrawing, you can see *reverse dollar cost averaging* if you sell shares for income. The ups and downs will *cause* massive erosion to your principal, ending in you running out of money. (Unless you die first, then the problem is solved) And we are only now beginning to understand the damage caused by the COVID lockdowns and the effect of a *$38 trillion debt* (impactful music) on our economy.

Your Oxygen Tank Explosion event

I am not worried about a crash since the markets will always come back, eventually. I am worried that *your* account will decline because of a market crash, causing you to delay your retirement, erode your savings, or reduce your retirement income and lifestyle. (Play the game show 'You Lost' music.) See illustration 3.3

In an interview in early 2023, Elon Musk said the following:

"In the past, when there's been a recession … it's amazing – it's flipped like a light switch. I mean, David, do you remember this when from PayPal, you know, the ex-PayPal days? When we raised $100 million in March of 2000,
we literally had the demand so high, and we had people like VCs (Venture Capitalists), just literally without even a term sheet, wiring money into our account. They literally were like, sleuth out our bank account number and just wire money in. And we're like, where did this come from? There was literally fire-hosing money in March of 2000.
In April of 2000, the market went into freefall. Raising money went from trivial to even good com panies could not raise money in a month."

The problems on Apollo 13 started with Swigert flipping the oxygen tank fan switches. The mission went from normal to disaster in a moment. The mission changed from exploration to survival.

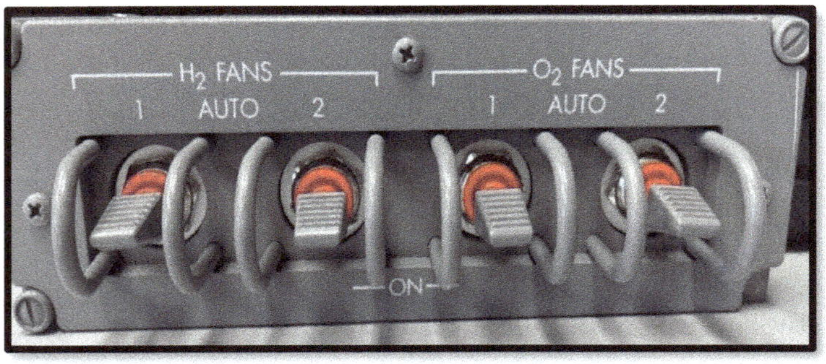

(A replica of the fan switches on the Command Module that started the oxygen tank explosion on

We will cover common investments in Chapter 6, "Launch Day Your Spaceship Awaits You." Whether you are realigning your portfolio for the Transition or Distribution stage, it is time to focus on 'I' and not the 'G.' Discard it like a used-up rocket stage. Also, you need an advisor passionate about the 'I' type of investments. This check item is important.

Understand what is happening when you are distributing funds from your account. You are either selling shares to cover income or distributing *cash flow*. (Again, say that like a late-night DJ)

"In inflationary times, all of a sudden, quality really matters.
Cash flow matters, distributions in the form of dividends matter…"
—Kevin O'Leary[91] Shark Tank Investor

91 CNBC.com Boring is the new black – Kevin O'Leary on how he's investing in a rising inflation environment Jan 21, 2022

You must sell shares to meet your income needs if you have a growth portfolio. That happens in illustration 2.2 of chapter 2; you are selling *shares* and *losing* money! If the value of your investments goes up, then you are fine. If history is any guide, a strong bull market is followed by a crash and a sideways market for years. Investing for growth is more volatile and inherently risky. As I explained, this is the retirement killer.

Real Estate Illustration

Let me explain it this way. Let's say you own 1000 acres of undeveloped land close to a suburb. It is producing no crop but has been going up in value. So, you slowly start selling off a few acres at a time. You look at the value of your land, and it keeps rising. You feel good; your property is a hot commodity. Then real estate prices collapse, and your land drops massively in value. Now, no one wants to buy your land. You continue selling acres for income only now at a much lower price, and you must sell more. The real estate crisis has passed, but the value of your acreage hasn't increased as much as you expected since you only have 500 acres of your original 1000. You realize that you are going to run out of land to sell.

Now, let us propose that the land is planted in a crop you harvest and sell. The value of the land isn't rising very much due to it being a farm. But you have the income from the crops. In drought years, you have crop insurance payments. But after some time, you still have the 1000 acres when you are ready to sell. You get income from the crops and some growth from the price of your acres. Isn't this a better long-term investment for retirement? (Retirement is the distribution stage).

Some market-based dividend investments (Dividend Stocks, Preferred Stocks, REITs, BDC, MLP, mREIT, and more) seem boring and may have a growth rate lower than the 'G' investments. In a market downturn, your market-based investments will lose value. However, the dividend stocks will likely still pay income. (Dividends can be reduced or cut completely, so selection and management is important) In the current interest rate environment, preferred stocks, government, and corporate bonds are interesting again and can be added to the 'I' portfolio.

Harvested cotton on my Hale Center ranch in 2009

⇦ To the left is harvested cotton bales.
To the right is lots in a subdivision. ⇨

"In investing, what is comfortable is rarely profitable."
—Robert Arnott, founder and chairman of the board of Research Affiliates, a 166 billion asset management firm.

Quoting Investopedia on Dividends

"Dividends are a major factor in reducing overall portfolio risk and volatility. ***In terms of reducing risk, dividend payments mitigate losses that occur from a decline in stock price****. However, the risk reduction benefit of dividends goes beyond that basic fact. Studies have historically shown that dividend-paying stocks outperform non-dividend-paying stocks during bear market periods.* ***While an overall down market generally drags down stocks across the board, dividend-paying stocks usually suffer significantly less decline in value than non-dividend-paying stocks."*** *-Quote from "5 Reasons Why Dividends Matter to Investors Updated January 31, 2022 -Investopedia.com"*

You may be sitting in an Apollo 1-built retirement and don't realize it. "But it was built by the largest and smartest firm on Big Wall Street, you say." Really? The smartest people-built Apollo 1. It didn't make it to launch day. Market history is clear: the conflicts of interest are working against you. You need to re-engineer before there is an explosion because there is always an explosion! The legendary Gene Kranz, flight director of Apollo 13, told his team, "Failure is Not an Option!" They were saving those astronauts. Likewise, I want to save your retirement! [92]

"Failure is Not an Option" -Gene Kranz, Chief Flight Director, Apollo 13

The Fiduciary planners use financial planning software programs that may have the purpose of keeping you invested in the 'G,' exposing you to the risk that your retirement fails. The fees seem to be higher in a growth portfolio. Just saying. Look at Illustration 2.2 in Chapter 2. Do you see the 4% withdrawal (remember the 4% rule?) and the erosion of almost 50% of the account value in 13 years? Here is the question,

"If it happened twice, could it happen again?"

What a Nobel Prize-winning economist said.

"The only way to avoid a catastrophe in retirement is to shift your mindset from asset value to income, not how big my pile is. How much reliable income can I count on."
—Robert C Merton Nobel Prize in Economic Science 1997

[92] This is not a guarantee to performance. All investments have varying risks that needs to be understood before investing.

The G is fine if you set aside one year of income -Myth.

Set aside one year of income to be invested in the money market. This assures you can stay invested in growth. When are we replenishing the income account? Hopefully, when the market is high? This involves timing. Who says market timing is an assured strategy[93]? In illustration 3.3, it took seven and six years to return to previous highs in the last two market crises. I contend a much higher reserve account is needed, or you will still have a severe chance of selling when your shares are down. A 6 -7-year cash reserve will reduce your performance pretty significantly. So, what is our procedure for this?

One year cash account is not good enough. There are better options; keep reading.

Large Stock Position or too much Cash

"Love your spouse, not your stocks." In 2000, a client brought a box of AT&T stock certificates into my office. These things looked like they came out of a museum. He had $400,000 worth of AT&T and every spin-off company AT&T had done. I have been telling people that it is safer and easier to transfer stock held in an account (when you die) than it is when it is held in certificate form. He emptied the safe deposit box at the bank and brought the certificates to my office.

I advised him to sell a good portion of the AT&T shares because it was too large of a position. He had worked for AT&T for 40 years; the answer was no, and if I brought it up again, he would move the account. So, I shut up about AT&T. 2002 was not a good year for telecommunication companies, especially AT&T, and in 2003, my client died, and his kids came in to settle Dad's accounts. The $400k was now worth $150,000. The kids initially thought I mismanaged Dad's account. I showed them how much AT&T lost, and they came around. They decided to sell AT&T stock at a huge loss.

My client made an emotional decision based on misplaced loyalty to the company he retired from.

The lesson is not to love any investment. Love your wife not your investments.

Inheritance is also difficult. Your money needs to follow *your objectives,* not your parents.' Also, too much cash can be a serious issue. In Chapter 6, I will discuss liquidity, but too many uninvested funds are losing ground to inflation. This issue is usually caused by an investor's

---

93 See Investopedia 'What is Market Timing'

phobia about investments. But if you follow the checklist and approach investments with the right philosophy, you can be confident about your decisions.

Remember, Stocks are worth what someone else is willing to pay when you are ready to sell.

Summing it Up

We recommend changes to your investment strategy when entering the Transition and Income stages. Failing to do this can force you to change your retirement date or significantly reduce your standard of living. Can you be cavalier about this? Some see the good years in the market and don't want to stop a good thing or miss out on the next best stock.

Your account gains are paper gains until you turn them into cash or income. A lot of people had a bad feeling about Apollo 1. When the accident happened, it was too late. Good men died. But we have seen the market explode before. *We know a major market decline will happen again; we don't know when.*

- ***How would 2008 style losses affect your daily life and relationship with your spouse?***
- ***What do you want to give up (Golf, ladies' lunch, travel, etc.) when another crash happens in retirement?***

Now is the time to develop a strategy that doesn't depend on others to buy your shares at all-time high prices. If the option is no income or to sell at low prices, this strategy can cause you to run out of money.

"Hope for the best, prepare for the worst." -Elon Musk, CEO of Tesla, X, SpaceX, and others.

✓ Review of Your Advisor(s)

When you were a kid, you had a pediatrician doctor. When you became an adult, you switched to a family doctor. Nothing was wrong with your pediatrician, but it was time for a change. We have seen many people who realized their current advisor was not suited to help them at this stage of life.

Then, there is the firm your advisor works for. Before becoming an Independent Wealth Manager, I worked for several large firms. I had a good year at one firm, and my manager sat down with me to discuss next year's production goals. I had sold a pretty diverse list of investments. I focused on my client's needs and recommended what was in their best interest. (Wow, amazing, right?) My manager set my next year's goal for the company's proprietary product. "Ok," I said, "how much do you have in mind?"

“Let’s plan for your current year's production (all investment types combined) into the company’s proprietary product as next year’s goal.” I was essentially told to sell only the investment that made the company the most money. The proprietary product wasn’t a bad investment, but was it the right advice for everyone? It was then that I decided to exit the firm.

This tug-a-war goes on all the time in your Big Wall Street firms. Your broker’s entire business model may be to invest in Stocks, Mutual Funds, and Proprietary Products that maintain the broker firm’s revenue stream and company objectives, not yours. If you have a fee-based Fiduciary advisor, he may need to take risks with your account to justify the fees being charged. (Imagine Marlon Brando saying this line.)

"It’s not personal, Sonny. It’s strictly business," said the voice of the Godfather Marlon Brando.

This is not a discussion of loyalty or friendship; it’s business. It is about who is uniquely suited to plan your retirement income (or transition) stages and is philosophically aligned with you and your best interest.

Hey, you don’t have to ‘whack’ anyone. (You might feel that you want to after losses in your accounts.) Can you see why you need to be objective about the advisor(s) you work with? This question should never be about friendship or loyalty. The issue often is not the advisor but his firm and business model, which may not align with your interests.

I see the statements from other firms come into my office with the firms’ favorite mutual funds or a random list of stocks all the time. When we run our analysis, these portfolios often stress test badly or fail the income test. Remember, smart people designed and built Apollo 1. You shouldn’t risk your retirement with an Apollo 1 design.

My Cancer Scare

I was diagnosed with prostate cancer in 2019. My family physician referred me to a local urologist. He did the tests and confirmed the cancer, then recommended removing the prostate. His approach would have been messy and caused a long recovery. I asked about radiation, and he told me it would likely cause more cancer and additional health problems. This doctor did many of these procedures, and I am sure he was good at them. However, once I did more research, I found his views were outdated, and he made money from the invasive surgery he recommended only. If I were 75, maybe it would have been fine. I'm not close to 75.

I researched and consulted several other doctors. The second one also wanted to remove the prostate with much less invasive surgery using a robotic process with minimal bleeding. I agreed to have him do the surgery, but I keep reading about the radiation treatments. I did another consultation with the robot surgery doctor and asked him why I didn't do the radiation treatment. This procedure had fewer long-term side effects. He said, "Yes, your cancer is very small; that would likely work." Why didn't this doctor mention radiation before? ***Because he gets paid to do robot surgeries only.***

I ended up with External Beam Radiation Therapy, and now I am cancer-free and have a few side effects. My point in this story is that doctors, as do financial advisors, have conflicts of interest. It doesn't mean that my doctors were crooks. Their primary practice revolved around one treatment. Understand the outcome you need. Many advisors' business models assume that you can take more risks. The firm may determine the investments or advice your advisor offers. (Yes, even fiduciary advisors.) They are not crooked, but following their advice might have a life-altering effect on your money. In many cases, higher risk means they can push you into portfolios that generate higher revenue for them, and everything is fine until it isn't. Some investments may not even be considered as they are not offered by the firm or are deemed as non-fiduciary accounts. Thus, your objectives are ignored.

The doctor I chose had a lifetime effect on my life, and so will your financial advisor.

Investments Only Advisor

Then, there is the question of whether your current advisor(s) will actually take a planning approach to your retirement. Please remember that nearly everyone in the industry is now calling themselves a fiduciary and a planner, but they may be neither. Many advisors focus on investments only and may not align with your retirement needs. Performance is tricky and sometimes fleeting. This guy wants you to trust in the markets and his ability to make you money. This selling-shares approach may have a mission-ending effect on your retirement.

Remember, Past Performance does not guarantee Future results.

"I gave my advisor $100,000, and she doubled it," said one client. I showed him a chart showing the S&P 500 cumulative return during the bull market from 2009 to 2020. The market increased by 401%. The reality is that a drunk monkey could make money during that time. Looking at past performance is like driving while focusing on your car's side view mirror. Remember, the mirror says items are closer than they appear. You need to look through the windshield at what is coming.

Let's say you had a portfolio of technology companies in 1999, and I told you that it is time to reevaluate your risk and prepare for retirement in 2001. (Which we say all the time, preparing for a 10 to 40-year retirement.) But you say your advisor has made me so much money!

However, when you ask your growth advisor about a retirement portfolio, he recommends staying where you are. Then, he offers you a questionnaire to fill out for a retirement plan. He returns with the 120-page Plan, then tells you your standard deviation is lower than the S&P 500. With a twinkle in his eye and the knowing smile of a winner, he tells you you're all right. Stay the course, and you will be rich. A wink seals the deal.

Most of us know what happened when the dot.com bubble burst and 9/11. Deciding to delay retirement after half or more of your portfolio goes away is a terrible, terrible plan. I say this because in 1999 a financial advisor told me to stay away from the dot-coms and invest in Cisco and Yahoo tech stocks. He said I would be just fine. It's a good thing I wasn't retiring in 2000, since tech stocks took 15-17 years to recover after the dot-com bubble burst. You read that right, 17 years![94] If you retired at 65 and faithfully did 'buy & hold,' you were 82 when those stocks returned to pre-2000 price levels. (Where did the income you lived on come from?)

Your advisor can instantly go from a genius to a village idiot.

Could he have known this was going to happen? Yes, market history bears this out! (It's not a typo.) Market declines always come as a surprise, but they do come. But many advisors cling to 'buy and hold' like it was holy scripture! This is not just a crazy story; I have seen it happen. The arrogance of some advisors when everything is going well is amazing. What are your market meltdown procedures? The answer is always to buy and hold for the long term as if it were some kind of religion. Where do you get retirement income?

"The road goes on forever, and the party never ends." —Robert Earl King.

[94] S&P 500 Information Technology Index was 988.5 in March of 2000. It lost nearly 80% of its value bottoming out at 170 in September of 2002. It broke the 2000 high in July 19, 2017.

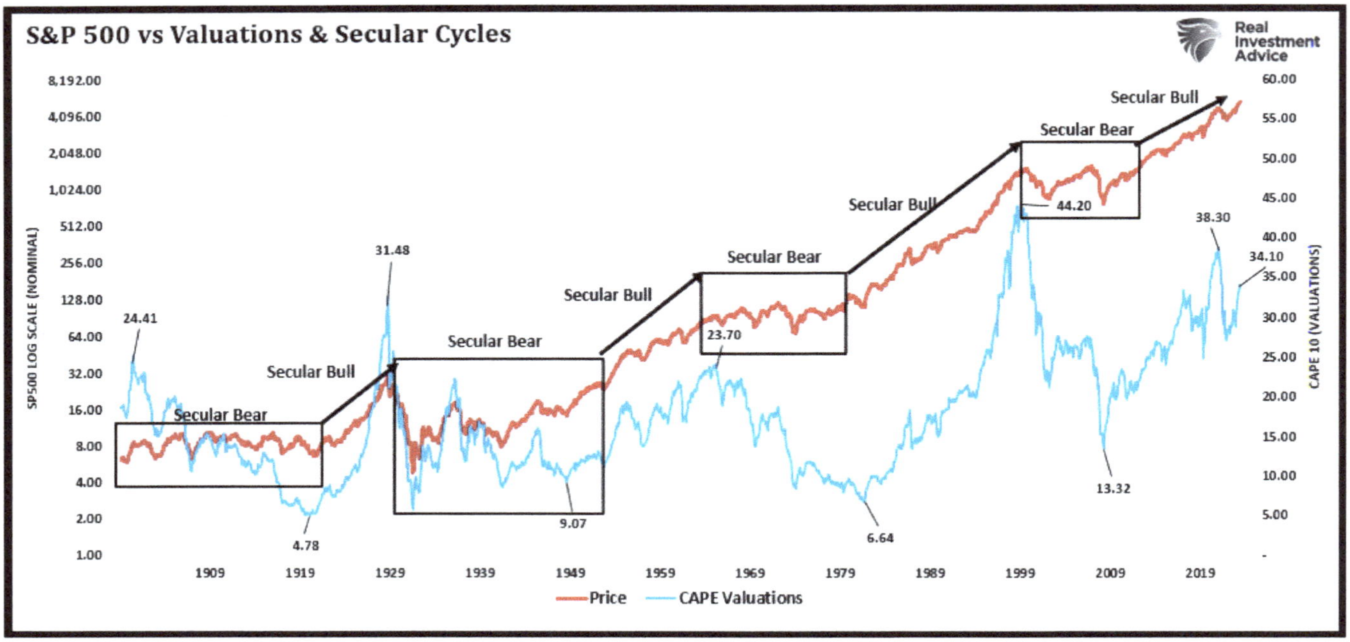

(The above chart uses CAPE[95] valuations based on data from Dr. Robert Shiller.)

Historically, long periods of 'secular bear' markets have followed 'secular bull' markets.[96] Falling into the wrong time period can have a detrimental effect on your retirement.[97]

Advisors who want to be Outperformers instead of Income Planners

Another problem that many advisors struggle with is trying to be outperformers. They are drawn to accumulator-style investing and the equity markets. Many made careers out of the bull markets in 2010 -2020, which conditioned them to be risk-takers. Many advisors may even be ignorant of how fixed income works! Because during that time, interest rates were near zero! It is like bonds became a lost art. I have listened to Brokers who are more loyal to a mutual fund company than they are to their wives!

As I have laid out, priorities should change in the transition and distribution stages of retirement. It is imperative that you have a retirement that doesn't blow up on the launch pad or

95 "CAPE ratio is a valuation measure that uses real earnings per share (EPS) over a 10-year period to smooth out fluctuations in corporate profits that occur over different periods of a business cycle. The CAPE ratio, using the acronym for cyclically adjusted price-to-earnings ratio, was popularized by Yale University professor Robert Shiller." -Investopedia.com

96 The prevailing trend in a "secular bull" market is "bullish" or upward-moving. In a "secular bear," the market tends to trend sideways with severe drawdowns and sharp rallies. -Seeking Alpha 'The Next Secular Bear Market May Be Upon Us' by Lance Roberts

97 Chart source: Real Investment Advice. I would like to thank Lance Roberts at RIA Advisors for allowing me to use this chart

during the next major market downturn. Too many advisors push clients into a more aggressive risk tolerance profile.

"Risk is our business!" -said in the voice of James T Kirk (Star Trek 'Return to Tomorrow' 1968)

Even the 'Fiduciary' advisor may want you to accept a higher risk profile to allow him to pursue a riskier portfolio (and receive a higher fee). Gasp! But a Fiduciary is legally required to operate in my best interest; they could never do something selfish!

Big Wall Street encourages advisors to pursue a "Risk is our business!" investing strategy. As long as you have a 10+ year time horizon, then you can be stock-aggressive. Abby Colen (legendary economist & Goldman Sachs analyst) once told a group that Goldman makes 3x the revenue on growth equity investments. Even in retirement, the firms push the advisors to recommend stocks. Then, the advisors recommend growth investments since you are not going to withdraw all the money at one time, but over the next 20 – 40 years, you can still have an equity portfolio. Have faith in Buy and Hold. (They will charge a larger fee for your stocks)

Let me tell you my friend, *this is an Apollo 1 design.*

"Greed, for lack of a better word, is good."
—Movie 'Wallstreet,' Michael Douglas as Gordon Gekko 1987 [98]

Greed is a dangerous trait in your advisor. Proverbs 16:18 says,

"Pride goes before a crash and a pretentious spirit before a tumble."
—Proverbs 16:18 (Byington Bible)

Pride and greed are closely related. If your retirement goes to zero, your advisor can get another client, but at 70, you may not be able to get more money. If your advisor is cavalier about risk, it could affect your health and lifestyle!

Is Risk *Your* Business?

The Apollo program always considered the what-ifs and developed procedures to deal with the 'ifs.' This preparation saved the men of Apollo 13 from suffering the fate of Apollo 1. During one of the simulation sessions (prelaunch), a massive service (SM) module failure was thrown at the astronauts in the sim. After that, they devised a procedure to use the lunar module

[98] I don't agree with this sentiment.

(LM) as a lifeboat in case of a massive SM failure. Everyone thought this was a one-in-a-million disaster scenario unlikely to happen. Nevertheless, the procedure was written down, saving the crew's lives when the Service Module exploded. They quickly turned the Lunar Module into a lifeboat.

Who knew the service module would blow up when stirring the oxygen tanks?

And that is why they had the lifeboat procedure ready; they saved precious time and the crew's lives. They went through the checklist quickly. What are your procedures if you have a financial emergency? What if the market goes through another 13 years with no growth period? Is the plan to buy and hold? Will you need to reduce your income? Resolving these issues is essential. This is financial planning, not turning your portfolio into a risk

Too often, financial planning turns into a model portfolio of mutual funds with no focus on dividends or interest, while depending on selling *shares* for retirement income.

Holding on to an advisor or investment due to *past performance or loyalty* is dangerous and might derail your retirement plans. "But no one can predict when the market will drop," you say. I respond with, "Nay, Nay! The markets drop all the time; the problem is when. Accumulator-style investing is a young man's game (I mean a young person's game. I'll sign up for the 'Why all men are Misogynistic' course) and carries an incredible amount of risk for a pre-retiree or a retiree." Imagine what would have happened if Apollo 13 hadn't shed its stages. Would that have gone well?

Recently, a new client we onboarded said he asked his last Advisor (who was with a Big Wall Street firm. I won't say their name, or they will sue me) to get him out of the market. She (past advisor) talked him out of it. His gut told him to sell since he recently retired. (She was a loyal disciple of the Buy and Hold cult, please don't tell them where I am. They looking for me.)

He lost $100,000 over the following eight months. During the checklist review with us, we discovered that, in addition to his losses, the amount he was withdrawing was unsustainable and would likely result in zeroing out his account in less than ten years—zero, zero, nada retirement.

We followed our checklist and developed a plan that he and his wife felt comfortable with, focusing on risk and income. Unfortunately, the damage was already done, and they had to make some lifestyle changes and take on part-time jobs in retirement.

In the story I just shared about my client's former advisor, I wouldn't say the advisor was stupid or corrupt. She was nice and had excellent credentials working for a top-tier Big Wall Street firm (whose name I won't say). His advisor was, however, an *accumulation advisor*, as so many are, unable to serve his best interest. The firm was vested in the offerings they recommended in the managed account service. Incidentally, the advisor was a Fiduciary.

Many Big Wall Street firms use persuasion, incentives, or pressure on their advisors to promote what is in the firm's best interest. Many of the advisors don't even realize that this is happening.

For example, do you continue seeing your pediatrician if you need a general practice doctor? Or when you need a cardiologist or OBYN? There was an episode of the sitcom 'Friends' where Ross (an adult in his late 20s) continues seeing his childhood pediatrician. Silly, right?

It can be difficult to change advisors. It's better to do it before you lose $100,000. Too many advisors think making as much money as possible is their job.

I can't tell you how many clients have told me that their advisor made this statement (or something similar): *"I have reviewed your accounts. You are fine, Trust me."*

"It's not that I don't trust you; generally, I don't trust anybody."
—Rick Harrison, Pawn Stars

Why are you Fine?

Really? Why? Ask yourself the following questions:

- Do I have any contractual guarantees?
- How much income does my portfolio produce?
- Do I need to sell shares to collect retirement income?
- How much dividends or interest after costs am I collecting?
- When you ran the stress test, what kind of risk did my portfolio show, and did it match the risk I wanted to have?
- What are my total costs? (All of them, advisor fees, third party manager fees, ETF or mutual fund fees and more)

What are my fees?

When evaluating your investments, **the fee drag is important to consider**. What is a fair advisor fee? I have talked with advisors who brag about their value. As an Investment Advisor, I feel I have value too. I have always aligned our fees with the work we do, taking into account other portfolio costs and the level of research and monitoring required. Most firms are targeting 1.5%, not including the Separate Manager Fee of another .30% - 1%. We think that is high. Notice this chart because I love showing you charts. It makes me feel smart. The lifetime fee drag (if very high) can potentially cause an account to run out of money.

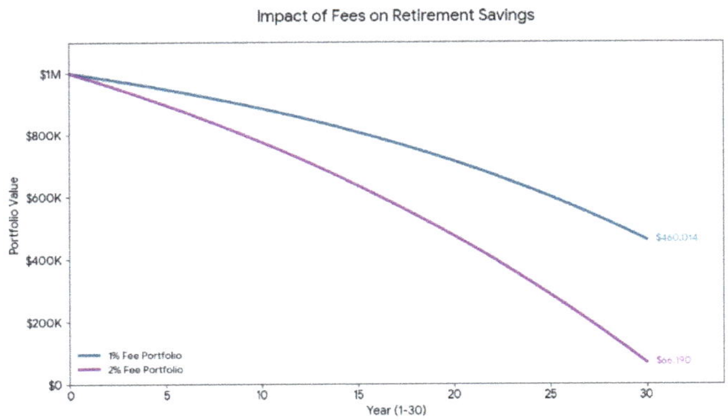

Starting Balance: $1,000,000.

Withdrawal Rate: A standard 4% initial withdrawal of $49,628, approximately 5% of the starting balance, without an annual inflation increase.

Net Returns: The "1% Fee" line calculates growth at 4% net, while the "2% Fee" line calculates growth at 3% net.

Nobody works for free

Studies have shown that a financial advisor can add value and return to your portfolio and be instrumental in managing your retirement. In our portfolio analysis that we do for clients, we often see total costs over 2% or even 3% with returns not matching the market averages and the stress test showing very high risks. ***If you are making half the return of the S&P 500, you might expect you are taking half the risk. This is often not the case.*** That is why we stress test your portfolio. Your actual risk profile might be higher than you expected.

If your advisor is earning his 2% that is fine. I charge more for clients who have me implement more intensive trading strategies. If your advisor is truly working for you, (higher fees should have higher performance) that should overcome the "fee drag."[99] ***"Vanguard estimates that the value of using an advisor is around 3% additional net annual gains for the investor."***

But at the end of the day, 1% seems standard, with reductions for multi-million dollar accounts seeming reasonable. I will talk about Exchange Traded Funds in Chapter 6. This move from mutual funds can reduce portfolio costs a lot in my experience. Finally, lowering or removing trading costs

What You're Not Going to Do is Jack up my Costs

---

[99] Source: Putting a value on your value: Quantifying Vanguard Advisor's Alpha. See Chapter 6.

We have reviewed many portfolios with high costs, high risks, and below-average returns. In some cases, it seems the client is slammed into a portfolio of mutual funds or other investments without regard to risks or income objectives. Paying above-average total costs for the privilege of investing.

"I have a portfolio of institutionally researched stocks," you say. Unfortunately, the Big Wall Street firm may have a conflict of interest in the selection of the companies they bought for you. Even if they don't, measuring the return and risk (meaning how much you would have lost in past market downturns) may reveal an underperforming portfolio with little cash flow and high loss potential.

What is my Cash Flow? (say that like a late-night DJ)

Like the doctors I saw for my cancer treatment, their advice was based on the kind of medicine they practiced. It didn't matter if it was the best for me. All the doctors I interviewed seemed competent. Only one could give me the treatment I was comfortable with. It must be practical and easy to understand if you are taking a planning approach. The income needs to be based on cash flow and not dependent on an always-rising stock market. Because we know the stock market doesn't always rise.

Ask your Advisor/Broker to please show their work; otherwise, the trust me statement above means nothing.

The markets don't care about your feelings.

I can do that (Now, you say that?)

Finally, be careful if your current advisor says, *"I can do that. I can help you invest for income first, reduce risk,"* when discussing what I am sharing with you. Then why didn't he already recommend that? ***Your advisor may not specialize or even believe in income-producing investments***. (Back to my prostate story, my first two doctors would have left me peeing on myself and no sex drive.) Even if the broker claims to be a fiduciary, he may continue to recommend the past winners, sell for shares for income, depend on average returns, growth style investments, push prepackaged investments, or firm recommendations without *procedures* for market declines, except to say, to have faith in "Buy and Hold with diversification." (meaning have a lot of investments and don't sell anything) I can't emphasize enough the need for an advisor specializing in the 'I' (income) for retirement.

Now, A Horse Story

I used to ride horses when I was a teenager. My neighbor had a Quarter horse that was a retired barrel racer. It was a beautiful brown quarter horse that lived to run! We would walk trails and come up to a green field. He would take off at a full run if I weren't careful. That horse was hard to control and took me on some terrifying rides. I had to keep the reins tight, and many times, I had to pull on one rein to run this horse into a circle so he would stop running. I never knew when this horse would take me for the ride of my life. (How I never fell off must have been God.)

An Advisor who settles for income investing when he has done his business on investing for growth may be like that barrel racing quarter horse, dying for more risk and to take you on a full crazy gallop in the growth markets. I don't blame your current advisor; he is under a lot of pressure to offer the investments the firm is promoting. (Even fiduciaries)

I have seen how some Big Wall Street firms pressure advisors. Ah, the allure of growth investing is intoxicating for some advisors. Often, they encourage you to accept a more aggressive risk tolerance. It's fun and games until you face-plant into the dirt. I would rather not have your retirement suffer a Christopher Reeve accident.[100]

The Danger of FOMO

This is the Fear of Missing Out. You are missing the market growth. You could have made so much money! Then, you finally sign the paper, agreeing to a growth portfolio. Living with this kind of risk is no way to retire. A higher-risk portfolio may also allow for a high advisory fee for the advisor, but don't worry; your advisor is a fiduciary.

The reality is that your advisor may be lost in the past bull markets. He may be stuck in accumulator style thinking and investments. Now, what about your advisor's firm? His Big Wall Street firm can exert enormous pressure and incentives for him to be a team player. We have screened or developed these investments to be in your client's best interest, they say. What the Big Wall Street firm thinks is best, happens to be also most profitable for the firm.

---

[100] Christopher Reeve played Superman in the 1980s. In 1995 he was paralyzed after being thrown from a horse in an equestrian competition.

The future of your happy retirement may depend on you making a change to an Advisor that is philosophically aligned with you and focused on your desire for Income Investing in a sustainable retirement.

This decision can be difficult, especially when times are good. Especially when you have made money! Why mess with success? Past performance does not guarantee future results!

You need the correct people to control your mission. It is a mistake to try to repeat the last mission! Your advisor(s) need to believe in and specialize in income-producing investments and have procedures in place for market downturns that don't require you to reduce your lifestyle. Sadly, no matter how 'nice' your current advisor is, he or his firm may not be suited for this investment stage of your life.

Note on Growth. I will discuss this in Chapter 6, but a mix of Growth and Income can make sense in your retirement planning. It needs to be more than a mutual fund label. The Income portion needs to stand on its own for the cash flow to be able to buffer down markets and provide a base of income. This will provide you with income that you can rely on in retirement. I recommend growth investments after your income base (cash flow) has been satisfied.

Failure is not an Option!

We recommend you follow a process and develop 'procedures' for when things don't go right. This is your retirement; failure is not an option! By helping you develop your objectives and understand the risks you are comfortable with. Look at your launch checklist again.

- ✓ Social Security Income estimates and optimal filing dates
- ✓ Income Sources for Retirement
- ✓ Retirement Asset Inventory
- ✓ Retirement Objectives and Risk Tolerance
- ✓ Retirement Expense/Debt review
- ✓ Your Ideal Retirement Life
- ✓ Retirement Income Needs and Wants
- ✓ Tax Strategies to employ now and later
- ✓ Investment Strategy (Moving from the G to the I) *Cash Flow, say like a late-night DJ.*
- ✓ Review of your Advisor(s)

In the next chapter, we will discuss Social Security. Social Security is the gateway to retirement and the most important one. I am a Registered Social Security Analyst[101] and I am uniquely suited to help you with this cornerstone topic. So, if you're ready, this pre-launch brief is over; it's time to proceed to *"Pre-Launch Planning, Social Security."*

Checklist Review

- Retirement launch should follow a checklist. Apollo missions launched in stages; likewise, your retirement must move past the accumulation stage.
- Selling shares for retirement income causes a reverse dollar cost average.
- The transition stage ensures you retire on schedule no matter what happens in the markets.
- The transition stage begins planning for retirement by positioning your ship for the income mission.
- Past market crashes have taken 7 and 6 years to recover from.
- Selling shares for income can erode your retirement and cause you to run out of money.
- Simulate market downturns, income amounts, and fees on your portfolio to follow the best procedure for retirement planning.
- Follow your checklist.
- Beware of real estate investments and small businesses in retirement.
- Often, it makes sense to sell the properties and invest in assets that will be easier to manage and pass to heirs (when you die) after retirement.
- Beware of Large Investment Positions or too much Cash
- Reduce Stress in Retirement.
- Know yourself. Being able to handle higher risk financially doesn't make it is best for you emotionally.
- Come to terms with your spending.
- The Financial 'Day of Reckoning' will come for your children. If it is after your funeral, you won't be able to guide them through it. Better, the tough love comes from you. Cutting off a child financially is difficult. Remember, we learn through adversity and hard times. If your child loses a house or has to live in a low-rent district, they will learn and be better for the lesson.
- Identify your ideal retirement life.
- TR = I + G If you want retirement to be stress-free, invest for the I and not the G!
- Dividends and Interest matter!

---

[101] Designations like RSSA and securities registrations require constant continuing education and meeting filing requirements. Go to NARSSA.com to see my current registration status.

- If it happens twice, it can happen again. (2001 & 2008)
- The best way to avoid a train is to get off the tracks.
- The only way to avoid a catastrophe in retirement is to shift your mindset from asset value to income, not how big my pile is. How much reliable income can I count on.
- Is your procedure for a market crash to suspend income and live on less?
- Accumulator-style investing is a young person's game and carries an incredible amount of risk for a pre-retiree or a retiree.
- You risk running out of money by trusting in the Bob Marley financial planning anthem.
- Volatility Matters.
- When it comes to Advisers, Past Performance does not guarantee future results.
- An accumulation advisor, like a barrel racer horse, always wants to run!
- Your advisor and his or her firm may have conflicts of interest.
- Do you want to do more in retirement than sit in a chair, in a dark house, watching Jeopardy, and paying bills?
- Consider Growth investing after your Cash Flow needs are taken care of.
- Many Big Wall Street firms use persuasion, incentives, or pressure on their advisors to promote what is in the firm's best interest. Many of the advisors don't even realize that this is happening.
- Total Costs or 'fee drag' can cause you to run out of money in retirement.
- The future of your successful retirement mission may depend on you changing your Advisor to one who is philosophically aligned with you and focused on your desire for Income Investing.
- Remember, *Cash Flow* (said in a late-night DJ voice)
- Failure is not an Option!

Chapter 4
Pre-Launch Planning Social Security Benefits

"The Social Security claiming decision…
is the cornerstone decision of retirement planning."
—Martha Shedden, RSSA, CRPC, president for the National Association of Registered Social Security Analysts

I carry the Registered Social Security Analyst designation. I decided to sign up for the designation in 2020 during the Covid 19 lockdowns. My reason for taking the courses was to demonstrate my competency in the subject of Social Security. We previously ran seminars on this topic, and I thought we would have higher attendance if I carried a Social Security designation. (This turned out to be very accurate.) What I learned about Social Security stunned me. Allow me to repeat a statistic from Chapter 2 of this book.

96% of people get less than they should from Social Security

$111,000 is lost by the average American household[102]

As I said previously, 96% is *everyone!* Further, the average person receives $300,000 from Social Security over their lifetime, and some couples receive as much as $2,000,000.00[103]. Many retirees do not have $300,000 in their retirement accounts. According to AARP, "Americans are woefully under-educated about Social Security." Being uneducated in Social Security ends here and now. This chapter will get you up to speed to get your Social Security right.

The following information may not include all the details that affect eligibility and benefits. This information is intended to be an overview of Social Security. I recommend consulting a trained Social Security expert, like an RSSA credential holder. (No arrogant and nasty letters correcting me, please.)

---

[102] Source: The Retirement Solutions Hiding in Plain Sight. "Capital One United Income June 28, 2019
[103] Source: National Association of Registered Social Security Analysts (NARSSA)

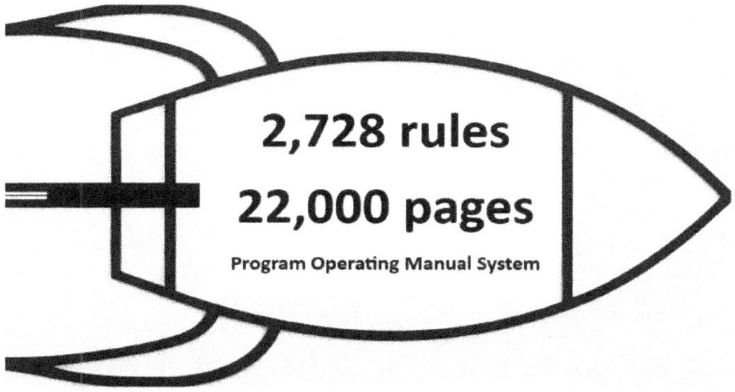

Consider how complex the SSA bureaucracy is. There are 2,728 rules and 22,000 pages in Social Security's Program Operations Manual System (POMS). The space shuttles were launched on a 12,000-page manual. Let that sink in. So, it's complex, to say the least. There are thousands of claiming strategies you can employ. The problem is that how most people, including financial advisors, view and approach filing for benefits is like a laundry list item.

"Today, I need to go to the grocery store, pick up the dry cleaning, get the oil changed, and file for Social Security benefits. Check, check, and check." This is no Beuno[104].

Would you enter a courtroom with a felony charge and no lawyer?

A bad ruling would mean lifetime consequences. In most cases with Social Security, your actions are irreversible and one-time decisions. Likewise, you need professional help to avoid losing thousands of dollars to bad Social Security planning or filing mistakes. I would beware of self-taught Social Security experts. Those who hold the RSSA credentials have been trained and tested and have access to the National Association of Registered Social Security Analysts (NARSSA) for post-certification support.

Providing the resources to break through the bureaucracy of the SSA.

104 Spanish for No Good.

The most terrifying words in English are: I'm from the government, and I'm here to help." - President Ronald Reagan.

What about going down to the local friendly Social Security office?

"The SSA local office will help me; that is why they are there to help," you say.

Let me explain it to you in Italian Guido style: "Don't ask for no stinking help. Take a number, ask your question, and don't cry on my desk, or it might get ugly."

For context, most SSA offices have armed security in the waiting room. Armed! Wow, what customer service for age 62+ people looking to start retirement benefits and the disabled looking for disability! What is going on? Don't carry a weapon into a Social Security office. They don't like you to do it, just them.

Let's return to the 'help' part: ***SSA staff is not allowed by law to offer advice. They can answer your questions and help you fill out the forms***[105]. (Answering a question is drastically different from getting advice). God bless you if you find a friendly and helpful SSA officer. The SSA staff rarely explains anything and tries to push you to sign and go. Why the SSA is this way can be supported by a quote from the 22,000-page SSA[106] Program Operations Manual System (POMS):

"Social security representatives are instructed to explain that "individual employees who administer the program are not at liberty to substate their own judgment or opinion for rulings, regulations, or the law ...Do not attempt to explain the rationale for any particular operational guidelines, nor go to any great lengths to justify them."

This is the direction and training for the SSA. I won't paint all Social Security employees with the same brush. But as a group, they are under-trained, understaffed, and bureaucratic. (You understand what it is like to interact with government officials, right? Being a tyrant is a common trait) To make things worse, SSA officers often are wrong about Social Security. I can tell you some crazy information my clients told me they received from the SSA office. The book 'Get What's Yours Social Security' relates numerous stories of SSA officials telling people wrong information.[107]

---

[105] Quoted from "Get What's Yours Social Security" by Laurence J. Kotlikoff PhD, Philip Moeller, & Paul Solman

[106] Social Security Administration

[107] I recommend "Get What's Yours Social Security" 2016 edition for a recommended read on the topic. My comments can be sourced to this book written by experts (Laurence J. Kotlikoff PhD, Philip Moeller, & Paul Solman) in the field of Social Security.

Office of Inspector General Report for 2019

$131.8 million in underpayments involving beneficiaries who filed for survivor benefits

The Social Security Administration Inspector General (IG) is reporting an estimated 11,123 Social Security beneficiaries were eligible for higher benefits had they delayed claims until age 70;

however, they were misinformed by employees of the Social Security Administration

resulting in about $131.8 million in underpayments and another $9.8 million in annual payments for those under age 70. The IG's report says, "SSA policy states its employees must explain the advantages and disadvantages of filing an application and the filing considerations so the claimant can make an informed filing decision."

How can the SSA employees explain what they don't understand? They don't have the time to research every topic. This is an observation based on the antidotes being reported.

Source: This box is quoted from the Social Security Report- "SSA Inspector General reporting $131.8 million in underpayments."

The problem at the heart of the IG report (box above) is that ***survivors*** are permitted to file a Restricted Application that, in many cases, would provide increased Social Security checks. SSA employees mistakenly told (and continue to tell) widows that this strategy is unavailable. (More on survivor benefits later in this chapter) What did the SSA do to fix this? Did they go back and pay these *widows* the benefits they could have gotten? What do you think? You would be correct if the words 'don't hold your breath' come to mind. According to the IG, it's still going on!

Getting 'Qualified' assistance with Social Security could not be more crucial. I had a client tell me their previous advisor referred them to a Social Security specialist. This person helped them fill out the paperwork to file for benefits. However, this person was just a form pusher and did not provide actual planning advice. You need to understand when and how Social Security integrates with your other income and investments.

On the other hand, if the Social Security office staff gives you wrong information or tells you No, you can't do that; t*he only way you are fighting back is if you know for a fact you are right*.

It would be best if you had benefits analysis and advice provided by an RSSA designation holder.

The book Get What's Yours Social Security tells the story of a 67-year-old woman who went through 8 levels of management at the SSA and was denied a strategy she was allowed to use. Only when one of the authors called SSA to tell them he would highlight her story on a television broadcast did SSA suddenly remember that the strategy was allowed.

Exodus 22:22: "Do not take advantage of the widow or the fatherless. -Holy Bible NIV

In Chapter 2, I examined retirement planning as ineffective and straight-up marketing by financial firms and fiduciaries. Do you want to guess what I will say about Social Security planning? Yes, it's not going to be good.

Why is information on your Social Security benefits so important?

In meetings with a financial advisor, the focus is often on the investments, particularly growth investments with some bond-type funds to moderate risk, the old 60/40 portfolio model.[108] Using a basing approach, you would need to calculate how much income you need in retirement. Social Security benefits are an important part of this. How much risk you can take, and the income you will need from your IRA, 401 (k), Pensions, Annuities, and other accounts, will depend on how much Social Security income you can expect.

Your advisor needs to be competently trained in Social Security because this income forms the base of your retirement.

In the Certified Financial Fiduciary program (at Toro Bravo, we are Certified Financial Fiduciaries), one of the requirements of our code of conduct is:

Practice the Duty of Good Care – There is a fundamental obligation to exercise the skill of an expert and only advise in those areas where expert skill level has been obtained.[109]

Again, your planner should be able to demonstrate an in-depth competency in Social Security. I am unconvinced that the current curriculum offered by many professional designations adequately covers Social Security, and there isn't a post-certification support mechanism in most cases. An RSSA designation holder does have this education and support.

Planning and filing for Social Security are vital to a successful retirement launch.

When setting a launch date for the Apollo spacecraft, they determined that mandatory tests had to be conducted or the launch would not proceed. It would be best if you were running

---

108 60/40 portfolio refers to a portfolio that is 60% stocks and 40% bonds.
109 Source: Nationalcffassociation.org Code of Conduct

calculations on your benefits starting in the transition stage of retirement. For example, if you are self-employed, test what happens if you run more revenue through the company as wages. This slight tax increase may be worth increasing your Social Security check. There are two problems with the Social Security projections made in many retirement plans. Here they are.

Social Security Software Projections are Often Wrong

After reading the last two chapters of this book, you are probably not shocked by this statement. In the book Get What's Yours 'Social Security,' the authors cite that most do-it-yourself Social Security projection software provides inaccurate numbers. You need two things when running a Social Security projection. The person entering information must understand Social Security and terminology. The software you use must require your earnings history and calculate the same way SSA does.

"We took the numbers off the Social Security statement," you say. Unfortunately, the Social Security statement will be off by 10% or more. *What? You say how is that possible?* Yes, your statement is not accurate for long-term planning. Too much is left out. According to the Social Security Intelligence website, written by Devin Carroll, RSSA:

"The SSA does inflate past earnings two years prior to the statement year. So, if the statement year is 2020, your earnings through 2018 have been indexed for inflation. But the problem is that when they estimate your future earnings, they assume that what you earned in the last year is what you'll earn in the future... Since the system is progressive and rewards a higher benefit for a higher earnings history, not paying attention to these additional earnings is a serious oversight." -Devin Carroll, RSSA[110]

The previous quote describes how SSA uses today's formula in its calculations. This formula has increased every year since 1979, but SSA assumes it will stay the same after 62.

These numbers need to be accurately calculated for a reasonable projection. The amount of risk and selection of your investments should depend on correct Social Security planning. Most financial advisors are not competently educated in this area of Social Security; instead, they rely on software without understanding how it works.[111]

Our software calculates your Social Security. It needs to use your full earnings history and not the statement. You can find this information on the Social Security website. Go to

---

110 Devin Carroll is one of the best experts in Social Security. I recommend his podcasts to expand your knowledge.
111 social Security forecast software will be able to predict your benefits to the dollar. Assumptions around inflation, formulas and social Security taxes paid may change. Having complete data can improve the future social Security estimate accuracy.

https://www.ssa.gov/myaccount/ to get a statement AND your full earnings history. (You have to scroll down the page to find it.) You ask, "Isn't the earnings history on the statement?" It *used* to be on the Social Security statement until they condensed it. It would make you think that Social Security was trying to prevent you from getting accurate Social Security income benefit projections, but that's just conspiracy theory talk, right? The Government is always there to help.[112]

How Social Security Benefits are Calculated

To qualify, you need to have 40 credits. You can get a maximum of 4 credits in a year. The value of credit differs for every year, but in 2026, you get one credit for every $1,890 of covered earnings.[113] If you can make $7,560 in one day in 2026, you'll get 4 credits. But since your Social Security check is based on your countable wages for the year, it's best to return to work tomorrow. It takes a minimum of 10 years (40 credits) to qualify for Social Security, but there is more!

Social Security looks at your full earnings history and uses your ***top 35 years*** to calculate your benefits. If you have a zero year in your top 35, well, then it sucks to be you. Each year, they apply a multiplier to your wages based on an index called the Average Wage Index. Your wages are indexed to the average wage level *two years prior* to the first year of eligibility, which is 62. Knowing that they don't do this after age 62 is essential. I will explain later.

The point of this is to account for wage inflation. Next, average by adding up the top 35 *index years* and dividing by 420, and if you are laughing, 420 is the number of months in 35 years (420 is also slang for time to smoke marijuana. This term has been around since the 1970s. Makes you wonder if there is a connection?) then divide by 12, and that produces … wait for it… the AIME or Average Index Monthly Earnings. Next, they run that number through bend points. Yeah, bend points, but not the rubber glove treatment that comes later. That total number is the PIA or Primary Insurance Amount. Whew!

Social security has all kinds of stupid acronyms, but PIA is important because it is your monthly check at the average retirement age (FRA). Oh, that got your attention?

---

112 Totally sarcasm.

113 Covered Earnings are income on which Social Security taxes have been paid. They refer to the total amount of an employee's pay that counts toward calculating retirement benefits.

In 2026, the maximum you can get (based on maxing out Social Security taxes for 35 years) [114] is as follows. The maximum monthly check at age:

Age 62 $2,969 FRA (Full Retirement Age) - $4,152 Age 70 $5,181

Now you know, so stop complaining, or I'll call the armed security.

Social Security Analysis That Works

I have used retirement planning software *extensively* in my career. Some retirement programs do have an option to enter your entire earnings history; step one is complete. Some, however, rely on the Social Security statement. But before becoming an RSSA, I only entered what was on the Social Security statement. Without realizing it, we had inaccurate Social Security estimates. My partner and I were using professional planning software, which we were trained to use, but we lacked at the time the specialized training for Social Security. This is a common problem for many financial planners. Further, because Social Security is such a complex labyrinth of rules and exceptions, it is easy to get this advice wrong.

NASA is always looking for the 'right stuff' in its astronauts and systems, and so should you. It starts with the software used by your advisor. It should base its analysis on your earning history or top 35 years, not your Social Security statements. Is this really a big deal? What would happen if we forgot to include a $100,000 IRA in your asset inventory? Would that change what you can expect for income in retirement? (I refer you to the study I mentioned earlier that says the average household is underpaid $111,000 in Social Security benefits).

Practice does not make perfect. Only perfect practice makes perfect.' -Vince Lombardi, Legendary Former Head Coach for the Green Bay Packers.

Next, you must answer other basic questions, such as whether you have a disability or if a spousal benefit will be used, and when your spouse should file for benefits.[115] This is where a complete understanding of how Social Security works is required. I know I already stated this, but the emphasis is essential here. Even if your advisor holds a financial planning credential, their training may not have adequately covered Social Security, or they may lack practical software training or post-certification support. You need to do 'perfect' benefits calculations. The RSSA educational program includes a dedicated course on correctly using software to run Social Security projections.

---

[114] Source: FAQ.SSA.gov What is the maximum Social Security retirement benefit payable? KA-01897

[115] Covered income is income that Social Security taxes were paid. Uncovered income was exempt from paying Social Security taxes (FICA or SE).

Here is a quote from my friend Dwight Rich, a Financial Advisor interviewed on the podcast Financial Lab by Dalbar.

"I have been a Certified Financial Planner (CFP) since 2007 and in the business now for 28 years; I got to be honest with no disrespect to the Financial Planning board because the training I got was absolutely fabulous, but the deep dive on Social Security could be improved."

—Dwight Rich, CFP, RSSA, Financial Advisor.

Your Advisor may also lack the ongoing resources needed for complex planning questions. I reiterate that searching for an RSSA may be in your best interest. (Go to https://rssa.com/find-an-rssa/ to search your state and locality or call my office. Actually, scratch the first part and call my office).

Planning when to file for your Social Security benefits and having an accurate income number are the first items on the checklist from Chapter 3.

Social Security Income Estimates and Optimal Filing Dates

This is a necessary step for another reason. Social security is a lifetime, inflation-adjusted income on which your retirement depends. Too many people file for benefits too soon and lock in a low payment for life. You can see the increased lifetime Social Security income you get for waiting, and maybe you can use your savings for the initial retirement years to allow benefits to grow. This is the opposite of what most retirees do. Most want to preserve their retirement savings and get the 'free money' first.

But remember, Social Security is not a welfare or 'free' money. You paid into that system for 35 or more years. Your monthly check is based on the taxes you (or your spouse) have paid into it.

"For which of you, if he wants to build a tower, does not first sit down and calculate the expense, whether he has enough to carry it through." Luke 14:28 Living English Bible

Use Your IRA First and Let Social Security Grow.

Give me some rope on this one before you say no. Let us say you are dead set on retiring at 67, or maybe you were 'retired' by your company before you planned. (Sucks to be you) You may have increased benefits if you wait until age 70 to file.

If you wait past FRA until age 70, you get 8% per year in delayed credits. If your FRA is 67, you can get an additional 24% of Social Security benefits by waiting until 70 to file. (If spousal benefits are involved, it may be better to file at 67.)

Consider whether it is possible to start income from your retirement accounts *first* and allow your Social Security check to grow; then, you will be in a better position for the rest of your life and your spouse's life. This takes actual planning and a mature understanding of how Social Security works.

Here is a simplified example of the math.

File at 67 @ $2,484/month or

File at 70 @ $3,036/month

Waiting until 70 earns you an additional $6,624 annually or +**$66,240.00** for ten years. (You would need to live past 80.8 to exceed what you would get filing at age 67.) If there isn't any reason why you or your spouse (if there is a surviving spouse benefit) wouldn't live into your 80's or 90's, it would be worth the cost of delay.

How Much Is It Going to Cost You?

The point is to figure out if you will get more than it costs you to wait until age 70. Statistically, if you are 62 or older, there is a 50% chance for men to reach 85 and a 50% chance for women to reach 88.

"What if I don't make it to 80, you say?" Then, your spouse can qualify for up to 100% of your benefit upon your death, which is higher because you made a plan to wait to file for benefits.[116] More on this later.

This is meaningful planning if you understand how Social Security works. I am sorry to say that many advisors do not have a comprehensive education in Social Security, even if they hold a financial planning credential. This can have a detrimental effect on your overall retirement. Even if they received a solid education on Social Security, they may use the number on the statement instead of running a detailed and optimized analysis.

Retiring from work and filing for Social Security are not required simultaneously.

---

[116] Assuming your benefit is greater than your spouse's social Security.

Working might not help. Waiting usually does.

There are 2 elements that can increase your Social Security benefits. Current wages and the year you file for benefits. (The longer you wait, i.e., age 70, the more you get.) If your **current** wages are not higher than your lowest top 35 years with average wage indexing, then your Social Security benefits will not increase the more years you work.

Example

You currently make $30,000/yr, and your lowest year in the last 35 is $60,000, then no increases from your current wages.

Filing Early Will Cost You and Your Wife.

There are many one-career households where the wife has spent her time as a homemaker and did not participate meaningfully in the workforce, then she can collect the spousal benefit if her benefits are less than 50% of her spouse's FRA. Which is 50% of her spouse's check (FRA amount). Yes, you can file for Social Security benefits starting at age 62. Depending on your birth year, you receive a 25% -35% *reduction* in benefits from your full retirement age.[117] See illustration 4.4.

If you were born in 1960 or later, your Social Security check will be reduced by 30%, and your spouse (if she files early) will get a 35% reduction. (One more bad decision she can remind you about.) Retiring early permanently reduces your Social Security benefits. The delay in filing for Social Security to at least FRA makes sense. But wait, there is more! If you work while collecting Social Security benefits, they might take them back. The penalty is called, 'Stop working and collecting social security, boomer![118] More on this later.

Primary and spousal benefits at age 62
(benefits based on a $1,000 primary insurance amount)

Year of birth [a]	Normal (or full) retirement age	Number of reduction months [b]	Primary		Spouse	
			Amount	Percent reduction [c]	Amount	Percent reduction [d]
1937 or earlier	65	36	$800	20.00%	$375	25.00%
1938	65 and 2 months	38	791	20.83%	370	25.83%
1939	65 and 4 months	40	783	21.67%	366	26.67%
1940	65 and 6 months	42	775	22.50%	362	27.50%
1941	65 and 8 months	44	766	23.33%	358	28.33%
1942	65 and 10 months	46	758	24.17%	354	29.17%
1943-1954	66	48	750	25.00%	350	30.00%
1955	66 and 2 months	50	741	25.83%	345	30.83%
1956	66 and 4 months	52	733	26.67%	341	31.67%
1957	66 and 6 months	54	725	27.50%	337	32.50%
1958	66 and 8 months	56	716	28.33%	333	33.33%
1959	66 and 10 months	58	708	29.17%	329	34.17%
1960 and later	67	60	700	30.00%	325	35.00%

Illustration 4.1 Source: SSA

---

[117] If you are born on January 1, use the prior year. January 2 uses the year of birth. Who makes these rules?

[118] My compliance department is forcing me to tell you, that is not what the work penalty is called. I say you have figured out the jokes by now. My son called his mother a boomer, once. The court won't let me say more.

Spousal Benefit be careful

A spouse can receive 50% of the other spouse's FRA but there are rules. Surprised?

- The other spouse must file for Social Security benefits.
- The spousal benefit will be based on FRA of the other spouse.
- It will be reduced if you file early.

Here is an idea. I will collect my Social Security benefit early and get the spousal benefit on my husband at FRA. Seems like a good plan, what could possibly go wrong?

If you file for a Social Security *spousal benefit* at age 62, there is a 35% reduction in the amount you receive. Let us assume your Social Security at age 62 is $200 a month (your benefit is reduced 30% for filing early. You calculate that your spousal benefit at age 67 will be $1,500. You plan to collect the $200 a month until you qualify for the spousal benefit at age 67. (Assuming your spouse has also filed for benefits)

Seems like a good plan, what could possibly go wrong? You don't understand the math, as your 8th-grade math teacher said. *The early filing reduction remains and is 35% for spousal benefits*. Because you filed early on your record that reduction carries over to your spousal benefit and is now 35%, ***your expected <u>$1,500</u> spousal benefit is now <u>$975</u>***. Sucks to be you.

That is a sizable reduction. The closer to FRA you can wait, the better off you are. By the way, filing early for Social Security on your earnings is only a 30% reduction but spousal benefit reduction 35%. Does Social Security have a war against women? Makes you think. **So don't file early if you are planning to receive a spousal benefit later.**

Break-Even Could Break You.

Many worry that if they wait to file for benefits, they will lose them if they don't live long enough. The break-even age for waiting to age 70 instead of filing at 62 is generally age 79. See the chart below.

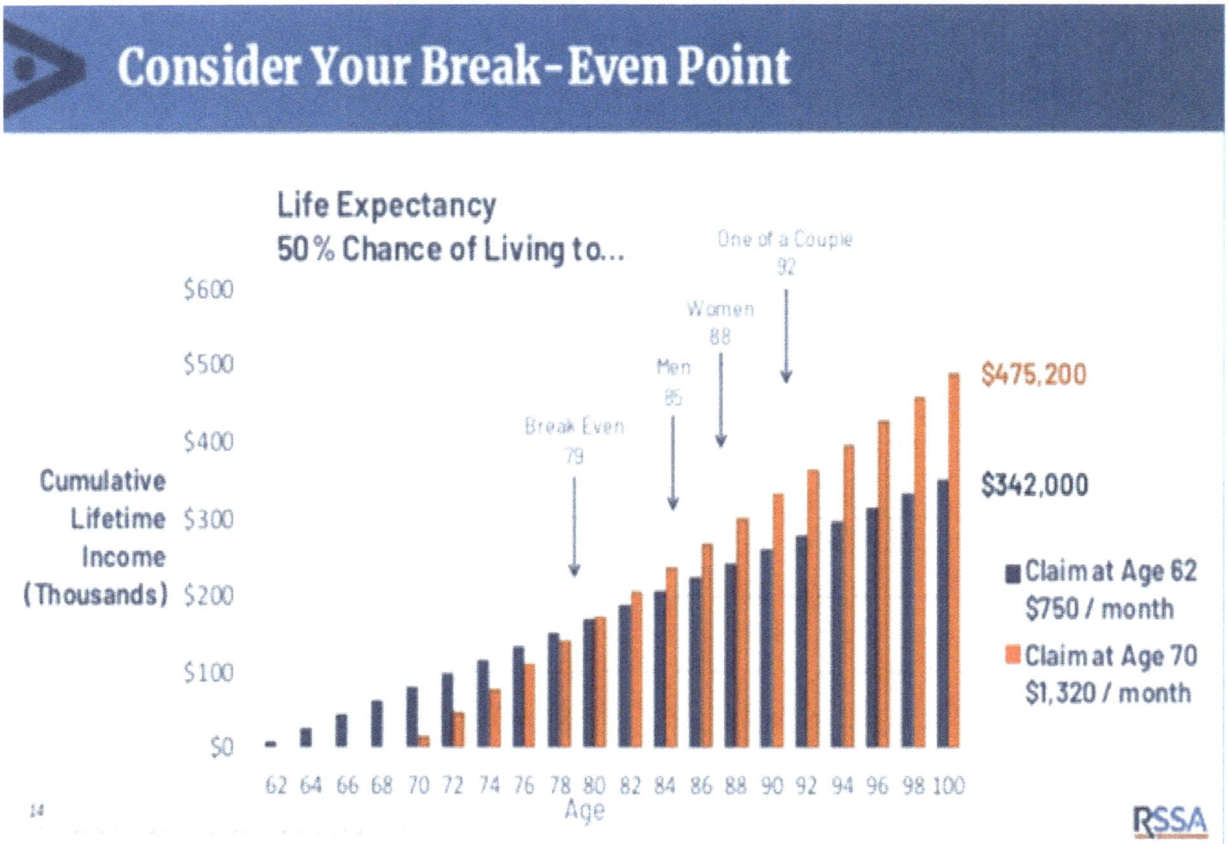

Illustration 4.2 Source: RSSA

Remember, your retirement accounts can be exhausted if you refuse to die early.

Your Social Security is a lifetime income you can't outlive. It protects you from longevity risk because income is guaranteed for life. It is also inflation-adjusted income. Retiring too soon and accepting too little in your Social Security check will have a detrimental effect on your long-term standard of living.

How many vacations, medicines, lunches with your friends/family, and rounds of golf can you afford on your current income?

The Survivor Benefit of Social Security because you are dead

Then, there is the survivor benefit. As I will discuss in more detail later, if you die before FRA your spouse can get 50% of your FRA benefit. If your full retirement age is 67 and your Social Security benefit is $3,000.00 a month, your wife (if she doesn't have a higher earnings record) will get $1,500.00 a month at her FRA. But if you die, she will get 100% (again, if she claims at her FRA) of your benefit. (Check those break lines before going to work)[119]

But wait, there is more! If you wait until age 70 to collect, she gets 100% of that number in a survivor's benefit! That's 100% of your age 70 benefit, not 50% of the FRA (66-67) amount she gets under a spousal benefit! You are worth more dead than alive. I will repeat this later.

Widow Rule

If you collect early, say 62, you get a reduction of 30% from your FRA amount. It also penalizes your spouse's survivor benefits. However, there is the 'Widow rule' when the higher-earning spouse files at 62 and then dies. (Your wife says, I told you so) The widow rule protects the lower-earning spouse by providing 82.5% of the deceased spouse's PIA,[120] increasing the amount your spouse will receive. (You got 70% of FRA she gets 82.5% of FRA) Pretty cool, right? But there is a whole formula calculation that is a bit screwy. There is no way Social Security is going to make it easy.

Tough Morning at age 70

Let us say you wait until you are 70 years old to collect Social Security. Because you are smart. The day the check comes in the mail, while pulling the check out of your mailbox, you have a massive coronary event and die with the uncashed check in your cold dead hands in front of your mailbox. Wow, tough day.

First, Social Security will take back that check. (Yes, out of your cold dead hands.) Then, your spouse (if she is FRA) will receive 100% of your age 70 income *for the rest of her life.*

Your retirement income was not wasted by waiting until 70 to collect your Social Security! Your wife/husband will get it. (If their own benefit is lower)

---

[119] Survivor benefits can be received as early as age 60 (50 if disabled) at 71.5% of the deceased worker's FRA. This percentage goes up every year you wait until you reach FRA. Filing for survivor benefits at or after FRA is 100%.
[120] The PIA or primary insurance amount" is the benefit (before rounding down to next lower whole dollar) a person would receive if he/she elects to begin receiving retirement benefits at his/her normal retirement age or FRA. (Full Retirement Age)

The higher amount you saved will benefit your spouse for the rest of her life. This is an important family planning tool to consider.

Did you get all this Math Straight?

So, you're not a beautiful mind.[121] You are thinking, "I am totally confused." That is why we run *your* goals through the *simulator* - or, more precisely, a good Social Security software program that is used correctly.

You give me the dates you are considering filing for benefits, and we determine the optimal times and strategies, and then I will give you the best options to choose from.

There is no right or wrong answer. It depends on what plan you can live with. You don't need to understand all this complexity if you have a good planning advisor.

Take this Job and Shove it! But Johnny Paycheck went bankrupt.

I remember this song when I was a kid. Everyone wants to punch the boss in the nose and then walk out cool as a cucumber. That is a bad idea. The musician Johnny Paycheck filed for bankruptcy, so his advice didn't work out.

Bankruptcy did not affect Johnny's Social Security benefits. Likewise, you won't lose Social Security if you file for bankruptcy. If you go to prison, yes, bankruptcy, no.

Sometimes, we become sick and tired of our job and want to cash it all in. If you want to get out of your job and start Social Security benefits, you need to run your simulation before launching retirement. (NASA calls this a go/no-go calculation.) You might reconsider once you understand the long-term consequences compared to the short-term incentives.

Consider a Life Change instead of Filing early

Still, you might need a change in life; if it's too early to retire, consider other choices. Rather than filing for Social Security too early, consider these three options.

1. Can you use your retirement savings first, adding part-time work and delaying filing Social Security benefits?
2. Can you consider changing jobs or starting a new business for a change of pace or

[121] Beautiful Mind is a 2001 movie about mathematician John Nash (who was schizophrenic) and based on the book by that name written by Sylvia Grazer.

3. Consider a 3–6-month sabbatical, then return to work, if possible.

As I said, retiring and filing for Social Security does not have to be done simultaneously. Make sure your launch window is doable. If you feel like Johnny Paycheck, you may need a change of environment instead of a bad retirement launch.

Remember that staying active is the most significant indicator of a long-life span.

Raising the bar and your check

Waiting to file for benefits is obvious; is there any other way to increase your Social Security check? Yes, here are four ways.

1. Increase your wages – if you are employed, have more of your business income come to you through wages. If you are an employee, make more money. (You are stunned by my advice.) By increasing your top 35, you could knock out some low years. You might see some zeroes in your top 35 years of earnings. If what you make now is higher than your lowest year in the top 35, that's good. This increases your Social Security check.[122]
2. Working full-time, gig, or part-time may cover your living expenses if you're modest, but you might be sacrificing your future Social Security benefits. Confucius said, "*Choose a job you love, and you will never have to work a day in your life.*" Take your experience and build something.
3. Work past 70 if you want—studies have shown that the longer you work, the longer you live. Even if you collect Social Security, they still adjust your top 35 years if you are still working and your earnings are higher than in past years. Your income could replace those low years and raise your Social Security benefits.
4. If possible, wait to file until you are 70. Less than 2% of Social Security recipients wait until 70 to collect. Be a two percenter.

The Benefit of Waiting to Age 70

+76%

[122] Important to note that if future earnings don't replace a low year of inflation indexed earnings, the benefit will not increase even though you continue to work.

Too many retirees file for Social Security benefits too early.

Social Security Questions You Have Answers You Need

The first thing I did after earning my RSSA designation was throw away the seminar PowerPoints I used for my seminars. I wrote a new seminar titled "Social Security Questions You Have Answers You Need, How the Lessons of Apollo 13 Can Help Your Retirement." (By

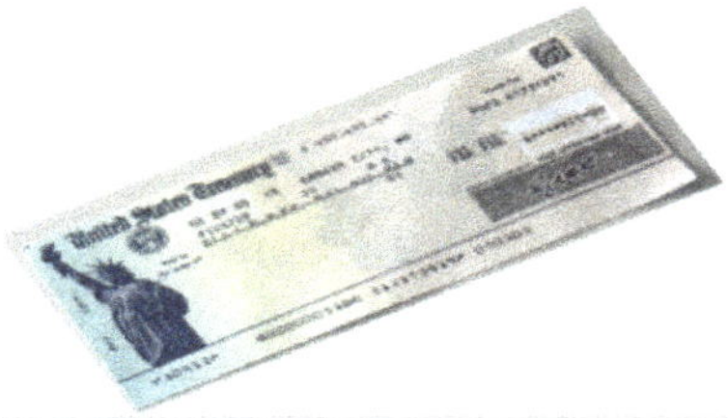

Waiting to collect until 70 years old earns you 76% more annually in lifetime retirement income! Less than 2% of filers wait until 70.

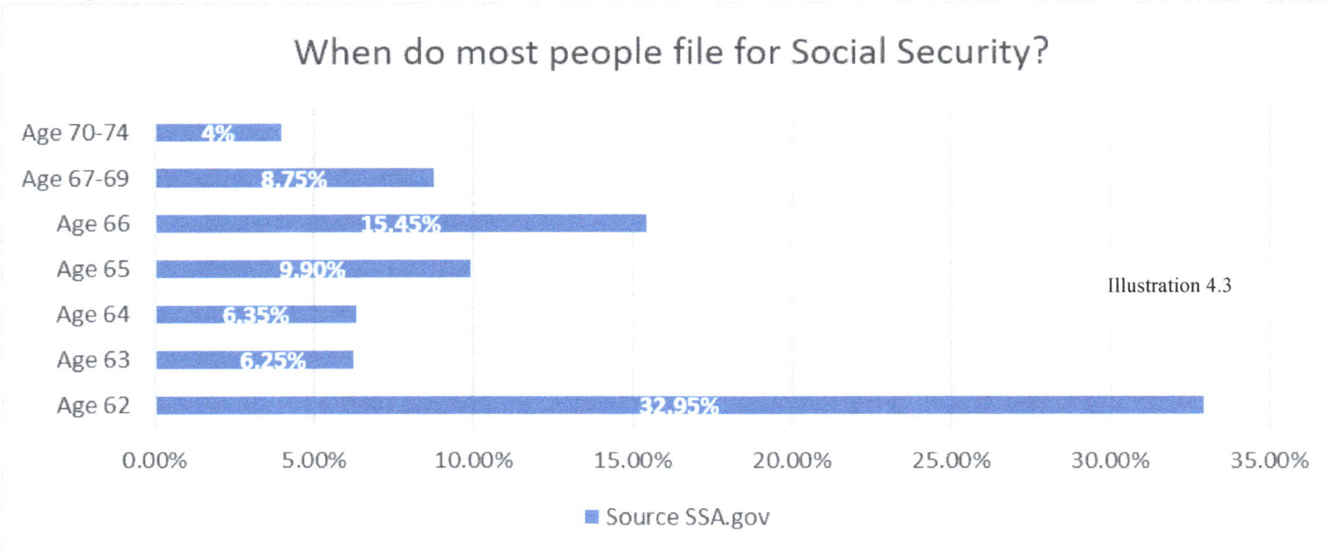

Illustration 4.3

now, you think I have a real thing for Apollo 13, and you'll be right. But Jim Lovell didn't have to file a restraining order; I was leaving.)

I focused the course on the big Social Security questions people ask, eliminating unnecessary junk. I also illustrated my points with the Apollo 13 story. Let's examine some Social Security questions and answers. Of course, I will also discuss the Apollo 13 parallels.

Get All the Money You Deserve!

Get your mind right.

First, ***I need you to get your mind right*** regarding Social Security planning. You need to

Get all the money you deserve!

I know that Social Security is considered an 'entitlement,'[123] but you earned this through the taxes ***you*** paid. Social Security is a progressive system that pays you more the more you pay into it. Your benefits, i.e., check, are based on your wages;[124] the higher they are, the bigger the check. The program has over 15 different types of benefits. Depending on your situation, you might qualify for benefits other than retirement. Social security is not welfare. ***Remember that maximizing your benefits is not 'gaming the system.'*** It is getting what is yours, what you paid for. If you wait to collect Social Security, it lets the government use your money in return for a higher benefit for you down the road. It's like giving the government a loan that gives you a return.

When Apollo 13 exploded, the crew had to refocus from a moon landing mission to a lifeboat mission. They had to use the Apollo spaceship in ways it wasn't designed for. First, they lost the batteries in the service module. They were left with the batteries in the Command Module (intended for re-entry) and batteries in the Lunar Module (designed for landing on the moon). They needed to account for and squeeze every ounce of energy out of these batteries to survive the 4-day flight around the moon and re-enter the Earth's atmosphere. (If, on re-entry,

[123] Entitlement a government program that provides benefits to any individual meeting eligibility requirements.
[124] It is possible for a Social Security benefits is based on another worker's earnings history, like a spouse.

the parachutes didn't have power, what was the point?) The simulators ran re-entry scenarios so they could develop the correct procedure for the post-explosion mission.

You need to squeeze every dollar out of Social Security for your retirement mission.

You will need it if you face an unexpected issue in your retirement, as Apollo 13 did. Falling short might not be life or death, but it could change your lifestyle and cause you to live on less. So, let's talk about how your benefits are calculated and some ways to increase your check and your spouse's.

Social Security's Zodiac

I never understood how your birth year determined your personality or your future in astrology. But someone at SSA said, "Hey, let's do the Zodiac thing! Your birthday will control your future! You can file for Social Security benefits as early as 62 years of age. SSA calculates your benefits based on your FRA or full retirement age, which is 66 – 67, depending on your birth year (See illustration 4.4). If you were born in 1957, I am sorry you carry the number of the beast from Revelation.[125] (I always get a laugh when I say that at my seminars. But it is Texas; bible jokes work.)

Birth Year*	Full Retirement Age
1943-54	66
1955	66, 2 months
1956	66, 4 months
1957	66, 6 months
1958	66, 8 months
1959	66, 10 months
1960 & On	67

Illustration 4.4 Source: RSSA

*If your birthday is January 1st, refer to the previous year. If your birthday is on the 1st, assume you were born the prior month. If the moon were in retrograde on your birthday, expect to be clubbed by SSA staff with cudgels.[126]

First, do you qualify for Social Security Disability?

If you meet the criteria for Social Security disability (and you know if you do), you will want to file for this benefit before filing for Social Security. Many people who qualify for disability decide to wait for FRA (age 66-67) to collect Social Security. This is a mistake. ***Understand first that Social Security disability is not welfare; it's insurance***. Social Security is insurance, and the payroll taxes that fund your retirement also fund disability payments. Just

125 Revelation 13:18: "Here is wisdom: let him who has intelligence calculate the beast's number; for it is a man's number. And its number is six hundred and sixty-six." -The Bible in Living English

126 Do I have to say it? Sarcasm, but who knows? Armed security might have a cudgel under his desk.

because some people have abused the system doesn't mean you should avoid filing for disability if you qualify.

Social Security Disability is typically based on your Full Retirement Age (FRA) amount. Collecting disability at 62 could add $200,000 to your lifetime benefits.[127] Again, not chump change, my friend. We must get your mind right on this to 'Get all the money you deserve.'

If you file for disability, get denied disability benefits, then file for retirement, and later on appeal if you get awarded disability, Social Security will make up the difference. Other family members may get benefits based on your disability numbers, which are likely higher.

This issue will take time and patience. Disability is a long process. You will need an attorney or advocate to do this, and they will want you to first be denied disability benefits. The SSA practically denies all first applications, but this begins the process. I am sorry to say you have to fight like hell to get it, and this causes many not to start the process. Getting an attorney will drastically improve your odds of getting approved, but you need to file and get the first denial before an attorney will take your case. (I said this at a Social Security seminar, and 2 people came up to me and said they got it on the first try. So there.)

Working and collecting Social Security before FRA is going to cost you

I would say 'the way it works,' but I prefer 'the way it screws you over.' If you are over 62 and collecting retirement benefits, you can only make **$24,480** for 2026.[128] After that, your benefits are reduced to $1 out of every $2 above the annual earnings limit. Here is an example;

If you have $70,000 earned income[129] -$24,480 = $45.520/2 for an annual penalty of -$22,760

If you get $2,000/month in social security benefits, you will lose $22,760 of your $24,000 annual check for working. So, you got almost nothing from Social Security.

The numbers change 'the year an individual reaches FRA'. Notice the wording. Not one year before, but the year you reach FRA with Social Security, ***the devil is always in the details***.

[127] According to Devin Carroll, RSSA.
[128] This number call earnings limit (work penalty basis) is adjusted each year for inflation. These amounts are for 2026.
[129] Earned income is money received as pay for work performed, such as wages, salaries, bonuses, commissions, tips, and net earnings from self-employment. -Investopedia.com Not your IRA, royalties, rental income, or other sources.

Now, you can earn **$65,160** for 2026, and your benefits are reduced by $1 for every $3. If your birthday is in February, the $65k is for January only. The year you turn FRA.

If you have $70,000 earned income -$65,160 = $4,840/3 for an annual penalty of -$1,613.

If you get $2,000/month in social security benefits, you will lose $1,826.66 of your $24,000.00 annual check for working within 1 year of full retirement age. I guess that is better.

Some adjustments can be made in the first year. For example, if you start collecting benefits in September, your employment before that won't cause you to be penalized. But you might need to communicate this to SSA properly.

Once you reach FRA, you are no longer penalized for working and collecting Social Security.

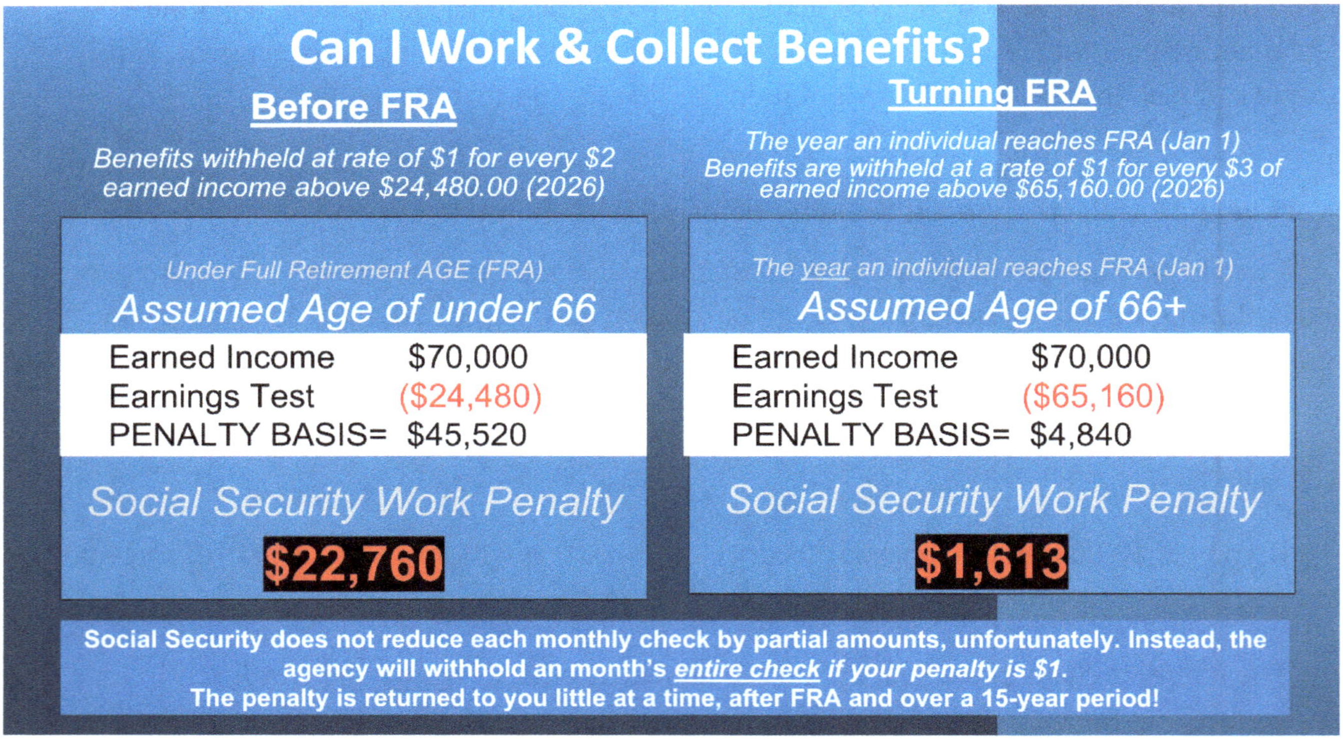

But do you get it back?

If your Social Security benefits are penalized, you will get it back. Ready for how this works? They will add a little to your check at Full Retirement Age (FRA) for about 15 years until you get it all back (without interest), unless you die before 15 years or switch benefits, so it is a 'sucks to be you' situation.[130] It's something, I suppose. This usually requires you to live past 82. Also, if you switch benefits and start receiving, let's say, a survivor benefit, then you lose the penalty recapture.

Be careful!

Here is another Social Security crap sandwich. Let us say your penalty is a few dollars, no worries, right? Except (it's never good news after 'except'), you lose that *entire* month's check. If you are collecting $2,000 a month and the penalty is $5, bye-bye, $2,000. (Social Security doesn't do partials; don't get mad, or the armed security will escort you out).

Do I get Inflation increases if I wait to collect Social Security?

In 2023, this question was on many pre-retirees' minds because the inflation increase was +8.7%. So, if I delay getting Social Security, do I miss out? The answer is no, you don't; if you believe me, skip the next paragraph.

According to the SSA document "Your Retirement Benefit: How It's Figured," it says, and I quote, "You're eligible for cost-of-living benefit increases starting with the year you turn age 62. This is true even if you don't get benefits until your full retirement age or age 70. We add cost-of-living increases to your benefits beginning with the year you reach 62. Benefits are adjusted yearly to reflect the increase, if any, in the cost of living as measured by the Consumer Price Index." It hurts that you didn't accept my answer and read the paragraph anyway.

When you start collecting benefits, your benefits are subject to an annual COLA increase. COLA is a cost-of-living adjustment. It was announced in October, and your Social Security benefit will increase in January.

Here is the last Cost of Living Increases from 2016 - 2024;

2019	2020	2021	2022	2023	2024	2025	2026
+2.8%	+1.6%	+1.3%	+5.9%	+8.7%	+3.2%	+2.5%	+2.8%

Negotiate the Price, not the Payment!

130 This applies only to retirement benefits. Dependent, spousal, and survivor benefits are not credited.

Years ago, my past wife and I went shopping for a Dodge Grand Caravan with the Sto-n-Go seats. We were visiting her sister in Austin and thought, with all the dealerships so close, maybe, just maybe, we could find a deal.

Being a finance guy, I told each dealership that I would only negotiate the price of the car. They would say, "OK, but what payment can you afford?" I would respond, "No, you psycho, I just said, what is the price of the car? The payment will be a mathematical formula based on the interest rate and length of the loan." We ended up walking away from many dealerships that refused to talk about the price of the minivan. Not negotiating the PRICE of the car will generally cost you thousands of dollars. That's why dealerships try to talk about payments.

Likewise, you should walk away from financial advisors who want to talk about investments only, not income, taxes, and retirement planning

You can make the same mistake with your Social Security. If you consider the monthly payment only (look, I am dangling something shiny, wouldn't you love a $1,500 check every month? Come on, come get it), you may be throwing tens or hundreds of thousands of dollars in the garbage by chasing a monthly benefit. Allow me to share examples;

Single Person Helen

Helen is 60, with an FRA of 66 and a PIA of $2,000 per month. Due to the longevity of her mother and grandmother, she is comfortable with a life expectancy of 90 years. (She will have 30 years of retirement if she dies when expected.) Consider how much she will get at 62, FRA, or age 70.[131]

Lifetime Amount

Claim at 62 (28 years x $1,500/month) $504,000

Claim at 66 (24 years x $2,143/month) $617,184 +**$113,184**

Claim at 70 (20 years x $2,657/month) $37,680 +**133,680**

Can you afford to throw away $113,184 or $33,680?

[131] Source of information is the RSSA.

Income Couple Terri & Ted

Terri and Ted are 61, with an FRA of 66 and a PIA of $2,300 for Terri and $1,900 for Ted. (I guess Terri worked harder.) They settled on a life expectancy of 90 for Terri and 85 for Ted. Let us consider how much they will get at 62 or 70.[132]

	<u>**Lifetime Amount**</u>
Claim at 62	$972,900
Claim at 70	$1,180,080

Can you afford to throw away <u>$207,180?</u>

Does this seem like a lot to remember?

So many details go into Social Security planning. No one should do it off the top of their head. I use software called Roadmap, which is provided by guess who? Yes, the RSSA.[133] This program, if used correctly, will help me help you.

Apollo 13 Explosion

When the oxygen tanks exploded on Apollo 13, mission control took their best people and formed a tiger team. Between the tiger team and the people in the simulators, they devised plans and did the 'correct' math. Most know that Apollo 13 landed safely, but the astronauts did not do it alone, nor did they hang on until they returned. They planned, analyzed the risks, and simulated every step of the post-explosion mission. They made course corrections and rationed resources. Because of this, Jim Lovell, John Swigert, and Fred Haise survived. It wasn't the mission they intended, but they came back safe.

I used the Apollo 13 story (besides being a space nut) to illustrate retirement planning. When making plans, something always goes wrong. What is your procedure for that? You need the correct planning and procedures with ongoing investment management if you want retirement to be a success.

"No plan survives contact with the enemy."
—Helmuth von Moltke, German Field Marshal 1800-1891

---

132 Source of information is the RSSA. I guess laughing old people slipped into the book. Sorry, I am too tired to replace the picture.

133 You're probably asking how much the RSSA is paying me for this chapter. The answer is nada. For full disclosure, Martha Shedding gave me a signed copy of her book. She scribbled out the name of the person she had planned to give it to.

Uncle Sam: We are sorry for your loss.

Let's talk survivor benefits. I already touched on this in previous paragraphs, but there is so much more, like anything connected with SSA! This is often a major reason to wait until 70 to file.

If you die (sucks to be you), your spouse is eligible for up to 100% of your benefit. Here is how it works. He/she can claim it as early as 60 years old (50 if disabled). With survivor benefits, if she claims at age 60, she will get 71.5% of your FRA and if she waits until FRA she will receive 100%. That is the first part.

Remember Spousal Benefits? It's better with Survivor Benefits.

Let's review the spousal benefits again. Remember what the max *spousal benefit* was? 50% of your FRA (age 66-67 based on your zodiac birth year). If your spouse waits until age 70, he/she *gets delayed credits of 8%* per year or 24% additional cash benefits (if FRA is 67) However, your spouse can't claim his or her spousal benefit until <u>you</u> begin Social Security benefits. Yes, she has to wait to collect spousal benefits. She can collect her Social Security benefits based on her earnings record; then, she will be eligible for the spousal benefits later when you file.

Does she get any delayed credits? Nope, at 70, you collect an enhanced Social Security benefit, and your spouse finally gets to collect 50% of what your FRA benefit was. Mind you, it's not what you are collecting at 70, but it is 50% of what you would have collected three years ago.

What your spouse gets because YOU waited

Do you remember 'The Survivor Benefit of Social Security'? Your spouse can get 100% of your *<u>attained age benefit</u>* (Provided she waits until <u>her</u> FRA to collect). This means she will get all the delayed credits if you wait as long as you can wait past FRA to file! (I wrote this addressing the husband as the primary wage earner again; Social Security is gender neutral; it doesn't matter who has the bigger benefit, husband or wife.)

Some men worry about losing Social Security if they die too soon. But you can provide a significant income source after you die to your widow (ex-spouse widow, also) by waiting to collect Social Security as long as possible or at 70. But if you file early, the Widow rule will limit the reduction to your surviving spouse. I'll explain that later in this chapter.

Again, I emphasize that the Social Security software lays out your options and shows the pros and cons of waiting or collecting earlier. These rules are built into the program.

Most married persons are concerned about their spouses being provided for when they are gone.

Social Security is gender neutral. If you are in a 'traditional family' where the wife's career is the family, her benefits might be low based on her work history. That is why survivor benefits are important. (Note: We see couples all the time where the wife has the higher Social Security benefit.) But first, let's get some qualifications for surviving spouses out of the way.[134] I am going to focus on retirement benefits and survivor benefits only. There are other benefits, but I was trying to keep this book under 22,000 pages.

Surviving Spouse or Surviving Ex-Spouse Benefit qualifications

- You must have been married for nine months (surviving spouse)
- If you are the divorced spouse of a worker who dies, you could get benefits the same as a surviving spouse, provided that your marriage lasted **ten years**. (They count out the months on this, so give it an extra day to be safe)
- You cannot have gotten remarried before age 60. After 60 is ok.[135]
- If you get remarried and that marriage ends, you can become re-entitled.
- If there are other ex or surviving spouses besides you, these will not affect your survivor benefits.
- Surviving spouse benefit starts at 71½% of the PIA at age 60; this benefit goes up monthly until FRA, then the surviving spouse gets 100% of the deceased's benefit amount. (***If the higher wage-earning spouse waits to collect this earns your surviving spouse or ex-spouse more social security benefits***)
- A surviving spouse or surviving ex-spouse who is disabled can file at 50.
- You collect on your deceased spouse's benefit, subject to the Widow limit, or if your spouse was not collecting, then your deceased spouse's FRA amount.

---

[134] See SSA.gov "If you are a survivor"

[135] Don't ask why because I don't know. Remember, this is for survivor benefits only. Ex-spouse benefits have different rules.

Don't cut the brake lines on your spouse's or ex-spouse's car. Social Security doesn't pay those who murder the worker or are in prison. Seems a bit judgmental.

Widow Benefit (again)

What if the deceased spouse had collected retirement benefits early? Here is the scenario. Your husband filed at age 62 and then died. So, if he had a PIA[136] of $1,000, his benefit would have been $700. After age 60, the widow is eligible for a *survivor benefit*. That benefit is impacted by the widow's limit (the widow's limit is the minimum a widow can receive. The widow's limit applies to an ex-spouse, too. This is 82.5% of the deceased spouse's FRA) I don't want to bore you with the math on this one; I have done enough of that. But if you think that at age 60 you will get $825, well, you are wrong. With Social Security, the devil is in the details, and you will receive $715.

But what about the Widow's rule? Those are the rules. Don't apply common sense to it.

If you love your spouse, consider waiting to collect Social Security as long as possible!

Remember the Inspector General report?

Earlier in this chapter, I related that widows have been given bad advice (from the SSA staff), costing 131.8 million dollars in lost benefits. If you meet the qualifications as a surviving spouse or surviving ex-spouse, you have a Social Security strategy that is unavailable to others. It is called Restricted Application. Here is where SSA staff may tell you wrong.

Restricted Application (this is important!)

Restricted Application[137] (or restricting the scope of this application) allows you to freeze either your own or the survivor's benefit, letting the other benefit grow while you collect the other one. You can switch to the higher benefit later (age 70, for example). Let me give you an example of how this would work. (I have rounded the numbers) For example, ***if you're a surviving spouse, age 62, you can choose between the survivor benefit and a benefit based on your work history***.

---

[136] PIA (Primary Insurance Amount) is what a person receives at full retirement age (FRA). This scenario assumes FRA of 67.
[137] https://secure.ssa.gov/apps10/poms.nsf/lnx/0200204020#e4

For Example,

Obviously, you choose the higher survivor benefit of $1,830/month. (Social Security calculates it this way: your benefit of $1,725 + an excess survivor benefit of $105= $1,830) But if you tell them (and insist on) a restricted application, you can take only the survivor benefit of $1,830, then at age 70, switch to *your* retirement benefit, which grew 76% from $1,725 to $3,036! That is a nice $1,311 monthly raise when you need it most.[138]

---

[138] I didn't include Cost Of Living Adjustments [COLA] in this example.

	Survivor Benefit	Age	Your Retirement Benefit	
	$1,664	60	$0	
File for Survivor benefit →	$1,830 ✓	62	$1725	
	$2,300	67	$2,300	
	$2,300	70	$3,036 ✓	← Apply to Your Benefit at 70

The results of the Restricted Application

What is the price of a restricted application? If we give the surviving wife a life expectancy of 85, she will collect $505,080 in survivor benefits. Not bad, not bad, you say. If she can switch to **her** retirement benefit at age 70 to her own higher benefit and she lives to 85, she will receive a grand total of $722,160 or **+$217,080** more. Yeah, baby, yeah.[139]

It's in there.

If you go to SSA.gov and look at "If you are a survivor," it doesn't mention restricted application. Here is what it does say under the "Other things you need to know";

"If you receive benefits as a surviving spouse or surviving divorced spouse, you can switch to your retirement benefit as early as age 62. This assumes you are eligible for retirement benefits and your retirement rate is higher than your rate as a surviving spouse or surviving divorced spouse." Pretty clear? I am unsure if I would understand what that means if I hadn't been trained.

"In many cases, a surviving spouse can begin receiving one benefit and allow the other benefit amount to grow until age 70."

Social Security might say No.

You must schedule an appointment at a Social Security field office for survivor benefits. When you show up, there is a good chance (even after the IG report) that they will say that "the Restricted Application option was discontinued under the Bipartisan Budget Act of 2015. Under the new Deeming rules, you are 'deemed' to be applying for all the benefits for which you qualify." (You sit in stunned and uncomprehending silence) Applying for one benefit, switching

[139] Ok, that is the last Austin Powers joke.

to another, or filing a restricted application is *prohibited*." (You lawbreaker) Then you add "*unless as a survivor.*" Restricting the Scope of the Application (official language) is an exception to the deeming rules.

And this is how the SSA is shamelessly screwing over widows. But it gets worse. Here is another "If you're a Survivor" quote on the SSA website.

Social Security will change your benefit automatically, you're welcome

"If you already receive benefits as a spouse, your benefit will automatically convert to survivor benefits after we receive the report of death." -SSA.gov "If you're a Survivor"

Whoa! Do they do this before you have a chance to run your options? Yes, you do have options! Because when you lose a spouse in death, the first thing you want to do is run down to the Social Security office. Fortunately, you have one year to change but must pay benefits back first. Some may not have the financial resources to do this if too much time has passed. (They may not be able to pay back the benefits in order to restart the filing.)

Social Security screws over the poor

I had a widow who I could have helped to get a higher benefit if she had seen me first. By the time I visited with her and discovered that a restricted application would benefit her, it was too late. She didn't have the financial means to pay back 9 months of Social Security checks and restart under 'restricting the scope of her application.' Thanks for the help SSA.

"The nine most terrifying words in the English language are: I'm from the Government, and I'm here to help."
—President Ronald Regan

See the following taken from the SSA POMS.

A. Statement to Restrict the Scope

When a widow(er) or surviving divorced spouse wishes to exclude RIB from the scope of his or her application, you must obtain an *unequivocal statement* to exclude the RIB, such as: **"I do not wish this application to be considered an application for retirement benefits on my own earning's record."**

MCS will generate this statement onto the application summary when the response is "No" to the question:

"If claimant is filing as a surviving spouse, is claimant filing for benefits on own record?"

This question is located on the Additional Benefits (ADDB) screen. For more information on the ADDB screen, see MS MCS 005.012C.

Again, here is where having an advisor who understands Social Security can significantly help. This mistake could cost you more than $100,000.

Do you see why it's essential for your advisor to be competent in this area of your or your spouse's finances?

To make a restricted application, Social Security wants an unequivocal statement to exclude your RIB application.[140] ***Does it seem like they are making it ridiculously complex on purpose?***

One More Thing

When you go to the local Social Security field office, you are going to need the following for your deceased spouse or ex-spouse:

Social Security number, Birthdate, Marriage license, Death Certificate, and Divorce decree.

SSA **will not** share this information with you due to privacy rules; they can be a real pain about it, too. Be ready with the info, and be sure to come away from your divorce with these documents. You are going to need them.

I know this is two more things, but there is a special lump-sum death benefit of $255. You need to claim it within two years of death. A surviving spouse or child can claim it with some requirements.

Divorce Read Carefully

---

[140] RIB -Retirement Insurance Benefits in other words your social Security benefit under your name.

Here is one often-asked question. I remember getting a call from a client who was madder than a wet hornet. He said, "That b**** is getting half of my Social Security!" ("Sigh," I responded)

First, an ex-spouse <u>does not</u> get half of your benefits. So slow your roll!

The ex-spouse's Social Security benefits do not affect your Social Security or the Family Maximum Benefit either. (The FMB limits how much benefits you, your spouse, and your children can get off your number.) So, slow your roll.

Another Story of Social Security telling it Wrong

Here is another story for you: a Social Security office told one of my clients that her ex-husband's one benefit (50% of the worker's Social Security) would be split up between <u>all</u> ex-spouses. (It's like they are making it up down there at the SSA) ***This is also not true***. As I have said, the Social Security offices are not a great source of reliable information. Now, let's go over the qualifications for *ex-spouse* benefits.

Ex-Spouse (Divorce) Benefits

First, you hate the jerk you are married to; it has been nine years and seven months, and you want this sham of a marriage to be over! Take a deep breath and wait five more months and a day. Because if you divorce <u>**before**</u> your 10th anniversary, it will cost you access to spousal benefits. To qualify for ex-spousal benefits or surviving ex-spouse benefits, you need **ten years and one day of marriage**. (They count the months so you have to have 10 years of marriage to the last month. Adding a day is to be sure) After 10 years, you must be divorced for more than two years, then you are independently entitled and can file for ex-spousal benefits after age 62. If you are divorced for less than two years, you can file for ex-spousal benefits if your ex-spouse has filed; if not, you must wait two years or until they file. See, it's simple. (Yes, sarcasm)

You are a Cougar

You married a younger man, good for you (or the other way around for the guy, but I think we call him a cradle robber. Women get the better slang on this one.) You won't be able to collect spousal benefits on that marriage until he/she reaches 62 and you meet the other requirements mentioned earlier.

If you get remarried (because you just didn't learn your lesson), you will not be able to collect an ex-spouse benefit, and will **lose** the benefit if you are already collecting.

UNLESS

You marry someone who is receiving Social Security widow(er)'s, mother's, father's, childhood disability, divorced spouses, or parents' benefits.[141] But wait, there is more! (With Social Security, there is always more and not the good kind of more usually)

If you do get remarried, you are eligible for spousal benefits on your new spouse's record after one year. If you remarry ***before age 60***, you lose survivor benefits and ex-spouse survivor benefits unless that marriage ends, at which point you can become re-entitled. After 60, you can get remarried without forfeiting Survivor or Ex-Spouse Survivor Benefits.

Remember, the remarriage-after-60 rule only applies to survivors' benefits. It's easy to mess that one up with the divorce rules. One more thing: you can only claim one benefit. I wonder what Liz Taylor's Social Security application looked like?

Grandparents raising grandchildren

In this day and age, many grandparents are raising their grandchildren. Did you know you can get additional Social Security benefits for that? If you are raising grandchildren on a permanent basis, you could be eligible for Child Benefits and Child-In-Care benefits. These benefits can be up to 50% of your FRA. In 2021, the SSA paid 2.8 billion in benefits to 4 million children.

These benefits are for children of retirees under age 18 or 19 (if still in school). There are also childhood disability payments if the disability began before age 22. According to the SSA pamphlet 'Benefits for Children,' "*Within a family, a child can receive up to half of the parent's full retirement or disability benefits. If a child receives survivors' benefits, they can get up to 75% of the deceased parent's basic Social Security benefit.*"[142]

A 'Family Maximum Benefit' formula is applied to these benefits, so you need to be aware of it.[143] The FMB will limit the amount you can get. These benefits could greatly help retirees raising children so late in life. In some cases, adoption might be necessary.

Filing Early Might Work.

When we start planning benefits for minor children, here is where your filing at 62 might make sense. Before benefits to children or the child in care benefits can be paid, the 'wage

[141] SSA Program Operations Manual System RS 00202.045
[142] Social Security Administration Publication No. 05-10085 June 2022 Benefits for Children
[143] The Combined Family Maximum Benefit applies when both spouses have their own retirement benefit.

earner' must collect benefits. Combined with your own, these benefits could be as high as 188%. To qualify, you may need to adopt the grandchildren. Remember when I said not to look at the payment but to look at the price? (Just remember the penalty for working and collecting Social Security applies.)

The total amount you get will be much higher if you retire at 62 and the family benefits apply.

Redemption: Some of your sins can be forgiven.

Let us say you want to repent of your sin of filing too early and start over. If it has been less than a year, you can withdraw your filing and pay back all benefits (including any Medicare part B if withheld and any taxes). But what if it's been over a year?

They might fight you on this: Suspending Benefits.

After FRA, you can stop your benefits and reapply at age 70. During this time, you will get the delayed credits. For example, a delayed credit from 67 – 70 is 8% per year or 24%. That would be a nice increase to your lifetime benefit. Why might they fight you? Because some of the staff don't know about suspending your benefits. Other filers have had to fight for this. Now I would like to think that when any organization screws up, they send out a memo reminding everyone of the problem, so it doesn't keep happening, but with SSA, not so much.

You don't look so good.

My good friend Carl Hicky, deceased.

Your health and the health of your spouse can be a big issue in Social Security planning. Some recommendations might be thrown out the window if your chances of making it to age 65, 70, or 75 are unlikely. That being said, let me tell you about my buddy, Carl. He was a former career Navy veteran. The doctors kept saying Carl was going to die. He had a dozen heart attacks and other health issues, but like a USS Battleship, he wasn't going down. I am sure there were doctors who lost money betting on how long Carl had to live. Each time, he survived. 'Carl is going to die' went on for over 15 years and 12 at the age of 80, probably under fleet orders. Don't be too dramatic; you [illegible] you expect even if your health is 'bad.'

You're not covered, man (said in the voice of Tommy Chong)

If you work for a public school, government entity, or another organization that doesn't pay into Social Security, you have two big problems. One is **WEP**, and the other is **GPO**.

Good News from President Biden and Congress: The Social Security Fairness Act

That statement seems like a typo. My autocorrect kept trying to change it. One of the last things Biden signed into law was the **Social Security Fairness Act**. (Thank goodness he didn't use the auto pen.) I erased a lot of content from this section since **the Evil Twins of WEP and GPO have been repealed**. This bipartisan legislation made a lot of sense. These programs reduced benefits for many retired schoolteachers and government workers. If you were worried about this, don't. They took it behind the barn and shot it. Chapter 4 is now shorter.

Not so fast

Even though WEP and GPO were repealed as of January 5, 2025, any overpayments or penalties before that date are still owed. So, pay up, bucko!

Your current earnings may not be helping you

We sometimes find that working might not increase your Social Security benefit. Why? The benefit is based on your top 35 years of earnings. If your current wages are below your best 35, then your benefits won't increase due to your work. However, they will increase if you wait to collect them. I know I already said this, but it's a common problem.

Albert Einstein was once asked what mankind's greatest invention was; he replied: "Compound interest."

You Need to Be informed

The IG report reprimanding SSA staff for short changing widows said the following:

"How can the SSA employees explain what they don't understand? They don't have the time to research every topic."

Wow! Now do you understand why you need to know the facts before you go into the SSA office or talk to them on the phone? If you don't, you may end up part of the 96% of people who get less than they should from Social Security. [impactful dramatic music]

I said before, no one (that is sane) goes to court with serious charges or serious money on the line without a lawyer. You need someone who understands the law standing next to you. You should likewise consider getting advice from an RSSA who knows Social Security before filing for your lifetime retirement benefits.

It is unlikely Social Security will correct mistakes THEY make in your favor. And will hunt you down like the felon you are if you are overpaid! So be informed. Reading this chapter is a good start.

My Social Security Success Story but first a report from '60 minutes.'

Let me introduce this by sharing a story reported in 60 minutes. In November of 2023, the news program 60 Minutes had a special on Social Security overpayments and the claw back of benefits by the Social Security agency. The people interviewed for the segment owed over $50k or $71k in benefits from overpayment by the SSA. One person who received benefits as a child (who went to his now-deceased mother) was being demanded to repay nearly $5k to the SSA. (This guy makes $25,000 a year.)

Social Security couldn't find the 'evidence' to prove the overpayment and still demanded the money from the adult child. The importance of getting Social Security right cannot be understated. If you are being overpaid, it is not safe to ignore it. SSA will come after you even decades after the fact. Overpayment notices at SSA were 1,228,389 in 2022. Social Security clawed back a total of $3.354 billion in 2022[144].

The people interviewed for 60 minutes had Social Security *reject all of their appeals*. Social Security ***can*** forgive overpayments based on 'Equity and Good Conscience,' but Social Security almost never allows that. In each situation in the '60 minutes' report, Social Security made the error, and the recipient would pay it back even years later. Interestingly, **when the 60-minute report came out, all three people interviewed received notices that their overpayment would be forgiven**. Wow, really? Just like that, after being told no and threatened previously.

---

[144] Source: Social Security

The report did comment that Social Security staff are motivated to deny benefits to control Social Security costs.[145]

Now, I will share my story because my editor says you like stories.

In June 2020, my client, whom I will call Lisa[146] received a notice from Social Security that her benefits were incorrect and had been overpaid by $18,000.00. The letter included convenient payment terms. By not repaying SSA, Lisa would have her benefits suspended until SSA reclaimed the overage. Lisa was 72 at the time. It was estimated that her benefits would be restored in 5 years.

How did this happen? Did Lisa misrepresent her financials to the SSA? No, the local field office made the error. They did not take into account her pension based on uncovered earnings. (Certain jobs in education or government do not pay into Social Security but offer a pension or a 403b/457 contribution plan instead, as I discussed earlier, but now is repealed) Lisa worked for a tax appraisal office that didn't pay into Social Security and had a 457 plan, which the Social Security field office knew about. That should have been an indicator to them.

However, Lisa had paid into Social Security during her life, but not enough to wipe out the effects of the Windfall Elimination Provision that reduces your Social Security benefit by up to 49% for non-covered school and government employees. As a government employee with non-covered earnings, she received a spousal benefit to make matters worse since GPO can reduce this amount by up to 100%. In her case, the Government Pension Offset would apply, completely wiping out her spousal benefit. We identified the mistake, but it was the field office that made the error. *However, that did not matter*. Lisa (age 72) sent the following email to me:

> *Hey Brian,*
> *I got this letter yesterday from Social Security. This just goes from bad to worse!! I just want to sit down and cry! I certainly don't have $18,000 to pay an "overpayment"!!*
>
> *What should I do now? The last page of this attachment is the front of two pamphlets included with this letter.*
>
> *Appreciate any advice you can give me!!*
>
> *Thanks,*
> *Lisa*

---

145 For more stories read "Social Security Horror Stories" by Laurence Kotlikoff & Terry Savage

146 Lisa is not my client's real name. She gave me permission to share this story however.

Lisa asked if I could help. At the time, I was studying my RSSA courses and said I would. We first called the Social Security toll-free number. The Social Security person would only say that the calculations were correct; Lisa owed $18,000. I asked questions about how these calculations were made. The lady on the phone refused to explain it. (Remember the earlier quote about not explaining things from the POMS?)

Then we appealed the decision. We waited months for a response. We called SSA to be sure they got the appeal, and then ***after a year***, Lisa received an appeal denial letter from SSA. We worked every angle we could and finally requested an in-person hearing.

In May of 2022, two years later, we received notice of a hearing before an administrative law judge for November of 2022. Yeah, a long time. This process had already taken two years, and Lisa wasn't collecting any Social Security money, so she continued to work her job, delaying retirement, and she was now 74. I was surprised that I could represent Lisa in these proceedings. I explained that I wasn't a lawyer and I had zero experience in what we were about to do. She said she had put it in God's hands and told me to do my best. Here is the email I sent Lisa:

> *Lisa,*
> *See the attached forms to appeal your benefit decision. I am applying to SSA to be a non-paid, non-attorney representative. I will send the paperwork to appoint me in a couple of days.*
>
> *As we discussed on the phone today, I need to disclose the following:*
>
> *I have no experience in SSA appeals or direct interaction with SSA.*
>
> *My qualifications as an RSSA are purely educational. My coursework did not cover SSA representation.*
>
> *I am not an attorney. However, I can testify on your benefit calculations, the Social Security rules for your case, and why Social Security has miscalculated your benefits.*
>
> *I have not been trained in argument and debate.*
>
> *There is a strong possibility that you won't win your appeal.*
>
> *That being said, I would not take this challenge if I didn't feel I would have a chance to represent you well. I also have resources through my affiliation with the RSSA organization that I am a member of. I believe that what we have already presented should have settled your case.*

It will not hurt my feelings if you decide to contact a firm on the list the SSA sent you. I recommend you call some of the organizations and see what they have to say. If you engage one of those firms, I can still support you as an expert. I want to reiterate that my contributions are free and will remain so. As a Social Security professional, I appreciate the experience of working with you on this in any capacity.

Please respond to this email that you have read and will call some of the advocacy organizations for your own due diligence's sake.

Be sure to submit the supporting documentation with your appeal form and get it registered and certified. Please do it by tomorrow.

I called the National Association of Registered Social Security Analysts and talked with Norm Haug, an RSSA. He gave me the idea to appeal based on equity and good conscience.

Brian Keith Moon, RSSA, CF2 - Wealth Manager & Chief Compliance Officer

There were many other emails from Norm at NARSSA (National Association of Registered Social Security Analysts). He gave me ideas and sources to consider as the hearing date approached. On November 7, 2022, we attended the proceedings by Zoom. Until now, I thought it would be some bureaucrats in a room that we would speak with. No, it was an actual Judge in a black robe and court reporters. In retrospect, it was in the name of an *administrative law judge*. I know, but hey, I am not a lawyer; what do I know?

But here I was, representing Lisa in court. (Without realizing I would be in court. I am glad I sent her that cover-my-butt email.) Before I proceed further, one piece of information I haven't mentioned is that Lisa and her husband had been lifelong farmers. In 2016, due to a 5-year drought that had hit the area, they had to file for bankruptcy and lost the farm, and four years later, she lost her Social Security, so wow. We included that documentation as well.

We made our case to the judge. We appealed on Equity and Good Conscience. (SSR 83-3a: Section 404.509) The judge asked many questions and asked us to fill out SSA-632-BK and submit that and other supporting documents to the court fax machine. A month later, Lisa received **a fully favorable decision**. The entire $18,000 was waived, and $5,800.00 already withheld by the SSA was paid to her.

I Didn't Do This Alone.

Success! But I didn't do this alone. As a non-lawyer and Social Security analyst, I had the help of NARSSA[147] staff. (I didn't even know of Equity and Good Conscience until Norm at NARSSA told me about the rule) **So, when I tell you what the RSSA program can do and how NARSSA supports its designation holders, do you get why you want the help of an RSSA for your Social Security and Retirement planning?** If you are a financial advisor who does retirement planning, you should complete this training and certification, even if you already hold a planning designation.

Before You Ask

One last point I need to make. I do not take cases to appeal adverse SSA decisions. I am a Wealth Manager, and Social Security planning is included in our retirement planning services.

But I will help existing *clients* with Social Security issues and appeals.[148]

Foreigners, Getting Social Security?[149]

That title likely triggers a surge of bias, either for or against (which's why I wrote it like that). There are a lot of issues when someone marries a non-citizen, lives in a foreign country, or is a non-citizen living in the USA. So, let's talk about this hot topic.

Can a Non-US Citizen Receive Social Security?

Yes, but it isn't what you think before you get mad (or glad). **Remember, everyone who receives Social Security benefits does so based on taxes they paid or on someone else they are related to who paid taxes**. (As an example, in the case of a spousal, ex-spouse benefits or survivor benefits.) To get Social Security benefits, you must have a Social Security number, have paid in at least 40 credits (10 years), or be a spouse of a taxpayer, be a lawful permanent resident, and have permission to work in the USA.[150] Here is the bottom line: Social Security does not pay benefits to undocumented workers. Surprised? Due to massive illegal immigration

---

[147] National Association of Registered Social Security Analysts

[148] Social Security planning normally involves running reports to optimize benefits. Representing clients on Social Security issues is discretionary and, if offered, may involve additional fees or costs. I am not an attorney, and we do not advise Social Security disability unless it is part of the retirement planning process.

[149] The following information is based on the RSSA continuing education module, written by Martha Shedding, RSSA, CRPC (Chartered Retirement Planning Counselor) and president for the National Association of Registered Social Security Analysts

[150] U.S. Citizenship and Immigration Services (USCIS) would grant this permission through a green card approval.

in the US, you probably thought we were giving Social Security to everyone. I can report that Social Security maintains these standards as if they were Republicans.[151]

Update: I wrote the preceding before DOGE audited the social security rolls and discovered that illegal immigrants were indeed collecting social security benefits. Sorry, I should not have believed the government. My bad. Social Security isn't Republican after all. While Social Security was paying some illegal immigrants retirement and disability benefits, it was taking away benefits from red-blooded Americans like Lisa. Seems wrong, no matter which side of the aisle you are on.

An illegal alien (undocumented worker) can get an ITIN number (Individual Taxpayer Identification Number) to keep track of his wages and pay taxes. Why would an illegal alien want to do that? For the following reasons:

If the person intends to gain legal status, showing they are paying taxes is a good step.
ITINs help individuals not eligible for SSNs comply with U.S. tax laws.
ITINs are issued regardless of immigration status.
ITIN is nine digits and starts with 9, with 7 or 8 in the 4th digit position.[152]

Earnings paid using an ITIN can be counted towards Social Security if the person gains legal status. Taxpayer privacy and the ITIN are not used for immigration purposes or reported to ICE.[153] Taxes paid while undocumented can count for benefits in the future IF the worker gains legal status and qualifies for a Social Security number. I personally don't approve of people not obeying the laws of the land, but most Americans support someone who makes things right.

I married a woman from the Philippines and have gone through the complex and lengthy process of legally bringing my wife and daughter to the US. It took over three years; my wife and my daughter had to wait the entire time in the Philippines. I don't have answers to the current problems except to say they need reform and streamlining.

I don't know how to put an illegal immigrant on Apollo 13 without it sounding racist, so I will move on.

---

151 If you are too partisan to appreciate that joke, then send your angry letter to Senator Ted Cruz.
152 ITINs are not easy to get, as I learned this when I applied for my wife, who is waiting for the marriage visa to be approved so she could immigrate to the USA. It is like the IRS fights you to get it. But have heart and keep trying.
153 ICE -Immigration & Customs Enforcement. The IRS does not routinely report ITIN holders to ICE. However, a 2025 IRS–ICE data-sharing agreement (after Trump was elected) created limited situations where ICE could request certain taxpayer information, and this agreement has since been blocked by multiple federal judges — meaning ICE currently cannot access IRS data from ITIN filers. This issue will likely go to the US Supreme Court.

Expatriates[154]

What if you decide to travel or reside in another country? US Citizens can live in foreign countries and collect Social Security Benefits. Nine countries are exceptions; they include Cuba and North Korea. Social Security will try to contact you to ensure you didn't die or something. I have read stories of expatriates having to come back to the US to 'fix' their Social Security benefits. You will want to keep a US mailing address and have someone access your mail.

The letter from SSA asking, "hey you dead?' will be important.

You can receive a spousal or surviving spouse benefit if you are a spouse or ex-spouse of a Social Security beneficiary. ***There is no citizenship requirement***, the non-citizen spouse must be in the USA **legally** to draw benefits. Here is another twist: if you are a non-citizen, you must be in the US at least once every six months for a month to receive Social Security checks. (Unless the home country has a treaty with the US).

If you are married to a foreign person, starting the citizenship process for your spouse makes sense. Could you see a future US government not renewing green cards (which must be renewed after 10 years) and sending those people back to their home countries? Why would they do that? There are several reasons, such as ending Social Security benefits to non-citizens from a stressed system. Protect your spouse; start the citizenship process right away.

Will Social Security be broke in the future?

The Social Security trust funds are currently on track to be depleted around 2032.[155] After that, the program will pay about 81 cents on the dollar. I have had my share of 'hair on fire' conversations about the problems with Social Security being there in the future. Some think it will be bankrupt, and others feel it will be fine.

I believe something will be done to protect those receiving and about to receive benefits. Why? For three reasons;

1) These people vote.

---

[154] An expatriate is a person who resides outside their native country. The term often refers to a professional or skilled worker who intends to return to their country of origin. However, it may also refer to retirees, artists and other individuals who have chosen to live outside their native country. -Wikipedia It can also refer to 50-year-old + men going to the Philippines or Thailand to get married.

[155] Source: Fact Sheet: 2026 Social Security and Medicare Trustees Reports

2) If Social Security is allowed to cut the payments to retirees by 19%, our economy will be thrown into a recession/deprecation not seen since the 1930s.

3) Homeless Elderly. According to studies, 50% of people receiving Social Security benefits indicate that it accounts for more than half of their retirement income. Do we want to be responsible for adding older people to the homeless population? Thanksgiving dinner at Aunt Margie's refrigerator box will be awkward. Please bring her warm socks.

If there were a cut in Social Security benefits…

If the Social Security trust fund reaches insolvency in 2032, we face an automatic 28% benefit cut. This is not a mere line-item adjustment; it is an economic earthquake. Based on current projections, roughly $480 billion in purchasing power would evaporate from the economy overnight. While a first-level analysis might view this as a ~1.5% hit to GDP, a seasoned economist looks deeper. Applying a standard fiscal multiplier, that initial shock could result in over $720 billion disappearing from the total economy. This is not just a recession; it is a permanent structural shock to the American consumer base. ***This is not just a recession but a broad base economic structural shock!***

I believe we will be forced to do something to avoid that. No, I don't trust or care for our political leaders, and I wish they would pursue options to fix Social Security sooner rather than later. Frankly, it is likely to be a crap sandwich for the younger people. There are actually a lot of fixes for Social Security that seem reasonable and doable.

Your retirement planning may include thoughts on your procedure if across-the-board Social Security cuts were implemented. This might affect how you invest your current retirement savings. I caution you against the 'collect now before it's gone' reasoning, which has become the rationalization to file early. If there were cuts to Social Security, you want your benefits to be as high as possible to minimize the damage to your retirement.

Good Morning, social security benefits will be cut -25%

Have a nice day!

If there was a 25% cut in benefits

If there were a cut of 25% across all Social Security benefits, how would that impact you?

If you collect at FRA, and your benefit of $1,500 is cut 25% = **$1,125,** or

If you collect at age 70, and your benefit of $1,875 is cut 25% = **$1,406**. Which is better for you?

If you are going to say collect early and save it, don't. It doesn't calculate, no matter how you slice it and few people follow through on that plan. It ends up being spent. The numbers don't add up. Taking this extreme view based on fear might cost you a lot in the long run.

A Few Words on Medicare

I don't sell or advise on Medicare. Like anything the government gets involved in, it is a confusing mess of rules, complete with gotcha's. Want to complain? Fill out the forms, and they will never get back to you, or until 60 minutes does an exposé on how terrible and stupid they are. That being said…

There are some key points you need to remember about Medicare. There is much more, but this will get you started. But first;

Medicare and Medicaid
Don't mix them up with other keywords

Medicare is health insurance for people age 65 and older, those under 65 with certain disabilities, and people of any age with ALS.

- Part A covers hospital insurance.
- Part B covers doctor visits and outpatient care.
- Part C (Medicare Advantage) plans are operated by private companies and combine Part A and Part B coverage, often including extra benefits such as Part D prescription coverage. Costs vary by plan, with different deductibles, copayments, and out-of-pocket maximums. (The maximum out-of-pocket limit for in-network services is $8,850 in 2024.)
- Part D is prescription drug coverage, also provided through private insurers.

Medicaid is a federal system of health insurance for those *requiring financial assistance.*

SSI is different from Social Security retirement. SSI is Supplemental Security Income. "Social Security administers this program [SSI]. We pay monthly benefits to people with limited income and resources who are blind, age 65 or older, or have a qualifying disability. Children with disabilities or who are blind may also get SSI." -quote from SSA.gov SSI Overview, I added the brackets for clarity.

When you turn 65 AND are already receiving Social Security benefits, you will be automatically enrolled in Medicare Part A. (You must sign up for Part B. Don't forget or it will cost you in lifetime penalties.)

You are not required to sign up during the initial enrollment period, but not doing so might cost you permanently higher premiums! (The penalty for late enrollment in Part B usually starts at 10% for each full 12-month period you could have had coverage but didn't sign up. That adds up quickly to some serious moola!) So be careful!

If you miss Medicare open enrollment, you could be without health insurance for a whole year!

The initial seven-month enrollment period begins three months before your birth month and then three months after your birth month.[156]

If you are covered by an employer health insurance plan, call your benefits administrator and ask if you need to sign up for Medicare. (**Some employer plans, usually in very small companies, are not considered credible coverage.**) You could find yourself without health insurance, and depending on when you discover the issue, it could take a year to get on Medicare and cost you more for filing late.

If you are not required to sign up during the initial enrollment period due to a work plan, you will be granted a special enrollment period once your work coverage or employment ends, whichever happens first.

Medicare limits what it will pay, so private insurance called Medicare Supplement (Medigap) is important. Medicare Advantage plans seem like a good option, but I haven't heard good things, so do your research on this option.

As they say, the devil is in the details — a good, licensed Medicare agent can help walk you through it all and service your plan.

The IRMAA Medicare Part B surcharge is sensitive to your earnings.

You paid into Medicare all your life, so now it's free? Oh, the laughter that statement causes. Of course, it's not free! (Part A is at no cost if you meet the work qualifications.) And if you make more money, you pay more for it! In the historical texts, there was something about the government being able to provide this coverage better than businesses could at no cost, but I digress.

Be careful asking AI, it seems to hallucinate[157] a lot.

"Tell me about the Senior Deduction in the OBBB."

---

[156] Go to https://www.ssa.gov/medicare/plan/when-to-sign-up for a calculator and more information

[157] AI hallucination refers to a phenomenon where an artificial intelligence system generates outputs that appear to be true or factual but are actually incorrect or fabricated.

"I can't do that Dave."
"Hey, did you turn off my A/C?"[158]

I can tell you from personal experience that AI doesn't have all the answers and makes up stuff when it doesn't know. I think I have met people like that. I actually had an argument with a popular AI program that refused to acknowledge that the OBBB was law and the effect on seniors' taxes. Here is a tip: when using AI for research, check the sources.

Here is the chart for the part B surcharge you will pay for 2026. (This cost increases every year and is based on your income and marital status.) Please look up these numbers since they change every year.

Medicare Cliff Hangers $1 is going to cost you a lot!

Going $1 over the $137,000 threshold for an individual (see chart on the next page) instantly increases the total monthly Part B bill by $144.70 ($1,736 annually).

The base Part B premium (joint income) of $202.90 represents a significant jump from 2025 (9.68%), largely due to rising costs of new specialty drugs and the shift of outpatient services onto the Part B program. Your Social Security inflation increase for 2026 was 2.8%. It doesn't line up, does it?

2026
Medicare Part B increase +9.98%
Social Security cost-of-living increase +2.8%

[158] 2001 A Space Odyssey reference.

*Note: your Medicare Part B premiums are based on your income from 2 years ago. The chart on the next page is the 2026 Medicare Part B premiums, but the Modified Adjusted Gross Income (MAGI) would be from your 2024 tax return.

2026 Full Medicare Part B and D Coverage Surcharges				
Single MAGI (2024 Return)	**Joint MAGI (2024 Return)**	**Part B Monthly Premium**	**Part D Surcharge (IRMAA)**	**Total Monthly Out-of-Pocket***
Less than or equal to $109,000	Less than or equal $218,000	$202.90	$0.00	$202.90
$109,000 to $137,000	$218,000 to $274,000	$284.10	$14.50	$298.60
$137,000 to $171,000	$274,000 to $342,000	$405.80	$37.50	$443.30
$171,000 to $205,000	$342,000 to $410,000	$527.50	$60.40	$587.90
$205,000 to $500,000	$410,000 to $750,000	$649.20	$83.30	$732.50
Greater or equal to $500,000	Greater or equal to $750,000	$689.90	$91.00	$780.90

You must pay the copay on Part B directly to CMS[159] or deduct it from your Social Security benefit check.

159 Centers for Medicare & Medicaid Services accessed through Social Security.

The red box shows your potential total monthly Part B + D premiums amount for 2026, which would be based on 2024 tax returns. This amount changes annually and is typically deducted from your Social Security check.

"And that's all I have to say about that." -Forest Gump, actor Tom Hanks.

Summing Up

As I have stated previously, Social Security has pitfalls. ***If your advisor can competently advise and plan (using accurate software), you might just squeeze every bit of retirement income you will need for a successful launch and retirement mission, avoiding the exploding oxygen tanks, like getting overpaid from Social Security.***

One of the reasons Apollo 13 was saved was the use of simulators to test and plan. The crew made the right decisions, turning a disaster into a success! We can do the same with your Social Security benefits.

You definitely don't want to go into Social Security uniformed or unprepared. A discussion on taxes is in Chapter 5, Pre-Launch Planning Taxes.

Social Security Review

- 96% of people get less than they should from Social Security. $111,000 is lost by the average American household
- Social Security is worth, on average, $300,000 to individuals.
- Some couples can receive $2 million over their lifetime.
- Social Security is a lifetime, inflation-protected income you can't outlive.
- Do not depend on the Social Security office or staff for planning or advice.
- Know the facts about your benefits before talking to the Social Security office.
- If you want the best planning and advice, your financial advisor should have specialized training in Social Security. Consider hiring a Registered Social Security Analyst (RSSA).
- Get all the money you deserve from Social Security!
- Remember that maximizing your benefits is not 'gaming the system.'
- Social Security income forms the basis for retirement income planning.

- Using correct Social Security software that uses your top 35 years and not your statement amounts is critical for accurate benefit projections.
- You can't lose Social Security in bankruptcy.
- Claiming early is costly, especially if you are still working.
- WEP and GPO, which traditionally affect teachers and those not paying into social security through their job has been repealed by the Social Security Fairness Act
- Working and collecting Social Security benefits for Full Retirement Age can result in benefit reductions
- You must be married ten years and one day to qualify for divorce spousal benefits.
- An ex-spouse <u>does not</u> get half of your benefits.
- Social Security can be likened to life insurance for your spouse or family.
- Couples should maximize the higher earner's benefit for the surviving spouse.
- Social Security is NOT lost when you die. Survivor benefits can provide for your spouse, ex-spouse, children, and parents.
- Spending your savings first and letting Social Security grow requires planning.
- If self-employed, consider increasing your wages to increase your benefits.
- If applicable, file for disability before filing for retirement benefits.
- Like Apollo 13, use simulators (software) to project your future benefits and lifetime benefits not just monthly.
- Consider the price of your Social Security over your lifetime.
- Beware of social security overpayments. Social Security is likely to come for them.
- You don't have to be a citizen to collect Social Security Benefits, but you do have to be in the USA legally.
- You can collect Social Security while living abroad, just not in Iran or North Korea.
- Remember to file for Medicare at 65 unless you are working with credible coverage or face penalties.
- Remember, studies have shown that the longer you work, the longer you live.
- The software lays out your options and shows the pros and cons of waiting or collecting earlier.

- You should correctly plan Social Security Benefits as the basis of your retirement income.

*If you get a phone call or email saying your benefits are being canceled, it is a scam.

*Note: I would like to thank Martha Shedding, President of the NARSSA, for her help, and Norm Haug, Vice President of Operations at the NARSSA, for his help once again. They spent a lot of time helping me edit this chapter.

Chapter 5
Pre-Launch Planning, Taxes

"Well, uh, if anyone from the IRS is watching, I forgot to file my 1040 return and I meant to do it today but..." —Jack Swiregt, pilot of Apollo 13

"That's no joke! They'll jump on him!" —Sy Liebergot -EECOM Mission Control.[160]

Now, we come to taxes. This area can change your retirement lifestyle by thousands of dollars a year. In one hand, they giveth; with the other hand, they taketh away.[161] Yes, your Social Security is potentially (frequently) taxable. I know the Social Security chapter seemed like one big crap sandwich after another but with taxes, we can do some actual planning that will help.

I want to be clear on something first. There is no product, loophole only the rich know about, or another strategy that completely avoids taxes. I see these ads, as you probably do that make outrageous claims about living off the tax grid. It's, to be blunt, a scam. That is not to say that you can't improve your tax situation, eliminate/reduce future taxes, or even add thousands of dollars to your retirement income by making some smart moves to lower taxes. Here is a great quote from a Chief US Appeals Court Judge:

"Anyone may arrange his affairs so that his taxes shall be as low as possible; he is not bound to choose that pattern which best pays the treasury. There is not even a patriotic duty to increase one's taxes. Over and over again the Courts have said that there is nothing sinister in so arranging affairs as to keep taxes as low as possible. Everyone does it, rich and poor alike, and all do right, for nobody owes any public duty to pay more than the law demands." -Judge Learned Hand, Chief Judge of the Federal US Appeals Court (1872 - 1961)

So now I need to cover my, um, backside on this issue by reminding you of the following message from my lawyer:

---

[160] EECOM (Electrical, Environmental, and Consumables Manager) controller and was responsible for the electrical and environmental systems on board the Command Module. See Wikipedia -Seymour Liebergot. These are actual quotes from the Apollo 13 mission.

[161] The phrase "what the right hand gives, the left hand takes" is derived from Job 1:21.

This is for informational purposes only. Though I believe my sources to be reliable, do not use the information provided here as your sole source of information and consult with a qualified tax or legal professional before implementing any tax or legal advice. Tax law is constantly changing, and it is possible that the tax strategies provided in this chapter are not updated or are obsolete. Further, the concepts discussed may not apply or be suitable to your individual tax or financial situation.

Finally, this information is intended to provide an overview of the tax subject and may not include all the details. I recommend consulting with a tax professional before acting on the information provided here.

Start Tax Planning with the End in Mind

Margaret Mitchel wrote 'Gone with the Wind' over a ten-year period. But she wrote the last chapter 1st. Likewise, it's best if you look at your retirement goals in the same way. Your IRA accounts are an IOU to the IRS. If you have a million dollars in your IRA, that is not your money. The IRS has a claim on a large part of it. There is no way to avoid this, but it might not be the biggest problem. There is a bigger problem. That taxes are going up, making the IRS claim larger. To complicate things further, our federal government is very interested in what you invest your money in. Moving away from IRAs is not the worst idea.

"I skate to where the puck is going to be, not where it has been."
—Wayne Gretzky, Pro Hockey player.

At one time, the top tax brackets in the US were 90%! Also, consider that we have a national debt of $39 trillion! Republican or Democrat, they are going to find the money, and guess what? There are $19.2 trillion dollars in traditional IRAs and 10.1 trillion in 401ks.[162] All Retirement Accounts total $49.1 trillion. That is a big, juicy pile of ol' money our government is eyeing. Where is the tax puck going?

It seems obvious that everyone should want to save on taxes, but too many wait until the tax filing deadline to inquire. A client once called me to say he withdrew his 401k during COVID. He was going to have to pay a lot of taxes and penalties. Had he called me when he made the withdrawal, we could have done things under the Care Act. It was too late now.

---

[162] Source: Investment Company Institute

After reading this chapter, you should have some goals you want to accomplish. Some may take years to complete, thus lowering taxes. So, know what you want to accomplish. Ed Slott encourages the following three goals in your planning; I added a fourth (Guess which one?):

- **More Control**
- **Larger Inheritances**
- **• Less Taxes**
- **More Income**

You need to consider what your future will be. Start your long-term planning now and know what your goals are.

Myth Buster- Taxes are lower in retirement.

Unless you retire on just social security benefits for income, this is rarely the case.

The avoidance of taxes is the only intellectual pursuit that carries any reward. —John Maynard Keynes, Economist

"401(k)s are Sitting Ducks for Higher Taxes; these plans have not yet been taxed, so they're sitting ducks for future higher taxes, and that's exactly what's going to happen."[163] —Ed Slott CPA, IRA and Tax Expert.

"One of my favorite tax resources, hands-down, is Ed Slott. Ed is perennially enthusiastic about Roth IRAs, —Christine Benz Morningstar writer.

"Ed Slott is the go-to expert on IRAs..." —Mary Beth Franklin, CFP InvestmentNews

"The tax code is written in pencil." —Ed Slott, CPA, IRA, and Tax Expert.

(Pictured here is Brian & Subhani ambushing Ed Slott for a picture at an industry conference in 2024.)

Effective Rate versus Marginal Rate

How much you spend on taxes can affect your living standard in retirement. In this chapter, I hope to give you a basic understanding of some strategies you can employ to lower taxes, have

163 Source: The New Retirement Savings Time Bomb: How to Take Financial Control, Avoid Unnecessary Taxes, and Combat the Latest Threats to Your Retirement Savings. I recommend you buy this book.

more control, and have a larger inheritance for children or charity. Let's review some basics so we are on the same page.

First, I want you to separate your *effective* rate from your *marginal* rate. The chart below shows your *marginal rates*:

2026 Ordinary Income Tax Brackets			
Tax Rate	Single	Head of Household	Married filing joint joint
10%	$0 to $12,400	$0 to $17,700	$0 to $24,800
12%	$12,401 to $50,400	$17,701 to $67,450	$24,801 to $100,800
22%	$50,401 to $105,700	$67,451 to $105,700	$100,801 to $211,400
24%	$105,701 to $201,775	$105,701 to $201,750	$211,401 to $403,550
32%	$201,776 to $256,225	$201,751 to $256,200	$403,551 to $512,450
35%	$256,226 to $640,600	$256,201 to $640,600	$512,451 to $768,700
37%	$640,601 or more	$640,601 or more	$768,701 or more

Illustration 5.1 Source: Internal Revenue Service

(I didn't include married filing separately since it is a bad filing status nearly all the time.)

Let's say your income is $100,000 (married), and looking at this chart, you assume you are at a 22% tax rate,[164] Right? But your effective rate (the amount of taxes you actually pay) might be 7-9% of your taxable income. Here is why: you have a standard deduction of $32,000 (in 2026, for joint filers; see illustration 5.2 below), and that income is taxed at a 0% tax rate. Next, remember that your *lower* income amounts are taxed at the *lower* brackets. You work through 10%, 12%, and so on until you reach your final tax bracket. That is why your effective rate is lower than the margin rate. In fact, at $100,000 of total income, after deductions, **not a single one of your dollars** would actually reach the 22% bracket. This is a common misunderstanding that leads to major mistakes in managing capital and retirement income.

Senior Deduction One Big Beautiful Bill

[164] Tax Chart and information is for 2026 and is adjusted annually.

There is an additional deduction for anyone age 65 and over. It's called the senior deduction and is set at $6,000 per person and will end in 2029 if not renewed by a future Congress.

Filing Status	Standard Deduction
Single	$16,100
Married Filing Jointly	$32,200
Head of Household	$24,150
Additional Amount for Married Seniors	$1,650
Additional Amount for Unmarried Seniors	$2,050
OBBB Senior Bonus (per person)	$6,000
Senior Bonus Wall (Complete phase out) married	$250,000
Senior Bonus Wall (Complete phase out) single	$175,000

Knowing this information helps you to make better tax planning decisions.

"Your effective tax rate is the average rate of tax you pay on all of your income and is always lower than your marginal tax rate. Knowing both is important so that you have the most complete picture of your tax situation."—Business Insider[4]

Capital Gains vs Ordinary Income

Tax rates are very different depending on the type of income you earn. Capital Gains, which are gains for selling an asset for more than you paid, will be taxed at a lower rate (potentially) than ordinary income. (Provided the gain is classified as long-term or is held over one year before being sold.)

Ordinary Income is taxed at your appropriate tax bracket rate. Qualified Dividends[165] (earned outside a retirement account) are generally taxed at the capital gains rate, and ordinary dividends are taxed at your ordinary income tax rate.

Capital Gains tax rates are not always the Best Deal

Let us say you have $200,000 ordinary income consisting of W-2 wages, annuity distributions, IRA distributions, and short-term capital gains; this will have an *effective tax rate* of 12.76%.[166] The reason? You perceive yourself to be paying 22%+ due to looking at the marginal rate. See illustration 5.1.

(The following is based on a married couple over 65 years old. The OBBB senior deduction is phased out, but they do get the 'Additional Senior Deduction' of $1,650 per person.)

Now, let us say (hypothetically) that in addition to the $200,000 in ordinary income, you also have $25,000 in long-term capital gains.[167] Capital gains are not included in your ordinary income amount since they are taxed using different brackets. If you focus only on marginal rates, you might consider a 15% capital gains rate a "real bargain" compared to a 22% or 24% marginal bracket. This thinking would change your planning in the wrong direction!

By directing capital toward capital gain-producing investments simply because "15% is less than 22%," you might inadvertently pay a higher rate on those specific dollars than you do on your ordinary income. Not looking at the effective rate can cause you to get hosed!

"In this scenario, your ordinary income is actually being taxed at an effective rate of about 12.8%, while every dollar of that capital gain is being taxed at a flat 15%. You thought you were gettin' a deal, but the IRS just took a bigger cut of your 'bargain' than they did from your regular paycheck. It makes you think, you know?" (Say that like a wise guy mobster.)

---

165 What Are Qualified Dividends, and How Are They Taxed? -Investopedia.com

166 Marginal vs. effective tax rate: Two ways to measure what you're paying the IRS -Business Insider Nov 3 2022 This number is an estimate and could be affected by other factors.

167 A capital gain is the increase in a capital asset's value and is realized when the asset is sold. Capital gains apply to any type of asset, including investments (Stocks, Bonds, etc.) and those purchased for personal use. -Investopedia Capital Gains: Definition, Rules, Taxes, and Asset Types. Capital Gains are taxed differently from ordinary income.

Now, notice my example below.

Example of inadvertently getting hosed on capital gains

Ordinary Income ($200,000)	Effective tax rate 12.15%
Capital Gains ($25,000)	Effective tax rate 15.00%
Total Income ($225,000)	Effective tax rate 12.46%

Or plan for more ordinary income and less capital gains

Ordinary Income ($225,000)	Effective Rate 12.76%

This concept of buying investments that are taxed as capital gains only can cause you to inadvertently pay higher taxes. There are advantages when you die, however, since capital gains investments get a step-up. But this comes down to objectives. ***Are you looking to generate income in retirement or produce a legacy?*** Both objectives can be true, so blending strategies is not a bad idea.

"Always pay taxes at the lowest rates!" —Ed Slott, CPA, IRA and Tax Expert.

Why?

I want you to have as much income in retirement as possible. Suppose I can save you $3,000, $5,000, or even $10,000 in taxes or more every year in retirement. A $3,000 tax savings is a cruise! That will be reflected in your lifestyle, the vacations you can take, the amount of traveling in your RV you can afford, and not worrying about how you will pay for medication, insurance deductibles, or medical treatment. Understanding the basics of taxes will also help you not be afraid to pay some taxes now to save more later.

A $10,000 tax savings is equal to the revenue from a $200,000 tax-free account earning 5% interest.

Last Dollar of Income Focus

I have read that many planners focus on the last dollar of income taxed issue. Once you are in the 32% bracket, every dollar of income is taxed at 32%. OMG, so stop everything! You are giving 1/3 of your income to the federal government! The reality is that every dollar is raising your *effective rate*. For example, let's say your effective rate is 14%. Why is this important? **Because it is not 32%!** Again, we are talking about your perception. If I ask you to do something that will cost you additional taxes now, you may hesitate if you don't understand your actual taxes. Always judge options based on effective tax rates. Don't let the tax tail wag the dog. (I'm unsure if that is a real expression, so I'll take credit for it.)

"You must spend money to make money." —Plautus, Roman playwright 254 – 184 BC.

Be careful of Tax-Free Bonds; they might be hurting you tax-wise.

We once met with a client with over a million dollars in tax-free bonds. The problem was that she was not benefiting from the tax-free interest her municipal bonds provided.

"The secret of change is to focus all your energy not on fighting the old but building the new. -Socrates

It Will Cost You- in Taxable Social Security

As I will discuss later in this chapter, tax-free bond interest is **included** in the calculation for taxing your Social Security benefits. The interest will be free of federal taxes but still cause you to pay taxes on your Social Security check. Nice right? (If you sell a tax-free bond for more than you paid for it, then capital gain is taxable) Here is where your financial advisor might not understand *your* tax situation. If he focuses on your marginal rate (last dollar rate) and not on your effective rate and the effect on your Social Security benefits, you might lose the benefit of tax-free interest. Tax-free bonds can also be subject to AMT,[168] Which might mean you lose the tax-free benefit anyway.[169]

Low Rate Not Much in Tax Savings

Remember, tax-free municipal bonds normally pay a *lower* interest rate than comparable corporate or government bonds. Holding tax-free bonds in taxable accounts might mean you are earning less interest and paying more taxes. (Due to the interest being a provisional income item for Social Security) This is fighting the old war and not the new war in retirement. (I am speaking of tax-free bonds in taxable accounts. You shouldn't purchase these instruments in an IRA, ever.)

Again, know your effective rate. If you think your tax rate is 20% (marginal) when it is actually 8%, it might cause you to think your tax-free bonds are a deal when they are not.

---

[168] "An alternative minimum tax (AMT) places a floor on the percentage of taxes that a filer must pay to the government, no matter how many deductions or credits the filer may claim." Source: Investopedia.com

[169] Certain types of municipal tax-free bonds are subject to AMT, but not all.

Taxes are a Moving Target.

Lastly, remember that your tax rates are a moving target. So, be careful not to lock in on one strategy every year. What works at one level of income might get blown up at another level.

Yes, that makes this subject hard, but that is why you should pay money for advice. The financial media constantly tells you that professional advice is unnecessary. (So, you will buy their subscription.) Still, every high-net-worth person that I know has accountants and financial advisors.

"With no guidance, a people will fall, But safety lieth in the greatness of the counselor."
—Proverbs 11:14, The Emphasized Bible.

Ceteris paribus is a Latin phrase for all other things being equal.[170]

Harvesting Tax Gains at a 0% Capital Gain Rate is Pretty Sweet.

I told you capital gains could be higher than your ordinary income tax rate, except when it's not. So here it is.

"In 2026, if your taxable income is less than $49,450 (Single) or $98,900 (Married Filing Jointly), you are at a 0% long-term capital gains rate."

If this applies to you, selling some investments in your portfolio (non-IRA accounts) might make sense to take advantage of 0% capital gains tax. We are talking about long-term capital gains, which apply to investments held for one year or more that generate a capital gain.

Important Caveat: These figures are Taxable Income (***Income after the standard deduction***). For a married couple over 65 using the $32,000 standard deduction and the $3,300 additional senior deduction, they could actually have a total "gross" income of nearly $134,200 and still potentially harvest some gains at 0%.

You want to be precise in your sell trades so you don't inadvertently push yourself into the 15% bracket. If you say, "*But that is an investment that is going higher,*" then great—repurchase it immediately! Wash trade rules don't apply to capital gains, only capital losses. Now, you have a new cost basis for future taxes or losses in that stock or investment.[171]

---

[170] I needed some Latin in this book, so you know how smart I am.
[171] I learned this concept from one of my first clients, Dr. Dwayne Dowell, a retired professor at Texas Tech. He taught financial statements

If you harvest a gain at a 0% tax, then immediately buy back the stock or investment for a new higher cost basis,[172] That makes you smart.

Take advantage of this if you find you are at a zero rate. But it would be best if you did it before the end of the year. Once January 1st rolls around, the 0% sale is over. Remember, the cost basis is what you pay for an investment and determines how much 'profit' you make, thus how much capital gain you have, and, finally, how much tax you pay. If you can push up your cost basis at zero tax, my God man, do that!

Example: $10,000 Stock you paid $4,000 = $6,000 Capital Gain
Sell it, then repurchase it at the same price on a $10,000 new cost basis.
0% capital gain on $6,000 profit = $0 taxes.

Stacking Rule (A Crucial Warning)

The "Stacking" Rule is one detail that often trips people up is that capital gains are stacked on top of ordinary income. If your ordinary taxable income is $90,000, you only have $8,900 of "space" left in that 0% bracket ($98,900 - $90,000). If you harvest $15,000 in gains, the first $8,900 is tax-free, but the remaining $6,100 is taxed at 15%. You don't just 'get' the 0% rate on everything; you only get it on the portion of the gain that fits under that $98,900 ceiling.

If you are a non-math person, you are starting to freeze up at this point. But stay with me! I'll tell more jokes!

Provisional Income problem

The "Stealth" Impact on Social Security. Selling stock to harvest a gain might not cost you anything in capital gains tax, but it could inadvertently trigger the "Tax Torpedo" by making more of your Social Security benefits taxable. This is why we use software to evaluate the total picture of your tax situation. More on Social Security taxes later.

Harvesting Tax Losses

Another before-year-end to-do item is to see what investments you have lost money on and potentially sell them. It's called 'harvesting tax losses.' You can sell a stock (or other investment) with unrealized losses and realize the loss[173]. If you like the stock, you can then repurchase it. But be careful of the wash rule on this one. Suppose you sell an investment and

---

[172] Cost basis is what you paid for a stock (but it can be any asset) or the purchase price, adjusted for stock splits, dividends, and return of capital distributions. If you sell it for more, that is a capital gain.
[173] These tips are for non-IRA/401k accounts that are subject to capital gains/losses.

buy a substantially similar one within 30 days before or after the sale. In that case, your loss is not deductible if you're thinking of being cute, selling in a taxable account, and repurchasing the stock in an IRA; this counts in the wash trade rules.

How many of your losers can you sell? You can offset all your capital gains plus $3,000 of excess loss. Losses exceeding $3,000 can be carried forward to future tax returns. So, you need to talk to your tax person[174] and a financial advisor in December to estimate your income, capital gains, and capital losses, and take advantage of the tax code. Not good at math? That's why you hired people like us.

But what if the stock shoots up during my 30-day wait period? Unless you have a hot stock in the middle of a run-up, your tax savings will likely be higher.

2024 Long-Term Capital Gain Rates

Tax Filing Status	0% rate	15% rate	20% rate
Single	up to $47,025	$47,026 to $518,900	Over $518,900
Married filing Joint	up to $94,050	$94,051 to $583,750	Over $583,750
Head of Household	up to $63,000	$63,001 to $551,350	Over $551,350

Illustration 5.3

Don't forget about Carryover Losses.

You can only deduct $3,000 of excess capital losses in a tax year. If you had $50,000 in capital losses in a tax year, you would first subtract that from any gains. The excess loss can be deducted up to $3,000. For example, let us say you end up with $47,000 of non-deductible additional losses for that year. You can carry this forward to other years until they are entirely written off.[175] Note: Losses in your IRA or other pre-tax accounts are not deductible.

---

[174] Tax person can be a Certified Public Accountant (CPA), IRS Enrolled Agent, or experienced tax preparer. Beware of preparers for the big Tax Prep firms. These folks many times lack training and experience to do much more than enter your information into software system.

[175] Source: Capital Losses and Tax -Investopedia.com

Donald Trump had losses in 1994 of nearly a billion dollars.

The carry-forward caused him to pay no taxes for over 15 years, which Hillary Clinton criticized him for in the famous debate before the 2016 presidential election.

Hillary Clinton said, "Maybe he doesn't want the American people, all of you watching tonight, to know that he's paid nothing in federal taxes."

Donald Trump responded, "That makes me smart!"

This is why you need a 'tax guy/gal.' It gets complicated, and you want to be sure not to miss out on ways to reduce your taxes.

"If you touch an IRA, you are already doing tax planning," said Ed Slott at a 2024 conference for financial advisors.

Your Big Wall Street firm advisor may be prohibited

Many financial advisors, particularly advisors of some Big Wall Street firms, do not advise on taxes even if they are qualified. It is a whole liability issue since the firm doesn't want to have lawsuits that make it liable for bad advice. This puts everyone in a strange spot as the firm's interests conflict with yours. Your advisor shouldn't have to dance around company policy. If the advisor is prohibited from offering tax advice but does it anyway, the firm can (often will) fire him for violating company policy. Do you care? I don't think you want a letter saying your 'advisor' is no longer with the firm. It is something to consider when working with a 'planning advisor.'

Your financial advisor should understand how to conceptualize tax planning and provide strategy ideas so that your accountant or CPA can verify that it will work for you and implement it on your tax filings. Depending on the complexity, they should work together to keep the taxes you pay as low as possible.

Unfortunately, I have seen some tax accountants or CPAs who lack any motivation or imagination to lower their clients' taxes. These accountants are tax form filers, not tax planners. Sometimes, you may find that you need to change your tax advisor. Separate the nice guy/gal issue from getting advice that could add thousands of dollars of income to your retirement. And don't be afraid to pay for a planning consultation with a CPA.

If your financial advisor is adequately educated and experienced, this will help you.

Double Standard at the IRS

Like Social Security staff, the IRS does not respect taxpayers but does respond to professionals. 'Do It Yourself' folks should think about this when facing off with the IRS. There is a lot at stake. I posted a video on my Facebook page @Toro bravo Investment Advisors on October 28, 2023, with Congressman Gary Palmer from Alabama's 6th district interviewing IRS Commissioner Werfel.

The short version of this exchange was that if a tax filer willfully misdirected or misreported his tax information, that would be tax fraud/evasion, punishable with incarceration of 5 years and fines of up to $500,000.[176] If an IRS auditor did the same thing (falsified documents), they would face nearly no consequence, not even being fired.

Another Personal Story

I married a Philippine lady named Nery in 2022 (the second time is a charm). I needed to file for a marriage visa to bring her and our daughter to the USA. We do lots of paperwork out of my office, but my experience with government bureaucrats told me if I wanted this to happen, I would need to hire an immigration attorney. So that is what I did. The marriage visa application is lengthy and filled with issues. The whole process took over 3 years. My wife and daughter were not even allowed a travel visa to visit me in the US (if customs sees you have an active visa application, they can (will) turn you away), so I have made 14 trips to the Philippines to visit my family. Many clients asked why I didn't send her to Mexico and let her walk into the US (pre-Trump). That is hysterical.

What is Your Tax Aggression Scale?

According to Shauna Werherlien, so-called 'Tax Goddess,' she said the following:[177]

"What is your aggression scale? … Zero to 10. Zero, meaning the IRS will never call me unless it's a random audit, which can happen. And 10, meaning we are all going to jail."

I am giving you advice on what I believe are 0s and 1s, maybe a 2, on this scale. You may want to ratchet up your tax aggression, and you do this with a specialist in this area. It would be

---

176 Often these penalties are increased for multiple counts.
177 Taken from Avoiding Social Insecurity by Martha Shedding.

best to look for a qualified CPA or EA (Enrolled Agent) who does tax planning. Your net worth and sources of income, combined with your emotional toughness, will decide how you proceed. A published audit accounting professor from Texas Tech University and Missouri State University (a very good friend and client, now deceased) once said,

"If you're not getting audited, you're not doing it right."
—James C Lampe, Audit Accounting Professor, PhD.

For the record, my advice is not to get audited, but Jim was a tax cowboy when it came to tax filing. He also championed ethics in accounting; there is nothing unethical about lowering taxes. I believe times have changed, and our government bureaucrats have become ruthless in enforcement. So be careful. But we don't have to annoy the IRS to make a difference in the taxes you pay in retirement. I'm just saying.

Remember how Apollo 13's mission control made operational decisions? Yes, by running it through the sims (simulators). The more complex your situation, the more we must test the plan's outcome to ensure success. Some situations are simpler than others when it comes to calculating the tax impact.

Your Social Security is Likely Taxable.

Many have mistakenly miscalculated how much Social Security will be taxed. If you add all your income, including tax-free interest. (So much for municipal bonds being tax-free) and then add half of your Social Security. You will find yourself in a bracket. (See illustration 5.4) Up to 85% of your Social Security benefits will be taxable. Note that 'other taxpayers' include widows, and they pay more. It doesn't take much income to see your Social Security benefits become taxable.

Many taxpayers see the income limit of $32,000 for marriage and assume that no more than that amount is safe to take from their IRA and not pay any taxes. I say, Nay Nay. (Nay Nay means no.)

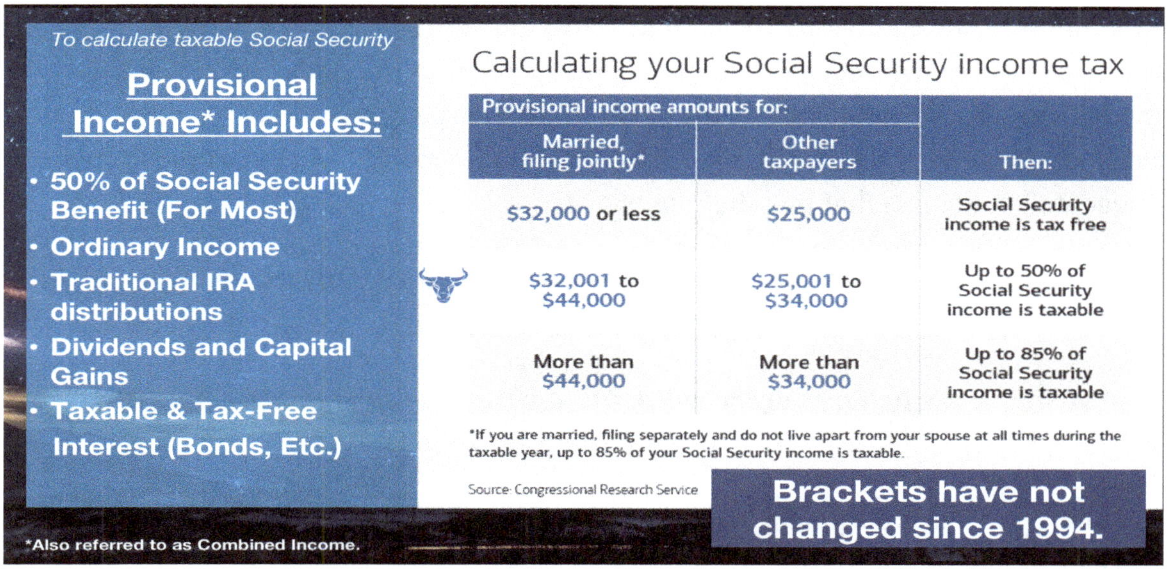

Illustration 5.4

Again, you must add all your income (except Roth IRA, including tax-free bond interest) and half of your Social Security. There is a three-part test to get the taxable amount of Social Security. If you're dying to know this, look it up. A fun fact: these Social Security brackets were set in 1994 and have not been indexed for inflation. I would have considered myself rich if I had made $32,000 in 1994.

Now, let me give you a quick tutorial on retirement accounts.

Qualified Accounts (Taxable Coming Out)

Traditional IRAs, 401k, 403b, 457, Simple, and SEP are funded with pre-tax contributions. This happened either through your paycheck at your job or as a deduction on your tax return. When you take the money out of these plans, it is taxed at ordinary income tax rates. If you take money before 59 ½, you pay a 10% penalty.[178] There are some hardship exceptions, like first-time home buyers, and other exceptions to the penalty.

Could we see an excise tax on certain 'wealthy' persons' IRAs? It's being tried, and though the promoters say it's for the billionaires only, it seems to filter down to the middle class. Also, remember that an increase in the marginal tax rates is a significant tax on your IRA accounts. If you say they won't do that, I remind you of the $39 trillion in debt the US is carrying (2026).

Moving money out of IRAs and paying the taxes now may allow you more control and fewer taxes now and in the future!

---

[178] 457 plans may allow penalty free withdraws after age 55.

But planning for taxes, income, and control of your retirement has never been more important. I see advertisements recommending all kinds of crazy schemes because the government is coming for your IRA. I urge you to be smart. Overreacting to sensationalism can cause serious financial mistakes and expose you to scammers. I am going to recommend some broadly accepted strategies that may help next.

"Every prudent man dealeth with knowledge: but a fool layeth open his folly." —Proverbs 13:16 KJV

"A simpleton believes every word, but a shrewd man considers his steps." —Proverbs 14:15 Byington.

Remember, you can't eliminate taxes you already owe, but you might be able to stop future tax increases from taking more of your retirement. The IRS has a claim on a part of your IRA. Ed Slott recommends exiting your IRA accounts now. Let's discuss the right and wrong ways to handle funds in your retirement accounts.[179]

"Stop contributing to IRAs and 401(k)s. This decades-old strategy no longer works. It's time to reduce IRA balances, not increase them." —Ed Slott, CPA Investment News 07-24-2023[180]

Protect the Capital[181]

Your retirement accounts (IRA, 401k, etc.) are the lifeblood of your retirement. Capital needs to provide you with income in retirement. Any loss of capital is significant and should be avoided. Interestingly, the mega-wealthy almost always have debt, even in retirement. It's managed, and it serves them. You should do the same thing. But note that I said the "debt is managed." Most people who accumulate debt usually do it through uncontrolled spending.

There is nothing wrong with making monthly payments on your home in retirement or financing large purchases in order to preserve your retirement capital, increase tax deductions, and reduce risks to your net worth. As I will discuss here, doing this makes financial sense in many situations.

The RV Purchase

---

179 When I refer to retirement account I am generally speaking of IRA's, 401k, and other pretax plans.
180 We recommend contributing to employer plans when matching funds are involved and other considerations.
181 I got to give credit to my friend Corey Maples a CEO of Legendary Capital for this quote.

One guy I knew withdrew all his 401k (approx. $250,000) and bought an RV. First, this caused his income to jump several levels up that year. He paid a lot of taxes to get a lump sum. Years later, he was in bad health, and the RV was rotting in the backyard. He was having trouble making ends meet. (His RV was worth a fraction of what he paid for it.)

Had he invested the 401k and generated a 4-5% income, from which he could borrow the funds for the camper purchase (yes, his credit rating was good, as is most retirees'), he would still have his retirement funds, and the camper would be paid for in 10-15 years. He would have budgeted the RV payments. Maybe he would have sacrificed somewhere else to make it work. **But he would still have his capital!**

But what about the interest? Yes, he would have paid interest on the loan; this could be balanced by what he earned in his retirement or at least a portion of it. If he could consider it a primary or 2nd home or a business asset, then the interest could be tax-deductible. Whatever he saved in finance charges, he most likely paid more than that in taxes that year. Carrying the loan would have preserved his capital. I repeat myself: most likely, he would have adjusted his discretionary spending because of the loan and still had his IRA capital.

He traded a permanent income stream for a temporary hobby. Now the RV is worth peanuts, the taxes are long gone, and the capital is a memory. Don't be the guy who burns the orchard down just to have one big apple pie. Keep the trees; eat the fruit.

It is almost always a bad idea to liquidate a retirement account for a big purchase.

Debt Free is not always the Best Advice

There is a misconception that you should enter retirement with no debt. Dave Ramsey and Suzie Orman promote this myth. This is not true. I did a Google search and found no articles recommending having debt in retirement. I did find videos by advisor Charlie Epstein (Yields of Dreams) that made compelling arguments for having debt on a home in retirement.

You want to pay off credit cards by using your employment income to reduce debt. This is an essential step in the transition stage. (Low fixed-rate loans like your mortgage should be paid last.)

What about taking a large disbursement from your retirement accounts?

"I identify 15 Myths People Have about Their Money. A Myth is "a false belief you have about a subject matter..." My Dad had this belief. When he retired at Age 68, he moved to Florida to build the house of his dreams on the golf course of his dreams for $500,000. He was going to pay cash. I told him to take out a mortgage for 30 years instead. "For 30 years,

he screamed, "I'll be dead before it's paid off." To which I said, "What do you care, you'll be dead." -Charlie Epstein "Yield of Dreams'

You want to retain your IRA capital whenever you can and use debt for these big purchases like RVs, boats, or a house. Let me give you a worst-case scenario.

Please, don't take money out of your IRA to pay off the house or buy an RV!

Your IRA Suit of Armor

Did you know that your retirement accounts (401k, IRA, etc.) have significant protections in bankruptcy and against creditors? Let's say you get into a tragic financial situation (no fault of your own). Your creditors could take your assets, but your retirement will be difficult, depending on the state you live in and the circumstances of the debt. There are federal protections for bankruptcy regarding your IRA and similar accounts. As of 2026, the amount is capped at $1,625,750 and is adjusted for inflation every three years.[182] Divorce, child support, Taxes, Criminal Penalties, and Civil or Criminal Judgments[183] are not afforded this protection.[184]

It is incredibly hard for creditors to seize IRA funds. Even the IRS generally views seizing an IRA as a "last resort" compared to seizing a vehicle or a bank account because of the complex legal hurdles and immediate tax implications involved. It would be best to look up the protections from creditors in the state you live. Texas has very strong protections. But as long as that money stays inside your IRA, 401(k), or life insurance, it's wrapped in a suit of armor.

If a series of unfortunate events causes you to lose everything, you might still have your retirement accounts and the income it provides. You should protect your capital and use debt for large purchases. Poo-poo havens in life. It makes you think.[185]

"Since this cap applies only to IRA or Roth IRA tax-year contributions and the earnings on those contributions, the bankruptcy law protects virtually all funds in IRAs." -Ed Slott, CPA, IRA, and Tax Expert. [186]

An Example

You purchase a $500,000 RV or a Yacht. Instead of removing that money from your IRA and paying high taxes for a depreciating asset, you instead finance it. Years later, after you have paid off half of the loan, you run into serious health and financial difficulty. The finance company repossessed the RV or Yacht. Let us say that you still owe $250,000. They place a

---

[182] Which Retirement Funds Are Protected from Creditors? -Investopedia, Is your IRA protected from Creditors? You may be surprised. Ed Slott March 9, 2016

[183] Civil or criminal judgments, in cases of your own wrongdoing against the plan see Michael T. Murray. "The Fraud Exception to ERISA's Anti-Alienation Provision: A Permissible Exercise of the Chancellor's Powers?

[184] Can an IRA Be Garnished in Texas? By Rebecca Lake

[185] Consult with an attorney if this is a serious consideration in your planning.

[186] Irahelp.com Slot Report "Is your IRA protected creditors you may be surprised"

judgment on your credit report and walk away. You still have that capital in your IRA, producing desperately needed income you need to live.

This is a terrifying story. Consider that a bad credit report is better than being impoverished. So, I ask you: why risk your retirement capital to purchase a home or another big-ticket item just to say you are debt-free? Why take a $200,000 distribution and raise your tax rates to see the funds disappear forever? It is one thing to pay taxes on a ROTH conversion. In this case, you still control the money, and your Roth is now forever tax-free. Taxable withdrawals are never refundable once spent.

"But I will pay interest," you say.

Okay, if we can earn the same or close to what you pay in interest on your account, won't you be better off? (Remember, some interest is tax-deductible if structured correctly.) Also, remember that structuring withdrawals can ***yield tax savings that offset the interest you pay.***

IRA withdrawals are taxable! Especially if you take a lump sum and shoot your tax rate up. It is a better deal to pay interest and let the bank carry the risk.

If you have a side business that involves the asset, you may be able to deduct the interest you pay from the business revenue. Obviously, talk to your CPA to be sure it is allowed. After the loan is paid, you will still have your retirement balance. Protect the Capital! Use other people's money to fund your lifestyle, and don't be afraid of debt in retirement.

"The 401(k) — or any retirement program — is the most powerful wealth-building tool out there, and I do not recommend withdrawing from those funds to buy a home." —David Ragland, CEO of IRC Wealth and a certified financial planner.

Civil Forfeiture is a Real Risk

You have your $500,000 Class A RV in your driveway. In a pre-dawn raid, the FBI, DEA, and local police swarm your property and arrest your grandson, who was selling drugs (unbeknown to you) in your camper. They hook up the RV and haul it away under civil forfeiture. Don't worry, they won't arrest you, but bye-bye camper and the $500,000 you took from your IRA to buy it. Forget asking for insurance to cover it. Folks, these are risks.

In civil forfeiture cases, it is nearly impossible to recover assets from the government. Your chances of the government seizing paid-for assets rather than financed ones are higher.[187] The bank's lawyers are the ones who have to fight the feds to get their money back. Let the bank take the risk.

As I mentioned earlier, the IRS can also seize assets if it decides you owe back taxes. But your IRA is harder to seize even for the IRS.

Protect Your Capital! Keep it in the Suit of Armor. Finance large purchases and homes in retirement and let the bank hold the risk. You can plan the payments.

How would you or your wife feel if you lost assets paid for with a lump sum IRA withdrawal?

Your fully paid for House is Dead Money

Another issue is buying an asset (like a house) and realizing that you can't access the capital. Here is my story. I bought a 70-acre ranch in Hale Center, Texas. I paid cash for it and improved it ***with cash***. I wanted a home equity loan to access my capital for more improvements. I discovered that Texas has a law that prevents me from taking out a home equity loan because I own more than 10 acres, mostly planted in cotton. I think the law was intended to protect farmers from losing their farms and homes to the bank. So, I had a dead asset, and my cash was trash because I spent it all. Had I financed it at the time of purchase instead of using my savings (that would have been ok), I wouldn't have tied up my liquid capital. Again, ***Protect the Capital! Don't be afraid to use debt in retirement***.

"For the vast majority of middle Americans, annuities and reverse mortgages will be the two products that will allow them to have a standard of living they desire in retirement." —Bob Merton, Nobel Prize winner in Economics. (Quote is from a Podcast with Robert Powell)

A reverse mortgage (HECM) is not a bad idea.

We have a Radio Show in Amarillo. It is NewsTalk AM 940 at 10 am on Saturday and Sunday. We did a show on reverse mortgages. (I have been waiting to work in my radio show plug) We interviewed Marina Watts, a Reverse Mortgage loan officer.

---

[187] Not legal advice. Consult an attorney in your state.

Many go into retirement with a fully paid home. Despite my eloquent argument to maintain a loan on your home in retirement, many will find it difficult to do so psychologically. A paid-for home is a wonderful feeling.

"I'm walking on sunshine (Wow!) And don't it feel good!" —Katrina & the Waves

But what to do about the capital that is tied up in the home? Enter Reverse Mortgage. What is a reverse mortgage? A reverse mortgage is a loan that you take out on your fully paid primary residence. You don't have to make payments on the loan, and the loan will be paid back after you and your spouse are deceased or no longer live in the home. We asked Marina several questions about reverse mortgages. Here are some of the important points.

- You have to be 62 or older to qualify for a reverse mortgage or have a spouse who is 62 or older on a HECM (Home Equity Conversion Mortgage). New proprietary reverse mortgages allow for homeowners 55 or older in some states)
- Creditworthiness is flexible. A high credit score is not needed.
- You must maintain property tax, homeowners' insurance, and any HOA fees.
- The home has to be your primary residence, and you can't be away from the home for more than 12 consecutive months at any one time.
- If you die or move to a nursing home, the loan will become due and can be paid back by you or your heir(s), refinanced, or the home can be sold and the loan balance paid off; any remaining equity belongs to you or your heirs.
- Your heirs, trust, or yourself will sell the home. The bank does not make a forced sale. You generally have 12 months to sell after death or lack of residency. Note: proprietary reverse mortgages become immediately due upon death, sale, or moving out of the home by all borrowers on the loan. See the terms.
- You can generally borrow 35%-60% of the home value depending on your age and the current interest rates.
- The fees range from $16,000 - $20,000 on a $500,000 value home.
- Interest rates are comparable to home loan rates.
- **No monthly loan payments are required**. However, property taxes, homeowners' insurance, and HOA dues (if applicable) must continue to be paid by the homeowner.
- The loan proceeds are **TAX-FREE!** (This alone makes up for the high fees)
- The loan proceeds will not cause your social security to be taxable.
- The loan can be a line of credit, so interest only accrues on the amount accessed.

- The only way to be forced to sell your home is:

  1) not paying the taxes, insurance, or HOA fees,

  2) not living in the home for 12 months, or

  3) not keeping up the home maintenance. (Most home insurance requires this anyway)

- Funds can also be received in cash, monthly payment, or any combination thereof.
- The equity (after the loan and interest are paid) is yours or will go to your heirs.
- If you have an existing mortgage(s), the reverse mortgage must pay it off.
- Many retired people have significant equity (dead money) in their homes; a reverse mortgage could free up significant retirement income capital. You can set a reverse mortgage as a line of credit years before you actually need it. Having this line of credit will allow you to access the funds as you need or want them. No one can force you to access the line of credit, so it is protected.
- The loan is also a non-recourse loan.[188] If you take out a Reverse Mortgage at 62 and live to 120, the bank will have to accept your house as a full payment even if the interest exceeds the collateral in the home.
- Reverse Mortgage and invest? I don't think that makes financial sense. At today's rates, you would be breaking even on the loan rate and interest rate at best. Establishing a reverse mortgage as a line of credit or for a monthly income to use as needed is a great idea! If you don't use it, then your heirs will receive more of the home's collateral.
- A home worth $1.5 million, a HECM will only look at the first $1,249,125; for anything higher, you would need the Proprietary (Jumbo) reverse mortgage
- Then, there is the Tax-Free status of the distributions. You borrow $300,000, which is tax-free and will not cause your Social Security to be taxed. Any tax-free financial instrument should be looked at carefully.
- If you want more information, email Marina Watts at mwatts@hightechlending.com or see her website at www.marinawatts.com.

If you still have a home loan going into retirement, you might be able to take out a reverse mortgage to pay it off and eliminate mortgage payments. If you take a $50,000 withdrawal from your IRA to fix the roof, you might pay 22% in taxes AND trigger a tax on your Social Security

---

188 "A non-recourse loan permits the lender to seize only the collateral specified in the loan agreement, even if its value does not cover the entire debt." -Investopedia Recourse vs. Non-Recourse Loans: An Overview.

check. If you take that same $50,000 from a Reverse Mortgage Line of Credit, you pay $0 in taxes, and your Social Security remains untouched. It's not just about the money you have; it's about the tax bracket you keep.

You could also use **tax-free funds** from a reverse mortgage (HCEM) to pay taxes on a Roth Conversion, invest in a long-term care annuity, or just provide another cash flow source for retirement.

Home Equity Theft

John Stossel did a piece on Home Equity Theft. Here are some key cases he profiled.

- Uri Rafaeli (Michigan): A retired engineer who accidentally underpaid his property taxes by just $8.41 because he didn't factor in interest on his debt. Oakland County bureaucrats foreclosed on his rental property and sold it for $24,500, keeping every cent.
- Tawanda Hall (Michigan): She lost her family's $308,000 house over a tax debt. The county gave the home to a private revitalization initiative—run by local officials—which sold it and kept the profit. Hall even tried to pay the debt in person, but officials reportedly told her they "didn't want her money; they wanted the house".
- Deborah Foss (Massachusetts): A 67-year-old woman who owed $9,626 in back taxes. Bureaucrats sold her house for $242,000 and kept the difference, leaving her to live in her car.
- Geraldine Tyler (Minnesota): A 94-year-old whose home was seized over approximately $15,000 in debt. The county sold it for $40,000 and pocketed the $25,000 surplus.

If your home is financed under a reverse mortgage, you will have federal protections that bureaucrats have to go through. It will make this kind of seizure very difficult. Like civil forfeiture, HECM loans (insured by the Federal Housing Administration, or FHA) add an extra layer of protection.

My kids won't inherit the house

In most situations, your 'kids' are going to sell that house after they put you in the ground anyway. Maybe you are worried that you will live long and all the equity will be eaten up, leaving no inheritance. Buy some life insurance with some of your tax-free proceeds for pennies on the dollar.

There is also HELOC

Home equity line of credit (HELOC). With this loan, you can access equity in your home as a line of credit. You have a 'draw' period that lasts up to 10 years, and you only pay the interest on the loan. After the draw period, you have the repayment period, usually 20 years, where you have to repay the principal and interest. There are tighter lending requirements on HELOC loans, but you can access up to 85% of your home value, compared to the 40-50% that you can access in a reverse mortgage. **HELOC distributions are tax-free!** But you have payments to stay current with. This is not an issue with a reverse mortgage.[189]

HELOCs or HECMs, either of these options to access your dead money makes sense.

Inherited IRAs Have No Protection.

In 2014, the United States Supreme Court in Clark v. Rameker, 573 U.S. 122, ruled that inherited IRAs are <u>not exempt</u> from creditor claims. If you make a child your beneficiary who has litigation risk, this may be a concern for you. When I say litigation risk, your child might have a high-risk business, be incarcerated, or have considerable debt. The IRA he inherited from you may go to creditors since SCOTUS has ruled against creditor protection. Inheriting money may not benefit them and end up in other hands. What can you do?

Annuities Offer Additional Protections.

You can roll IRAs and other pre-tax accounts (for example, 401k or 403b, etc) into an IRA annuity. This will afford you and your beneficiary protection from creditors and bankruptcy. In Texas, this protection is excellent as long as you're not being sued or going to be sued when you fund the annuity. [190] Remember, these rules vary state by state. But most states have protections for annuities.

Your IRA is a fortress, but an Inherited IRA is a tent in a windstorm. By using an IRA Annuity, you can upgrade that tent back into a fortress for your kids. Just remember to build the walls while the sky is still blue—don't wait for the storm to start before you try to protect your legacy.

---

[189] See Forbes Advisor 'What Is A Home Equity Line Of Credit, Or HELOC?' Written by Kiah Treece & Robin Rothstein
[190] Texas Insurance Law Creditor Protection Title 17 Sec. 1108.051. Consult an attorney.

Do You Remember Kenneth Lay?

Kenneth Lay was the former CEO of Enron before the Enron meltdown. At one point, he moved 10 million dollars into two variable annuities from the company.[191] After the Enron bankruptcy, Ken was sued for the 10 million in compensation he had deposited. In Texas, annuities are not protected from creditors if funded under a 'fraudulent transfer.' In other words, the sky must be clear and blue when you fund the annuity, and no one is going to sue you—a fraudulent transfer exception applied in this case. Ken died, and his widow battled with the Enron Recovery Trust for ten years. Ultimately, after ten years of litigation, Enron Recovery settled with Linda Lay for $10 million. We don't know how much the account made in that period, but I assume she had more than she started with after forking over 10 million.

If creditors find it challenging to pursue an annuity in a case of overwhelming fraud, as with Ken Lay and Enron, your chances look pretty good. Annuities do provide you and your heirs with more protection. See Chapter 6 for an in-depth discussion of annuities.

I discussed Texas law for additional protections above the federal, but if you live in another state, you must investigate the state laws for IRAs and Annuities there. Most states offer enhanced protections for IRA Annuities to a greater or lesser extent. If this topic is of concern to you, consult an attorney.

Downpayments

How about a down payment for a house purchase? If there isn't another option, you do what you must. Moving money from your IRA into a house is neither efficient nor a good use of capital. Remember, your IRA or Roth IRA has protections that other assets do not have.

To get a $100,000 down payment, you might have to withdraw $140,000 to $150,000 to cover the 2026 tax hit. You lose the capital, the future growth, and the legal protection. Don't be cavalier about taking large amounts out of your retirement accounts. Additionally, you must pay taxes on the withdrawal, reducing your savings.

Borrow From Yourself

One option (if you are under 70) is to consider setting up a Single or solo 401 (k). You can borrow up to 50% of the account value or $50,000, tax-free and penalty-free, and pay it back

---

191 More on variable annuities in Chapter 6.

over 5 -15 years.[192] You do pay an interest rate, but in most of these plans, the interest rate you pay is added back to your account. Your cost is relatively low. There may be commissions and fees, but the money loaned to you comes from your account and is not invested until you pay it back, so you lose market opportunity. But you return the funds to your retirement account with interest over time.

In the Single 401k accounts I have opened, the interest rate on the loan is put into your account. This means you paid yourself the interest rate instead of the bank! That is powerful. As I already mentioned, you lost the investment opportunity, but in the end, you protected your capital and saved interest expenses, penalties, and taxes.

I have helped many doctors, professors, and others to roll over from an IRA or 403b to a Single k based on a side business. (Your business can't have any employees in a single k except a spouse.) In most cases, they need the funds for a home purchase downpayment, but you could pay off credit debt with this method, too. You avoid paying taxes on the money taken from the plan, and if you are under 59 ½ years old, you also avoid the 10% penalty. Your monthly payments will return your capital to the account.

Be Your Own Banker

Instead of being a victim of the tax system, you become your own banker. You aren't 'spending' your retirement; you are 'leasing' it from yourself. By paying yourself interest instead of a bank, you turn a debt into a wealth-building exercise. Just ensure your side business is legitimate and you keep up with the paperwork, or the IRS will turn that loan into a very expensive, taxable withdrawal.

If you decide to end the repayment after you begin the Single 401k loan, you will pay taxes on the outstanding balance in the tax year you stop repaying the loan. (There are a lot of DOL rules on these plans, so watch for correspondence from the sponsor requiring affirmations and such.)

Paying Off Credit Cards

What about paying off my high-interest credit cards? Are we talking about a small amount? Sure, but what about a higher amount? Here is the problem, and I agree with Dave Ramsey on this one: Credit card debt is the enemy of your wealth and happiness.

---

192 General purpose loans are five years, and loans for a home are generally 15-year repayment schedule. Loans are not available after age 70.

However, it is not your credit cards but your spending habits that caused you to accumulate this debt; that is your problem.

"There are no shortcuts when it comes to getting out of debt," —Dave Ramsey.

If you pay that off with a withdrawal from your retirement, you will likely be right back where you started without severe changes to your spending habits. It is better to pay these debts off in the transition period in preparation for retirement or out of the income produced by your retirement investments, and build better spending habits that you will need. Setting up a repayment plan using Social Security and IRA income will preserve capital while paying off your debts. Dave Ramsey says that it takes 90 days to form new spending habits.

"This plan sounds awful," you say.

I agree. There is so much satisfaction from paying off debts quickly. But remember this:

Your IRA is temporal; it is how your younger self from the past takes care of the older person you are now. Only there isn't a cool DeLorean involved.[193]

Again, Protect the Capital! If you pay off your debt slowly while making positive spending choices, it will be self-imposed tough love, and you are less likely to reaccumulate debt. Financing large purchases does make sense, but carrying high-interest credit card debt does not. If you do decide to pay off your credit debt in one fell swoop, get therapy to recondition your mind to make sure this never happens to you again. (I am not joking about this) You may even want to cut up your credit cards if you can't trust yourself.

The reverse mortgage I talked about earlier may be a perfect tool to pay off your high-interest debt and start retirement fresh.

[193] Back to the Future reference.

At the time of this writing, the national debt is over 39 trillion dollars. Congress passed a bill (the Inflation Reduction Act, 2022) to hire armed IRS agents. Like Social Security, our government is arming itself against us. Your IRA is a juicy target for a revenue-hungry government. I start this chapter by stating that in 2025, there was over $19 trillion in traditional IRAs and 10.1 trillion in 401ks. Total Retirement Assets have reached $49.1

More and more people are choosing to remove significant portions of their pre-tax retirement accounts (IRAs, 401ks, and like accounts). There are rational reasons to do this beyond saving on taxes. I quoted Ed Slott earlier saying, "401(k)s are Sitting Ducks for Higher Taxes." Add the power play the Department of Labor is making for control of the investments you're 'allowed' to have in your IRA, which makes you think. How do you protect your capital? There are a couple of ways; let's start with Roth IRA conversions.

"If you've got a business, you didn't build that." —President Barack Obama

Because that is not your money

The IRS has a substantial claim on the money in your non-Roth retirement account. Congress can increase the claim at any time it wants to by increasing tax rates. I would not be surprised if a 'wealth tax' on undistributed IRAs is implemented in the future.

Roth IRAs (Tax-Free and invisible on your tax return)

Roth IRA contributions do not get a tax deduction when you deposit the money into the account, but distributions from a Roth account are tax-free. (You must have had any Roth account for more than five years and be at least 59 ½ to enjoy this benefit. Converted funds must have been held for 5 years from conversion (unless you have held the Roth for 5 years already, and you must be 59.5 years old to withdraw tax-free)

You can contribute to a Roth[194] if you have earned income. You know, from working and no, investment income doesn't count, so quit asking. In 2026, you can contribute $7,500 plus an additional $1,100 catch-up contribution if you're over 50. However, and you're going to love this, in 2026, if you earn more than $242,000 a year, you will be phased out and stopped from

---

[194] Investopedia.com "Roth IRA Contribution and Income Limits: A Comprehensive Rules Guide"

contributing to a Roth. This counts for your spouse, too, even if she doesn't have any income or hasn't contributed to an employer-based retirement account. If your employer offers a Roth option in the 401k, you should seriously consider having your contributions go to the Roth, as I will explain later.

I HAVE THE POWER![195]

Like He-man and the masters of the universe, the Roth is a powerful retirement income tool that defeats the IRS's Skeletor! (Except you don't get a sword with lighting flashing off of it.) Why? Because the Roth is entirely invisible on your tax return. It is one of the few truly tax-free things. Some deductions may run afoul of the AMT tax but not Roth distributions. Roth distributions are not included in Social Security tax calculations. You can pull the converted principal out the next day if you need to, and it is tax-free because you already paid the tax at the time of conversion. But if Roth is that good, won't Congress take it away or change it?

Sure, anything is possible, but Congress and Presidents have only improved the Roth over the years. Many industry experts are comfortable with the Roth in long-term planning. (Roth conversions are frequently villainized by certain congress members. It's possible that the feature could be lost or modified in future legislation.) Even the IRS has made favorable rules for the Roth.[196] I also repeat that Roth distributions are not included in Social Security tax calculations. This is a major benefit to retirees!

"Change your life by going from forever taxed in IRA, 401(k), 403(b), and 457 plans to possibly NEVER TAXED where the government has a hard time touching your precious wealth!" -
—Ed Slott, CPA, IRA, and Tax Expert.

"Then you will know the truth, and the truth will set you free."—John 8:32 NIV

If you are a sinner who hasn't been funding your Roth IRA, you're probably doing the math and saying, "Well, I screwed the pooch on this one." Guess what? There is time to repent and be forgiven! You can do a Roth Conversion! Convert and be saved taxes! There are no income limits, no earned income required, and no age limits. Yes, you can repent of your sin of not funding a Roth IRA by converting. (No bible study is needed.)

---

195 Quote from He-man cartoon. "He-Man is a superhero and the main protagonist of the sword and planet Masters of the Universe" First appeared in 1981 -Wikipedia I remember watching this after school in the '80's.
196 I am referring to rules allowing inherited Roth IRA's to be held for 10 years with no required minimum distributions by your beneficiary(s).

From the movie 'Oh Brother, Where Art Thou?'

Pete: "Well, I'll be a son of a b****. Delmar's been saved."

Delmar O'Donnell: "Well, that's it, boys. I've been redeemed. The preacher's done washed away all my sins and transgressions. It's the straight and narrow from here on out, and heaven everlasting's my reward."

Ulysses Everett McGill: "Delmar, what are you talking about? We've got bigger fish to fry."

Delmar O'Donnell: "The preacher says all my sins are washed away, including that Piggly Wiggly I knocked over in Yazoo."

Ulysses Everett McGill: "I thought you said you were innocent of those charges?"

Delmar O'Donnell: "Well, I was lying. And the preacher says that that sin's been washed away, too. Neither God nor men (*or the IRS*) got nothing on me now. C'mon in, boys; the water is fine."

Roth IRAs is New Windows on your Retirement Plan

If you take part of your IRA and convert it into a Roth with all the tax-free advantages, you will have to pay the taxes on the amount converted at ordinary income rates with no penalties, even if you're under 59 ½.[197]

"Whoa! I have to pay taxes," you say. "Turn the page on that!"

Here is where understanding your effective rate is essential. Depending on your situation, you could convert at a low rate (say 14% or lower) to move your money from "always taxed to never taxed!"

"I don't know," you say. "If I convert $100,000, that is $14,000 in taxes! Crap on a cracker, you're killing me here! Wait? Do you want me to do this for several years? Are you out of your mind?"

Allow me to illustrate in a non-Apollo 13 this time. Have you ever bought new windows, an HVAC unit, or other home improvement?

Was the energy efficiency that would generate energy savings you would get a significant factor in your decision? The windows would pay for themselves in reduced heating and cooling

---

[197] If you are under 59 ½ you will have to pay the taxes from separate funds. If you have the taxes withheld from the convert funds, then a penalty of 10% would be due the IRS.

costs in a few years, right? Or did the salesperson say, "This HVAC unit is 36% more energy efficient and will pay for itself and save the environment?" The same applies to a Roth IRA (except for the environment part).

Buying the windows (the conversion) doesn't just lower your bill; it changes the value of the house. Once that money is in the Roth, it is invisible to the formulas that tax your Social Security and determine your Medicare Part B premiums. ***You aren't just saving on taxes; you're insulating your entire retirement plan from future government 'utility hikes'.***

You're just not seeing it yet. Could taxes go up in the future? In 2024, we are in the 3rd lowest tax environment in the last 80 years! Moving taxable money out of your IRA now will allow you to control your tax bracket and reduce the taxes you pay on Social Security and Federal income in the future. (More control, less taxes, and more income). It's all in the sequencing, John.

Apollo 13 lost its batteries in the service module. They were down to the batteries in the Command Module and the Lunar Excursion Module (LEM). To stretch out the power they had left they had to sequence their power. Turning on some things and skipping others so they would have enough power to re-enter the Earth's atmosphere until the parachutes deployed.

In the movie Apollo 13, Ken Mattingly, played by actor Gary Sinise, is tasked with simulating the power-up procedure for the command module when it re-enters the earth's atmosphere. The spacecraft had a limited power supply to work with. Ken says in the movie:

"It's all in the sequencing, John. If we can skip what we don't absolutely need and turn things on in the right order, maybe it will work."[198]

Sequencing the power made it possible to successfully re-enter the earth's atmosphere and land in the South Pacific with their limited power. Remember, they lost the primary batteries in the service module. They had to use the lunar module and command module batteries to survive four days and land the ship. (They had to drastically reduce the power consumption by turning off nearly everything on the ship.) Apollo 13 would have been a different story if they had run out of power before the parachutes deployed.

---

[198] Quote from 'Apollo 13' movie. The is no confirmation that Ken Mattingly actually said this. Sequencing the re-entry procedure to conserve power was developed by the Tiger team and tested by Ken in the simulators.

How would saving thousands of dollars in taxes improve your lifestyle for you and your spouse?

Sequence where you take Withdraws

In retirement its very common to start withdrawing from your retirement accounts for income. Tax analysis of the different types of accounts you have is important. Each account type has its own tax consequences. The following graphic illustrates this.

Taxable Accounts (Single and Joint)	Taxable Retirement Accounts (IRAs)	Tax-Free Roth IRAs

Most just start taking money from their IRA. But a good analysis might shave off thousands in taxes by 'sequencing' where your retirement income is drawn from. Again, even a few thousand dollars of tax savings can improve your lifestyle.

$3,000 tax savings buys a cruise!

Sequencing your Income in Retirement

Still not convinced? Allow me to illustrate this for you. Imagine a married couple who wants a $100,000.00 income. We will call them Mrs. and Mr. Bennett. (See illustration 5.5 below) The husband has $30,000 of annual Social Security benefits, and his wife has $15,000. If they take $55,000 out of their IRAs, their total yearly taxes will be $4,541.00 (a 4.54% effective rate[199]) $34,475 of their $45,000 Social Security benefits is taxable.[200] But let's say they had a Roth IRA, and instead of pulling $55k out of the Traditional IRA, they took out only $25k from the IRA and did just $30k from the Roth. (Strategy #3 in chart below) This move will save **$4,541** in taxes.

199 Remember the effective rate is your gross income divided by your net taxes. The rate increases after the senior deduction sunsets in 2028.

200 Taxable means adding this amount of your Social Security check to your taxable income.

Tax Reduction Summary "It's all in the sequencing John." –Ken Mattingly

Married with $100,000 income goal, with a $45,000 coming from SS.

	Strategy #1	Strategy #2	Strategy #3
Taxable Social Security ($45,000 gross amount)	$34,475	$25,975	$8,975
Traditional IRA Income	$55,000	$45,000	$25,000
Tax-free Roth IRA Income	$0	$10,000	$30,000
OBBBA Deduction (Gone after 2028)	**$12,000**	**$12,000**	**$12,000**
Estimated Tax	**$4,541**	**$2,348**	**$0**
Estimated Tax post-OBBB	**$5,981**	**$3,761**	**$0**
Total After-Tax Income	**$95,459**	**$97,652**	**$100,000**
Effective Tax Rate (OBBB)	**4.54%**	**2.34%**	**0%**

Estimate only, other factors can influence taxable income calculation. Based on Married filing Joint, age 65, standard deduction and no dependents.

Illustration 5.5

The higher your income, the higher your taxes. In illustration 5.5 strategy 3, you see how the taxable portion of your Social Security goes down, with just 1/3 of your income coming from the Roth IRA. Do you also see how your overall taxes go down? Remember, in retirement, taxes on Social Security are an issue. Its called the Tax Torpedo but for this book its your exploding oxygen tank.

All space missions have procedures for all potential problems, as we discussed. When thinking about retirement, one problem that receives little thought is taxes after the death of a spouse. Is there anything you can do to help your widow when you're gone?

When you go from married filing joint to single, your taxes skyrocket!

Tax Reduction Summary "We wish to offer our sincerest of condolences." -Uncle Sam
$85,000 income goal with a $30,000 coming from SS.
Widow's Penalty -Taxes increase when you lose a spouse and become single.

	Strategy #1	**Strategy #2**	**Strategy #3**
Taxable Social Security ($30,000 gross amount)	$25,500	$18,100	$9,600
Traditional IRA Income	$55,000	$35,000	$25,000
Tax-free Roth IRA Income	$0	$20,000	$30,000
OBBBA Deduction (Gone after 2028)	**$5,400**	**$6,000**	**$6,000**
Total Tax	**$7,241**	**$3,226**	**$1,045**
Estimated Tax post-BBB	**$8,429**	**$3,946**	**$1,726**
Total After Tax Income	**77,759**	**81,774**	**83,955**
Effective Tax Rate (OBBB)	**8.52%**	**3.80%**	**1.23%**

Estimate only, other factors can influence taxable income calculation. The effective rate is calculated on gross income and total taxes paid. Based on a single, age 65, standard deduction, and no dependents. Calculator Source: Gemini AI

Illustration 5.6

Your living expenses after losing a mate rarely go down much. You might lose some healthcare and food for the deceased spouse, but all your other expenses will pretty much remain the same. So, let us revisit The Bennetts. Mr. Bennett dies in a bungee jumping accident. (It could happen) Mrs. Bennett decides to live on only $85,000 a year instead of the $100,000 she was getting. (Again, it's rare for a surviving spouse to afford this big an income reduction without a drastic lifestyle change.)

Mrs. Bennett now has her $30,000 Social Security; if she takes another $55,000 out of her IRA, her taxes will be $7,241.00! (That is an 8.52% effective rate, almost double when she was married; see illustration 5.6) and $25,500 of her $30,000 of Social Security is taxable. Are you seeing how much her taxes have increased? She is getting $22,000 less income and paying more taxes! Wow.

Ok, now, if she takes $30,000 from Roth and $25,000 from the IRA, she will save **$6,196** in taxes. Again, this is 35% of her income coming from Roth. Whoever dies first, the other is burdened with higher taxes. (Widow penalty). Investing (converting) in a Roth IRA will be a significant financial help to your surviving spouse. Its like buying windows for your retirement. Yes, there is a cost now, but the savings just keep coming as you -

Go from forever taxed to never taxed!

The Biggest Tax Increase you or your wife will see in retirement is from death or divorce.

Doesn't a Widow file as Joint for two years after the death of a spouse? Oh, my friend, you didn't look at the details; that is where the devil is. You can file as joint in the year you lose your mate in death. After that, you must meet the qualifying surviving spouse rules, and you only get to use the standard deduction for joint; you're not considered as filing joint.

Qualifying Surviving Spouse Rules

To be eligible to use the Joint standard deduction as a widow, the following applies:

- You can't remarry in the following two tax years.
- You must pay more than half of your home expenses.
- You have a qualifying dependent who lived with you the entire year.
- If you are raising a grandchild, then that child would most likely apply.

A ROTH conversion can save your spouse thousands of dollars in taxes as a widow. If you love your wife, you will start converting your IRAs to Roth now. If you don't, your wife won't love you, the government will get all your money, and your dog will die.[201]

Does knowing that you are doing all you can for your spouse after you are gone make you feel better now?

Reduce or Eliminate your RMDs.

Required Minimum Distribution or RMD. At age 73 or 75, you are required to take the required minimum distribution from your IRAs, 401k, 403b, 457, and other pretax retirement accounts. It starts around 3.75% of the previous year's December 31st value. By converting your IRA to Roth, you will only have RMDs on IRAs, 401ks, etc., to deal with since RMDs only apply to taxable retirement accounts.

---

[201] That is clearly a joke based on a Saturday Night Live Mr. Rogers comedy sketch. No angry emails, please.

Let us recap. Why does paying taxes now, on a ROTH conversion, make sense?

- Taxes will increase. The previous charts are based on 2024 tax rates
- Current Tax rates[202] are at multi-year lows.
- You can reduce the taxes you will pay on Social Security.
- You can better control what tax bracket you fall in.
- It will reduce your RMDs.
- At the death of either of you, a Roth will help reduce your widow's tax rates.

Think about what this means. You can add thousands of dollars to your income in retirement by saving on taxes. You can help you or your surviving spouse hold down your tax rates with Roth IRAs. Consider my windows illustration. Would new energy-efficient insulated windows pay for themselves in energy savings? Yes and the taxes you pay on your Roth conversion will pay for itself in terms of the tax savings you or your spouse will get in the future.

The quote following is from the sitcom TV show Big Bang Theory.

"What are the odds that two individuals as unique as ourselves would be connected by someone as comparatively workaday as your son?" —Sheldon Cooper

"Is that a rhetorical point or would you like to do the math?" —Beverly Hofstadter

"I'd like to do the math." —Sheldon Cooper

"I'd like that, too." —Beverly Hofstadter

Let's Do the Math for Saving Taxes

You decide to convert $300,000 from your Traditional IRA to a Roth IRA. To control the taxes, you do this over five years at $60,000 annually at an effective rate of 10%. That means you pay $30,000 in taxes to convert $300,000 from a Traditional IRA to a Roth. Stretching out the conversion helps keep your effective tax rate down.[203]

Let's assume you made no money on the Roth (unlikely), and you pulled $30k per year out for 15 years. From illustration 5.5, Strategy #3, you would have saved $4,440 per year in taxes

[202] As of 2026.

[203] Conversions can't be accessed for 5 years and you must be 59.5 without being taxable and penalized.

in retirement. That is a tax savings over 15 years of $68,115.00, or an additional **<u>$38,115</u>** in tax savings over what it costs you to convert. (It cost you $30,000).

Cost you $30,000 in taxes now- You Saved $38,115 in taxes later; this is a good deal!

Now, let's assume you die because of a brake line failure after telling your wife that she is gaining weight. (Definitely could happen) Now, as a widow, if she pulls out $30k per year for 15 years, she saves $6196.00 per year in taxes. (Illustration 5.6 Strategy #3) That is a 15-year total tax savings of $92,940.00 or an additional <u>$62,940</u> in tax savings over what it costs you to convert. (Remember, we are assuming current tax rates. Future rates may be higher!)

Cost you $30,000 in taxes now- You Saved $92,940 in taxes later; this is a better deal!

Even though it costs $30,000 to buy these 'windows,' remember that we are paying the tax with cash that could have been invested elsewhere. However, since the Roth allows all future growth to be tax-free forever—with no RMDs—the 'return on investment' from the tax savings usually far outweighs the lost interest on that $30,000.

You are saving your spouse over double what it costs you when assuming no growth of the Roth! That is amazing when you think about it. Now, those are energy-efficient windows that I want to buy! Even if you are a conservative investor, you will have additional tax-free money from interest, dividends, and growth when you withdraw the funds. Any growth in the Roth only compounds the savings you will get because (wait for it) it is all tax-free!

Illustration 5.7

What if Taxes Increase?

If tax rates increase (and they probably will), the amount you save in taxes will skyrocket. It makes a lot of sense to consider converting some (or all) of your IRA accounts to Roth. See the chart below and remember that 'I' is income.

Improve your Lifestyle in Retirement, and protect your spouse (or yourself).

By starting a Roth Conversion plan now, you can improve your future retirement lifestyle. Can you go on a cruise? How about loading up the camper and going to Florida or South Texas? (Stay away from California; the max RV speed limit is 55. Jerks) Maybe you will need to pay out-of-pocket expenses for medicines. Visit Las Vegas or enjoy some fancy restaurants.

It makes sense to plan now to add thousands to your retirement income. However, a single-year $300,000 Roth conversion will likely send you to the top of the tax brackets. (See illustration 5.1)

Start a Roth conversion Strategy now. Depending on your tax situation, converting an amount each year for several years to a Roth IRA makes sense, thus controlling the taxes you pay while moving money from ***"forever-taxed to never-taxed."***- Ed Slott, CPA, IRA, and Tax Expert.

Many people are reluctant to convert IRAs to Roth IRAs because you need to pay the taxes on the conversion. It is possible to pay the taxes out of the IRA, but that reduces the account value, and if you are younger than 59 ½, you will have to pay a 10% penalty on the taxes paid. If under 59.5, it is better if you can pay the taxes separately from the converted funds, then you avoid the penalty.

In retirement, taking a quarter to half of your income from a Roth IRA can significantly affect taxes and your retirement lifestyle! The effect is even more significant for your widow.

There is one problem with my numbers: they are probably wrong

Why do I say that? Because I based everything on the *current tax code*. Taxes are increasing and will likely continue to increase, making my numbers ultra-low. Returning to my hero Ed Slott (because Subhani and I are nerds), in his last conference, he revealed that he had converted ALL his IRAs to Roth years ago (2010). His reasons were taxes and government control of his accounts.

In an article entitled "Stop contributing to IRAs and 401(k)s" by Ed Slott, he wrote,

"This decades-old strategy no longer works. It's time to reduce IRA balances, not increase them.[204]" Ed points out that future tax bills will increase and require larger minimum distributions, resulting in higher tax brackets.[205]

Tax Planning Myth: Taxes are Lower in Retirement

I know I said this already. But the myth in tax planning is that your taxes go down in retirement. This is rarely the case for the middle class and up. This is where a Roth IRA is an important planning tool. The other myth is you need less income after the death of a spouse. The bills tend to be the same.

Roth IRAs are Awesome for Your Beneficiaries.

If you plan a legacy for your kids or someone else, the Roth should be key to your estate planning. First, it transfers to your beneficiary TAX FREE! That is right; they inherit the money tax-free. Second, your beneficiary can hold the Roth for up to 10 years. Think about that: if your child inherited a $100,000 Roth IRA and got a 7.2% average return for ten years, the account would be worth $200,000 tax-free!

10 Reasons You Don't Want to Convert to a Roth

I know; I just spent all this time trying to convince you to convert some or all of your IRAs into a Roth. But there are always exceptions. That's why you need to visit with a CPA or Financial Advisor in person to review your situation. Before you rush to convert to a Roth IRA, consider the following:[206]

1. Up Front Tax Bill –If you are under 59 ½, you will pay a penalty on tax withholding if it is taken from the amount converted. You must be able to pay the taxes now and separate them from the funds in the IRA. So, if you do it right, you will need to write a check for the taxes. Conversions are permanent and irreversible!

2. Tax Rates—Consult with a tax advisor to see if you will be pushed into an unreasonable tax rate. If you are married, don't compare it to your current rate;

[204] Investment News, "Stop contributing to IRAs and 401(k)s" by Ed Slott, CPA, IRA and Tax expert 07/24/2023
[205] The Tax Cuts and Jobs Act tax reductions will revert to 2017 levels in 2026. This covers Individual tax rates, Standard Deductions, Estate and Gift tax exemptions, and Child Tax Credit.
[206] Source: The New Retirement Savings Time Bomb ticks louder. –Ed Slott, CPA. Some of the text is directly quoted.

remember the widow penalty. You need to see how much it will cost you in state income taxes, too. (If applicable)

3. Beneficiaries' Tax Rate – The conversion could be ineffective if your income tax is high and your beneficiaries' tax rate is very low. (You would pay more taxes converting than your beneficiary would have paid on an inherited IRA).

4. Side Effects of Roth Conversions, Stealth Taxes – you could lose tax deductions like medical deductions, child tax credits, taxation of Social Security benefits, or loss of the 20% deduction for qualified business income (the section 199A deduction). You may also impact education tax credits. You will also increase Medicare Part B & D co-pays. Consider these expenses as part of the cost and see if it still makes sense.

5. Impact on Financial Aid – While retirement accounts are excluded from (College) financial aid, income is not. In this case, Roth conversions may need to wait.

6. When will you need the money? The tax-free benefits work best if they compound over several years. So, consider whether this makes financial sense. One important caveat to know.

   Roth Forever Clock. Unlike the conversion clock, this one starts with your very first Roth IRA establishment and does not restart with subsequent conversions or contributions. If you are over 59 1/2 and have 5 years in the Roth account, all your earnings are tax-free. Otherwise, your conversions must be held for 5 years to be tax-free. [207]

   If you convert to a Roth on your deathbed, the 5-year rule will also apply to your heirs. Unless you already have the forever clock completed.

7. Over 73 or 75 and subject to RMDs- if subject to required minimum distributions (RMD), this must be done <u>before</u> the conversion, which raises the tax cost because you must pay tax on the RMD.

8. QCD Effect – Qualified Charitable Distributions. Directing your RMD from your IRA to a qualified charity avoids the tax on the IRA distribution. Ed Slott recommends avoiding conversions unless you want to carve out a portion of your IRA for children or grandchildren. (I will talk about QCD later in this chapter).

---

[207] Source Ed Slott

9. Medical Expenses—If itemizing a large medical bill will benefit you, a Roth conversion will cause you to lose the deduction.

10. Obamacare subsidy- Many who retire before 65 might qualify for a subsidy and access to the healthcare marketplace. This could wipe out or reduce your health insurance costs. You would lose or reduce the subsidy if your income rises due to a Roth conversion.

Bonus reason not to do a Roth Conversion (Stealth Tax)

IRMMA (Income-Related Monthly Adjustment Amount) is a surcharge added to Medicare Part B and Part D premiums for higher-income beneficiaries. Yes, your Part B and D for Medicare could go up. This is re-evaluated every year (the look back is 2 years). Include the surcharge cost in your calculations to be sure that the future tax savings will be worth it. It usually is.

You may still convert some of your IRA even if some of these exceptions apply. You must consult with your CPA or tax professional to calculate how much tax or benefits are at risk. I already said this, but remember, Roth conversions cannot be undone. So, consult this list with your tax person to be sure the conversion won't cost you more than anticipated.

Divorce Considerations

Finally, if you are going to or are divorcing before the year's end, consider a Roth Conversion before December 31. If you file a joint return, you will have a lower tax rate. Your lawyer might put that in the divorce docs to be sure your spouse signs the tax return. A married filing separate tax return would be costly.

Strategies to Reduce Income in Retirement

"Did I read that correctly?" you ask. Yes, you did. A common issue I see is people retiring early and needing health insurance. You can qualify for Medicare insurance at 65, but what do you do if you retire at 62? The answer? Obamacare. But how do you qualify?

"While anyone can buy health insurance under Obamacare, those with household incomes between 100% and 400% of the federal poverty level (FPL) may qualify for financial assistance that reduces premiums and out-of-pocket costs. Using 2026 federal poverty levels, a family of four would qualify for subsidies with a household income of $32,150 to $128,600. A single person would qualify for subsidies if they made $15,560 to $62,600." (Federal poverty levels are higher in Alaska and Hawaii)

Accessing your IRAs or other pre-tax accounts will increase your income and reduce or eliminate your subsidy. If you are attempting to qualify for a Healthcare subsidy, you must keep your income low. One way is to sell some of the investments in your taxable accounts (not IRA or Employer retirement) and pay the capital gains taxes. It would be best if you did this a year or more before you retire. Then, you can spend those accounts with little or no recognizable income consequence. This keeps your income low and access to cash.

The other option is to access funds in a Roth IRA, which we have discussed extensively. When you think about it, the Apollo 13 spacecraft had to look for alternative power. They could extend the command module batteries during re-entry by accessing the Lunar module batteries. They had to shut down every non-essential piece of equipment to conserve power.

"You want your plan, not the Government plan. For you to sit there and do nothing is the Government's plan." **—Ed Slott, CPA, IRA, and Tax Expert**

Don't be afraid to pay some taxes.

In 2001, I had a client with a significant position in Cisco Systems stock. It was at $40 a share at the time. I told the client that Cisco was overpriced and likely to come down. The client agreed with me but said if he sold now, he would pay a load of taxes since he bought his shares at $20. That problem was solved when the stock price dropped to $12 a share a few months later. It was 18 years before it reached $40 again. That client died before that day came.

This has always been a tough conversation to have with my clients. Some are fiercely against paying **any** taxes. This is a problem. To share a proverb, I have heard since I was a boy:

"Don't cut off your nose, to spite your face." —unknown.

"I get along just fine when I am paying some taxes," —said a client.

If you can pay taxes now to save either paying more later or preventing your heirs from dealing with a tax bill, that is smart. If your tax rate is low, let us say lower than 10%, you paying taxes now might save your spouse or children, who will be at a higher tax rate.

Also, there are times when you need to reposition your investments. I have been wrong before on whether the stock will rise or fall.

Accredited Investor

An accredited investor generally has $1,000,000 of investable assets. These investors are considered to be financially sophisticated and have a lower need for the protections provided by regulatory filings.

For individuals, the main criteria to qualify as an accredited investor are:

- Income: An annual income of more than $200,000 ($300,000 for married couples) in each of the two most recent years, with a reasonable expectation of reaching the same income level in the current year.
- Net Worth: A net worth exceeding $1 million, either alone or with a spouse, excluding the value of their primary residence.
- Professional Certifications: Holding certain professional certifications, designations, or credentials, such as a Series 7, Series 65, or Series 82 license.

Certain entities also qualify as accredited investors, including banks, insurance companies, registered investment companies, specific trusts, and businesses with assets exceeding 5 million.

If you fit in this category of investors, there are Private Equity, Direct Participation programs, Equipment Leasing, Qualified Opportunity Zones, 1031 Exchange/DST, and other alternative investments that allow you to take a deduction (depreciation) against your income. The programs can be profitable but may require you to invest for 5, 10, or even 15 years. They also face real risks of total capital loss. To benefit from the tax benefits, you will want to include a CPA in the planning.

Offsetting a ROTH Conversion

You want to convert a $500,000 IRA to Roth. The taxes on this will be steep. But let's say you invest in the same year in a program that gives you $500,000 first year depreciation (active participant). The investment won't be the money you are converting but will be funded from separate taxable money. This strategy would nullify your tax bill while converting a large amount of IRA funds.

Planning like this requires coordinating with a CPA and conducting thorough due diligence on the investment involved. Private Equity and Alternative Investments have additional risks. **If the investment were to go 'belly up,' would that be an Oxygen Tank Explosion or just a reduction of your net worth? Would it change your retirement lifestyle?**

Now, let us consider more options in retirement.

Pay The Taxes and Buy Life Insurance.

Another option besides Roth Conversions is withdrawing funds from your IRAs and 401k and then moving the money into permanent life insurance. (There are other options, like a taxable brokerage account registered to a living trust.) **In purchasing life insurance, you have the option to eliminate taxes in the future**. It is also protected from creditors and is tax free to who ever inherits it. Ed Slott also recommends this strategy; why, you ask?

Whether you start Roth conversions or move to Life Insurance will depend on your objectives. If legacy planning is your major objective, you want to look at permanent life insurance. Structured correctly, life insurance can solve several retirement issues. Some folks have biases when it comes to the subject of Life Insurance. This is because insurance is sold. But don't let that hold you back if you can meet your retirement and estate objectives.

"I do not sell life insurance. I am a tax advisor. And as a tax advisor, I can tell you that the single biggest benefit in the federal tax code is the income tax exemption for life insurance."
—Ed Slott CPA, IRA, and Tax Expert.

We must first consider that "permanent life insurance is not an expense." (Ed Slott quote: I should have had him write this chapter.) We are not talking about term insurance. You can move large amounts of money into a permanent life insurance plan.

Ed doesn't sell life insurance, but I do. It has preferential treatment in the tax code, and it can solve many retirement and estate problems. Unfortunately, some folks have biases towards Life Insurance.

Wrong Tools for the Wrong Job

You don't show up with earth-moving equipment to fix the fence in the backyard. Understand your objectives and use the best tools to accomplish your goals.

From a pure cost and performance standpoint, funding a Roth IRA and converting existing IRAs to Roth is a smart move. Roth offers wider investment options and lower expenses, meaning better investment performance. You also maintain full liquidity at all times.[208]

Life Insurance will not let you invest in individual stocks. Variable Life has mutual fund-like options but will have a much higher cost. Compared to a Roth account with stocks, you will not transfer a set death benefit much higher than the account value to your heirs. (If your life insurance has a cash value of $100,000 and a death benefit of $500,000, in most cases your heirs get the $500,000 tax-free when you're gone).

Which is better, you ask? Neither, it depends on your objectives. You might even have both accounts. If you say you want to grow your money in low-cost income investments, and the 'insurance agent' offers you a variable life insurance policy, well, it's not going to work out well. You are going to be disappointed. Life Insurance has death benefits and other benefits that add cost and lower your overall return and use mutual funds as investment vehicles. In the next chapter, I will bum-rush mutual funds.

Many life insurance agents may only sell life insurance. I will comment on this in Chapter 7, but for now, I believe this sales pitch-originated approach leaves a distaste when it is discovered that your objectives might not have been met. Life insurance has advantages that you can't get in a Roth account. But these advantages must be needed for this to be a good move for you. I will now go over the benefits of a life insurance retirement plan.

Life Insurance to Reduce Taxes

Some of the 'get off the tax grid' advertisements have permanent life insurance policies, gold, or cryptocurrency as the answer to all your tax problems. In this discussion, we will focus on life insurance. Some of these terms are 'infinite banking' or 'become your own bank.' Here is the concept. Put your money into a Life Insurance policy and borrow against it 'tax-free' for the rest of your life. When you die, your heirs receive the funds tax-free. Everyone wins except the government. But there are some things to watch for.

Permanent life insurance builds up cash value as you pay the premiums. Your cash value earns an interest rate in the policy and accumulates tax-free.[209] Some policy interest rates are indexed (more on this in Chapter 6), and some offer mutual fund-like investments. These

---

[208] I am referring to a Roth IRA brokerage account. Some Roth accounts, like an Annuity, may have surrender charges. See chapter 6.

[209] If the policy is discontinued or cash value is withdrawn (non-loan) these funds would be taxable.

policies also have various charges and expenses. You need to pay particular attention to these costs, which affect your cash values and benefits.

Paying the taxes now on your IRA and lump sum investing of those proceeds in a life insurance policy will allow you to fund the policy right away. The amount of life insurance you purchase will be less, reducing the policy's overall cost. The fees and expenses will be important if you want the cash value to grow faster. For example, if you put $700,000 in a policy with a death benefit of $1,000,000, you would be paying for $300,000 of life insurance, not $1 million.[210]

You will want to deposit a large amount upfront. Your existing insurance may not be designed for this, so you might need to set up a new policy. It isn't uncommon to put $100s of thousands or even millions in a life insurance policy. You will want a policy that is designed for your objectives. The guarantees and costs are also important aspects.

Define Your Money Objectives.

Defining your money objectives is essential to making the right decisions. Life Insurance, retirement, and estate planning are complex. But this is a good thing. If you know upfront what you want to accomplish (start with the end in mind), we can design the right plan for you. We want to rank your investment purchase's top 2 or 3 objectives. Let's cover a basic overview without a financial planning course.

So, we will consider what permanent life insurance can do for you.

Some Money Objectives

- Principal Protection
- Growth
- Income
- Growth followed by Income
- Charity funding
- Legacy (heirs)
- Growth of Capital
- Long Term Care
- Tax Control
- Estate Planning
- Avoiding Probate
- Creditor Protection
- Asset Purchase in retirement
- Liquidity
- Creating Tax Advantages

[210] There are options that pay the cash value plus a fixed death benefit. If maximum death benefit is an objective, then this would be chosen. It would raise the internal costs and lower the performance of the cash value.

But life insurance offers benefits you can't get in a Roth account. People sometimes get all weird when it comes to Life Insurance talk. But remember, the wealthiest Americans use life insurance in their retirement, estate planning, and employment compensation packages. So have an open mind on this.

The six main benefits of Life Insurance are:

- Tax-free transfer of money to your family or charity after your death.
- Access to your cash value via tax-free loans that don't have to be repaid.
- Life Insurance can pay for long-term care or terminal illness care.
- Life Insurance is protected from creditors for you and your beneficiaries.
- Life Insurance has guarantees and safe investments.
- Life Insurance Retirement Plans do not have income limits.

Let's consider these benefits provided by Life Insurance.

Another word from my Lawyer (I really hate this guy)

This discussion is very general. Life insurance requires a level of 'insurability' in order to qualify, and it may not be guaranteed if the cash values underperform. Before investing, you must investigate the fees and expenses, review the company-provided illustrations, including the guarantees provided, research the company's credit rating/financial standing, and compare it with other companies. Cash values on lump sum deposits may take years before they are available for loans. Benefits may have restrictions or limitations.

Now, the benefits of Life Insurance.

1) *Tax-free transfer of funds to your family or charity after your death.*

Life Insurance death benefits are better than IRAs. Life insurance transfers to the next generation are tax-free. This is big and is better than sending funds from an IRA to your kids. If your children want to 'stretch the payments' on an inherited IRA to lower their taxes, surprise! The new stretch IRA rules limit this to 10 years. (There are exceptions, and I will go over that later in this chapter.)

"Don't give your kids ANY money; give them life insurance!"
—Tom Hega Best Selling Financial Author

2) *Access to your cash value via* <u>*Tax-Free*</u> *loans that don't have to be repaid.*

Depending on how your policy is structured, you can borrow from the cash value. This will come with an interest rate, which is extremely important, particularly if you plan to borrow from the cash value. You should review a company-provided illustration to see how the policy will fare if you withdraw funds via a loan and how much you can access.

Accessing money from your life insurance is generally tax-free. Loans from a Life Insurance policy, like Roth withdrawals, are invisible on your tax return. It also won't affect the eligibility of many government programs (except Medicaid).

In many cases (not all), it may take four years or more for your deposits to be available for loans. Again, have an insurance company-provided illustration before you purchase a life insurance plan that shows this. If this is one of your objectives, be sure the policies, loan rates, or costs don't make your policy go broke. (That isn't good because the loans become taxable if the policy lapses).

When it comes to life insurance retirement plans, how you plan to use them is essential. In most cases, when you die, your loans will reduce the death benefit, and the balance transfers tax-free to your heirs. There are many ways to set up life insurance to provide tax-free retirement income. This is a general overview just remember the options are nearly endless.

"Life insurance is the bedrock of any serious financial plan."
—Ed Slott CPA and IRA expert.

3) *Life insurance can pay for long-term care or terminal illness care.*

I don't have a long-term care plan. Wrong you do and its to be a burden on your kids.

The 3-word problem is "Long-term care (or LTC) and shut your mouth!" Many don't want to talk about it because they are not going to a nursing home ever! If I were to think back on the one topic where clients got nasty with me, it would have to be discussing long-term care.

Statistically, 70% of people who reach the age of 65 will need a nursing home at some point in their life.[211] So, who are these people going to nursing homes? I am not sure I have met them, but know this: you won't decide to go to a nursing home. Someone else will. Hopefully, it won't be your daughter-in-law.

If you feel passionate about this subject, get LTC insurance. The policies used to be quite popular, but the premiums have increased considerably due to increasing claims. But there is now another option.

Certain Life Insurance Policies Offer Long-Term Care Benefits.

This is a new benefit that only recently has been offered in permanent life insurance. It allows a percentage of the death benefit to be used for nursing home, assisted living, or at-home care. If you have an older policy, you can transfer the cash to a new policy designed with these benefits. You want to look at this sooner rather than later since the benefit is less attractive on policies issued after age 70.

I had a client that funded a Life Insurance plan with two objectives. Pay for her LTC expenses (if she should need it), and transfer the money to her children upon her death. This checked both boxes for her; the death benefit was more than her large single deposit amount.

Funding a life insurance plan would save you the expense of long-term care insurance and cost you nearly nothing since the benefit is part of the life insurance policy. You obviously need to investigate the coverage details, but it can be 30%—80% (or more) of the death benefit for long-term care costs. You also want to know how long it takes for these benefits to become available.

Depending on the policy you purchase, it may also cover terminal illness. Insurance companies' policies offer more substantial or lesser benefits. If you know what you want to cover, it is not hard to match you to the right coverage for your objectives. See chapter 7 on Insurance agents. One thing to note is that this coverage is difficult to get when the client is over 70.

---

[211] Source: Zippia.com 25 INSIGHTFUL NURSING HOME STATISTICS

4) Life Insurance protects you and your beneficiaries from creditors.

This depends on your state laws. These laws were written over 100 years ago to protect the deceased person's family from being sued for life insurance proceeds. (If Dad blew up the plant and himself, the company couldn't come after the widow for the insurance money).

Life Insurance protects the insured and beneficiaries from creditors. (State law may limit this, so check your state.) If you're concerned about how the money is spent, you can set up a trust to distribute the funds. I recommend engaging an attorney to do this.

Here is a story for you. A doctor bought a life Insurance policy. He purchased a 15-year paid-up policy. It had little cash value accumulation but was guaranteed as long as he made 15 years of premium payments. In year 12, he got cancer and died. His two sons did not like each other. The money was split between them and the stepmother. One of the sons sued the estate in an effort to stop his brother and stepmother from getting any money. However, the lawsuit was completely ineffective in stopping the life insurance and the annuities the good doctor owned from paying out. The son was able to freeze all the bank accounts. But over two million dollars were transferred to his brother, stepmother, and himself without any delay. Brother dropped his suit eleven months later.

4 out of 5 doctors say life insurance freshens your breath

Medical doctors often purchase life insurance retirement plans and fund them heavily to protect themselves from litigation. Since doctors could face malpractice litigation, safeguarding their assets from creditors is important. Additionally, doctors (and others) with high incomes may not be able to deposit money in their retirement accounts or may be limited in the retirement accounts they can fund.

5) Life Insurance can offer guarantees and safe investments.

There is Whole Life, Universal Life, Indexed Universal Life, and Variable Universal Life. These policies will have guaranteed fixed accounts. The interest rate may be declared annually or connected to a variable index, meaning the interest rate will vary between 0% and 10% or even higher. Your principal and credited interest are guaranteed by the insurance company. If you are transferring large amounts of cash to the policy, this may be appealing. If the life insurance is a variable policy, it will contain mutual fund-like investments with principal loss risk but higher potential returns. These investments need to be evaluated for investment worthiness and overall costs.

Remember, the guarantees provided by life insurance and annuities are backed by the credit and financial standing of the life insurance company. Life Insurance policies are <u>not</u> backed by any government agency, credit union, or FDIC. We recommend using companies with A- or higher credit ratings (or equivalent). There is a state guaranty association for life insurance and annuities. However, this coverage is usually limited (about $250,000 for annuities and is set state by state), and without going into details, you shouldn't consider this in your decision.

Choose an Independent Insurance Agent

Each type of life insurance has pros and cons, and it is hard to say one is better. Your insurance agent needs to be competent and independent. Why independent? This means your agent has the ability to represent a variety of companies to shop for the best customized deal for you. This is especially important when you have health issues. Some companies will cover an illness or provide a better rating class (i.e., your costs are lower the higher your classification) than others that may decline coverage. Some financial advisors only sell one or two companies. When it comes to investing in insurance, you want the right company and product for your health status and money objectives. If your advisor can shop the insurance market for the best plan, you will likely meet your objectives. In large cases, we have access to independent consultants who can help us design and select the company and contract that will meet your objectives. If your financial advisor is captive to an insurance company, I can't see how that is in your best interest.

6) Life Insurance Retirement Plans do not have income limits on your deposits.

If you earn more than $146,000 as a single filer and $230,000 as a married filing joint, you can't contribute to a Roth IRA even if you are not contributing to a workplace retirement like a 401k. Many high-income professionals use retirement life insurance plans as an alternative to funding other retirement plans, they may have 'income out of.' (This means you make too much money to invest in a ROTH IRA.)

These plans can be customized if self-employed, through an employer, or individually. A retirement life insurance plan can provide a tax-free income in retirement.

Caveat on Life Insurance Retirement Plans

I see too many people with incomes under $200,000 a year who use a life insurance policy for primary retirement accumulation. This is not an effective accumulation stage investing vehicle. Here is my wealth-building ranking:

1. Employer-Sponsored Plans 401k, 403b, 457, SEP, Simples (Get the free matching $$)
2. Roth IRA or Traditional IRA (I recommend the ROTH)
3. Cash Savings (3-6 months of living expenses)

4. Real Estate Investments (If you are an accumulation stage investor)
5. Permanent Life Insurance (after everything else)

If you have done all of this and you have enough income to properly fund a permanent plan over 20 years or can provide a lump sum investment, then you are likely to see advantages in permanent life insurance. Otherwise, buy a good term policy instead.

High Income Clients

I have had many clients with very high incomes ($200,000 + and high-risk careers that skip straight to #5. Their income knocks them out of meaningful participation in #1 or #2, and they don't have time to buy and manage real estate investments. Life Insurance offers strong creditor protection (doctors are usually concerned about lawsuits) and performs extremely well when properly funded over many years for retirement.

Older Life Insurance Needs to Be Reviewed.

You may already have permanent life insurance that you bought years ago from your college roommate. The problem is that it may not have been designed for any of the objectives I covered. It would be best to have your advisor evaluate how long your existing insurance will last, your benefits, the internal costs, and whether you need to add new money to the policy. This is done by ordering an illustration from the insurance company. Depending on the complexity of your insurance policy, experts may need to review it.

For example, Universal Life Insurance is a flexible premium. I have met many people who didn't realize that the payments they made over the years were insufficient, and now they would have to deposit massive amounts of new premiums to keep life insurance from lapsing.[212] These policies also lack benefits like Long Term Care or Critical Illness riders that new policies cover.

Another problem is that we have seen policies that charge high loan rates, making it hard to borrow from the policy without potentially causing the policy to run out of money and be canceled. Your life insurance policies should be reviewed, at least in the transition stage. ***The earlier problems are identified, the sooner they can be fixed.***

---

[212] Lapse occurs when premium payments are missed or the policy doesn't have enough cash value to support it. The policy is canceled and the Life Insurance coverage is lost.

Now, get rid of the Life Insurance!

After convincing you to invest in life insurance, I will now recommend that you get rid of it. What? Why? Here's another story: I had a client who had five separate life insurance policies. She had these for over 20 - 40 years. The total premiums were over $800 a month. In planning her retirement, I asked her why she kept the life insurance. Her children were now adults, and besides final funeral expenses, she didn't need insurance. However, she needed the income. We closed out four policies, removed $10,000 of the cash value, which she deposited into her bank for emergency funding, and increased her monthly income by $600.

Another husband-and-wife client had 7 policies between them, totaling over $200,000 in cash value. We looked at using the Life Insurance to make tax-free loans, but the loan rates were very high, at 8%.[213] After a discussion that included their grown daughter, they decided to close the life insurance policies and do a 1035 exchange[214] (transfer) of the money to an annuity for income. This kept them from paying taxes on the $200,000 proceeds immediately. They were able to increase their monthly income (now they didn't have to pay $2,000 a month in premiums) and had another $8,000/year of beginning lifetime income from the annuity. (More on annuities in chapter 6). They gave up the life insurance death benefit (which only benefits their children) in exchange for income and budget savings. The latter was more of a high-money objective for them.

Your advisor needs to understand more than just investments. Having an advisor who can objectively evaluate your finances will help you succeed in your retirement mission. We are networked with Estate Attorneys, CPAs, and Advanced Insurance experts who assist us in analyzing these situations, selecting the right insurance company and the best policies, and performing analysis on existing permanent life insurance policies. You want your premiums to end at some point (usually early in retirement). That is why a single premium or a 15-year (or less) premium policy is attractive.

Give your grandkids appreciated stock.

If you own appreciated stock, you can gift it to family members and let them sell it at their tax rate. Consult a CPA on gift taxes if applicable.

---

213 When you borrow money from a Life Insurance policy it charges you a 'loan rate.' If this rate is too high it will cause the policy to collapse years later making your 'tax free' loans taxable.

214 "A 1035 exchange is a provision in the Internal Revenue Service (IRS) code allowing for a tax-free transfer of an existing annuity contract, life insurance policy, long-term care product, or endowment for another one of like kind." - Investopedia

Summing Up

Planning to lower or move all your money out of IRAs and like accounts is not a terrible idea if your goal is to go from 'forever taxed to never taxed.' You have two main options.

1. Converting IRA accounts to a Roth IRA or
2. Buy permanent life insurance.

You are paying the taxes on both options and you eliminate future taxes. If under age 59.5, you pay a 10% penalty to remove money from an IRA, consider a Roth conversion instead.

Obamacare Subsidy

Is it wrong to lower your income to get a healthcare subsidy? It isn't a secret that you have IRA assets. The government could disqualify early retirees from accessing subsidies based on retirement balances or liquid assets if they wanted to. This shouldn't bother you as long as you are honest and transparent in providing the requested information. Since the bureaucrats, Congress, and the President's office make these rules, there is absolutely nothing wrong with arranging your affairs to benefit from them. I point to the quote from Judge Learned Hand at the beginning of this chapter.

QCD (Qualified Charitable Distributions) lowers RMD, taxes, and your taxable estate!

At 73 and older, you must take distributions from your IRA, 401k, and other retirement accounts. The only exception is the 'Still Working' in an active employer-sponsored plan. (For example, your 401k where you work if not retired.[215]) You are not required to take money out of these accounts at 73 or older if you are still employed with the employer sponsoring the plan!

If you are 73, your Required Minimum Distribution will need to be met. Generally, the first year's withdrawal is 3.75% of your retirement account balances. This withdrawal is taxable income and possibly affects your Social Security taxes.

Donating to a qualified charity directly from the IRA avoids paying taxes on this amount. Yes, it is tax-free distribution! Due to changes in the tax code, it has become harder to deduct charitable contributions. But guess what? You don't need to itemize deductions to do this. QCD also decreases your estate size tax-free.

---

[215] There is a couple exceptions to the exception. You can't be a 5%+ owner including your spouse , parents, children or grandchildren.

Consider this: You have a $300,000 IRA account. You have to take 3.75% out at age 73, which is $11,250 of taxable income. Your Social Security benefits might be taxable because of an RMD. But if you are already donating to a church, Save the Animals fund, or some other charity, doing a QCD instead allows you to send these funds (thus meeting your RMD) to the charity or church and avoid paying taxes in this withdrawal at the same time.

The QCD details:

Here it is—the when, how, and what of Qualified Charitable Distribution (QCD). First, you can start doing QCDs after you turn 70.5, not before. Each year, you and your spouse can send up to $100,000 directly from your retirement accounts to a qualified charity for a total of $200,000.[216] (Do not withdraw funds and write a check; it won't work. The money must be sent directly by the IRA custodian to the charity. I can't emphasize this enough).

The Secure Act made it possible to contribute to an IRA after 70 <u>if</u> you have earned income. (Income from working) If you contribute to an IRA, these amounts will be subtracted from any QCD. For example, Joe is 75 years old and still working. He contributes $7,000 to a pre-tax deductible Traditional IRA and in the same year, he decides to do a $10,000 QCD. Only $3,000 will be excluded from taxable income. Joe lost $7,000 in deductions. If you already contributed to an IRA, you have until the following year to remove it.[217]

QCD is a great way to contribute to charity and have the funds taken from your IRA tax-free. You can still convert a portion of your IRA to Roth while leaving funds in your IRA to give to charity.

Dangers of DIY:

DIY means 'Do it yourself'. Many people, including me, get personal fulfillment from doing their own work. Maybe you are a DIY. In some areas of life, you need professionals involved. One client told me that his father had done his own trust work. He had made errors that caused delays in closing his estate. Closing the estate took 20 years and over $70,000 in legal fees.

The same caution can be applied when doing a DIY Roth conversion. One problem is that the Tax Cuts and Jobs Act eliminated the ability to recharacterize Roth conversions. It is now

---

[216] See IRS.gov "Reminder to IRA owners age 70½ or over: Qualified charitable distributions are great options for making tax-free gifts to charity"
[217] See Coordinating QCDs With Post 70 1/2 IRA Contributions Under The SECURE Act by Jeffrey Levine, Kitces.com

one and done. No take-backs or changies. (I think 'changies' is in the IRS code) The following paragraph is based on an article published by Ed Slott.

Bad Day for a DIYer

One IRA owner intended to convert a portion of his 2-million-dollar IRA to Roth. He missed a decimal point and converted the entire account! What are the taxes on a 2-million-dollar income? A lot, 37% (at this level, the effective rate is only slightly lower) for the federal and whatever your state tax rate is. (Many states are at or above 10% income tax) The effective rate would be lower, but this was still a massive tax bill.

It would be easily corrected if a financial advisor or the financial institution made this mistake when acting on his client's orders. Getting a private letter ruling from the IRS based on good conscience is possible, but that is costly and time-consuming, and the IRS may refuse to provide you with relief. So, get help.[218]

"Had either of these two people worked with a professional adviser, instead of taking a DIY approach, there's a good chance these errors and the resulting tax disasters could have been avoided." -Ed Slott, CPA "The perils of do-it-yourself IRA" Investment News.

Remember Your Spouse

You may have had success in trading and financial management of your money. Would your spouse do as well? Would a savvy broker perhaps prey upon her or him? ***Hiring financial advisors who are philosophically aligned with you now will help your spouse and family when you are gone.***

Dunning-Kruger Effect

This is a researched, measured, and known problem. "The Dunning–Kruger effect is a cognitive bias in which people with limited competence in a particular domain overestimate their abilities," quote from Wikipedia.

This is an interesting topic to read up on, and I believe some DIYers can suffer from it to the point they see success even when they have messed up royally.

---

[218] The perils of do-it-yourself IRA transactions by Ed Slott publish at InvestmentNews.com

My IRS Story

Twenty years ago, I used an established tax strategy to amend some of my past tax returns. Rulings in tax court supported this strategy. I amended 4 years of tax returns and used them in the current year (2006); however, the IRS refused to accept my deductions in 1 of the four years. No reason was given. I wrote a letter and made numerous appeals (like Social Security, IRS explains nothing, just a denial letter). My only option was to go to tax court for relief. I had submitted $1,400.00 in tax reductions that were being denied. I decided to drop my case due to the time and cost of fighting for this for a small gain. Now, I wish I had pursued it, but I was not confident in my ability to represent myself then, and hiring a lawyer would have cost more than the gain I hoped to get. Now, it is spilled milk under the bridge.

If I had hired a good CPA, this situation would have likely turned out differently. The crazy part is that I knew several excellent CPAs. But I am smart; I can do it myself. (Dunning-Kruger effect) I don't need to pay these people! My DIY attitude this time cost me $1,400, more than I would have paid a CPA. Nearly 20 years later, I have a professional prepare our taxes. Even though I consider myself advanced in tax strategy, I lack practical application. My CPA is Thad Reid, at Lewis, Kaufman, Reid, Stukey, Gattis & Co., P.C. in Plainview, Texas. He prepares and files our taxes and listens to all my crazy tax ideas.

Tax Review

This was a lot, so let us review some high points.

- Start with the end in mind.
- Main goals: more control, larger inheritances, less taxes, and more income.
- Focus on effective tax rates, not marginal.
- Always pay taxes at the lowest rates.
- Capital gains are NOT always lower than ordinary income taxes.
- Annually harvest capital gains and losses for lower taxes.
- In December, harvest your losses to lower taxes.
- Harvest your gains and take advantage of a 0% capital gains rate by selling profitable investments and repurchasing them for a new lower-cost basis and a 0% tax rate.
- Tax-free bonds may tax your Social Security and give you a low rate of return.
- Protect your Capital; debt can be good in retirement.

- “Take out a mortgage for 30 years instead. ‘For 30 years, he screamed, "I'll be dead before it’s paid off.’ To which I said, "What do you care, you’ll be dead." -Charlie Epstein

- Roth IRAs are invisible on your tax return.
- Remember, the IRS owns a portion of your IRA.
- Pay taxes now and convert to a Roth IRA.
- Go from Forever Taxed to Never Taxed.
- Taxes will increase in the future.
- You want your plan, not the government's. The Government's plan is for you to sit there and do nothing.
- Use debt for large purchases to Protect Your Capital!
- Your IRA is temporal; it is how your younger self from the past takes care of the older person you are now.
- Credit card debt is the enemy of your wealth and happiness. However, it is not your credit cards but your spending habits that caused you to accumulate this debt; that is your problem.
- Remember, the IRS has a claim on your IRA.
- Plan to move your IRAs and 401ks to Roth or Life Insurance.
- Roth IRAs are tax-free and do not tax your social security.
- Roth IRAs are invisible on your tax return.
- Your heirs will receive a larger inheritance from a Roth IRA.
- Remember the 5-year rule on Roth conversions.
- Roth conversions cannot be undone.
- Don’t be afraid to pay some taxes now to save more money later.
- Taxes are a moving target, so be careful not to lock in on one strategy every year.
- A tax strategy that works at one income level might get blown up at another level.
- Alternative investments may reduce taxes if you understand the risks and can assume potential losses.
- Sequence your withdrawals from Taxable accounts, Tax-deferred accounts, and Tax-free accounts for a lower tax rate.

- Roth IRA conversions can help you or your spouse to pay lower taxes after becoming a widow.
- Please, don't take money out of your IRA to pay off the house or buy an RV!
- Define Your Money Objectives.
- Main goals: more control, larger inheritances, less taxes, and more income.
- Permanent life insurance is not an expense but rather an investment.
- Cash values on lump sum deposits may take years before they are available for loans.
- Benefits may have restrictions or limitations.
- Costs, loan rates, index options and many other features are important to consider for the right plan for your objectives.
- Compare Life Insurance illustrations before purchasing a policy.
- The six main benefits of Life Insurance are:
    1. Tax-free transfer of money to your family or charity after your death.
    2. Access to your cash value via tax-free loans that don't have to be repaid.
    3. Life insurance can pay for long-term care or terminal illness care.
    4. Life Insurance is protected from creditors for you and your beneficiaries.
    5. Life Insurance can offer guarantees and safe investments.
    6. Life Insurance Retirement Plans do not have income limits on your deposits.
- Evaluate older policies and cancel what you don't need or replace with a newer one.
- Use Qualified Charitable Distributions (QCD) to lower taxes on your IRA while meeting your RMDs and reduce your taxable estate.
- For QCD, do not withdraw funds and write a check; it won't work. The money must be sent directly by the IRA to the charity.
- DIYers find financial advisors who are philosophically aligned with you now to help your spouse and family when you are gone.

Now is the time to inspect the spaceship you will use for your retirement mission.

Chapter 6 is about building and launching your retirement. We will cover the issues, investments, and strategies you should consider to achieve sustainable, reliable retirement income and launch your retirement mission. Next chapter: **Launch Day, Your Spaceship Awaits You.**

Chapter 6
Launch Day Your Spaceship Awaits You

"Rockets are cool. There's no getting around that." —Elon Musk

Retirement Income Planning is "The hardest and nastiest problem in finance." —William Sharpe, Economist & Nobel Prize Winner

This is the Chapter you have been waiting for: investments. We need to build you a ship that will provide you with success in your retirement mission. There are many ways to build this ship, and I will discuss most of them.

The overarching principle is simple: retirees need income in retirement.

If your portfolio is based on income investments in retirement, I believe you will have a more secure retirement mission. I need to get some disclosures out of the way, so here it is.

A Word from my Lawyer (Listen up, or he will put a TRO[219] on you and your dog)

This information is not intended to be used as the primary basis for investment decisions, nor should it be considered as advice designed to meet the specific needs of an individual investor. Economic and market information has been obtained from published sources. While we believe such sources to be reliable, neither I nor my firm, Toro Bravo Investment Advisors, LLC, assumes responsibility for the accuracy of such information. Investments contain risks and could be subject to loss. Losses could be short-term or permanent. Please consult your advisor before initiating the purchase, sale, or hold of any investment or investment strategy. Some of the information here are my views and opinions and may conflict with other established sources. And always remember,

Past Performance is not a guarantee of future results.

Ok that's out of the way let us get started. I introduced the chart below (illustration 6.1) in Chapter 2. The point was that, over the 13-year period of no growth from 2000 to 2012, with a 4% withdrawal rate, you would have drawn down half of your retirement savings. If you were 65 in 2000 with a $1 million (say it like Dr. Evil) at 78, you now have $514,132 left. (Say that like Scooby Doo with a Ruh-Roh-Shaggy) The next years are very good in the market (2013-

---

[219] Temporary Restraining Order

2020), but after 13 years and down nearly 50%, any rational person is going to rebalance to be more conservative, reduce income to a sustainable level, and likely miss the uptrend.

After all, bull markets last 3-4 years on average. (Looking at the chart 2009-2013, these were bull market years) If you are evaluating what to do in January 2013, you see that the market has posted four consecutive years of gains. Rationally it's time to find shelter before another recession hits.

No one has this much faith in Bengen's 4% rule.[220] You either get more conservative by reducing your stocks for low-yielding bonds or similar investments, or you reduce your withdrawals, or both. (Interest rates are at nearly zero so the safe money is nearly no money.) Maybe you move your investments into money market accounts and wait while the market plays out the longest bull market in history.

Market History

DATE	BEG. CAS	S&P 500 Total Return	**WITHDRAWAL**	**END CASH**
1/2000	$1,000,000	-9.10%	40,000	**$871,496**
1/2001	$871,496	-11.89%	40,000	**$728,734**
1/2002	$728,734	-22.10%	40,000	**$531,372**
1/2003	$531,372	28.68%	40,000	**$637,080**
1/2004	$637,080	10.88%	40,000	**$663,272**
1/2005	$663,272	4.91%	40,000	**$654,123**
1/2006	$654,123	15.79%	40,000	**$713,949**
1/2007	$713,949	5.49%	40,000	**$713,041**
1/2008	$713,041	-37.00%	40,000	**$418,385**
1/2009	$418,385	26.46%	40,000	**$480,779**
1/2010	$480,779	15.06%	40,000	**$508,140**
1/2011	$508,140	2.11%	40,000	**$479,099**
1/2012	$479,099	16.00%	40,000	**$514,132**

Illustration 6.1

220 See Chapter 2 for a discussion on the 4% rule.

In retirement, you are confronted with a new reality. This money is all you've got, and no more is coming. Going back to work for what you used to make is not going to happen. The reality is that the market is too volatile for retirement savings.

The Apollo program dealt with the same issues of risk. Once the spaceship is launched, ground control can do nothing but advise. They can't say, "Hold on, boys. We are sending up some oxygen tanks, copper wire, and some Snickers bars."

That brings us to consider solutions to the retirement-income question that Nobel Prize winner William Sharpe called "the hardest and nastiest problem in finance." My 29 years of experience have revealed this investment secret that, frankly, everyone already knows.

"The most important aspect of retirement planning is to estimate your retirement income and ensure that it is adequate to cover your projected retirement spending."
—Robert Merton Nobel Prize Winner Economics.

Income Investing for Retirement

As I discussed in retirement, focusing on interest and dividends will lower risk and increase your likelihood of retirement success. I call this *cash flow* (say that like a late-night DJ). Why is cash flow so important? Allow me to regurgitate some quotes on dividends. (Some of the quotes I already used in previous chapters of this book).

Some Dividend Quotes to consider:

- "If you want retirement to be stress-free, invest for the I, not the G." -Pat Pearson, Public Speaking Trainer.
- "In inflationary times, all of a sudden, quality really matters. Cash flow matters, distributions in the form of dividends matter…" -Kevin O'Leary Shark Tank Investor
- In terms of reducing risk, dividend payments mitigate losses that occur from a decline in stock price... Studies have historically shown that dividend-paying stocks outperform non-dividend-paying stocks during bear market periods. While an overall down market generally drags down stocks across the board, dividend-paying stocks usually suffer significantly less decline in value than non-dividend-paying stocks." -Investopedia
- "Over the last 40 years, 71% of the market returns came from dividends, not capital appreciation. -Kevin O'Leary Shark Tank Investor.

- I hate gold. It does not pay a dividend, it has no value, and you can't work out what it should or shouldn't be worth," he said. "It is the last refuge of the desperate. -Jeremy Grantham, British Investor and father of the first Index funds.
- "The true investor… will do better if he forgets about the stock market and pays attention to his dividend returns and the operational results of his companies." ~ Benjamin Graham, Professor and American Financial Analyst, is known as the father of value investing. Author of "The Intelligent Investor."
- Do you know the only thing that gives me pleasure? It's to see my dividends coming in. -John D. Rockefeller, American business magnate and philanthropist.
- I rarely think the market is right. I believe non-dividend stocks aren't much more than baseball cards. They are worth what you can convince someone to pay for it. -Mark Cuban Shark Tank Investor.
- The great thing about dividends is that they can't be faked; they are either paid or not paid, increased or not increased. –Investopedia

Apollo 13 mission success was enough power to deploy the parachutes bringing the astronauts home alive.

Similarly, your mission success goal is not to run out of money in retirement.

Apollo 13 Command Module

Why <u>are dividends or interest</u> necessary for retirement?

In illustration 6.1, you see the devastating effect a 13-year no-growth market has on your savings and income. Now, notice what happens if you have the same S&P 500 volatility with a 4% dividend (*cash flow*) instead of 4% withdrawals (selling shares for income).[221]

---

[221] Illustration 6.2 chart is hypothetical. The 4% dividend is not the actual S&P 500 dividend yield. This number is a hypothetical dividend of 4% while assuming the historical S&P 500 performance. S&P 500 returns are calculated using the month-end price of the SPTR index published by the CBOE. This chart also assumes no costs.

After 12 years of no growth and $480,000 in withdrawals, you still have $967,152 left!

Remember, being retired makes you unlikely to earn more money. Like being launched into space this is it. These are the resources you have to survive. Losing it would be mission-ending. We are trying to avoid your retirement situation being, sitting on the couch in a cold, dark house, paying bills, and watching Jeopardy.

Market History

DATE	BEG. CAS	**S&P 500 Returns**	**4.0% DIVIDEND**	END CASH
1/2000	$1,000,000	-9.10%	40,000	$894,909
1/2001	$894,909	-11.89%	40,000	$773,850
1/2002	$773,850	-22.10%	40,000	$589,209
1/2003	$589,209	28.68%	40,000	$740,704
1/2004	$740,704	10.88%	40,000	$805,132
1/2005	$805,132	4.91%	40,000	$829,031
1/2006	$829,031	15.79%	40,000	$943,663
1/2007	$943,663	5.49%	40,000	$980,458
1/2008	$980,458	-37.00%	40,000	$606,142
1/2009	$606,142	26.46%	40,000	$748,431
1/2010	$748,431	15.06%	40,000	$844,273
1/2011	$844,273	2.11%	40,000	$847,187
1/2012	$847,187	16.00%	40,000	$967,152

Illustration 6.2

This is what cash flow (say it like a late-night DJ) looks like.

Understand what is not happening; you are not selling shares for income!

Imagine getting through one of the worst 13-year periods with your account value intact and $480,000 of income collected. There are no buckets, no selling shares at a loss, no cutting your income to preserve your retirement, and lower stress and worry. (You still have some wicked volatility see 2002 and 2008) I have railed against buy and hold previously because when you are retired with a growth style investing strategy because you are violating 'hold' to sell shares for income! ***But consider if you collect cash flow (late-night DJ voice) when times are bad then you can leave your shares alone.*** This is why dividend portfolios are considered to have less risk. This is also why a dividend portfolio is better suited for retirees. Compare this with illustration 6.1; in order for selling shares for income to work, you must have a rising market, or you risk eroding your account value significantly. Next time, there might not be another powerful bull market in your lifetime to save your retirement mission.

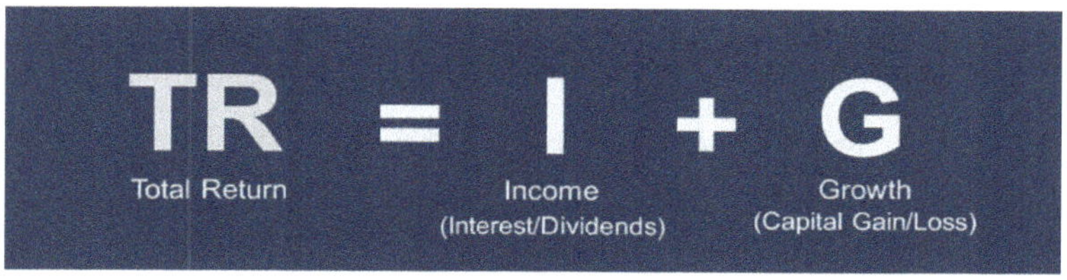

Illustration 6.3

Revisit the formula.

I need to give credit where credit is due. David Scranton, CEO of the asset management firm Sound Income Strategies,[222] introduced me to this formula. Frankly, it's a "why didn't I think of that" type of thing.

Most advisors and Big Wall Street firms focus on past performance and growth when it comes to building a portfolio that will provide your standard of living in retirement. These 'baseball card portfolios' (to use Mark Cuban's quote) depend on a rising stock market. What happens when the market is in decline? It's a selling shares situation with erosion of your capital in progress. This can cause a lot of stress in retirement. It makes sense to shift from growth investments to income investments in retirement.
Unfortunately, this is not the typical Big Wall Street advice; why?

Baseball Card Portfolio

3 Reasons for the Shift from Bonds to Stocks

1. Bonds paying interest have had extremely low yields. (2009 – 2022)
2. Recent extraordinary Bull market performance, especially in technology stocks.
3. Big Wall Street firms, Financial Advisors, and Fee-Based Advisors make more money on a growth stock portfolio.

---

[222] My firm Toro Bravo Investment Advisors, LLC employs Sound Income Strategies as a third-party manager for our clients' portfolios.

What most people understand about the markets is incorrect. They see it as a casino or a lottery ticket. Many want to get rich from the markets.

This takes two things:

1. Investing over long periods of time (10 years or more),

2. Shrewd risk-taking, and

3. Impeccable Market Timing.

As retirees or pre-retirees, you don't have 30 years to let things play out, and can you afford to lose it all in crazy, aggressive investments? And relying on timing in or out is inconsistent for even the best investors. **There are many advisors telling their clients that they will get them out before the 'poo-poo' hits the fan.** Notice the quote from legendary money manager John Fogle.

"The idea that a bell rings to signal when to get into or out of the stock market is simply not credible. After nearly fifty years in this business, I don't know anybody who has done it successfully and consistently".
— John Bogle, Founder of Vanguard Group.

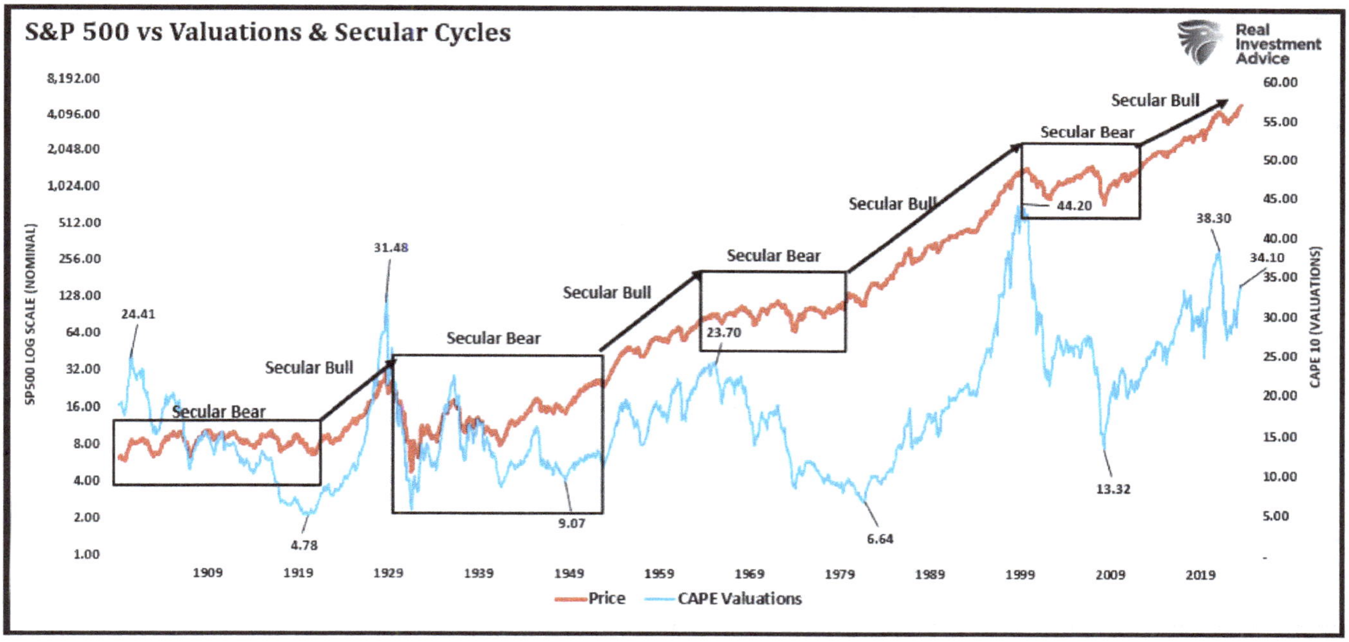

Illustration 6.4

(The chart from the previous page uses CAPE[223] valuations based on data from Dr. Robert Shiller. I would like to thank Lance Roberts at RIA Advisors for allowing me to use his chart.

---

223 "CAPE ratio is a valuation measure that uses real earnings per share (EPS) over a 10-year period to smooth out fluctuations in corporate profits that occur over different periods of a business cycle. The CAPE ratio, using the

Historically, long periods of 'secular bear' markets have followed 'secular bull' markets.[224] Falling into the wrong time period can have a detrimental effect on your retirement.[225]

But the Markets have been Good

Look at market history over the last 100 years. A decade of plenty is almost always followed by a decade of want. Is our current bull market 'long in the tooth'? I believe it is. We have had over a decade of plenty. We are at a high point now, and this is not the time to chase a baseball card portfolio for your retirement mission.

Following advice based on the last 10 years of past performance is dangerous.

I fell for this early in my career. In 2001 was hopped on Oracle stock. It was a value trap. It eventually came back but it took almost 2 decades to see. But the past 10-year performance in 2001 was awesome!

And I have seen this happen before! Brokers showed the past performance of stocks like Oracle, Microsoft, and other growth companies after the crash in 2000. These companies still had incredible past performance histories. But it took over 17 years to see a recovery in Technology stocks. Is Artificial Intelligence in a similar bubble?

"There are to be seven years of great abundance in all the land of Egypt. But seven years of famine will certainly arise after them, and all the abundance in the land of Egypt will certainly be forgotten, and the famine will exhaust the land. And the previous abundance in the land will not be remembered because of the famine afterward, for it will be very severe.

—Genesis 41:29-31

I am going to discuss the investments and strategies for income that are available to you. We want to build the best ship for your retirement mission. The next chapter will be about your mission control crew and flight operators (i.e., Financial Professionals) for your mission. But I need to address the elephant in the room. I have taken shots at Fiduciaries in the previous chapters, but now is the time to discuss it.

---

acronym for cyclically adjusted price-to-earnings ratio, was popularized by Yale University professor Robert Shiller." - Investopedia.com

224 The prevailing trend in a "secular bull" market is "bullish" or upward-moving. In a "secular bear," the market tends to trend sideways with severe drawdowns and sharp rallies. -Seeking Alpha 'The Next Secular Bear Market May Be Upon Us' by Lance Roberts

225 Chart source: Real Investment Advice.

(The following narrative on regulation is, in my opinion, interwoven with accepted facts.)

The Fiduciary Debate

What is a Fiduciary? At Investopedia[226] it says,

"Fiduciaries are persons or organizations that act on behalf of others and are required to put the clients' interests ahead of their own, with a duty to preserve good faith and trust. Fiduciaries are thus legally and ethically bound to act in the other's best interests... When a party knowingly accepts a fiduciary duty on behalf of another, they are required to act in the best interest of the principal (i.e., the client or party whose assets they are managing). This is what is known as a "prudent person standard of care," which stems from an 1830 court ruling, Harvard College vs. Armory, and is found in many state laws via the American Law Institute's Uniform Prudent Investor Act from 1994."

"Fiduciaries are legally bound to put their client's best interests ahead of their own," —Investopedia writer Adam Hayes.

"The prudent see danger and take refuge, but the simple keep going and pay the penalty." —Proverbs 22:3 NIV

The Prudent Man Rule. Now, the Prudent Investor Rule.

In 1830, Judge Samuel Putnam formulated the Prudent Man Rule, now called the Prudent Investor Rule, and we know why (you misogynistic woman hater). He wrote as a judgment in the Harvard v. Amory case:

"Do what you will, the capital is at hazard...All that can be required of a trustee to invest is that he shall conduct himself faithfully and exercise sound discretion. He is to observe how men of prudence, discretion, and intelligence manage their own affairs...considering the probable income, as well as the probable safety of the capital to be invested."

After the Great Depression

After the Great Depression, several Acts of Congress were created to create rules and regulate investments and investment advice.[227] These Acts attempted to remove fraud from the

---

226 Fiduciary Definition: Examples and Why They Are Important by Adam Hayes

227 The Securities Act of 1933, the Securities Exchange Act of 1938, and the Investment Company Act of 1940.

markets, which was desperately needed. I am giving you a general overview here, so forgive me if I don't get bogged down in the details.

IARs vs Brokers

The two main types of finance professionals are Investment Advisor Representatives (IARs working for an RIA or registered investment advisor) and registered representatives (RRs), commonly called brokers working for a Broker/Dealer. IARs are fiduciaries and are subject to higher legal standards of care and loyalty than brokers. In the olden days, only those with considerable assets would hire an IAR who served their account in a fiduciary capacity.

In the past, IARs might charge management fees, commissions, or other revenue. This only needed to be disclosed. However, the SEC changed this. Now, a fiduciary is paid with one or a combination of the following: a flat fee, an hourly charge, or a management fee as a percentage of assets under management.

All have to be fair and reasonable. And there it is, defining fair and reasonable. This change was significant and has caused some of the issues we are dealing with. ***Since commissions could no longer be considered as compensation for a fiduciary, this was an industry game-changer.*** (There is a way for an IAR to charge commissions as part of compensation, but no one is chancing it. One securities attorney said to me, "Try it and see how your audit goes.")

We won't ask the court for a ruling

The SEC likes to clarify the rules through **enforcement**. Here is the process the SEC follows: It sues firms for what it believes are violations. The company being sued by the SEC doesn't want a long, drawn-out lawsuit that damages its reputation and may even limit its ability to conduct business. So it settles without admitting they did anything wrong and pays a fine (since that is much cheaper than court and lawyers, and it looks bad to clients to have a battle with the SEC), and bam, the violation is settled by capitulation. No court ruled on whether the SEC was right or wrong! In other Supreme Court cases, the government is often wrong.

They had a gun to my child's head

Elon Musk described the settlement he made as a "gun to his child's head," explaining why he settled with the SEC over a twitter he made about "Funding Secured." Because Tesla was in a precarious financial position, the banks threatened to cut off the company's capital if he did not resolve the dispute with the SEC quickly.

What is happening in the securities industry is the same, and it has been more about politics and social engineering than about orderly, secure markets. I will explain why this is important later. Here is a concise history of investing and advice.

Registered Representatives or Brokers

Before the Great Depression, most people hired a broker to manage their investments. This person received a commission for every transaction you made. In the early days, the brokers met under a buttonwood tree *on Wall Street* to trade stocks. Coming to our day, if you bought a stock for $10,000 and paid a 2% commission to the broker, that cost you $200.

Here is the problem: you are not even sure the advice to buy or sell wasn't to make the 'broker' money. (Baby needs new shoes or a new Porsche) The self-regulatory organization FINRA[228] (formerly NASD) was formed to make rules, keep brokers honest, and protect investors. However, there were many conflicts of interest and problems for investors by Big Firms.

One issue was the suitability rule. As long as the investment offered was 'suitable' for the investor, there was no issue with offering it. Even if it was risky or the Broker's firm (called the Broker/Dealer) had a conflict or a separate revenue agreement. (i.e., additional money paid to the broker or his firm outside the commission you paid for promoting the stock or bond.)

Regulators (SEC, FINRA, and individual state securities commissions) have been trying to redefine fairness and protect investors from predatory practices. The goal is to make markets fair, orderly, and free. However, **that is not the opinion of all who work for these regulatory organizations.**

Attitudes about Profit

Karl Marx, who developed Communism, wrote that "Profit was excess price." He believed this should be returned to the people (proletariat class). These beliefs infect a great many people who don't understand how free markets and capitalism work, especially for poor people! You can't deny the wealth of the USA. I have been to many countries, and nowhere can individuals rise to the level of prosperity they desire like here in the USA. Immigrants sacrificed their lives to make it to America and, as a group, were more likely to become millionaires.[229] A Thai business owner who operates the Bangkok Tokyo restaurant in Amarillo, Texas, told me she would have worked as a servant if she had stayed in her home country of Thailand.

---

[228] FINRA is the Financial Industry Regulatory Authority. FINRA is a not-for-profit organization authorized under federal securities laws and registered with the Securities and Exchange Commission (SEC). Alongside the SEC, FINRA oversees U.S. member broker-dealers and their personnel, including individuals who recommend or sell securities products to the public. FINRA's mission is protecting you, the investor, and ensuring the integrity of our country's securities markets. -FINRA.org 'What It Means to Be Regulated by FINRA' APRIL 22, 2024

[229] Source: The Millionaire Next Door- Thomas Stanley, Ph.D & William Danko, Ph.D

I asked a missionary who had been to Eastern Europe, Africa, and South America in his 30 years of missionary work: "What country is best for someone poor?" He said unequivocally, the United States. Our system is not bad for the poorest, but it also doesn't end poverty. (No Government can or has ended poverty.)

That isn't to say we have a utopia or a perfect society. The Japanese have bidets on every toilet. Why don't we? Bidets are awesome! (My editors are saying TMI) Here is my point: Some people see successful people and want them punished for crimes against society. You add the tribalism among political parties that has reached levels never seen before. The belief that excess prices must be eliminated and redistributed to others has infected many people. This never works in any society that has tried it—the end.

My point is that some people in charge of administering government regulations are pursuing socialistic agendas, not upholding the law or what makes money and business work. Socialism may not be the stated mission of the regulator, but more of an 'intent' of individuals involved in regulation.

The Change to the Fiduciary Model

After 2000, advisors began switching to the Fiduciary model of doing business. Ending commissions for transactions and managing client assets for a percentage fee of the money entrusted to them. Why did they start changing their business model? Four reasons:

1. FINRA became punitive and aggressive in its enforcement of 'rules.' (RIAs are not regulated by FINRA but are regulated by the SEC or Individual State Securities Commissions)
2. More clients like the idea of their advisor being a Fiduciary instead of a broker.
3. Broker/Dealer firms could annualize and even out their revenue stream.
4. The hope was to reduce compliance violations that cost the B/Ds fines, like account churning.[230]

Brokers and Broker/Dealers are regulated by FINRA. I agree and believe that customers need someone to keep firms and brokers in line and accountable. What FINRA does is necessary for fair markets and honest advisors.[231] However, as more and more Marxist views are accepted by individuals, an attitude of punishing achievers prevails. The regulatory bodies have begun

[230] Churning is the illegal and unethical practice by a broker of excessively trading assets in a client's account in order to generate commissions. -Investopedia

[231] I have always believed that we should break up FINRA into 2 or 3 self-regulatory agencies. The competition could reduce the tyranny of the regulator.

shifting from keeping everyone honest and fair to social engineering based on social philosophy. With the trend of FINRA enforcement becoming cruel and punitive, more and more brokers worry about being eviscerated by FINRA for errors (particularly individual advisors). Compliance has become difficult and expensive. For these reasons, we have seen a migration of brokers out of the broker channel to form Registered Investment Advisors and represent their clients as an Investment Advisor Representative (IAR).

*Note: many IAR's are **dual-registered**. Meaning they are Registered Representatives (Brokers) AND Fiduciary Investment Advisors. So, they switch back and forth from being under a Fiduciary standard and the broker's 'best interest' standard. More on this in a moment.

Incentives Matter (so say all one-armed Economists)[232]

That being said, the shift away from the transaction model to the fee-based model is not necessarily a bad thing. When your advisor is paid fees to manage your portfolio, it aligns the advisor's interest with your own. The advisor's incentives will be tied to stable or rising account values. Remember, if you see a 10% drop in the value of your account, your advisor (if your fees are an asset-based percentage) sees a 10% cut in his fee. If you decide to move your account, a broker loses future commissions, but the advisor loses current revenue.

Consistent Revenue is Great for the Firm!

Thus began the change. Brokers/Dealers began forming RIAs and shifting some client accounts to that model. The industry preferred fee-based models to avoid the appearance of conflict, even though dual-registration remains a standard (albeit highly scrutinized) practice.

Granted, more and more customers liked this and wanted this, and it was a great deal for the Brokers/Dealers. Instead of revenues (i.e., commissions) going up and down with the market, they could now see a more stable revenue stream. Many firms forgot to rid themselves of the legacy back-room conflict of interest deals that went against their clients' interests. So, the SEC and State Securities started enforcement actions to clean it up.

Some unfair enforcement and some rules through enforcement have resulted, but overall, this has cleaned up the business and has definitely been good for clients like you. But the SEC now had a problem. Are they going to eliminate the broker channel completely? Are we saying

---

[232] Easter Egg -mail me a short note stating the reason that is funny, and I will mail you a puzzle of the book's cover with a smart alec comment. Limitations and exclusions that I will make up later apply.

commissions are an evil plague? Is the fee-based model the only model good for clients? Is that even constitutional?

The Broker/Dealers are needed for markets to function and the US capital markets to work. Destroying that channel would crush the US economy and is unnecessary. Allow the investors to decide is my answer, just keep everyone honest. But if you're trying to change capitalism, you can't possibly allow that, can you?

RIAs hate FINRA, and Brokers are afraid to say what they think

A few years ago, a suggestion was made to use FINRA to share some of the regulatory burdens at the SEC. This caused massive outrage among RIAs, who generally dislike FINRA. Many left the Broker channel because of FINRA's perceived unfair rulemaking and enforcement.

Before we go further, if you believe investment advice and service should be free, then I can't help you. If you want it to be a win-win and fair for all involved, then continue reading.

Which is better, Fees or Commissions?

Allow me to demonstrate the difference in cost.

Fees vs Commissions for 10 year holding period assuming 5% annual growth

$100,000 principal invested x 7% commission = $ 7,000.00[233]

$100,000 principal invested x 1% annual fee = $12,577.00

$100,000 principal invested x 1.5% annual fee = $18,866.00

You can see that there is a solid argument for the commission model's cost. 7% would be the total maximum commission.[234] Interestingly, you will find articles claiming that certain financial products pay enormous commissions, lining the agents' pockets, like what the fee-based guys do, is charity work.

---

[233] I will assume the investment product would pay the commission (not the client), thus allowing 100% of the capital to be invested.

[234] This is a hypothetical illustration and isn't inclusive of other costs that could be involved.

Who is doing better, the commission guy or the fiduciary? Unfortunately, commissions have become a political philosophy for some rather than a discussion of the client's (you) best interests or even what is the best value.

However, in the war to fundamentally change financial advice and investments, it is in the best interest of certain Big Wall Street firms. They want everyone to stay on their trading platforms and pay regular fees. In a moment, I will discuss the 'Income-Producing' investments. Some investments pay the advisor a commission, while others you invest in under a fee arrangement.

Which is better?

I will explain in a moment, but first, let me tell you how the SEC saved the commission broker model and how the Department of Labor is trying to destroy it.

Best Interest (Reg BI) Rule to Save the Day

If you read the articles about the business of providing investment advice and services, you will see a lot of high-minded articles about the abuses of the Bourgeoisie[235] brokers. Ok, they don't use those words, but the idea that the SEC needs to take the profits away from these brokers is clear. Why? Because the working man will have more money if they did! Look at every country in the world and see how this line of thinking has worked out.

How would the SEC fix the conflicted advice that is common in the broker channel? Ban certain investments? Allow only fees? Is a commission always bad? Some of those advocating a sweeping Fiduciary requirements believe this will eliminate corrupt practices in the investment industry and reallocate profits to the non-wealthy.

In the US, we have this thing called the Constitution and Bill of Rights. They couldn't make the broker channel fiduciaries. Why? Because they already said fiduciaries couldn't charge commissions for one reason. What is the answer? The SEC came up with the Best Interest rule.

A lot of the high-minded financial commentators did not like this, as it didn't force brokers to be fiduciaries. The Best Interest rule essentially says you are a fiduciary without *being a* fiduciary. Treat your clients fairly, disclose their options, and plan based on the client's financial objectives and situation to sell or offer investments *in the client's best interests*. (If two investments are essentially the same, but one costs more and pays the broker more, then the

---

235 Karl Marx referred to the Bourgeoisie as a class of business owners and merchants. His description was they were abusive, evil, and the people needed protection from them.

broker is obligated to recommend the one that is in the client's best interest). Finally, brokers and dealers must eliminate conflicts of interest, not just disclose them. (I love the legal talk that tells you how they are screwing you).

The Best Interest Rule was definitely an upgrade from the suitability rule and drastically improved commission-based advice. Now, I am leaving out a lot of details, and the Best Interest rule has many flaws. That being said, I believe the best interest rule saved the broker channel business while providing clients with disclosure and protections they previously didn't have, without making Brokers fiduciaries!

Shouldn't everyone be a Fiduciary?

Here is the bar fight. Let me illustrate: Is your local grocery store a fiduciary? Of course not. They make a profit on the products you buy. That's how they stay in business and provide you with choice and selection. Some products pay the store to be on the shelf. This would be a conflict, right? (Try shopping at grocery stores in other countries; you'll see the difference) If there are other stores competing for your business, the prices will be as low as they can make them, or they will offer additional services to improve your shopping experience. Should the government make the grocery store a fiduciary? End conflicts? That is obviously ridiculous.

What if you hire someone to buy your groceries for you? Should that person be a fiduciary? I would say yes. He shouldn't accept money or gifts to shop at preferred stores that are against your interests.

Here is my point: We shouldn't turn the fiduciary issue into a Philosophical Quasi-Political Social Issue. ***See where you need a fiduciary and where you don't.***

Many of the Big Box Big Wall Street firms have embraced both businesses. (Dual-registered advisors. Fee-based model and the broker model) If you read your statement carefully, you see the broker accounts that charge commissions and the advisory accounts that charge fees. Which one is better for me, you ask?

Fee or No Fee: that is the Question

Let me cut to the chase, as the expression goes.

I believe how you pay your advisor should be based on what is involved in managing your account and aligning the advisor's incentives with your interests.

I don't hate anyone who makes a profit off me as long as it is fair and reasonable and gives me the service I need. If you ask someone to manage a portfolio of stocks and bonds, what is your expectation? Does he or she monitor the account? Are they conducting ongoing research on your holdings? Does he or she recommend you sell investments that look too risky or stop meeting your objectives? Does he or she answer your phone calls and meet with you when you request? Do they do what is in *your* best interest?

Do you think a broker who is paid when there is a transaction would do all this enthusiastically? (Unless you're buying/selling, the service is 'free work'.) If you have a strong buy-and-hold portfolio with no management expectation, then a commission-based broker would be cost-effective for you.

But as I described previously, a portfolio of equities[236] and bonds need active management.

In my opinion, you clearly want a fee-based fiduciary advisor. Since fees are paid as you go, there is an incentive for the advisor to provide the service and management. You want the trust that transactions are in your best interest and not to generate revenue, especially if you have given discretion (meaning permission to buy or sell without informing you first) over your account.

If your account loses value, the fee-based advisor will receive a lower fee, but what will the broker say? "Let's sell everything and buy new stuff." You lose money, and he has a good month thanks to a down market. (Commission Brokers, in my experience, are more aggressive risk-takers.) The fiduciary *is likely* (not guaranteed) to be more proactive and risk-averse, and if the answer is to sell everything, it is more likely the advisor's recommendation is in your best interest.

For assets that need ongoing evaluation and management, a fiduciary relationship in a fee-based portfolio aligns your interests with the advisor's, allowing you to leverage the advisor's experience, resources, and education to meet your investment objectives.

What if you have a 10-year investment product? (I will go into detail later on this) All the work of choosing the right one and setting it up properly is done at the beginning. After that, an annual review is all that is needed. Is it in *your* interest if the advisor is paid a commission at the beginning? I would say that is reasonable and likely in your best interest.

Fee-only vs. Fee-based

---

236 Equities are typically ownership investments like Stocks, Exchange Traded Funds, Mutual Funds or others.

"A fee-only advisor's only source of compensation is the fees they charge their clients, most frequently as a percentage of the investments they manage… A fee-based advisor's income, on the other hand, can come from several avenues, such as fees and commissions on products they sell to their clients."[237] A fee-based advisor cannot offer non-fiduciary products as an outside business, but a fee-only advisor cannot.

This means that the 'fee-only' advisor can offer investments that might be in your best interest if they don't pay him correctly. I believe this is a problem since it assumes that only fee compensation is always the best model. Because he is a fiduciary. **Set aside that the fee model pays more! Over time and may require more risk!** After all, he is a fiduciary.

Pawns in the Social Warfare

The media is controlled or influenced by Big Wall Street companies. I don't feel I need to convince you of that one. The drumbeat is for fee-only fiduciary advisors. Is it a surprise that the investments in which they make the most money are promoted as the good ones? Even if they have more risk than the invest want's to take on?

The media, in many instances, have become useful idiots to Big Wall Street firms trying to keep their Baseball Card portfolios and trading platforms going, profiting, and investing.

The large firms also want your money exclusively on their platforms. They make money on order flow, transaction charges, loaning on margin, and other fees in addition to the advisory fees charged to your account.

This is an interesting problem. That begs the question: Is the fiduciary fee-based advice conflict-free?

The media narrative is that anyone who isn't a fee-only advisor is a dirty wolf of Big Wall Street. I can tell you that everyone in the investment business has conflicts, some more than others, and some that directly go against your objectives and interests. And here is the other dirty secret: A fiduciary might not work in your best interest but rather against it.

How is that possible, you ask? Allow me to expand. If your fee-only fiduciary offers only mutual funds in his discretionary fee-only account, are you getting the best advice? I am getting ready to explain investments in this chapter. Some investments are not offered by a fiduciary. If your 'fiduciary' is restricted in his offerings, you might not have what is in your best interest

---

237 Forbes.com Fee-Only Financial Planner vs. Fee-Based: What's the Difference? By Amy Fontinelle

despite having a fiduciary advisor. Some Fiduciaries go on the offensive, declaring these 'other' investments as bad and exposing the 'truth.'

Who does best by not rolling over your account?

Big Wall Street firms and the 401 (k) providers want you to stay with investments offered on their platform. (Blackrock, Vanguard, Fidelity, State Street, and JP Morgan) These firms are looking at the long game in this relationship, and they make more money from fee-based accounts over time than from commission accounts or products with fewer compliance issues. Commission products ultimately pay them less. (When considered over a 10-year time horizon.)

I was contacted by a Big Wall Street firm in 2021. They were offering me a lucrative deal to move my business to their platform. I do business in guaranteed non-market investments outside of fee-based equities and bonds. The recruiter made it clear they were not interested in the non-market investments, and if I joined that firm, all my clients would invest in 'only' in the money managers, stocks, bonds, mutual funds, and ETFs, they offered and I would be a 'fiduciary,' still, despite potentially not offering an investment that may be in clients best interest. I contend that fiduciary advice doesn't necessarily protect your interest if the advisor is restricted in what he can offer.

"Those who would give up essential Liberty, to purchase a little temporary Safety, deserve neither Liberty nor Safety" —Benjamin Franklin.

The Department of Labor enters the Battlefield.

Starting with the Obama administration, he charged the DOL to use ERISA[238] to change 401ks and IRAs. Obama wanted real change in investment advice. We are back to the fear that fees and commissions would reduce retirement accounts, leaving less for the proletariats, I mean retirees, to retire on. The narrow view is that all the excess prices in the form of commissions and fees are messing up your retirement. They needed to do something. So, they hired the best socialist lawyers they could find to work at the DOL on this problem.

---

[238] ERISA is the Employee Retirement Income Security Act of 1974. is a U.S. federal tax and labor law that establishes minimum standards for pension plans in private industry. It contains rules on the federal income tax effects of transactions associated with employee benefit plans. ERISA was enacted to protect the interests of employee benefit plan participants and their beneficiaries ... -Wikipedia.com

ERISA's purpose

This act passed in 1974, was intended to ensure that employer-sponsored plans (401k's and Pensions) and health plans were fair for all employees.

The passage of this bill was in response to the collapse of the automaker Studebaker. When it closed, 10,500 current and former employees lost their pensions, receiving only 15 cents on the dollar of what was promised.

This legislation was intended to protect employees from self-serving employers by assuring access to retirement plans and health plans and that they were managed in the best interests of the participants and not for a select few. This legislation is being expanded to control all retirement accounts.

Why go through the DOL? Why not use the SEC to change the system? If making advice fair and eliminating conflicts were the goals, then that would be the best option, and the SEC was already working on that goal. However, eliminating brokers and commissions was proving difficult. Why? The Constitution keeps getting in the way. The DOL wanted a ban on commissions; it is their view that this is the source of all our problems. The simple change that anyone touching an IRA had to be a fiduciary was mission accomplished! (IRAs and 401ks account for $20 trillion in assets).

Frustratingly, the SEC was working on a best-interest rule, and the DOL knew the SEC did not intend to turn everyone into a fiduciary. Elements of our government want a strict fiduciary standard to eliminate product salespeople, insurance agents, and others from offering investment advice or selling investments. This would also slow rollovers out of employer plans. (A lot of Big Wall Street firms like that idea) Next, they could regulate the advice and be sure you have only the investments the government approves. Is that chilling? It should be. Consider that the sale of government bonds funds our massive deficits. (US debt in 2026 is $39 trillion; there are only 400 million stars in our galaxy, we have more debt than stars) What if they required you to buy treasury bonds in order to protect you? Remember, there are over $20 trillion in IRAs and 401k accounts. Is this too conspiracy for you?

The Department of Labor came out with the DOL rule. The first iteration was a hoot. The DOL planned to allow attorneys to enforce the rule through litigation and class action lawsuits. (Guess whose idea this was?) Currently, most disagreements are handled through binding arbitration through FINRA or another arbitration organization. The settlements typically settle for actual damages or less with little punitive damages. In the Broker channel, FINRA looks carefully at these cases to see if more attention is warranted for the advisor or the broker/dealer firm.

The DOL knew what would happen. Every down market, an attorney would gather up clients who lost money in their accounts and sue the advisor or his/her firm for non-compliance with the DOL rules, of which there are many. (Trial lawyers loved this one.) The effect of this would be that small clients would be forced to stay with the large retirement plan providers, and rollovers would slow to a trickle. Advising rollovers would have been risky for Broker/Dealers, Insurance Companies, and others. The big asset managers would benefit the most from these regulations.

Many brokers saw a wave of angry Braveheart lawyers coming over the hill because of the Fiduciary Rule. Most financial advisors I talked to (at that time) said they planned to drop all clients who had less than $250,000 in assets, and many financial advisors would have exited the business (i.e. lost their jobs). The 5th Circuit Court invalidated the rule, and disaster was averted. Trump became President (2016), and the DOL re-tried a rule requiring brokers who provide one-time rollover advice to disclose conflicts of interest and follow impartial conduct standards instead of having fiduciary status.

The main argument for why all this is needed is the cost. The argument is that the DOL rules will reduce costs for investors. Billions would be added to retirements. These cost savings will add to your retirement. If that were really true, then I would be all for these savings. ***It never works that savings are produced by reducing choice.*** Asset Management companies love broad-based mutual funds, such as target-date funds. After all, they are easy to manage. If that is what you want, I say 'fine,' but why do I have to be reduced to a few investment options to reduce 'imaginary' costs? Unfortunately, the Financial Elites believe that you can't be trusted to make that decision. You might choose to be crazy and leave the stock market. OMG!

Here is the interesting point: If you roll your 401k to a commission-based account, the narrative is that you are charged absorbent commissions that are destroying your retirement **unless** you roll to a fiduciary charging a 1.5% advisor fee with separate 1% mutual fund costs. Huh? Isn't that more costly? The bias here is obvious. And that is why Big Wall Street firms are pushing for this: **to protect their business**.[239]

239 Ok I am not going all 'conspiracy' here and saying the big asset managers was complicit in the DOL attack on IRA freedom of choice, but I didn't see them fight it either.

Be careful of what you ask for.

"But didn't you say you were **for** a fiduciary approach to retirement planning?" you ask. If that is all this is about, I say sure, we need honesty, fairness, and standards in retirement advice. There are abuses, but restricting choices and individuals from making their own decisions won't make everyone rich and happy.

Be careful watching the wolves devour your enemies. Guess who is next when they are done.

The DOL changed its strategy after more losses in court and implemented additional rules (not as ambitious as the first go-around) to curb free choice. To this date, courts have invalidated much, but the DOL keeps coming back. The last rule (2024) was literally rammed through by the Biden administration and defeated in court.

"Are the DOL rules about protecting investors? No, they are not."

This has always been about changing the way you invest. The largest Big Wall Street firms and their 'platforms' stand to benefit from the DOL rules. Consider this: the US had $39 trillion in debt in early 2024. (Try not to choke on that) Who are we borrowing this from? Can we expand the list of those willing to loan money to the US? How about your account? If your funds are stuck in a 401k because there are no other options, it would be easy to next require that 35% of your account be invested in safe and secure treasury bonds for your safety. (I know I said this already, but I am making a point here.)

The rulers of the state are the only persons who ought to have the privilege of lying, either at home or abroad; they may be allowed to lie for the good of the state. —Plato

Also, the US politicians have always used the Stock and Bond markets as a gauge of economic health. Elections can turn on the declining markets. If your money leaves the stock market, is that a risk to politicians? I found this quote interesting:

"I continue to believe the DOL is conducting an ideological campaign to ban commissions, as evidenced by their inflammatory and offensive framing of this rule when they initially proposed it, the un-American and absolute disgrace of the lightning pace at which they have pushed this rule through, and the lack of questions or even spirited debate on the substantive issues within this rule," —Finseca CEO Marc Cadin speaking of the rule introduced in 2024.

Are advisors who are paid by commissions a bad deal for you? The answer is no. But we have a system that allows freedom of choice. Certain circumstances might be better for you if you have the option for lower-cost commission-based investments.

We want our regulators to ensure fairness and honesty and support a vibrant market. Standards of conduct and reducing/eliminating conflicts of interest, make sense. We also want them to fight fraud and misconduct. But not make our choices for us!

I have criticism for the regulatory system, but it is needed, and they are doing the job for the most part. What we don't need is social engineering under the guise of safety.

Update: It's Over, for Now

The election of Donald Trump and repeated court losses have ended the DOL Fiduciary rule. We are back to the 5-part test that determines if a person or entity is an investment advice fiduciary under ERISA. I nearly erased this entire section, but decided that you need to know. After 15 years of battle, the DOL is back where it began. Your choice of what to invest in and whether to roll over your IRA or 401(k) is entirely up to you, for now.

How you invest should be your choice; whether you hire a fiduciary and pay a fee or invest in a product that pays your advisor a commission, that should be your choice, and I will describe the advantages of both. One thing I know is that it never goes well when the government gets between you and your money.

What was that all about?

Now you're wondering why I took time to tell you all of this. The reason is that there is an ideological war going on to control your retirement account in the name of customer safety and cost. When elements of the media speak against investments and strategies that 'Big Wall Street' sees as a danger to their business model, they will have the government get involved in order to 'protect you' and save you money. When it comes to retirement planning, costs are not the only factor.

There are abuses when clients don't understand what they are investing in or the important elements of the investments being offered. Educating yourself is better than having elitists make choices for you. It is also important to know the agenda and bias that exist in the media and government bureaucrats. Remember, for the government, ***it is easier to control you by controlling your advisor.***

Frankly, I agree with many of the principles the DOL said it was pursuing. I distrust their real purpose. It is my passion to educate everyone on Income Investing for retirement.

Frog Boiling

I will wrap this up by explaining to you how to boil a frog. You don't throw the frog into a pot of boiling water—he will bounce out. You put him in a pot of cold water and slowly turn up the heat. Once everyone is a 'fiduciary,' it would be easier to control what a 'fiduciary' is allowed to say or offer to you. That is when the frogs really feel the heat. Don't worry it is for your protection. That is what we are seeing now, and as I described in Chapter 5, many retirees are choosing to cash out their retirement accounts, paying the taxes now, and funding Roth IRAs, Life Insurance plans, or other investment accounts for the retirement mission.

"And both these kings' hearts shall be to do mischief, and they shall speak lies at one table…" —Daniel 11:27 KJV

Do financial advisors have worth for your retirement?

Do financial advisors make a difference? Fidelity conducted research that I found interesting. It said the following:

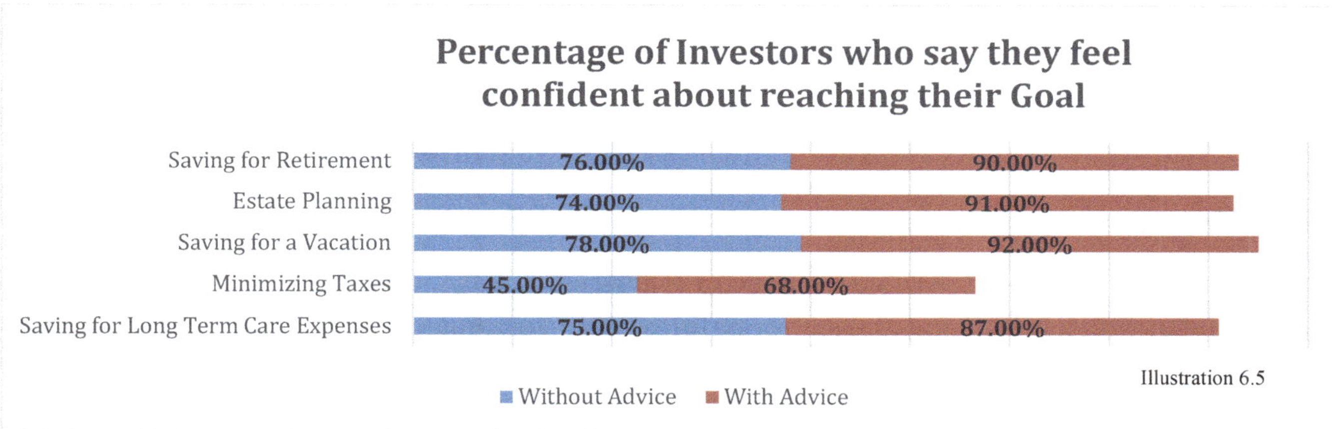

Illustration 6.5

"Financial advisors deliver value of 5.2% annually or more each year to their clients in a relationship that extends beyond investment-only advice." —Russell Investments[240]

240 Source: Think Advisor "How much value does a financial advisor deliver?" -Michael S Fischer

"Vanguard estimates that the value of using an advisor is around 3% additional net annual gains for the investor." —Putting a value on your value: Quantifying Vanguard Advisor's Alpha

The Vanguard scored seven categories of advice and service with netted +3% after fees. Often people focus on whether an advisor can outperform the markets. That is not what you need to consider. This relationship should help you avoid behavioral mistakes with your money. Donald Trump once said in his book, 'Art of the Deal,' that "Sometimes your best investments are the ones you don't make." Expecting your advisor to score big gains for retirement means more risk. You should be looking for the opposite of that.

I have personally talked many clients out of many bad investments or even scams over the years. Having a professional on your payroll, to say, is a benefit to you and your family.

Even if you are an amazing investor/trader yourself, having someone who is philosophically aligned with you will benefit your spouse and family when you are gone.

The advisor relationship could make a difference in saving and retirement, but anything requires you to be selective in the advisor you select. There is tangible value in the client-advisor relationship. This topic will be covered in the next chapter, 'Choosing Mission Control.'

You're probably thinking, "Wow, the last few pages weren't all that funny." Yeah, talking about politics takes the oxygen out of the room. So, I am going to take a shower and hose this off me, and let's move on to how you can have a successful retirement mission.

Certified Financial Fiduciaries [241]

Subhani and I became Certified Financial Fiduciaries in 2021. You get how I feel about the whole issue of fiduciaries being abused for political purposes and to reformulate capitalism as we know it. So why would I become a Certified Financial Fiduciary? Here it is. Because we agree with standards and loyalty to our client's interests, whether or not we are fiduciaries in the SEC definition. Here is the Certified Fiduciary Code of Conduct.

[241] Go to https://nationalcffassociation.org/ for more information on the Certified Financial Fiduciary designation.

The Certified Financial Fiduciary code of conduct is as follows:

- Practice the Duty of Loyalty – first and foremost, always put the client's best interest first.
- Practice the Duty of Good Faith – there is a fundamental obligation to treat all clients fairly.
- Practice the Duty of Good Care – there is a fundamental obligation to exercise the skill of an expert and to only advise in those areas where expert skill level has been obtained.
- Educate First – provide comprehensive and unbiased education to clients prior to making specific suggestions or providing advice.
- Holistic Approach – consider all aspects and factors that affect a plan prior to making suggestions or providing advice.
- Full Disclosure – fully divulge all fees and commissions as well as disclose any conflicts of interest and disciplinary actions.
- Confidentiality – protect and keep all clients' information confidential and securely stored and transmitted.
- Professional Behavior – practice in a manner that does not bring disrepute to the profession, the Certified Financial Fiduciary® mark, and fellow professionals.
- Keep NACFF Informed – report on professional practice management and any disciplinary actions taken by regulatory bodies to NACFF to ensure that the above standards are being met at all times.

This is what we are about! We are committed to doing what is right & lawful for our clients and their families, no matter what kind of investments or advice is in your best interest.

Building the Right Spaceship for You 

There isn't a perfect investment. Everything has pros and cons. We start this conversation with your objectives. The Apollo spacecraft was built to go to the moon. That was the objective. The Space Shuttle was built to orbit the Earth and launch and recover satellites. SpaceX docks with the International Space Station and eventually will go to Mars.

Your retirement mission has objectives. What are you trying to accomplish? Chapter 3 was about working on your checklist.

✓ Social Security Income estimates and optimal filing dates

✓ Income sources for retirement

✓ Retirement asset inventory

✓ Retirement Objectives and Risk Tolerance

✓ Expenses/debt review

✓ Identify your ideal retirement life

✓ Retirement Income needs and wants

✓ Tax Strategies to employ now and later

✓ Investment Strategy (Moving from the G to the I)

✓ Review of your Advisor(s)

Your objectives are important. We screen objectives twice. The first time, we keep it simple by asking you to rank the following <u>3 objectives</u>:

___ Generating income to meet or exceed your retirement goals.

___ Make sure your risk is appropriate for you.

___ Maximize growth for a large purchase or to leave a legacy.

Next, we need to revisit your risk tolerance. Below are the percentage losses and imaginary statement values:

Loss	Hypothetical Account Value
0%	**$1,000,000**
12%	$880,000
25%	$750,000
37%	$630,000
50%	$500,000

Illustration 6.6

In Chapter 2, we discussed volatility. If you review illustration 2.1 under The Effect of Volatility on Your Retirement. I make the case that volatility can be the '**exploding oxygen tank**' in your retirement, which drastically changes your lifestyle in retirement. Your choice is important.

The consequences of accepting a risk of -25% or more could mean reducing or suspending your income when your accounts lose money. Less golf, ladies' lunch, gifts to grandchildren, charity or traveling.

Let's say you are comfortable with -12% or less. We take note of that. Finally, we determine your target income and the base income you have (Social Security, pensions, and other income, not including investment income), then the assets you have to make up the target income. (If legacy is a primary objective, a dollar amount of income is not at issue except to lower risk.)

Once we start the investment strategy meeting, we need to re-evaluate your money objectives or MO.

Determining your MO

We use the following Money Objectives:

- Income
- Principal Protection
- Growth followed by Income
- Charity
- Growth

1. ______________

- Legacy (heirs, charity)
- Long Term Care
- Tax Control
- Estate Planning
- Risk Reduction

2. ______________

- Creditor Protection
- Asset or Large purchase
- Liquidity
- Growth of Income
-

3. ______________

Your MO (Money Objectives) will determine the investments that will best meet your mission parameters (goals).

Now, we will discuss the investments that we can consider for an Income Portfolio. We will consider each investment on its merits, not on whether it's fiduciary or not. Every investment has pros and cons.[242] We will also consider procedures for what can go wrong.

---

[242] The pros and cons of something are the arguments for and against it. When you're considering the pros and cons of something, you're thinking about its good and bad points. -Languagetool.org

Before I talk about investments, another reminder from my Lawyers

The following information is for Educational Purposes only and is not a recommendation to buy or sell any security or investment program. This information is not intended to be used as the primary basis for investment decisions, nor should it be considered as advice designed to meet the specific needs of an individual investor.

Investments contain risks and could be subject to loss, which could be short-term or permanent. Selling existing investments may involve the following considerations: capital loss, tax implications, loss of benefits or features, increase in costs, surrender periods with early withdrawal costs, opportunity loss, and other considerations.

This information is general in nature and may not include all the details that are needed to make a prudent investment decision. Elements in your financial situation may cause some of this information to be completely unsuitable for you. Please consult your advisors (financial, tax, or legal) before initiating the purchase, sale, or holding of any investment or investment strategy. Some investments require a thorough review of a prospectus before investing.

Past Performance is not a guarantee of future results. Some investments may not be offered as a fiduciary. Some of my comments, views, or opinions may differ from those of other established authorities.

Income-Producing Investments

As an Independent Fiduciary Advisor, everything is on the table for your retirement. I am going to list the common investments first, and provide a brief description. Then, we will discuss how to put together a portfolio to meet your target risk and income objectives.

"Investors should purchase stocks like they purchase groceries, not like they purchase perfume."
—Benjamin Graham

"If you have trouble imagining a 20% loss in the stock market, you shouldn't be in stocks."
—John Bogle, founder of The Vanguard Group

Stocks

There are about 10,000[243] publicly traded stocks in the US. Every day, they are bought and sold. What are they worth? So much research, books, formulas, and other theories have been produced to define the value of stocks. Here is the secret of what stocks are worth. Ready?

"Stocks are worth what someone else is willing to pay for them at the time you are ready to sell."

Illustration 6.7 Source: Google Finance

Many people invest for growth. They look for companies that will be worth more in the future, regardless of dividends. Earnings are the most watched measure. How much will a company make now and in the future? Sometimes, investors will tolerate a company that loses money if they believe it will be profitable in the future.

Consider one of the most successful stocks in our time, Amazon. Amazon started in 1994 and went public[244] in 1997 but did not have a profitable year until 2003.[245] After that, it went in and out of profitability, essentially not becoming profitable for 14 years.[246] Investors keep pushing up the stock price in the hope of the future of online shopping. This is the growth poster boy. You notice the volatility in the stock's price, like when it crashed in December of 2022 or during years of no growth. As we discussed previously, investing in growth is risky for retired investors. You don't have time on your side as the accumulation investor does. A market crash or a no-growth market could cause you to run out of money.

Can you invest in stocks for retirement?

You can absolutely. If you focus first on how much income in retirement you need, you will see if your pensions, annuities, and social security can make up your base income. If you need more income from your stock market investments, then a dividend stock focus makes sense. If you need to reduce risk, then dividend stocks can (if selected well) provide less volatility (amount of potential loss). Dividend stocks will be higher risk than bonds.

There are 1,500 US companies that pay dividends.[247] One risk with dividend stocks is the company can reduce or eliminate the dividend during difficult times. The selection and

---

243 Source Motley Fool The Biggest Companies on the Stock Market: A Guide November 27, 2023
244 A company that goes 'public' means you can buy the shares on the exchanges.
245 Source Business Model Analyst.
246 QZ.com It took Amazon 14 years to make as much in net profit as it did last quarter by Griswold and Karaian
247 Source: DiscoverCI "The Complete List of Dividend Paying Stocks"

monitoring of these income investments would be critical. We target a 3-5% dividend yield for a safe *cash flow*. ***Dividend stocks also have growth potential in their dividend yield and share price.*** This makes them an inflation hedge as well. Collecting the yield (*cash flow, say it in a late-night DJ voice*) for retirement income while you hold the shares is sustainable but comes with market risk.

"In these markets, you need companies that actually make money and don't just give you hype, I mean cash flow." —Kevin O'Leary, Shark Tank Investor

If you go back to my hypothetical chart in illustration 6.1, I show the no-growth period from 2000 to 2013. Assuming the same S&P 500 volatility but a 4% dividend (illustration 6.2) instead of a 4% withdrawal, you can see the account maintains its value. In financial literature, there is a very specific difference between a dividend and a distribution. The SEC will jump on companies that mislead on this.

You notice in my hypothetical that you are close to the same ending value (during the 2000-2012 period) with a dividend portfolio. Why?

That is the difference between selling shares and collecting cash flow in the form of dividends.

Because of the risks I mentioned, you absolutely shouldn't buy dividend stocks based on past performance, and ***you must understand whether the dividend a company pays is sustainable and whether it is a risk worth taking***.

High Yield Dividend Stocks

Some stocks pay a very high dividend. However, these stocks contain a higher level of risk. It's important to recognize that the market has sold off the stock, causing the dividend yield to be high. You need to be cautious here. There is a real risk that the company can't sustain the dividend, and a dividend cut will result in a loss of capital and income. As a rule of thumb, a yield above 7% in 2024 would need careful consideration of the risks of this investment.

That is not to say the market is wrong for some companies, resulting in mispriced stock and creating an opportunity to invest with a high dividend income. If high-yield stocks are in your portfolio, you would want to limit the position(s) to 5% - 15% of your invested account, if any at all.

"Diversification is the only free lunch in investing."
—Harry Markowitz Nobel Prize Economist

Diversification is Needed

Having many different stocks (or other investments) in a portfolio takes away your single stock risk from taking down your whole retirement. Companies can go bankrupt, including very large companies. (If a company survives bankruptcy, the common and preferred stock shareholders will usually lose their equity position, and the bondholders become the new common stock. When GM went bankrupt, the Union went before the bondholders. Which was unprecedented.)

Here are some corporate bankruptcy examples:

Over the years, clients have called to ask me to invest in a company in bankruptcy. I fielded a lot of calls on GM. I had a client who wanted to buy GM for .25 cents a share after it announced bankruptcy. The shares traded on the exchange for a couple of months before they were delisted, and eventually, the company was transferred to the bondholders and the union. The moral of the story is, don't buy companies in bankruptcy. It will only end in tears. Yes, GM survived bankruptcy, but the stockholders saw their investment flushed down the toilet. Actually, the bondholders only did a little better.

How to Diversify?

If you invest in stocks, you should own a portfolio. How many? It really depends, but 5 – 50 or more, depending on the amount of money you have to invest. Academic research indicates that diversification is achieved when you own 25 -30 stocks.[248] (If you include international, the number goes up to 70.) After that, you risk over-diversification. The problem is keeping track of these companies. This takes time and resources. Opinions on how many positions are the 'right number' are varied. What is the best way to diversify?

"Wide diversification is only required when investors do not understand what they are doing."
—Warren Buffett legendary investor.

[248] Elton EJ Gruber M.J. Brown S.J. & Goetzmann W.N. 2010 Modern Portfolio Theory and Investment Analysis.

My 2008 Sucked Story

The Mutual Funds Sharp and Savvy Guys

Going into 2008, I was a Mutual Fund guy. I managed a portfolio of well-selected (fee-based & commission-waived) mutual funds for my clients with a few individual stocks. I looked for lower cost, six-year manager tenures, and top 20 percentile rankings. I had the best 'sharp and savvy' guys on Big Wall Street managing my client's money. As the markets crashed in 2008, being fueled by fraud in the real estate investments held by banks, I watched my well-chosen 'funds' do nothing but lose money and not perform very well when the markets began to recover.

One expectation of owning a mutual fund is that the 'sharp and savvy' guys will take less risk than doing it yourself, while giving you diversification. The S&P 500 dropped 37%, and my accounts, on average, were off by under 30% that year.[249] I can assure you that the reason some of my clients outperformed wasn't my portfolio of sucky mutual funds.

I went 20% cash in early September. My reasoning was to have some dry powder in case the market dipped. But we had a full market meltdown instead. My mutual funds had no excess performance or reduced risk. These Apollo 1 money managers blew up on the launch pad.

Over the next two years, I reinvented my process and moved away from mutual funds completely and used exchange-traded funds (ETF) instead. My performance increased significantly due to this one simple change.

Mutual Funds are costly and inefficient on a good day.

When I entered the business, I was trained to sell mutual funds. These investments were considered the best option for retail clients. By hiring professional managers (the sharp and savvy guys) to buy and sell stocks or bonds, you eliminated single stock risk and they did it better than you or your advisor could. If the fund underperforms the index[250] It's ok. Why?

---

[249] This is an average. I remember some of my clients lost more than 90% of their value due to the extreme market conditions, margin loans, or bankrupted investments. The memory of my performance should be considered anecdotal only.

[250] A market index is a hypothetical portfolio of investment holdings that represents a segment of the financial market. The calculation of the index value comes from the prices of the underlying holdings. Some indexes have values based on market-cap weighting, revenue weighting, float weighting, and fundamental weighting. Weighting is a method of adjusting the individual impact of items in an index. -Investopedia You can't invest in an index.

Because the fund is taking less risk as measured by modern portfolio theory statistics. If you are saying "Ruh-Roh Shaggy" (Scooby-Doo), then you're already starting to get it. Let's look at a few issues for mutual funds.

(This discussion will assume mutual funds purchased under an advisory account. Mutual Funds purchased under a commission arrangement incur either an upfront commission of 5.75% or less, depending on the purchase size, or have an increased expense ratio. Additionally, mutual funds purchased under a commission charge have additional costs like 12b-1 fees.)

Costs

According to one study, the average expense of mutual funds is +1.19%.[251] If you are paying your fee-based advisor 1% (most Big Wall Street firms charge up to 1.5% or more), that is 2.19% - 2.69%. But there is more! According to the Financial Analysts Journal, I'll quote: **"Funds incur a host of "invisible" costs that are less transparent to investors—most notably, the transaction costs associated with implementing changes in portfolio positions."**

In this article, they pointed out that the trading cost averaged at +1.44%. This trading cost (in addition to the fund's expense ratio) is charged to the fund and is made up of three components: 1) brokerage commissions paid by the fund for trading, 2) paying the asking price from dealers (this is higher than the bid price and represents profit to the dealer) and 3) price impact when they enter large trades and move the price of the stock higher. These costs are hidden and impact your performance.

Cash Settlement

What happens when an investor sells his shares in a mutual fund? When you sell a stock or bond, we send your order to the exchange, and someone else buys it in exchange for cash. Not so for a mutual fund, it is redeemed to the fund, and they give you cash based on the fund's value, called NAV or Net Asset Value, based on the day's market close.

The mutual fund has 3 ways to come up with redemption money: 1) use the cash on hand, 2) offset redemption requests from new investor funds, or 3) sell some of the holdings in the fund. Most mutual funds don't borrow, so that is not an option. If #3 is selected, some stocks or bonds are sold to meet redemptions. The losses or gains are felt by <u>all the fund investors</u>. Most

---

Indexes are often used as a benchmark or comparison for the performance of other investments.
[251] Shedding Light on "Invisible" Costs: Trading Costs and Mutual Fund Performance -Roger Edelen, Richard Evans & Gregory Kadlec Financial Analysts Journal, Volume 69, 2013

redemptions are requested during declining markets, so it sucks to be a mutual fund investor at that time.

You may be a stand-up, buy-and-hold guy, but is your mutual fund doing the same?

No, it is not! If you look at the average turnover rate, you will be shocked! It is 63% - 115%.[252] WTW! The mutual funds might blame all this buying and selling on you. (You unsophisticated rube, you are why we can't have nice things!) But even if that is the case, it is still a problem for long-term investors if, on average, over 60% of the fund's holdings are sold and then bought again.

Inflows and Outflows: Do They Affect Performance?

This is a difficult argument to make since the research seems undecided. I believe that mutual fund inflows and outflows can affect the fund's investment performance more than is reported. One study by Morningstar stated that funds with high inflows stood a lower chance of outperforming peers. So, a popular fund may underperform? Mutual funds have performance issues that have nothing to do with making good investments.

Here is a disclosure that appeared in a PIMCO Total Return fund (PTTAX) in 2015. It stated that purchases and redemptions "*may cause funds to make investment decisions at inopportune times or prices or miss attractive investment opportunities. Such transactions may also increase a fund's transaction costs, accelerate the realization of taxable income if sales of securities resulted in gains, or otherwise cause a fund to perform differently than intended. While such risks may apply to funds of any size, such risks are heightened in funds with fewer assets under management.*"[253]

My point is that the money going in and out can affect <u>your</u> performance.

Tax Inefficiency

If you hold a mutual fund in a taxable account (non-IRA), you might get a taxable capital gain distribution. Except that there may be a problem, you lost money on the fund. WTW! What the World is going on? Do you remember the redemption request that the fund had to sell investments for? What happens if they sell a stock that has a gain? That is capital gain, and they

---

252 Source: "What is turnover ratio?" Investopedia.com
253 Source Seeking Alpha 'How Do Fund Flows Affect Fund Performance?' by Zack funds.

distribute it to fund investors. What is worse, that gain might have been there before you invested in the fund. So, you get to pay taxes on gains you didn't get. Here is how that goes.

You buy the fund for $100 per share. The market goes down immediately after your investment, and now your fund is $85 per share. Yeah, it sucks to be you. Then, in December, you get a notice that they are distributing $8 per share in capital gains. This is a good news/bad news announcement.

The good news is the capital gain is distributed in cash, and if you reinvest it, you will buy more shares at $77 per share. (You have to deduct the capital gain distribution from the share price.) "The bad news is the capital gain is taxable. The even worse news? Your cost basis is now $108, but the shares are only worth $77. You've effectively paid taxes to 'gain' on an investment that is currently deep in the red. Wow, it really sucks to be you!

"According to Morningstar, the average cost of mutual funds' tax inefficiency is about +1.10%." -Forbes How Much Do Mutual Funds Really Cost? -by Kenneth Kim

It sucks… ok I won't say it again.

Window Dressing, Burying the Bodies and Cold IPO's

Oh yes, the plot thickens with mutual funds. Mutual Funds report their positions at the end of every quarter. So, let's say there is a hot stock in the market. The fund might buy this stock so it is in the top ten holdings even if they determine the run is close to over. As investors look at the fund's top holdings, they see the darling that, frankly, the fund just purchased.

Now, let us say the mutual fund purchased a stock that died. The fund manager and his associates stare at the stock that they just lost a bunch of money on. The fund manager pulls a burner phone out of his pocket and dials Tony Soprano's phone number. "Hey, send Pauly over to pick up his mail." The loser stock gets buried in the woods, and we don't talk about it again.

Mutual Funds sometimes get rid of losers before the quarter ends so the shareholders don't see the losses on the holdings list. (Burying the Bodies) This is shortsighted for a fund that claims to hold positions for long-term growth or value.

Here is another scenario: a mutual fund manager is having lunch at a swanky Manhattan restaurant with his good buddy at an investment bank. The friend laments that their latest IPO[254]

---

[254] An IPO is an initial public offering, in which shares of a private company are made available to the public for the first time. An IPO allows a company to raise equity capital from public investors. -Investopedia

is undersubscribed due to the share price being too high. The fund manager agrees to buy the 'cold IPO' to help out his buddy ol' pal, with your money.

Just a small example of the shenanigans going on with mutual funds. The incestual relationship between mutual funds and some Big Wall Street firms is pretty sick. Some Big Wall Street brokerage firms allow their favorite mutual funds to pay convention or meeting costs so they can pitch to fiduciary (and commission) advisors, brainwashing them into thinking their fund is good for their clients.

According to the study I referred to earlier, these behaviors account for about +2.49% in additional cost.

"Higher Sharpe ratios, in and of themselves, do not necessarily imply better investments."
—Kenneth Kim, PhD, & William Nelson, PhD quote from 'Mutual Funds Exposed'

Diversified to the Max

Finally, mutual funds own 100's or thousands of companies. Remember how I said that researchers agree that diversification is met at 35-40 stocks? There isn't much benefit after that. Why do mutual funds over-diversify? You have to when you have $50 million, $1 billion, or $100 billion in asset value. Being large does not help you make money.

Add it Up

According to the research, if you add up the cost (1.19%, + 1.44%, + 1.10%, + 2.49%) that is +6.22% in cost plus the advisor fee. Is that right? Some of these numbers could be debated, and maybe some funds hold high standards, thus avoiding some of these costs; however, the reality is that there is a lot of cost and inefficiency in mutual funds. The reality is that mutual funds don't make any sense as an investment vehicle for your retirement.[255] I am not convinced by the 6.22% additional costs that the study came up with, but the average cost with hidden trading costs would explain the underperformance issues. The costs involved in mutual funds are simply not worth it. Remember, the average turnover rate is 60%. That is a lot of buying and selling! How do these mutual funds describe themselves as conservative buy and hold with huge turnover?

---

[255] See the article by Kenneth Kim at Forbes.com "How Much do Mutual Funds Really Cost." Sept 24, 2016

Yet Big Wall Street firms are in love with mutual funds. Not just the 'commission brokers' but also the fiduciary advisors. What facts are they using to decide these 'funds' are in their client's best interests?

Brokers/Dealers and RIAs (the fiduciary) sign selling agreements with mutual fund companies. Many of these companies have the following motive; "If we promote the mutual fund, they will pay for our once-a-year party in Vegas," says the Big Wall Street broker firm executive.

Making my Point

Look at the share classes of most mutual funds. Notice there is an institutional share class that usually requires a million dollars or more to purchase. In my experience, these shares have better performance and lower fees. They still have to deal with redemptions, but larger investors are less likely to liquidate. Vanguard lowered its minimum investment in its institutional target date fund from $100 million to $5 million. The exodus caused massive capital gains to investors who were still in the fund. The Massachusetts Secretary William Galvin stated. "These extraordinary capital gains were caused by Vanguard's conscious decision to benefit ultra-wealthy shareholders over Main Street investors." Why did the ultra-wealthy dump the fund when the minimum was reduced to a paltry $5 million?[256]

The washed didn't want to be sullied with the unwashed, and they left the capital gains to others to deal with.

My Conversion Away from Mutual Funds

I made a change away from mutual funds in my practice in 2010. Once I ignored the hype and brainwashing that I suffered at my former firms, I was able to see that I wasn't meeting my clients' objectives, particularly in factoring risk and performance with mutual funds. I saw that the best funds that I could select performed really badly in 2008. I lost my faith in the 'sharp and savvy' guys of the mutual fund machine. But to my defense, no one was really using ETFs before 2008. ETFs had $417 billion invested in 2005, they crossed over $1 trillion invested in 2009[257] and has grown to the $19.2 trillion+ in 2025. So, I wasn't the only one to figure this out.

In Chapter 3, I discussed the conflicts in the Big Box Big Wall Street firms. It is hard for some clients to move away from these relationships they have had for many years. Likewise, it

---

256 Source Wealthmanagement.com 'Vanguard to Pay $6M Over Target-Date Fund Investigation'
257 See www.marketsmedia.com/global-etf-assets-reach-record-21-2-trillion/

was hard for me to realize that my training was flawed and conflicted. My change put my clients ahead of anything else (even my own ego). Do you think changing advisors to establish an income approach in retirement is in your and your family's best interest?

After all, you made money!

You have so much more in your account today than when you started. I had a new client tell me that his mutual funds had doubled in value in the past ten years. He had done well, except I showed him that the market had gone up fourfold in the same period. The reality was that he had made money, but his funds failed to do as well as the markets had with the same risk or possibly more.[258]

Early in my career, I was mentally conditioned to believe the 'sharp and savvy' guys would be the safest place with the best returns for my clients' investment dollars. Underperformance was the premium of conservative investments. Sure, they didn't make as much as the index, but it was because they didn't take the raw risks of the market. You are safer with the 'sharp and savvy' guys. It took 2008 for me to come to Jesus and learn the truth. The mutual funds I used lost as much money as the market and more. I used all the modern portfolio theory statistics, MorningStar© fund analytics, and benchmarking measures in my selection. My fund costs were mostly below .75% lower than the average of 1.19%. I wasn't careless or random in my research or choices.

My move to ETFs and individual stocks drastically improved my overall performance for my clients.[259] My ETF portfolio (currently) costs an average between .20% - .35%.[260] A fraction of what mutual funds charge in costs and hidden costs. It hurts my heart when I see portfolios full of mutual fund investments when going through our onboarding process. By moving away from mutual funds to individual stocks or ETFs could boost your performance and align your objectives.[261]

Why do you want to Rollover your 401K, 403b, 457, or other Employer Sponsor Plans (ESP)

---

258 We expect a dividend portfolio to underperform growth investments during a bull market and have less volatility during bear markets while maintaining cash flow for income or reinvestment. This client had a market growth expectation that his mutual funds drastically underdelivered.

259 My memory of performance should be considered anecdotal only.

260 This percentage can change. Currently, our highest ETF in the portfolio cost .85%.

261 Past Performance is not a Guarantee of Future Results.

The market has brought down the expenses of employer-sponsored plans. Some plans at large companies have low-cost funds. According to the 401k source, plan cost as a percent of assets is 1.12%.[262] Even if the cost is .40%, you know that isn't all of it. There are the hidden costs of mutual funds to consider. So why don't Employer-Sponsored Plans (401ks) use ETFs?

It's the administrative and record-keeping challenges. 401ks and the like are not set up for intraday trading. With mutual funds, the plan gets the money with your investment instructions and submits it before 4 pm EST. This is not so easy with ETFs. Some small plans are able to use ETFs. I have seen an ETF mutual fund in some plans. (A mutual fund that invests in ETFs only and totally NOT the same as investing in an ETF!)

There are better options outside of the ESP. If you are in the transition stage and your plan allows it, do an ***in-service rollover*** to a Rollover IRA. Most plans allow this after age 60. How do you find out if an in-service rollover is allowed in your plan? Don't ask HR; call the customer service number on your statement. Sometimes, you can initiate the rollover on the phone. Try to have the money go directly to your IRA. If they mail you the check, do not cash it, sign it, or look at it. Forward it to your IRA ASAP. You are allowed to do as many direct rollovers in a calendar year as you want, but only one *indirect rollover*. If you get 2 checks from any IRAs and deposit them in your bank, then write a check to your IRA (within 60 days), the IRS will disallow the second amount you received. That will be taxable, and if under 59 ½, have a 10% penalty. If both checks are categorized as indirect, then the second will become taxable. Make sure you do this correctly.

ETFs: The Basics

Exchange-traded funds (ETFs) are built on transparency and diversification. Unlike the internal "black box" of some mutual funds, an ETF's basket is established by clear, rules-based parameters. If a stock is added or removed, it isn't done on a manager's whim—it's done by a committee following a strict, transparent index. This essentially eliminates the "style drift" and high-turnover shenanigans that often plague mutual funds.

One of the biggest perks is that an ETF trades throughout the day on an exchange just like a stock, while mutual funds only settle once a day after the market closes. While you own shares of the ETF rather than holding the individual stock certificates of the companies yourself, the ETF trust does physically own the underlying securities to back your investment.

---

[262]Source:401ksource.com/wp-content/uploads/Infographic-Breakdown-of-Small-Plan-Fees-100k-22nd-Edition.pdf

The Tax Efficiency "Secret Sauce"

The real magic of the ETF is its tax efficiency. ETFs use a specialized "in-kind" exchange process to handle redemptions. Instead of selling stocks for cash—which triggers the capital gains taxes that haunt mutual fund investors—the ETF swaps shares of the stocks themselves with market makers. Because this isn't a "sale" in the eyes of the IRS, capital gain distributions are rare and usually very small.

When you sell your ETF, you'll still owe capital gains or losses based on your specific purchase price, but you won't be hit with "phantom gains" from other people's trading.

Lowering the Temperature

While an ETF's price will still fluctuate based on the market value of the stocks it holds, you gain stability through broad diversification rather than betting on a single company. The internal costs are incredibly low, and there are no hidden "back-room" trading fees.

Because the basket follows a strict index, you can target specific industries or income styles with zero deviation. For our strategy, we focus on high-yield dividend ETFs that produce consistent cash flow. Combine the high tax efficiency with the lack of "manager churn," and I say: **winner-winner chicken dinner.**

Warning! The mutual funds are scaling the walls.

In 2005, there were about $441 billion invested in ETFs; by early 2026, there was $21.2 trillion! A new player has entered the arena; however, it is called the Active Traded ETF. Active ETFs are like a mutual fund in an ETF costume. Mutual Funds wanting to get in on the ETF craze made an ETF. They've fixed the tax problem, but they kept the high fees and the manager's ego. They don't target an index or basket of securities but have portfolio managers (sharp and savvy guys again) that make investment decisions for the portfolio but charge 2 – 4xs more than passive ETFs. Understand? I don't like them either. They are still more efficient and less costly than most mutual funds. Active ETFs account for 5.5% and growing of the ETF market.[263]

---

263 According to ETFGI (ETF and ETP research and consultancy firm) see the article "The unlimited potential of actively managed ETFs" StateStreet.com

If you're looking for a Capital Fortress, why pay for a 'sharp & savvy guy' to guess when the ETF does the same job for pennies? Stick to the passive side—it's more predictable and lets you keep more of your hard-earned cash.

SMA

This one took me a while to come around to. Separately Managed Accounts are professional asset managers who manage your account in individual stocks and bonds. The is usually an amount of customization involved and you own the stocks and bonds in your account. It can be like owning your personal ETF. Firms offering this service in the past would charge 1% to 3% in management fees but now many are in line with ETF charges.

Some SMAs do frequent trading, while others look for triggers when selling their positions. If your advisor recommends an SMA, beware of the costs and investment philosophy, and not just the past performance. Also, beware of the 'this is only offered to clients with 1 million dollars' pitch. We all have SMAs with $1 million minimums, just saying.

The million-dollar minimum SMAs are not necessarily better because they are stroking your ego.

I say this because I have met some clients who thought that their million-dollar minimum SMA advisor was private club status. Guess what? They put their pants on the same way everyone else does. (At Toro Bravo we stand up our pants and jump in) Is the advisor doing typical asset allocation or investing for *cash flow*?

SMAs are widely different, but depending on your situation, they can bring a high level of professional trading and management with tax efficiency. Our SMAs focus on *income* investing across bonds and stocks. Surprised? Look for the philosophical alignment with the SMA and be less impressed with their size and importance.

As your fiduciary advisor, we evaluate the process and performance of the SMA firms we employ and ensure the agreed-upon objectives are being met.

The bigger they are, the harder they fall.

1. **Long-Term Capital Management** —This fund was led by smart elitists (the ones who want you to give up eating beef for cricket protein, but they will still eat beef) with 1 billion of investor money (in 1998). Nobel-winning economists and Big Wall Street traders ran the shop. They promised they could take your risk to zero but ***nearly caused a global financial crisis in 1998***. The Federal Reserve bailed them out in September of that year. **Nobel prizes don't stop market crashes.** Peak assets $125 Billion

2. **SAC Capital** —Steve Cohen, a politically connected hedge fund manager, had nearly $50 billion under management. The SEC raided SAC's offices and convicted eight employees of securities violations, including insider trading. They paid 1.8 billion in fines and stopped managing outside funds. Steve Cohen was never charged with anything. ***Politics and connections don't always make you money unless you are Nancy Pelosi.***

3. **Amaranth Advisors** – Nicolaus Maonis started the fund in 2000 and had amassed $9 billion by 2006. The fund folded in 2006 due to derivative bets causing losses of 6.6 billion in losses. (Wow sucks to be them.) ***Don't bet the farm on one commodity.***

4. **Marin Capital-** a California-based Hedge Fund that did credit arbitrage. It brought in $1.7 billion in capital. Debt arbitrage involves investing in convertible bonds that can be later converted into common stock of the company and sold for a profit. I imagine they bragged about how safe their strategy was. This strategy is considered low risk except (now you know it is not good when you see accept.) Marin loaded up on GM convertible bonds. GM credit was lowered to junk credit status four years before GM went bankrupt. The 'low risk' fund was crushed and closed on June 14, 2005. ***"Low Risk" is often a marketing story when investing in stocks.***

5. **Archegos Capital Management-** This fund had charismatic manager Sung Kook 'Bill' Hwang, who lied to all of Big Wall Street, causing over $100 billion in losses to companies in its portfolio while sinking his own $36 billion fund in 2021. (But he was a Christian, and so was Judas) ***Charisma is not a substitute for compliance.***

6. **Melvin Capital** -Due to the GameStop short squeeze in the first three months of 2021, Melvin Capital lost 49% of its value. Prior to that, between 2014 and 2020, they had seen annual returns of 30 percent. In response to this hemorrhaging, Citadel and Point72 provided a $3 billion bailout. On May 18th, 2022, ***Melvin Capital closed because of a video game store (GameStop) and a bunch of belligerent subreddit kids. Never underestimate "meddling kids" with a smartphone. Sorry, that's hilarious!***

"I'd have gotten away with it too if it wasn't for you meddling kids!"
—every unmasked criminal in Scooby Doo.

Don't be impressed with size or advanced degrees as your only criteria to invest with any manager. Many garages seem to be the birthplaces of awesome companies.

I didn't include Bernie Madolf in this list because he was a fraud who was not conducting a legitimate business.

Bond Mutual funds

My late career mentor, David Scranton, in his book 'The Retirement Income Stor-e,' talked about Bond Funds. They seem like good investments. Bonds are good, but mutual funds—oh, that is where it falls apart. First, let's consider why you want a bond.

Bonds are loans to businesses, states, cities or the government. You get a fixed interest rate and your principal is returned at the end of the bond term. Thanks to our markets you can sell a publicly traded bond at any time.

The price of a bond is pretty much controlled by interest rates. (Other factors can also influence a bond value. For example, if a corporate bond has its credit rating cut, the bond price will suffer.) The chart below shows what would happen if interest rates were to go down; the bond price would rise. (Coupon is the interest rate of the bond) The opposite would happen if interest rates were increased. See illustration 6.8. The Federal Reserve Bank (the Fed) sets the interest rates.

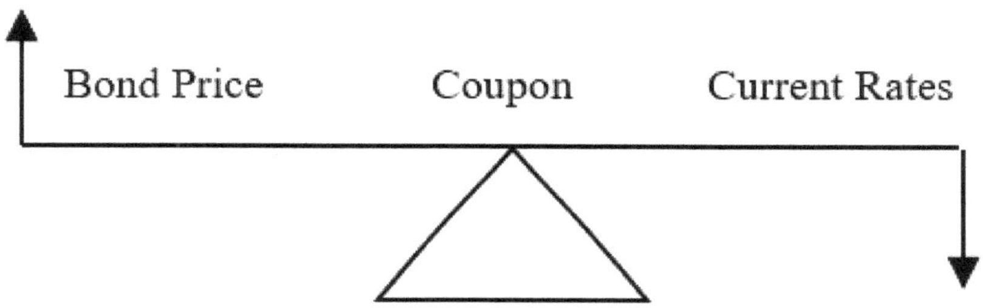

Illustration 6.8

Now compare the features of an Individual Bond to a Bond Mutual Fund[264]

Individual Bonds

- Permanent Income -yes
- Definite Maturity -yes
- Return of Principal -yes
- No Management Fees
- Know What You Own -yes

Bond Mutual Funds

- Fixed Income -no
- Definite income -no
- Return of Principal -no
- Management Fees -yes
- Know What You Own -no

[264] The following was taken from 'The Retirement Income Stor-e' by David Scranton, CFA, CFP, CLU, ChFC

"The definition of a bond mutual fund is shares of a stock that own bonds." —David Scranton CFA, CFP, CLU, ChFC

Remember how I said mutual funds cash settle redemptions? Outflows are even more devastating in a bond fund. The difference is that there is unlikely to be any growth to get back your losses. Stocks can increase in value, but losses in a bond are likely to be permanent. (Okay, I won't say it again.) A bond fund is not the same as owning bonds. You don't have any of the features of a bond and additional risks.

You can't rely on the interest income since it can be cut in a bond mutual fund. A bond can't cut its coupon (except in bankruptcy). A bond fund has no maturity date, no principal return guarantee, and charges you fees. You are already paying a fee to your advisor, so why not cut out the fund and invest directly in bonds? An advisor who specializes in income should be able to do this. In a fund, it is difficult to know what you own. The end of the quarter report could have already changed. A portfolio of individual bonds in your account is easy to see.

If you don't own bonds individually, a bond ETF is far better than a bond mutual fund.

"It ain't what you don't know that gets you into trouble. It's what you know for sure that just ain't so." —Mark Twain

Annuities

The financial media is clearly biased when it comes to this topic. Why? Here is a reason: they depend on Big Wall Street firms for advertising dollars and market intelligence for the articles they write. Big Wall Street needs you to stay on their platforms. (That's one likely reason they did not fight the DOL rule) There was an RIA firm that did a whole media campaign with the statement, "I hate Annuities." Of course, he makes his money on assets (i.e., stocks and bonds) invested on his platform. I found his comments on annuities to be incomplete and misleading.

Even if you never invest in annuities, you can't deny them as a powerful retirement income solution. One problem I see with the annuity discussion is that they are often sold through a sales pitch instead of a retirement planning process.

Now, before some smart-alec says, "I knew it; it's an annuity book," I say in response, "Stick it in your ear." The research indicates that Annuities should be part of a retiree's base income, like Social Security. Annuities are income-producing investments. Some retirement ships will use them, and some may not. I don't judge.

Now, without bias, let's discuss the topic of Annuities.

"I would be careful with a Fiduciary to this respect because, unfortunately, there are a lot of fiduciaries out there who are not doing what's in their client's best interest because they're not using annuities, life insurance, or long-term care." —Tom Hegna Economist, Financial Writer, Retirement Expert and PBS host of the 'Don't Worry Retire Happy' show.[265]

Retirement Researchers like Annuities

I started this chapter with Nobel prize winner William Sharp's quote, "Retirement income planning is 'The hardest and nastiest problem in finance.' Why is this? Because of the way most retirements are planned, you have a high risk of an Apollo 13 'oxygen tank' explosion during your mission.

Before you say so? Volatility can be a retirement killer. It can change your life.

Whether it takes one year or fifteen years for a retirement-altering event to happen, you risk running out of power (money) before the parachutes deploy. Hitting the ocean at terminal speed is a 'nasty' problem.

So, as the financial media deride annuities and the DOL tries to discourage you from using them, what are the retirement income researchers saying? Here is some actual research to consider. —Dr. Michael Finke

One of the most consistent voices on this topic is Dr. Michael Finke, a professor of wealth management at The American College of Financial Services and the Frank M. Engle Distinguished Chair in Economic Security. (I know I promised to avoid whitepapers, but sometimes you have to go to the source!)

In his research, specifically the whitepaper *"Portfolio Income Insurance: Understanding the Benefits of a Contingent Deferred Annuity,"*

---

[265] Source: Avoiding Social Insecurity by Martha Shedding.

Dr. Finke argues that an annuity shouldn't just be viewed as an investment—it should be viewed as

Portfolio Income Insurance.

Dr. Finke highlights four critical "retirement leaks" that this type of insurance is designed to plug:

- **Longevity Risk:** As lifespans stretch, retirees face the very real danger of outliving their savings, especially if the market underperforms in the early years of retirement.
- **Sequence of Returns Risk:** Significant investment losses early on can permanently strain a portfolio's ability to provide a reliable paycheck for a 20- or 30-year retirement.
- **The Spending Squeeze:** Without a protected floor, a retiree may be forced to significantly slash their standard of living to avoid running out of money during a market downturn.
- **The Guarantee:** Insuring the income stream guarantees that you can spend a fixed, predictable amount throughout retirement, regardless of how "belligerent" the markets behave.

In Dr. Finke's whitepaper (I know I said I tried to avoid whitepapers, sorry) named "Portfolio Income Insurance: Understanding the Benefits of a Contingent Deferred Annuity."[266] He makes the case for annuities in your retirement. (I had the chance to discuss this section with Dr. Finke. He indicated that he had more recent research on this topic. I will keep what I found.)

Whitepaper Highlights & Quotes

- If you lose -30% in the first year of retirement, the probability of maintaining your spending is 37.4%. (4.5 % withdraw rate)
- If you make 0% in the first year of retirement, the probability of maintaining your spending is 75.9%
- If you make +30% in the first year of retirement the probability of maintaining your spending is 91.8% (The Apollos or any NASA program would never launch with an 8.2% chance of failure.)
- "Buying insurance trades growth in wealth over time for income certainty."

---

266 This article covers one type of annuity but the principals apply to other annuities.

- "A risk-averse individual accepts a modest decrease in wealth in order to avoid the possibility of a significant and random negative event."
- "Portfolio insurance allows a retiree to maintain a lifestyle free of the possibility that spending today could jeopardize their ability to live well later in retirement."
- "...the CDA gives the retiree a license to spend their savings in retirement while unprotected investments demand greater caution."

In other articles, Dr. Finke shows that he is not a fan of the 4% rule.[267]

"The real degree of safety with the rule depends a lot on when you retire and whether you get unlucky or not,"

As Dr. Finke puts it, "if you wouldn't leave your home uninsured, why would you leave the income that pays for that home to chance?"

The "Professor of Longevity": Moshe A. Milevsky

If Michael Finke provides the "insurance" logic, Dr. Moshe A. Milevsky provides the raw mathematical proof. As a tenured professor with a Ph.D. in financial economics and a master's in mathematical statistics, Milevsky doesn't deal in "stories"—he deals in probabilities.

In his book, *"In Defense of Annuities: From Accumulation to Decumulation,"* Milevsky argues that the greatest risk to your retirement isn't the stock market—it's **longevity risk**. He posits that an annuity is the only financial vehicle capable of generating "mortality credits," a technical way of saying the insurance company rewards you for the simple act of staying healthy and outliving the "averages."

Mortality Credits.

What they are: This is the "secret sauce" of annuities that no other investment has. It's the extra return you get from the pool of people who don't live as long as expected. According to Milevsky, "Mutual funds give you market returns. Annuities give you market returns plus mortality credits. It's the only investment that pays you more just for staying alive."

Milevsky's research shows that by "pensionizing" a portion of your nest egg, you aren't just buying a product; you are hedging against the uncertainty of time itself. As he often notes, you can't manage what you can't measure—and you can't measure exactly how long you'll need your

---

267 Think Advisor 'Ask the Retirement Expert: Michael Finke on Rethinking the 4% Rule' By John Manganaro

money to last. In Milevsky's argument, as the "Science of Sustainability." He believes that for a retirement plan to be mathematically sound, it must include a life annuity to act as a personal pension.

How Tom Hegna illustrates it

Tom Hegna defines mortality credits (which he also calls longevity credits) as the "secret sauce" of retirement planning—a unique form of "Retirement Alpha" that only life insurance companies can manufacture. His definition centers on the idea that mortality credits are a financial reward for living longer, generated by the pooling of risk among a large group of people.

The "5 Ladies" Story

To make the concept easy to grasp, Tom Hegna famously uses his 5 Ladies story.

1. "Five 90-year-old Ladies" analogy: Five 90-year-old ladies go on vacation and each put $100 into a box (Total = $500).
2. They agree that next year, whoever is still alive will split the money in the box.
3. The next year, unfortunately, one lady has passed away. The remaining four ladies open the box and split the $500, receiving $125 each.
4. They just earned a 25% return in one year. He then asks: "How much was invested in the stock market? Zero. What was the interest rate? Zero."

The "return" came from mortality credits, as Milevsky describes in his research.

"An annuity is the only math-based solution to that problem." —Dr. Moshe A Milevsky

Wade Pfau: The Architect of Safety-First Planning

If we are looking for the scientist who mapped the modern retirement landscape, we look to **Wade Pfau**, Ph.D. As the director of the **Retirement Income Certified Professional (RICP)** program at The American College of Financial Services, Pfau's research has dismantled many of the myths Wall Street tells retirees.

In his *Retirement Planning Guidebook*, Pfau makes it clear that annuities aren't just an "option"—they deserve an equal seat at the table with any other strategy. He identifies

Longevity Risk as a key threat that an income annuity manages more effectively than a standard portfolio of stocks and bonds.

Solving the "Annuity Puzzle"

Pfau often speaks about the "Annuity Puzzle"—the mathematical mystery of why more people don't use a tool that is so efficient at funding retirement. In an interview with *ThinkAdvisor*, he noted that many advisors are stuck in a "Total Return" mindset, relying solely on the stock market because they want to keep "optionality".

My Take: While Wade is polite about it, I'll be blunt. That "optionality" often translates to asset-based fees for Big Wall Street firms. They want your money sitting on their trading platforms where they can shave off their percentage every year. An annuity is their "hated enemy" because it prioritizes your paycheck over their profit margin.

As Pfau told *Annuity.org*: *"If you're trying to fund your retirement, the annuity is a very efficient way to do that"*. When the guy who wrote the textbook on retirement income says it's efficient, it's time to stop listening to the sales pitches and start looking at the science.

"Annuities deserve an equal seat at the table with any other retirement income strategy."

"The whole idea that annuities mean giving up something is not true."

"Longevity risk is one of the key risks which can be managed effectively by an income annuity."

Wade said this in a Think Advisor interview:[268]

"Many advisors have one retirement income style in mind: total return. That is, they're comfortable relying on the stock market as a funding source for retirement, and they want to keep as much optionality as possible and make changes in the future. But that style doesn't apply to everyone."

I have said that this thinking of 'Annuities Bad' comes from the Big Wall Street firms and RIAs wanting to maximize their earnings. Asset-based fees and the revenue produced by assets residing on their trading platform make the annuity investment a hated enemy. Wade didn't say that, but I did. Remember, they make more money if they invest you for a 1.5% fee in market-based securities.

---

[268] ThinkAdvisor: Wade Pfau finding the best retirement Income Strategy for your client September 28, 2021

"The annuity puzzle is just that — if you're trying to fund your retirement, the annuity is a very efficient way to do that. And it's puzzling why there's not more use of commercial annuities," —Wade Pfau, author of "Safety-First Retirement Planning," quoted to Annuity.org.

Dr. David Blanchett: The "Retirement Spending Smile"

Dr. Blanchett is a researcher who works closely with Wade Pfau and serves as the Head of Retirement Research for PGIM (and formerly Morningstar). He is the one who proved that retirees don't spend the same amount every year—a concept he calls the **"Retirement Spending Smile."**

- **The Insight:** His research shows that spending typically drops in the middle of retirement (the "Slow-Go" years) before rising at the end due to healthcare.
- **The "Annuity" Connection:** Blanchett's math shows that because people spend more early on (the "Go-Go" years), having a guaranteed floor from an annuity allows them to spend more confidently when they are young enough to enjoy it.

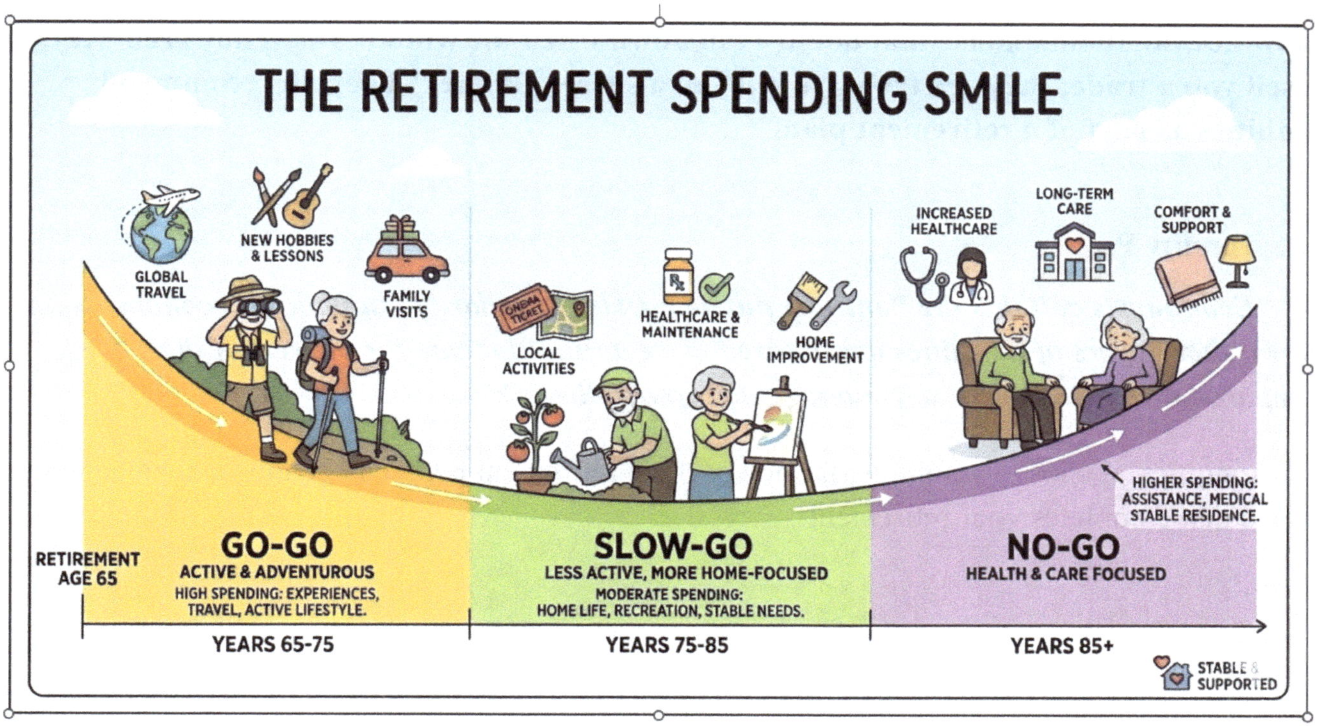

The Nobel Prize Solution: Richard Thaler

Nobel laureate Richard Thaler famously noted that economists are stumped by the **"Annuity Puzzle."** Using standard mathematical assumptions, they've proven that people who use annuities are guaranteed more annual income for life than those who try to "self-manage" through the ups and downs of the stock market.

So, why is it a puzzle? Because despite the math, many people still hesitate.

The Real Secret: Thaler's research into behavioral economics suggests we are our own worst enemies. We are afraid of "losing control" of our money. Big Wall Street firms exploit this fear, convincing you to keep your money in high-turnover mutual funds so they can collect their fees. But as Thaler points out, an annuity isn't about giving up control; it's about **taking control** of your lifestyle by insuring your income.

As we've seen from the "Hall of Shame"—from Long-Term Capital to Melvin Capital—even the "smartest guys in the room" can't guarantee a return. But an annuity, positioned correctly within your retirement plan, acts as the final piece of the puzzle that completes your "Capital Fortress." It turns "maybe" into "mandatory" when it comes to your retirement paycheck.

Wall Street is a high-stakes casino, and these professors are the master architects who know how to build a house that doesn't fall down when the wind blows. They aren't trying to sell you a trade; they are trying to sell you a successful life." They all recommend annuities as part of a retirement plan.

The Annuity Puzzle

"Economists call this the "annuity puzzle." Using standard assumptions, economists have shown that buyers of annuities are assured more annual income for the rest of their lives, compared with people who self-manage their portfolios..." [269]

Annuities, if chosen within the framework of a retirement plan, can be the final piece in the puzzle that completes your retirement.

---

[269] The New York Times 'The Annuity Puzzle' By Richard H. Thaler

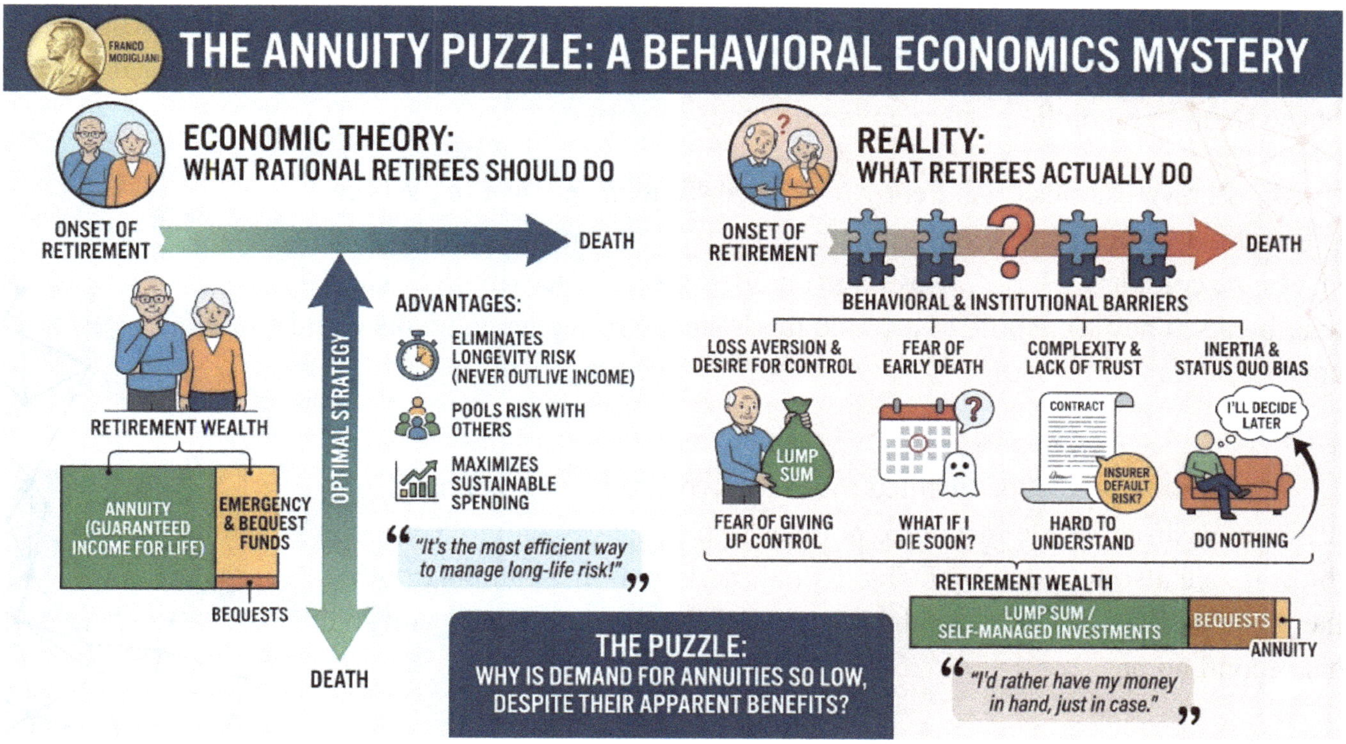

"The basic idea is that you must have enough guaranteed lifetime income to cover your basic living expenses in retirement. Once your 'Paychecks' are secure, you can use the rest of your money for your 'Playchecks'—the things you want to do."
—Tom Hegna, Economist, Financial Writer, Retirement Expert, and PBS host of the 'Don't Worry, Retire Happy' show

Life Insurance Companies are Generally Safe

As I discussed in Chapter 5, Insurance companies are generally viewed as safe for your capital. However, remember the following:

Remember, the guarantees provided by life insurance and annuities are backed by the credit and financial standing of the life insurance company. Life Insurance policies and annuities are <u>not</u> backed by any government agency, credit union, or FDIC. We recommend using companies with A- or higher credit ratings (or equivalent).

Insurance companies survived the Great Depression and helped iconic businesses with capital. But for context insurance companies can go bankrupt and the government bailout AIG. These seem to be outliers. Here are some other examples:

JC Penny - James Cash Penny took massive loans against his Whole Life policies (1929) and kept his business afloat. It is worth noting that insurance companies have always been more conservative with their capital over banks. They were able to provide funds to JCPenney when banks could not.

McDonalds - It's documented that Ray Kroc borrowed against two different cash-value life insurance policies to pay his key employees along the way. He also founded McDonald's hallmark branding campaign using the precious liquidity provided by his whole life insurance policy and sold his second home.

Disney- Walt Disney used his whole life policy to provide the necessary liquidity to fund his dream.[270]

Annuities are Tax-Deferred and Protected from Creditors

If you have taxable money in a Non-Qualified Annuity (meaning non-IRA), you will not pay taxes on the interest earned until it is withdrawn. (The interest comes out first, so it can be taxed. Thank you, IRS) It will be considered ordinary income and not capital gain income. Go back to Chapter 5 about how the taxes work. Your effective rate might be lower than the capital gain rate, so be careful not to make snap judgments on taxes you might not owe.

If you have a Non-Qualified Deferred Annuity, and you want to change to another annuity you can do a 1035 exchange, avoiding a tax bill on any earnings you have in the contract.

Also, you have enhanced creditor and bankruptcy protection (depending on your state) for you and your heirs. Inherited IRAs are not protected from creditors. An IRA that passes to your

[270] Source: Banking Truths.com Famous Entrepreneurs Who Used Whole Life Insurance as their own Bank. (Some of the texts was directly taken from this article.)

heirs via an annuity would be protected if your heir was being sued or filing for bankruptcy.[271] It also transfers outside of probate after your death.

You can invest your 401k, IRA, 403b, 457, or other employer-sponsored plan into an annuity, but there is no additional tax deferral for doing that.

Think of Annuities like Cars

The biggest problem with annuities is understanding them. Many articles define annuities as a series of payments over one's lifetime, which is literally one type of annuity.

If you tell me, "I am looking at an annuity," it is like saying I am looking at a car. What information are you giving me? All you really said is you are looking a box with an engine and four wheels. That's it. I effectively have no idea what you are looking at. Is it a 4-door, 2-door, pick-up truck, minivan, cargo van, full-size van, sports car, electric car, luxury car, and so on? There are numerous annuities as well. I won't get into the weeds with the details, but just know your money objectives and risk tolerance factors into this decision. After that, we will discuss how to design a portfolio customized to your individual situation and desired outcome using some of the options in the Income-producing investments.

This is why dogmatic statements about annuities are ignorant. There is a lot of variety and difference. Like fees, some have high fees some have no fees. Finally, since this is an overview, I won't cover all annuities available, just the ones I see commonly used for retirement.

Annuities Get a Bad Review in the Media

So, let's get this straight: the Financial Planning Academics like annuities, particularly for income benefits and risk reduction, but much of the media does not. Could the fact that asset companies own significant positions in the media companies like Comcast, Sky, Disney, Warner Bros., and Fox affect their coverage?

---

[271] In Texas the protections for heirs are the same as the owner of the annuity. You might need to check the protections provided if you live in another state.

As of early 2026, the landscape of media ownership is defined by a "Big Six" media companies that dominate the market, with names like Vanguard, BlackRock, and State Street appearing at the top of the shareholder lists for almost all of them.

Summary of Top Shareholders (Estimated 2026)

Media Giant	Top Shareholder 1	Top Shareholder 2	Top Shareholder 3
Disney	Vanguard (~8%)	BlackRock (~6.5%)	State Street (~4%)
Comcast	Vanguard (~9%)	BlackRock (~7%)	State Street (~4%)
Paramount-Warner	Vanguard (~10%)	BlackRock (~7%)	State Street (~6%)
Fox Corp	Murdoch Family*	Vanguard	BlackRock

Asset managers have an interest in funds NOT leaving their platforms or the stock market. It is hard to believe they don't influence the Media to support their interests. Fidelity is the fourth pillar.

Digital giants like Amazon (MGM) and Apple (Apple TV+) are "self-owned" in the sense that they are too large to be dominated by a single asset manager, though Vanguard and BlackRock remain their largest shareholders as well.

My Point is

The major asset management companies influence the financial media. They don't want your money to leave their platforms. It wouldn't be the first time institutions influenced the media and government to do their bidding. Earlier in this chapter, I discussed how quiet the asset managers were as the Department of Labor attempted to take over investment advice and the ability for retirees to make their own investment decisions.

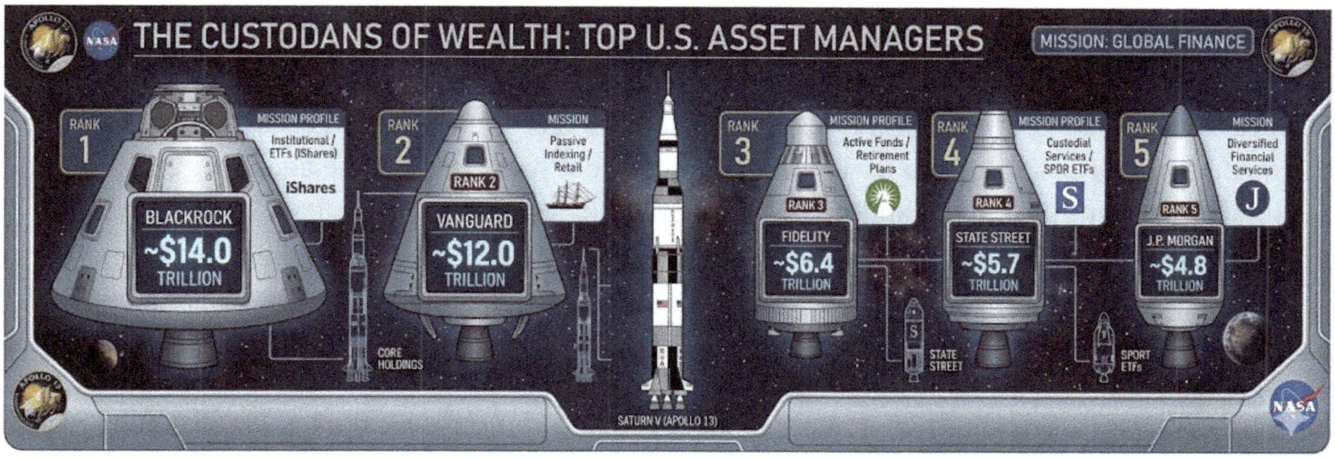

Summing Up

I believe annuities should be used for three primary purposes. Generate guaranteed and sometimes lifetime income, portfolio risk reduction, and tax deferral. (There is no additional tax deferral in IRA annuities)

The Types of Annuities[272]

SPIA- (Income Investment)

Single Premium Immediate Annuity. This is your classic payment for the rest of your life. You give your money to the insurance company, and they pay you a check (monthly, quarterly, semi-annual, or annual) over your lifetime or a specified number of years. The biggest caveat here is you lose control of the capital. For example, if you give the insurance company $100,000, you will get a payment of 6-8% of the amount (depending on your age) for life with a 10-year certain payout. What if you die? You can guarantee at least ten years of payments to go to your heirs.[273]

If an SPIA is a consideration in your retirement ship design, then 'SHOP IT' around. Different insurance companies have better or worse offers. Sometimes, the minimum payout (if you die) is less than you gave them, so be careful. I rarely recommend an SPIA for retirement income due to losing control of your principal. For older folks who expect a long lifespan, the payouts can be generous. I have not seen a SPIA with inflation adjustment either. That means you get a fixed payment that won't go up.

---

[272] Not inclusive of all types of annuities.
[273] All kinds of terms can be specified in these contracts. This is one example.

Fixed Rate Annuity- (Less Boring than CDs, Income Investment)

This is structured like a CD but is not a CD. Annuities are NOT FDIC insured. You pick the number of years, and you get an interest rate. The principal is stable and guaranteed by the insurance company. You can defer the interest or have it paid to you. The agent is generally paid a commission by the company and not by you. So, 100% of your deposit is at work for you. In fixed-rate annuities, there are generally no asset management costs either. Since the account isn't managed, the advisor's getting a commission doesn't go against your interest and is less costly than paying a fee to the advisor.

These interest rates are often generous, but be careful. The devil is in the details. Here is a personal story, in 2002 (I am guessing here, but it was a long time ago), I had a client who wanted to get the best rate on an annuity. He showed me an annuity with a 5% rate in a postcard ad. The best rate I could find was 4%. Then I looked at the deal more closely. It would pay 5% for 3 years and then the best rate they would offer new clients for 3 years after that. (6-year contract) I pointed this out, and he said rates will likely be higher, so no problem.

One thing about insurance companies is that they always follow the contract (that they wrote) to the letter.

After three years, the company would come out with another contract with the same name and #2 at the end. The rate on the old contract is now 3%, which they don't sell to anyone, so it's the best rate. New clients are offered product #2 at a much higher rate. The client was right. Interest rates were higher, except his rate went down. If he liquidated, he would pay a surrender charge and lose money trying to switch. I don't mean to be cynical, but don't depend on the generosity of the insurance company. They will follow the contract.

Another problem is fees. There could be all kinds of ridiculous and costly fees (like a fee to withdraw funds or to set up an auto draft of interest) in the contract. The good companies don't do this. If you have a seasoned and knowledgeable independent advisor who can sell any company, not just one or two, he or she will get you a good contract with a highly-rated company with the best rate available. Ask for comparisons and tell the agent you're shopping. (Suddenly, your advisor is looking for the best rate instead of offering the company he is comfortable with).

We use field marketing organizations to shop for the insurance companies that meet our criteria when selecting a company for a client who wants a fixed-rate annuity. We can also avoid companies that pull the shenanigans I spoke about.

One additional problem. The rate you get is only good until the term ends. Then you have to find another contract if the renewal rate stinks. Can we permanently solve the income problem with another type of annuity that has lifetime income? Keep reading.

Fixed Rate Annuities need to be shopped for new rates after the term expires.

This could be a problem when you reach your 80's. Insurance companies may not offer their products if you are 80 or 85 years old. I have seen some elderly with fixed annuities paying only 1%-2% because that was the renewal rate. One of the reasons we recommend longer-term Fixed Index Annuities. I will describe these later.

Variable Annuities (VA) - (Born to Be Wild with Risk, Growth Investment)

Brokers love variable annuities. I used to, as well. Here is the pitch and reality. A variable annuity can only be sold by a broker registered with FINRA or, in some cases, with an RIA. You deposit your money (or rollover an IRA account) into the VA. The VA will have a list of mutual fund-like investments called subaccounts. (If it walks like a duck and talks like a duck, then it's a Sub Account!) These non-mutual funds are very similar to mutual funds, and now your money is in the stock market, oh yum. (No dividend funds or dividends in the VAs.)

*Note: When buying a VA, you should ask for a fact sheet, a company-produced illustration, and a prospectus. Your income amount will be reflected in the illustration, so you can see what that looks like. As always, past performance does not guarantee future results.

Next are the benefits. Some VAs have no benefits at all but may have a really low-cost structure. Most offer a return of purchase payment (if you die) minus withdrawals minus fees. Others lock in the quarterly or anniversary value if it is higher than the previous value. In a volatile market, if you die reading the statement, your family will get one of these values. I have seen many clients' heirs get more than the statement value due to the death benefit.

Income Benefits

Now comes income benefits. VAs are all over the board on this one. Let me give one example. You get a 5% living benefit. Income starts at 5% of your original deposit and goes up when the value of the subaccounts rises (calculated on the anniversary date). If there is no growth or withdrawal, your lifetime income will remain the same. If you suffer from bad performance or you live too long, the income will continue for your lifetime even if the account goes to zero. Each company has a variety of twists on this income benefit. So, the devil is in the details.

Here is the problem with VA's. They are usually expensive. (There are a few that are very inexpensive and have no benefits) but again, we are back to owning mutual funds, and you know how I feel about that! (Oh, not mutual funds, I mean sub-accounts. I keep messing that up) So how expensive? If you get one with the living benefits (the death benefit is usually not a big concern unless you die, then it sucks to be you), ***you are looking at 2.5%-3.5% in total annual costs***. (They waive the annual $30 account fee if you invest over $50,000, oh goody)

Let us work this out. If you invest in equities and earn 9%-3%=6%. Wow, that sucks. What if you earn 15%-3%=12%? Ok, and your benefits increased, too. Wonderful. I sold these plans during the great bull market, and the majority of my clients took a high-risk profile. We made money, and a bunch of us have really good lifetime income guarantees as a result. Here is the problem: these policies are going to be volatile. Yes, you have a guaranteed lifetime income,[274] but when the markets experience problems, your account value may plummet, and you will only have your benefits to hold on to when you are sad and lonely.

These costs are only worth it if you invest in 100% equity (stocks) and take full metal jacket market risk. The lifetime income benefit will act as a safety net, providing income regardless of how long you live or if you have lousy market performance. But this protection is not cheap, and if you don't invest aggressively, you are going to perform poorly. (Aggressive, is what brokers love!)

Imagine a $500,000 investment and a 25% market decline. Your statement arrives saying you have $375,000 in your VA with $3,281.25 in quarterly benefit costs. (Not including the fund charges) Your family might need the death benefit if you die while reading the statement. Do you want that kind of risk and volatility in your retirement mission?

We review VA statements frequently; it is not uncommon for us to see 1% - 3% performance during a bull market! WTW! Why? Often, the advisor invested in a 50/50 portfolio with 50% low-yielding bonds (during a 0% interest rate period) and 50% stocks. The account never had a chance to make money. The advisor may have accurately determined your risk tolerance to be conservative. However, the VA is born to be wild with risk. This is frankly too aggressive for most retired investors. **You can only get over the high-cost hurdle by going 100% aggressive growth.** Then, your living benefit guarantees may grow, allowing you to earn a much higher lifetime income, possibly. (If there isn't a market crash or sustained bear market) **Once you start to access the income benefit, you will be selling shares for income**.

Unless you have a bull market to your back, your account will risk going to zero, and the income growth will stall.

Meaning not grow any larger as you watch your account value go to zero. ***The stress of volatile markets and the risk of a future no-growth market make Variable Annuities a poor choice for retirement.*** The very high costs will make it difficult to make money except when pushing equity exposure to 100%. But guess what? Not all VAs even let you invest in 100% equity. They may require you to invest 30% of your capital in bond funds or low-volatility funds. (Ruh-Roh Shaggy) Now you have a really expensive balanced fund.

No Living Benefits or Management

[274] Backed by the credit and claims paying ability of the insurance company. Not backed by any government agency, credit union, or FDIC.

The majority of the variable annuities I offered had a living benefit for lifetime income. I had a few for tax-deferral purposes (non-IRA), but they were low-cost contracts. I am always amazed when I see an annuity with no benefits (or a small death benefit) and high costs. There are better options.

The other big problem I see is that brokers do not actively manage these accounts. Why? They usually are paid a commission up front with a 4-to-7-year surrender schedule. There is no incentive for the broker to research the 100+ sub-accounts and build a forward-looking portfolio. Do you remember earlier, I mentioned that you should pay a fee (to a fiduciary) to manage stocks and bonds? ***There are VAs that are accessible to fiduciaries on a fee basis***. If you want the benefits with access to mutual funds, I mean sub-accounts, with lifetime income to act as a safety net on an aggressive growth portfolio, then the cost *could* be worth it. I do not think they are worth the costs. I have seen the statements yo-yo during a long Bull market; I fear what could happen if we enter another no-growth period, which seems likely at some point. With a VA, you are always selling shares for income. No Bueno.

I got lucky; my clients wanted the benefits, and we made money during a time when the markets went up 401%.[275] (No, we did not beat the market as a benchmark, and we had pretty significant volatility along the way) I called everyone 1 -2 times a year to rebalance, and I stayed popping fresh on the mutual funds (sub … you know). But I am looking through the windshield for my retired clients and not the rearview mirror. VAs contain too much risk, stress, and cost. Further, there are other annuities with the stability of principal and guaranteed income. More on that later.

Death Benefits of a VA

Variable Annuities sometimes have an enhanced death benefit. It might be a return of your deposit minus fees and withdrawals, or it might increase your earnings by 25% or more. We have run across VAs with 2.5% - 3.5% costs and a death benefit of $50,000 more than the client put into the VA. We believe (other factors are involved, so I will make this simple) that there are usually better options. You may be holding on to the VA because of the death benefit only instead of transferring it to a more cost and investment-efficient plan.

Consider the dollar cost of the fees. In one case, the fees after 5 years would equal the death benefit amount. Pretty substantial, right? Can you get a life insurance policy to replace the lost

---

[275] I speak on average. It is likely some lost money in their investment accounts for a variety of reasons. I am not claiming that all my clients made money in these instruments. These comments should be considered anecdotal only. Source: FactSet, S&P, J.P.Morgan based on the S&P 500 index Mar.9, 2009, to Feb. 19, 2020, +401%

death benefit? Finally, review your MO. Do you have 'legacy' as a money objective? If not, another account type or annuity might be in your best interests.

Registered Index-Linked Annuity- (Buffer the Volatility Slayer, Growth Investment)

The boys in the back room have been working on something. They are asking how we can lower risk while letting you participate in the stock market with no fees. The RILA was born. It is sometimes called a Buffer annuity. The first thing you need to know is that this annuity is not for income. (Recently, we seen new contacts that do offer Income) Yes, you can draw 10% annually or (on most I have seen) the earnings. This would be selling shares for income, so if income is your objective, you will want to move on. However, if you want growth with reduced risk, then this could be something to look at.

The basics of this annuity are that it usually has a 6-year surrender period. The insurance company limits your risk by providing a 'buffer' on the downside. There are usually a couple of options to choose from. You can get 10% - 20% protection from loss. For example:

1. You invest $100,000, and after 3 years, you are down -7%. If you have a 3 year 10% buffer, you will return to your original principal amount of $100,000
2. You invest $100,000, and after 6 years, you lose -24%. If you have a 6 year 20% buffer, you are restored only 20%. You still see a -4% loss in your account.
3. There is usually a ceiling on how much you can make. This has gotten generous in recent years, but it can be a 10%+ cap on how much you can make.

Some of the RILAs also have enhancements that say if you lose 5%, that annuity will gross you up 10%. So, your original deposit of $100,000 could be $105,000. These benefits vary drastically from contract to contract.

If your objective is legacy or growth, this annuity gives you access to the S&P 500 or the Russell 2000 indexes (other market indexes could be offered) as your investment. Here is what a lot of people like: there are usually *no asset fees*.

How do they pay the rent? I assure you the insurance company is taking little risk and making money using options to make good on the upside and pay for potential downside to you. This is usually a commission product (the company pays the broker), but since there is little to no management involved, that could be in your best interest. There are now fee-based programs if you purchase through a fiduciary advisor with an advisor fee. (That is how we offer RILAs)

*Note that not all Buffer annuities are free of costs. There could be investment costs, death benefit rider cost, or Income rider costs. The ones I have seen and sold have no costs (not including the advisor fee on non-commission products), but you need to check this. Ask for a company-produced illustration, a fact sheet, and a prospectus to review. The illustration should give you an idea of the potential performance but remember this does not guarantee future results.

Final note on RILAs as the '**Buffer the volatility slayer**,' but you must consider the following fine print:

'This annuity provides a level of protection from SOME downside risk; if the negative return is in excess of the selected buffer, there is a risk of substantial loss of principal.'

Bad Scenario: If after 6 years your account is down, let's say -40%, and you have the 20% buffer, you are still down -20%. Some RILAs offer a principal return death benefit (if you die reading the statement) for an additional cost.[276]

Fixed Index Annuity (FIA): The one they are all talking about, Income or Growth Investment

Now, we come to the popular annuity that all the cool kids are talking about. In 2023, FIA sales were $95.9 billion, up 20% from the previous year.[277] Total annuity sales for 2023 were $385.4 billion. Why are FIAs so popular?

First, understand that the Fixed Index Annuity (like the other annuities discussed) is a contract between you and the insurance company. They drafted the contract, not you, so you need a competent and experienced planning advisor to help you do this right and comparison shop. An independent advisor can offer most companies and isn't captive to one or two companies. Ask how many companies the advisor can offer.

Principal Protected

FIA is principal-protected, which means your principal is guaranteed by the financial strength and claims-paying ability of the insurance company. The insurance company is tightly regulated by the state's insurance regulators to ensure they have the ability to pay your principal,

---

[276] "What is a RILA? What to Know Before Investing" By Bryan Kuderna - The Street.com
[277] Source: Limra.com LIMRA: Record-High 2023 Annuity Sales

interest, and benefits.[278] The company may buy safe underlying assets or invest in the company's general account.

The interest isn't simple.

The insurance company makes the interest rate by buying institutional daily options on indexes. Your interest rate is not based on these 'option trades.' It is based on an 'index'[279] that you choose from the list. The annuity will have several indexes that you can tie to your interest rate. Here is where it gets complex. Some indexes have caps, meaning the most you can make is maybe 3.5%, as an example. Some are uncapped but have a participation rate of, let's say, 65%, so if the index makes 10%, you make 6.5%, and some operate on a spread. If the spread is 5% and the index makes 10%, you earn 5%.

If you wait two years to get interest, the participation rate (also called the Par Rate) offered might exceed 100%. Over 100% participation? So, if the par rate is 150% and the index makes 20% (over 2 years), I get 30%? How do they pay the rent? Don't worry. The insurance company does just fine, and they are incentivizing you to wait 2 years to get your interest. Guess what happens if you take out 10% before the interest is credited? They don't have to pay on that amount you withdrew. This is earnings to the insurance company. This is why you need liquid accounts in addition to your annuity. You want to use your annuity as designed to get the most out of it.

If you say, "All this makes my brain hurt," keep reading, and I will show you how to evaluate an FIA with ease later. But remember, you do not own a security. You own an annuity contract. Your money is not in the market; the insurance companies' money is.

Is 10 Years Too Long?

One major issue frequently brought up is the 10-year surrender period. (There are 4 and 7 year options but the best deal is usually the 10 year contract) That is a ridiculously long time to commit to an investment, so says a financial writer. When I took my first training class with Edward Jones, they said that to invest in equities, you must have a 10-year time horizon to be successful. Most bonds that have any kind of interest rate are 10 years to maturity or more. You have liquidity during the ten-year period in the 10% free withdrawal amount. But consider most people do not liquidate their accounts in retirement but take income. Short-term investments

---

[278] Backed by the credit and claims-paying ability of the insurance company. Not backed by any government agency, credit union, or FDIC. Investigate credit ratings before purchasing.

[279] The S&P 500 is a common index but there are other indexes in most FIAs.

rarely solve your income problems when you retire. Finally, FIAs don't charge you a commission. The company pays the advisor. But that is why there is a surrender charge to recoup their costs if you liquidate early. If you don't fully liquidate within the first 10 years (except for income or the 10% free-out amount), then you won't pay a surrender charge.

What do FIAs make?

Robert Ibbotson[280] wrote a paper in 2017 Fixed Indexed Annuities Beat Out Bonds.[281] His research showed FIAs Hypothetical Return (1927-2016) at 5.81%, compared to Long Term Government Bonds at 5.32%. What fixed annuities didn't beat were stocks. But you don't get a principal guarantee with stocks.

According to a LIMRA[282] study, 2011-2020 FIAs averaged 3.23%. Gasp! That is terrible! Except during that time, CDs earned less than 1.5%[283] and 10-year treasuries averaged 2.26%.[284] But don't FIAs do well in Bull markets, you ask? That answer is no. They do well in high-interest-rate markets. Remember, the insurance company has to secure your principal. When they buy higher-yielding bonds for their general account, that means they have more ability to give you better terms, caps, spreads, and the other confusing language they use.

Remember, the interest rates that affect your account are at the beginning. That is when they buy the bonds. If interest rates fall after that, it shouldn't affect you. If lower rates help the markets, that does help you since your interest rate is tied to market indexes. (Market indexes may be composed of stocks and bonds.)

If you ask for an illustration showing past performance on an FIA (with no income guarantees, just growth) in 2024, you might see 7%—14% on a 10-year past performance. That was not available in the past 10 years. It is now because the contracts are working on interest rates of +4.46%.[285] Those interest rates drive the FIA's index rate potential. Never compare your FIA's performance to the equity market. It is not designed to do that.

---

280 Roger G. Ibbotson (born May 27, 1943) is a Professor Emeritus in the Practice of Finance at the Yale School of Management. He is also chairman of Zebra Capital Management LLC. He has written extensively on capital market returns, cost of capital, and international investment. He is the founder, advisor, and former chairman of Ibbotson Associates, now a Morningstar Company. -Wikipedia

281 See article at Wealthmanagement.com Ibbotson Fixed Indexed-Annuities beat out bonds

282 LIMRA- Life Insurance Marketing and Research Association is the world's largest association of life insurance and financial services companies. Founded in 1916, it operates as a global research, consulting, and professional development organization.

283 Bankrate.com Historical CD interest rates: 1984-2024 - 6/1/2011 5-year CD was 1.68% & 5/1/2019 a 5-year CD was 1.49%.

284 Macrotrends.net 10-Year Treasury Rate – 54-Year Historical Chart 2010 – 2020 average rate.

285 See CNBC.com/US-Treasurys/ US 10 year 4.46% 05/22/2024.

FIAs do not beat the market except when the markets go negative or lose money. In that case, your interest rate stops at zero. No negative returns. There are no investment losses in a FIA. This will improve your average rate of return when compared to the equity markets. (Remember fees can reduce your account value below your initial investment amount.)

When the markets lose money, your Zero is a Hero!

Please review illustration 6.9 on the next page.

Hypothetical Return Comparison of $100,000 in the Markets and FIA with no withdrawals:

Year	Hypothetical Stock Market	FIA
1	30% - $70,000.00	0% - $100,000.00
2	+20% - $84,000.00	+6% - $106,000.00
3	+20% - $100,800.00	+6% - $112,360.00
4	-5% - $95,760.00	0% - $112,360.00
5	+25% - $119,700.00	+7% - $120,225.00

When you eliminate that downside, you don't have to make as much on the upside.

To repeat myself, FIAs will not beat the markets, especially when the markets are good. However, it will eliminate the sequence of returns risk, protect your principal, eliminate volatility, or establish a lifetime income. If you are looking for an alternative to bonds with guaranteed income or other benefits, FIAs may be a way to lower risk in your portfolio.

FIAs can't make you rich, but they will keep you from being poor. And if you refuse to die, they can continue providing lifetime income.[286]

Equity Index: we don't talk about it

When FIAs began in the late 1990s, they were called Equity-Indexed Annuities. I think this name came from the marketing department who had a 2-whiskey shot minimum because it was a terrible name compliance-wise. Insurance agents ran around telling people that they could get equity performance with principal guarantees. In the beginning, people got crazy returns, but then the rates started going down. Ruh-Roh Shaggy. Why were FIA's making less money? It had to do with interest rates. The more money the insurance company had to put into the bonds to secure your principal, the less they had for the option pool and the less they could make. So, the caps and participation rates went down, and so did the amount of interest clients earned.

FIA companies use the excess funds (gains) from the options trading account to do the following;

- To generate the interest rate, they will pay you
- Set aside reserves for any benefits they are offering and
- Make a profit. (You can call Greta Thunberg to have her say, "How dare you charge excess price!")

This option account is not in any way connected to your FIA. The company has to pay what they agreed to pay whether they make the money or not. (They always make the money.)

*Note: Some FIA companies use a general account that is considered high credit quality. The cash flow would pay the benefits and option premiums needed to generate your return and/or income.

I don't know when they stopped using the name equity index for fixed index; it might have been around 2008. But your principal was never in the market, options, or equities of any kind. The company contract promised to pay you what the selected index made (with all the complexity) I just laid out, protect your principal, and pay whatever benefits were promised.

The Insurance companies started retraining the agents to say that FIAs were bond alternatives and to quit referring to them as some kind of equity, or they (so help me God) would

---

286 Some FIAs do not offer lifetime income benefits. Each product is different in design. Understanding your Money Objectives will help you choose the right annuity for your best interests.

send the Sopranos over to smack them around. (The SEC at the time wanted to regulate FIAs as a security.)

What are your Money Objectives? (MO)

Some insurance agents' unreal descriptions of FIAs may have contributed to the FIA reputation some financial journalists talk about. But remember, Big Wall Street firms also don't like your money leaving them either. So, they are on the offensive. The biggest problem I have seen with FIAs is insurance agents who are pitchmen and don't follow a retirement planning process or match the annuity design to your *money objectives*. (But the same can be said of the sales process at Big Wall Street firms. So bad advice is not an annuity problem).

Yes, you can design an FIA. Each company offers differing contracts, with pros and cons. If matched correctly, you will have an FIA that is right for your MO. Correctly designed, FIAs can be a powerful planning tool. Too often, the agent is selling and not planning, and this is something you need to watch out for. Let's start with some examples by returning to your money objectives.

Don't Invest without an Insurance Company-Provided Illustration

Remember all the moving parts of how your interest is calculated and ultimately credited to your account? Participation rate, caps, no caps, and spreads? How do you understand this? You don't need to. The advisor should provide an Insurance Company Produced Illustration. This illustration should be based on the insurance company's software not the advisor or a third-party analysis. Study it and have the advisor explain it.

- **Here are key points to consider regarding the Insurance Company Provided Illustration:**
- Look at the **minimum guaranteed income** page and the income based on past performance. (Remember, past performance is not a guarantee, just a guideline. You might only get the minimum if the indexes perform less than expected.)
- Are there fees?
- What kind of account value growth might you see? (Remember this is a hypothetical based on past performance, and past performance doesn't guarantee future results.)
- Is a no-bonus FIA actually better than a bonus FIA? (This requires an apples-to-apples comparison)
- What other benefits are offered? (Death Benefits, Critical Illness Benefits, etc.)

- If married, is the Income guaranteed to you and your spouse?

The illustration should make it easy for you to see what's possible. For example, let us say the advisor goes on about how this contract has (some esoteric concept you don't understand), and it would make a super awesome investment! You turn to the past years' return in the illustration, with the average rate of return, and it says 2%. You say, "The best this can do is 2%?"

You may need to hold off on signing anything. This guy is pushing products and not shopping the annuity market. You should also ask for a comparison or two. (Or look for a better advisor) Now let's look at how you use your MO (money objectives) to invest in an FIA.

What do you want your money to do? (How about not die?)

When looking at illustration 6.6, how do we get to a maximum loss of -12%? We can use bonds to lower the risk and pass the stress test, but we can also use FIAs. Remember, the principal is protected. They also reside outside of the equity markets. Yes, you can remove stock market risk from some of your retirement and provide lifetime income benefits. Let me give a few planning scenarios that FIAs can solve for you.

These scenarios are designed with annuity products in mind. However, I will not reference the Insurance Companies or their product names. As an independent agent, I present the company(s) that meet my client's MO (money objectives).

FIA Annuity Solutions based on your Money Objectives

Money Objectives: 1. Income 2. Income Growth 3. Principal Protection (No Legacy Needed)

Annuity Solution 1: You get a rising income with a reasonable rate of return. (These numbers are usually NOT guaranteed but rely on the interest your account earns. This rate of return could be **zero.)** The starting distribution rate[287] usually starts around 3.5% -5% of your principal. Your income should grow as you age, and you are guaranteed to receive it for your lifetime. The illustration might show a distribution of 10% or higher of your original deposit at

[287] Distribution is how much the company is distributing from your account. If the distribution is higher than the interest rate over time, then you will see erosion of your principal. Your principal in most cases will erode to zero if you live past 85. This could be acceptable to you if your MO is lifetime income guarantees and you do not need a legacy to pass on to your children or someone else.

some point in the future, due to growth of your account value or index growth. Some annuities stop increasing your income at age 80-85, and some have no maximum age.

The negative is that the insurance company will liquidate *your cash values first*. (Some might actually show a positive account value throughout your life) If your illustrated account value shows zero (usually around 85+ years old), and if you just won't die, the insurance company will continue paying you your income to you (or your spouse if joint income). This means your family won't receive an inheritance. Why do this, you ask?

Many clients tell me that legacy to their children is not a consideration or that they have life insurance for that objective. If you have a spouse, the income can be structured as joint, providing this income for whoever is more stubborn about dying. If the income grows, you could be at a ridiculous distribution rate—let's say 10%+ of the original principal. This gives you an inflation-adjusted growing income for life. The principal will be gone, but the *cash flow* continues, baby. If you're not planning for an heir, this meets your MO!

"Don't leave the kids any money. Leave them life insurance! You can do that for pennies on the dollar!" **—Tom Hegna Economist, Financial Writer, Retirement Expert and PBS host of the 'Don't Worry Retire Happy' show**

Annuity Solution 2: You get a **level income** that is much higher than Solution 1 (5-9% of your deposited amount after one year, depending on your age). Like Solution 1, this income is lifetime and will liquidate your cash value (to zero) first, but the income will continue until, well, you know. This section is getting dark. Level Income usually doesn't grow, but starts off much higher. If you need a higher distribution of income, this is worth considering.

Both of these solutions provide income, which is first on the MO. When we calculated the amount of income you needed (from the checklist), the choice became clearer.

Frankly, you can't get this kind of guaranteed income from the stock market.

Since the amounts are guaranteed[288] that means no market correction (your oxygen tank explosion event) is going to change your retirement. We can also help you with your income needs and wants.

How do they pay the rent?

---

[288] Backed by the credit and claims-paying ability of the insurance company. Not backed by any government agency, credit union, or FDIC. Investigate credit ratings before purchasing.

It is insurance. There are Mortality Credits that not everyone is going to keep the policy; some will die too soon, and a few will live too long and get into the insurance company's pocket. The insurance company hires brainiacs from Warton and MIT to crunch the numbers, and then they set aside reserves for claims—basic insurance 101. There is more to say, but this is an overview. A good planning advisor can walk you through this.

The law of large numbers benefits you in the case of annuities.

Money Objectives: 1. Growth 2. Principal Protection 3. Long Term Care (LTC)

Annuity Solution: You want to exit the stock market, and you don't need the income. One option is to invest in a liquid bond portfolio.[289] Consider that bonds can lose value during rising interest rate periods or in market illiquidity. In illustration 6.8, I show how bond prices rise when rates go down; conversely, bond values go down when interest rates go up.

Bonds can lose value before they mature. This limits your liquidity.

This is a principal risk to consider. Other firms trained me to say you need to have a 10-year + hold expectation on a bond portfolio. A bond portfolio doesn't have a surrender charge if you liquidate early; however, you could still *lose money* in bonds if your timing is bad. The FIA may have a surrender period; however, you get a 10% free withdrawal provision. Meaning you can access 10% of your money with no cost or market value losses. Bonds are worth what the market says they are worth when you sell them. So, you could lose money on your so-called 'safe' bond account.

Annuity Solution: But can an FIA account value grow? Actually, yes, it can. But that is not guaranteed most of the time. Usually, your long-term interest rate is guaranteed at zero.[290]

FIAs without Income benefits usually have better growth potential.

The next feature to consider in this solution is the interest rate potential. In my experience, the rate of return on FIAs that offer lifetime income guarantees seems a bit low when compared to a Growth FIA.[291] However, you might be able to get a much higher rate of return on an FIA with no income provisions. But you can generally take withdrawals of 10% or the earnings at no

---

289 Liquidity -refers to investments that can be easily turned into cash with little penalty or loss of value due to the sale. Bonds can lose value due to interest rate risk and other risks. Selling a bond when it shows a loss would make that loss permanent.
290 Some insurance products could offer guaranteed growth but the devil is in the details. See the conditions, costs, and other considerations.
291 Growth FIA is our term and it refers to a FIA that has no income benefits. You access the account through withdraws.

cost to you. If withdrawing funds is not your goal, you can let the account grow until it is needed. What about long-term care? When this is a concern, you have a couple of options in plan design.

Some FIA (with income benefits) will increase your income (2x, 4x or higher) if you are unable to perform two of the six ADLs (Activities of Daily Living). The benefits may have an additional fee associated with them. You might have to wait two or three years for this benefit to kick in, so READ THE EXCEPTIONS AND EXCLUSIONS carefully and have it explained to you. ***In some cases, you can access your funds without a surrender charge if you need LTC.***

Money Objective: Long Term Care (LTC)

If you are concerned about paying for LTC and an LTC insurance policy is not an option, your deposit could help you secure additional funds for nursing home or home care coverage. For example, if you deposit $100,000, the annuity may provide $200,000+ of Long-Term Care coverage. Be sure to understand the details. Usually, there are waiting periods involved.

If you have earmarked funds for a nursing home or for costs associated with custodial home care, then you can shop for an annuity designed for that purpose

> **What are ADLs?**
>
> ADLs (Activities of Daily Living) trigger the care benefits and terminal illness benefits. The trigger is your inability to perform two out of six ADLs as certified by a physician.
>
> The ADLs are feeding, toileting, mobility, grooming, dressing, and personal hygiene (bathing).

Money Objectives: 1. Growth followed by Income 2. Principal Protection 3. Legacy

Solution: You purchase an annuity with a bonus that increases your lifetime income guarantee after ten years. Meanwhile, the bonus can be paid out to your heirs when you die. Your principal is protected and will pass to your heirs privately (meaning outside of probate), protected from lawsuits or creditors.[292]

Some FIAs offer enhanced taxable death benefits rather than a bonus. Again, this may require the beneficiary to take payments over a 5-year period or more. (Sometimes it is available immediately as a lump sum) You want to understand this and have the advisor show you the fine print. In an earlier solution, we max out income, which depletes your account to zero, usually

---

[292] This depends on the protections your state affords annuities. Not legal advice seek a qualified Attorney for your situation.

around age 84-85, but you (or your spouse) still receive the income for life. When a legacy is an issue, we can make sure the account value is sustained by paying out only the interest earned, thus maintaining a balance to be inherited. Some FIAs may offer guaranteed income with the potential (non-guaranteed) account value if the indexes generate positive interest rates.

If you buy a permanent life insurance policy for your heirs, that legacy is now guaranteed and tax-free. This gives you the "license" to spend every other dime of your savings on yourself during your "Go-Go" years without feeling guilty or worried about leaving the kids with nothing. —Tom Hegna Economist, Financial Writer, Retirement Expert and PBS host of the 'Don't Worry Retire Happy' show

Fees aren't Necessarily Bad if they pay for something you Want

Most FIAs do not have any fees, and some advisors (pitchmen) sell that hard. However, some annuities charge for income benefits, nursing home riders, enhanced death benefits, and other benefits. These fees can reduce your account value *below* what you invested. "Whoa, you say!" I thought this was principal-protected. It is, but fees can reduce your account value below your deposit due to costs. Let me share another story.

I had a client who bought an annuity with enhanced death benefits. There was a 1.2% annual charge for this, but it gave him or his wife a guaranteed 20% increase if either died in the first five years, then a 40% increase in the next five years, and finally a 60% increase after year 10. The heirs had to take the money over five years. The first year he owned it, his index made no money, and the $100,000 he deposited was now $98,800. The next year, the account made money and was over what he invested. My client would tease me that this contract didn't make what his other FIAs did, but he held on to it. In year 6 of the contract, his wife passed. This annuity paid him 40% more than his cash value (including interest) in a five-year payment stream. The contract worked as promised.

Remember, in most cases, Death Benefits paid by annuities are taxable to your heirs. Life Insurance death benefits pass tax-free.

Ask your advisor for multiple companies to compare

Look and compare illustrations. Ask the advisor what other contracts he considered. I have sometimes found that a contract with some fees may perform better than other contracts we compared it to, even with the same company. Some advisors (not the Right Stuff advisor I will talk about in Chapter 7) are operating on a sales pitch. "Hey, no fees! Sign here!" But the contract with a fee might actually be better for your money objectives. Comparison is important and needed. Leave your bias at the door.

Benefits instead of Performance

In some cases, the annuity offers a high lifetime income guarantee but a meager performance of the indexes. (Sometimes you find this out after you invest.) **If your #1 objective was income**, this might be better for your situation.

Income FIAs protect against longevity risk through Mortality Credits. If you take the maximum income allowed for life, your account balance will go to zero, usually between 82-85. (If the index averages 3% and you're getting 7%, you can see what is happening.) When the income is guaranteed by the insurance company, you continue to collect it as long as you keep breathing. In an annuity that offers low potential interest but a high lifetime income, this might be better for you even if the account value goes to zero at 81 instead of 85.

If your advisor is doing his job and planning by carefully analyzing the contracts for the best design for your MO, you have a keeper. Many 'annuity salespersons' don't do this. Instead, they might yell, "Hey, this has no fees, so it's better!" They are pitchmen and not planners. If you know your objectives, pay a fee if it is better for what you want to accomplish. You can see the effect that a fee has on the company-produced illustration.

If you secure lifetime income and principal protection in some of your portfolio, this could allow you to be more aggressive in your market-based investments. I still recommend focusing on cash flow, but dividend-producing stocks produce cash flow with growth but have higher risks.

Be careful of Bonuses.

This is where the illustration and a comparison FIA help you. I have found that in some contracts, the bonus might have a 10-year waiting period. If your MO is growth followed by income, this might work. Further, the bonus might only enhance your benefits! Because it's not cash. If the advisor is overly happy with what the bonus can do for you, he may be a pitchman instead of a planner.

Some bonuses are cash with a vesting period and may help you increase your income benefit right away. In these annuities, the bonus will vest over a 10-year period, could be a day-one cash value vest, or at the end of the 10-year period. (*Ask the advisor to show you the marketing materials and the company-produced illustration*[293] *with the fine print on this*) Which one is better is subjective and dependent on your situation.

---

293 I refer to company-produced illustrations repeatedly. The insurance company has software that shows the guarantees and past performance of the contracts based on the amount you invest. These reports are scrutinized by

A comparison with a <u>non-bonus</u> annuity might reveal that the bonus annuity ultimately performs <u>lower</u> than the non-bonus annuity. Think about that: you might make <u>more</u> money without a bonus. (After all, there is no free lunch)

Why you might want a bonus

If you are trying to get out of a poor-performing annuity, the bonus may help you recoup surrender costs or other losses. Another consideration is your life expectancy. If the 'Bonus Annuity' pays the bonus as a death benefit (read the fine print on this. It could be a 5-year payout with no interest) and you suspect your life expectancy is limited, the bonus annuity might make more sense.

If the agent is jacked up on the bonus the FIA pays, I wouldn't walk but run from him.

Please remember that these are guidelines. ***You must ask questions, review the company-produced illustrations, and be sure your annuity design meets your money objectives.*** There are many kinds of contracts, and the details are important. If your advisor seems clueless, then you probably need a more experienced advisor.

The Illustration Looks Really Good

During the low-interest rate period of 2008 – 2021, FIAs averaged 3.23%. This seems low, except bonds and CDs were lower. The new illustrations after 2023 show very high potential returns. Remember, today's FIA has not been available in the past 10 years. Why? Remember, the FIA has better rates to buy protection. When rates are high, that leaves more money for the insurance company to invest to generate interest (paid to you), reserves (for benefits), and profits. Use bonuses as a tool, not expecting a free lunch.

Choose the right contract design for your Money Objectives!

Too often, the advisor is selling and not planning. You need to make sure your advisor has access to multiple annuity companies and matches your Money Objectives to the right contract for your situation. You shouldn't buy an FIA or any annuity because it has a bonus only; rather, it should meet your top concerns for your money.

---

lawyers and regulators to be accurate and truthful. If the agent is using third-party software to illustrate how the policy will work, I would recommend you not walk but run from that agent.

Curb Your Enthusiasm

The future 'return,' which is based on past performance, depends on another bull market happening that is similar to the past ten years. Many analysts are calling for another no-growth period in the markets moving forward. If you see an average 8 -12% return on the illustration, that is assuming the market repeats itself in the next ten years. ***If you are looking at a future income based on this past performance, it could end up being lower***. Look at the guaranteed page. Can you live with that income if the performance doesn't pan out?

I hope the markets and your FIA do well, but you may need to curb your enthusiasm. If the advisor is a 'pitchman,' you might need to be sure you understand what you are getting. If investing for income, when does it start? If you end up with a couple of zero years, will that change your plans? If the markets are challenging, the FIA may be the best investment for you; just don't count on a high return or a higher future income amount. Past Performance does not assure future results.

Don't compare performance.

When the markets are doing well, the performance of the annuity will nearly always suck in comparison. Remember why you bought the annuity. It would be a false statement if you were told it would outperform the S&P 500.

This is your 'safe' money with benefits, not your growth money with risks.

Paying for Benefits You Don't Need

We had a client who had a large Variable Annuity. She had had the account for over 14 years, and it had a substantial 'living benefit' income that was very high. She was in her 80s, and if she didn't start the income now and live another ten years, that benefit would not be worth the costs she paid. In our meeting, we went back and forth as I tried to get her to start income and she resisted taking any. I stopped, went to the whiteboard, and started to review her money objectives with her. They were:

1. Principal Protection 2. Long-Term Care 3. Legacy

I stared at the board. No income was needed. She planned to use this money for the nursing home or for her children to inherit. She didn't want to be a burden on them if she needed to go to a nursing home, and she was uncomfortable with being invested in the stock market.

Her variable annuity was costing her over $10,000 a year for the lifetime income benefit she wasn't using and didn't plan to ever use. We needed to get her out of this expensive product for something that aligned with her objectives. We found a growth FIA that allowed free withdrawals without surrender charges if she went to a nursing home and posed no risk to her principal. The FIA she invested in also had no fees and, importantly, no income guarantees that she didn't need. The 10% annual withdrawal provision was more than she ever planned to take from the account. The fees we saved were over $13,000 a year.

I preach about money objectives all the time, and for a moment, I couldn't see the forest for the trees.[294]

"Freakonomics pushed a study out on social media conducted by the University of Chicago, which looked at people who bought lifetime annuities versus people who didn't. The study found that people who bought the annuities lived longer than those who didn't."
—Tom Hegna, Financial Writer and PBS host 'Don't Worry, Retire Happy.'[295]

Putting It Together

Now, it's time to build a portfolio. I listed a number of income investments that can be used. The mix should be a mix of investments. Some of my clients will use annuities, and others won't. How you put this portfolio together depends on the risk tolerance that makes your life good and the income you need or want. Having an advisor who offers stocks, bonds, ETFs, CDs, ***and*** annuities is in your best interests.

"***When you are a hammer, every problem is a nail.***"

Advisors who are 'insurance agents only' may be focused on selling insurance products and lack a full toolbox of financial products and investment tools to solve your problems.

First, let us talk about Liquidity

Depending on your total net worth, you should have between $10,000 - $50,000 in the bank. (Business liquidity is separate and depends on what the business's needs are) Why the bank? The transactional value of cash. Banks are accessible immediately, and emergencies are usually immediate. "But I won't make any good interest on that money, and inflation will erode it," you say. ***Mark Cuban, in an interview, spoke of the 'transactional value of cash.'*** What you lose

---

[294] The client paid no surrender charges on this transaction and it financially improved her situation and risk tolerance.
[295] Source: 'Avoiding Social Insecurity' by Martha Shedding.

due to inflation, you gain in the quickness and ease of access. Keep this cash liquid and separate from your investment accounts, preferably in a bank account.

If you have $500,000 that needs to generate income and you have $50,000 in the bank, can I invest this money in an annuity? No, not all of it. The max should be 75%. The rest should be in a brokerage account that has daily liquidity. The investments can be Stocks, Bonds, ETFs, or CDs. The reason is that annuities have surrender periods and liquidation charges.

The benefits usually depend on your withdrawing a fixed amount set by the contract to maintain your guarantees. Life has a tendency to change, and you may need to access funds beyond your bank cash. You want to leave the annuities alone and access the income you planned. Ideally, the $500,000 would be split into a $375,000 annuity and a $125,000 brokerage account. If you need income right away, (most annuities require a one-year cooling-off period then you can withdraw your first year from the brokerage account.

Mix of Investments

How much income do you need for your retirement mission? If you need $1,000 a month and you have $100,000 in savings, that won't be a sustainable income flow. Next is the risk tolerance you desire. If you said a maximum 12% downside loss, it would be difficult to do that in a dividend stock portfolio. You need 50% - 70% in bonds or annuities to reduce your market volatility.

In market sell-offs, dividend stocks can lose as much money as everyone else. They call it correlating to 1. However, we typically see dividend stocks recover first as the big money moves to 'yield' as they wait for the recession to end.

When dividend stocks become accidental high yielders.[296] The market eventually sobers up and rectifies the situation. I saw this in 2008. All stocks (bonds, too) went into free fall. In January 2009, dividend stocks rallied hard.

Do remember that **dividend stocks can cut their dividend during a company crisis**. A number of our model portfolio stocks (particularly real estate investments) suspended dividends in 2020 during the Covid crisis. That was, frankly, a scary time. Normally, cutting or suspending a dividend is a deal breaker. We managed through that and came out on the other end okay. We like preferred stocks, but if a preferred cuts its dividend, you still pay taxes on the yield (in a

---

[296] Accidental High Yielder is a stock with the ability to maintain its dividend sells off due to market volatility. The reduced share price means a higher dividend percentage than what is historically average.

non-IRA) even if you are not collecting it. We call it a stealth tax. This is why professional management of your stocks is important.

Your mix of stocks to bonds/annuities will determine your risk percentage and the amount of income you need. We stress test to test the right mix and what yield we can achieve. The decision on the annuity is important. The reason is the annuity can give you a guaranteed income stream, now or in the future. This income stream (depending on your age) could be 4 - 9% of the principal deposited. With higher guaranteed income coming from the annuity, this gives us the ability to take more risk on the 30-40% in a managed portfolio. Then, we will conduct a stress test to see if we are hitting your desired risk percentage.[297] Bonds can be used in place of an annuity but with lower income and some fluctuation of value.

When they planned the Apollo missions, their options were to handle the risks. It's called T.E.A.M.

Transfer it

Eliminate the risk

Accept it

Mitigate it

You have options on how you deal with risk.

- Annuities **Transfer** the risk of living 'too long' and market risk to the insurance company through mortality credits and principal protection.
- Cash **Eliminates** some risks.
- Investing in growth **Accepts** it.
- Bonds & Dividend Stocks **Mitigate** the Risk.

Remember how Apollo 13 tested everything in the simulators located in Houston? They tested whether the plans would work and what issues they needed to overcome. It should be no different with planning your investments. We need to work on the checklist. Notice that the investment strategy is in the 9th position? There are many issues that need to be worked out first before changing your investment strategy.

Many advisors go to investments first because they are pitchmen, even if they claim the title of fiduciary.

Annuities make excellent Retirement Assets, and you live longer, too.

In chapter 2, I talked about how investment stress can affect your health. According to Mark Stibrich, PhD,

[297] We can't guarantee you won't lose more than your target risk tolerance percentage. We use historical data and analytical software to make educated investment decisions.

"Research shows that overreacting, constantly worrying, and living in a state of perpetual anxiety can reduce life expectancy."

According to The LIMRA Secure Retirement Institute Study (2016) it found 73% of retirees who own an annuity believe they can live the lifestyle they want, compared to 64% of those who don't. It also noted that annuity owners have significantly higher confidence that they will not outlive their money.

"Retirees who are surrounded by their family and friends — and who also have a substantial check coming in every month for the rest of their lives — are much happier, according to an article published in Time and The Big Wall Street Journal. Studies show that they also live longer."

—Kiplinger, December 2020 writer Ken Nuss, Retirees with a Guaranteed Income Are Happier, Live Longer.

Adding Annuities to your Pensions and Social Security to secure your '**base of income**' can reduce stress in retirement. Your income is secure from the worries in the world around you.

Is there no room for Growth Investments?

The objectives and risk tolerance are the keys here. Let us say you have no need for income and feel you can handle a higher risk tolerance. What then? I still recommend a portion of your investments in bonds/annuities and dividend stocks, but you definitely have the flexibility to include higher-risk growth investments as a percentage of your assets.

If you can meet your income needs and want targets with room to spare, then you have the ability to allocate to some growth as well. The Apollo missions that did land on the moon brought back moon rocks. They had space, weight allowance, and fuel to afford this. They made sure the primary mission would succeed first. This was obviously scrapped in the Apollo 13 mission.

Secure your Income First

If you can secure the retirement income you need (including Social Security, Pensions, and other sources of income) using 70% of your capital with income investments, then you could invest the remaining 30% in more aggressive growth investments without worry of retirement changing economic situations affecting you. Again the 'Oxygen Tank Explosion' that changes your retirement mission.

70/30 - 80/20 - 90/10

What percentage of income to Growth is right for you?

"That you may make sure of the more important things, so that you may be flawless…"* *—Philippians 1:10 NWT

If you don't need income, you may want a lower-risk portfolio. An accumulation FIA with no income benefits but offering principal protection and volatility control can reduce your overall risk. If you choose a maximum -12% volatility, a high percentage in an accumulation annuity will reduce your portfolio risk.

What about Gold?

Gold (and Silver, too) are Baseball cards. You hope someone is willing to buy them for more than you paid when you sell. Gold isn't a growing business and doesn't have a maturity value or a dividend, and frankly has a terrible long-term return history. When gold is good, it is good! This quote from Advisorpedia I found interesting,

"Gold is a speculative asset. Accordingly, it can rise and fall, and at times violently, based solely on the whims of traders and speculators."
—Is Gold Warning Us or Running With the Markets?'

If you want gold or silver anyway, we recommend investing in gold or silver ETFs. Holding physical metals is costly and involves high commissions, but holding gold coins in a safe in your home could be useful when the zombie apocalypse begins.

When the Zombie Apocalypse happens, you'll be glad you bought a flamethrower. Works against the hordes of the undead or your money back. —Elon Musk

Commemorative doesn't mean Valuable

Be careful of commemorative gold and silver investments. The collectibles market is tricky and often results in lost capital from buying overpriced collectibles. Your lack of knowledge could cost you. There are gold clubs that sell all kinds of gold coins, solid gold notes, and such. They promote that these have value above their 'melt' price. Watch a few episodes of the TV show Pawn Stars, and you will see how nuanced the collectible market is. In the end, gold is worth its weight per ounce minus commissions. Any more is retail and likely not the price you will get.

Here is another client story on buying physical gold.

We had a retired Cowboy who listened to our radio show and set an appointment. He had bought physical Gold (over $300,000) in his IRA. It was held at a custodian specializing in alternative investments and sold to him by a gold broker. What they did was sell him US Mint gold and silver coins bought directly from the mint at the retail price. The retail price was almost double the 'melt' price.

Melt price is the real price of gold. The value is set by the trading on the commodities markets. The best price we could get for these coins was 10% above the melt price. (We weren't sure if that was accurate or a scam, frankly.) Additionally, the "Gold" broker charged a 25% commission for this service. The sad part of this was that he was down by our estimates 50% while gold ran up over $2,500 an ounce. Plus has enormous custody fees to pay.

The Gold Brokers promise a market for the Gold coins, but we didn't see one. Other Gold Brokers required you to open an account before they shared prices, and they were clearly not interested in buying or selling their existing gold. ***If you want to invest in gold (or any other metal), do it inside an ETF in a brokerage account. It's liquid, low-cost, and legitimate without the scams.***

Taxes are Higher for Gold & Silver

If you own physical gold or silver outside a retirement account like an IRA, you will pay higher taxes. Capital Gains are 0 -20%, but your precious metals will be taxed at the higher collectibles rate of 28% if you cross the 22% margin rate. If you're a Higher-Income individual ($250,000 married, $200,000 single, and $125,000 married filing separately), you might be subject to the 3.8% Net Investment Income Tax (NIIT), which could bring the effective federal rate on collectible gains up to **31.8%.**

This is avoided if you buy your Gold or Silver in an ETF. You're back to ordinary Capital Gains.

They shall cast their silver in the streets, and their gold shall be removed: their silver and their gold shall not be able to deliver them in the day of the wrath of the LORD: they shall not satisfy their souls, neither fill their bowels: because it is the stumbling block of their iniquity.
—Ezekiel 7:19

Summing Up

- There is an ideological battle going on for your retirement account.
- The overarching principle is simple: retirees need income in retirement.
- Past Performance is not a guarantee of future results.
- Selling Shares for Income only works in Bull Markets
- In retirement, you are confronted with a new reality. This money is all you have, and no more is coming.
- Dividends matter in retirement.
- Cash Flow is dividends and interest.
- TR= I + G (Total Return = Interest/Dividends + Growth/Loss)
- Historically, long periods of 'secular bear' markets have followed 'secular bull' markets.
- Falling into the wrong time period can have a detrimental effect on your retirement.
- Commissions cost you less than an annual fee.
- See where you need a fiduciary and where you don't.
- How you pay your advisor should be based on what is involved in managing your account and aligning the advisor's incentives with your interests.
- There is tangible value in the client-advisor relationship.
- Even if you are an amazing investor/trader yourself, having someone who is philosophically aligned with you will benefit your spouse and family when you are gone.
- Certified Financial Fiduciaries follow a code of conduct that transcends fees and commissions.
- The advisor relationship could make a difference in saving and retirement, but anything requires you to be selective in the advisor you select.
- Follow your checklist and money objectives.
- Hiring a fiduciary doesn't mean you will get your money objectives met.
- Your MO (Money Objectives) will determine the investments that will best meet your
- mission parameters (goals).
- "If you have trouble imagining a 20% loss in the stock market, you shouldn't be in stocks."

- "Stocks are worth what someone else is willing to pay for them at the time you are ready to sell."
- Dividend stocks also have growth potential in their dividend yield and share price.
- Diversification is achieved at 30 -40 stock positions.
- Mutual Funds are operated by sharp and savvy guys.
- Mutual Fund costs, hidden costs, turnover rates, and other issues make them undesirable investments.
- It is not how much you made but compared to what.
- Rollovers from employer-sponsored plans make sense.
- ETFs accomplish the goals of mutual funds without the costs and shenanigans.
- SMA gives you individual positions and a level of customization not available elsewhere.
- Large firms like hedge funds can fall hard.
- Stocks can go bankrupt.
- The definition of a bond mutual fund is shares of a stock that own bonds.
- There are serious potential risks of running out of money in retirement.
- Using standard assumptions, economists have shown that buyers of annuities are assured more annual income for the rest of their lives, compared with people who self-manage their portfolios.
- Annuities with income guarantees allow a retiree to maintain a lifestyle free of the possibility that spending today could jeopardize their ability to live well later in retirement.
- "Don't leave the kids any money. Leave them life insurance! You can do that for pennies on the dollar!"
- If you have earmarked funds for a nursing home or for costs associated with custodial home care, then you can shop for an annuity designed for that purpose.
- Variable Annuities are costly and full of mutual fund-like investments.
- Registered Link Annuities are best for growth with some downside protection.
- Bonds can lose value before they mature. This limits your liquidity. Annuities are liquid and permit 10% free withdrawal without surrender charges.
- Fixed Index Annuities can be designed for your money objectives.

- When you eliminate that downside, you don't have to make as much on the upside.
- What do you want your money to do?
- Use a company-produced illustration when evaluating an FIA.
- Beware of Bonuses. Make sure they actually help you.
- Don't walk but run from an advisor who is over-promotional on annuity bonuses.
- The media, in many instances, have become useful idiots to Big Wall Street firms trying to protect their Baseball Card portfolios and the platforms they are traded on.
- Test your plan in the simulator.
- Advisors who are 'insurance agents only' may be focused on selling insurance products and lack a full toolbox of financial products and investment tools to solve your problems and meet your Money Objectives.
- Hire an advisor who follows a planning process, not a pitchman.
- Make sure your living expenses and retirement goals are covered by Pensions, Social Security, and Annuities with Income Guarantees.
- If you want to invest in gold (or any other metal), do it in an ETF inside a brokerage account. It's liquid, low-cost, and legitimate without the scams.
- Physical gold might be useful when the zombie apocalypse begins.

Now, you are building your retirement ship for your retirement mission. There is a lot to consider when making investment choices. Remember, this was a general overview. Using a financial advisor to carefully plan the investments that will carry you through retirement or to the next generation takes careful consideration and good planning. Hiring an advisor and not a pitchman will make all the difference in retirement.

Now, let's talk about Choosing Mission Control next.

Chapter 7
Choosing Your Mission Control

The following conversation happened before Apollo 13's reentry and recovery.

NASA Director: "This could be the worst disaster NASA has ever experienced."

Gene Kranz Flight Director: "With all due respect, sir, I believe this is gonna be our finest hour."

Every NASA mission has mission control. Apollo 13's lead flight director was Gene Krantz.[298] He led a room of engineers, doctors, and scientists. Everyone had a particular job and came together to achieve a successful mission.

Your mission control will involve an attorney(s), CPA or Accountant, and financial advisor(s). By now, you may understand that a successful retirement launch and mission should be based on income and *cash flow*. Your CPA and advisor need to communicate to optimize your taxes.

However, the most important position you will fill is your Financial Advisor. Some folks have only one advisor, and some will have multiple advisors, but everyone will have a primary advisor who is your go-to person. The advisor's principles will guide your retirement ship for good, stress, or disaster. Hiring advisor(s) with the 'Right Stuff' can improve your retirement mission success.

The Right Stuff

The Right Stuff was a book written by Tom Wolfe and later a movie directed by Philip Kaufman starring Ed Harris, Dennis Quaid, and others. The story followed the men who test-piloted jets and eventually worked in US Space programs like the Apollo program. Astronauts are referred to as having the 'Right Stuff.'

10 Signs Your Advisor Has the 'Right Stuff'

[298] I recommend Gene Kranz's autobiography "Failure is not an Option."

Does your primary advisor have the right stuff? Here are ten signs to look for. The right stuff we are looking for is an advisor who is an actual 'Income Specialist.'[299] Many advisors sell investments or (for so-called fiduciaries) sell portfolios. Whether you are investing in dividend-producing investments, interest from bonds, or annuities,

"You need an advisor who can say 'cash flow' in the coolest & sexiest late-night DJ voice.

The 'Right Stuff' advisor shows how important income is for a retirement portfolio. I describe the advisor using male pronouns, but this obviously applies to female advisors equally. (Please note, if I see 'misogynistic' anywhere in your email or letter, I will trash can it. If you are a lady and you send me a picture of yourself, my jealous Filipina wife will burn it on your front lawn).

1. The 'Right Stuff' Advisor Listens to You and Your Spouse.

When you interview a new advisor, is he waiting for you to finish what you are saying so he can start his sales pitch? If you ask your advisor to reduce your portfolio risk, does he remind you of the buy-and-hold and long-term performance of stock markets? Does your advisor have confidence in equities above all else, including Grandma?

Then you may not have an Income Specialist.

Big Wall Street firms train many advisors (myself included) to love, love, and love stocks for growth. After 2008, when interest rates dropped to near zero, bonds became completely uninteresting, with an average yield below 1%.[300] Bond trading desks run by large firms closed. Advisors began to look to the stock markets for a larger share of their clients' accounts.

Many advisors were conditioned to recommend growth investments primarily in mutual funds, which are overpromoted investment vehicles that provide free lunches, pay-for-company conferences, and other freebies. These advisors, fiduciary and non-fiduciary, seem more concerned with the revenue stream they generate than with the income you receive, and they become addicted to chasing growth. When you get that statement that is down 10-20%, you are riding that little brown barrel racer horse (story from Chapter 3), and you are hanging on for dear life, hoping not to fall off!

So, it is important to listen to you and your goals in retirement. Ask about the lifestyle you want and the amount of income you will need. What investments match your money objectives?

---

299 Income Specialist is not an official designation or degree. It indicates the advisors focus on income investing.

300 See Macrotrends.net "Federal Funds Rate - 62 Year Historical Chart"

It is not about selling products, investments, or even the company the advisor works for. ***Is your advisor tuned into your unique retirement mission?***

If Mom isn't Happy nobody is Happy

Equally important is listening to your wife. I don't want to come off as misogynistic here but when we meet potential married clients, I'd say 80% of the time, the husband drives the meeting, which excludes the wife (most of the time, I don't think this is meant to be intentional), but it is not good. She will also live with these decisions, obviously. Her views should be sought out.

Men, by nature, are risk-takers, and women are nurturers. If the advisor insightfully involves your spouse, this can help you achieve a balance that allows unity in the family. However, some male advisors may not be sensitive to this dynamic. They may have the confidence but not the 'Right Stuff' to take care of your family when you are gone. Many women who stay uninvolved in the financial decisions of the household retirement plans are at a disadvantage when they lose their spouse in death.

If your wife has entrusted you to make the right decisions on investments and planning, you owe it to her to choose the 'Right Stuff' advisor who will have the compassion and respect to advise your spouse as he would you. One client who has operated a number of successful businesses recently told me, "My wife has little business acumen, but over the years, I found her advice on who I should do business with has been spot on. I would have saved $100s of thousands of dollars of losses if I listened to her."

"The three things I tell all young men to look for in a woman: Can she cook? Can she carry the Bible? And does she have a sense of humor? If you find one that has all three, you better marry her." —Phil Robertson, Duck Dynasty

2. The 'Right Stuff' Advisor Always Puts Your Interests First

Investment professionals are being pushed toward a fiduciary standard that puts your interests first. Is that happening? We have fiduciaries who won't sell annuities even if that would best meet your objectives, and we have some insurance agents who only recommend annuities, no matter what your objectives are. Some fiduciaries push clients into growth portfolios where they can generate a higher fee, while brokers and fiduciaries often sell mutual funds that their firm promotes with no regard for better alternatives.

Many 'Big Wall Street' firms restrict what ETFs and Mutual Funds may be offered to you. At first glance, this seems like a 'quality control' to ensure that you have access to the best offerings. ***The firm may actually be colluding with the funds against your interest.*** Revenue-sharing and selling agreements may require a certain purchase level (company-wide) in certain flagship funds. To achieve the 'firm's goal', they restrict what the advisor is 'allowed' to offer you. Thus, ensuring the funds that provide the best revenue for the firm are sold to you.

My partner and I were invited on a recruitment trip for a Big Wall Street firm. They flew us to Dallas, Texas, put us up in a nice hotel, and fed us a really lovely dinner, so I won't trash their name. However, during the 'What We Can Offer You' presentation, I raised my hand to ask what I thought would be a smart-alec question. (I see you're shocked that I am a smart-alec.) Subhani and I see this firm's statements all the time. They contain mostly mutual funds with a peppering of ETFs. So I said in a nice and non-arrogant voice, (cough) I said, "We do not offer mutual funds but rather ETFs. Would we be able to do that at your firm?" The answer I got shocked Mr. Subhani and me. The corporate rep said, "Yes, we offer all the publicly traded ETFs on our platform." (This turned out not to be true since they had a limited list of ETFs that could be sold.)

I looked at Subhani, and he looked at me. Our brains telepathically linked up on a spiritual dimension. We said WTW! (What the World?) Who in this company is buying ETFs? We don't see them on the statements. Is this firm doing what is in the client's best interests? The realization that they had the ability to choose ETFs and didn't was shocking to us. We assumed it was the firm that limited ETF selection. However, selling mutual funds (even as a fiduciary) is the culture of that firm.

We took the pledge as Certified Financial Fiduciaries in its code of conduct to put our clients' best interests first. The National Association of Certified Financial Fiduciaries sent a white panel van to our office and abducted us, putting black bags over our heads, and then they took us to an abandoned amusement park to swear the fiduciary code of conduct[301] on an Indian grave or die! After that, they took us for ice cream, so overall, it was a lovely evening.[302]

Doing retirement planning should involve the items on the checklist in Chapter 3, and it is necessary if your interests are to be truly followed. The investments should likewise be in your best interest.

3. The 'Right Stuff' Advisor Never Pushes Proprietary Products

Again, big financial media tells you that only a fiduciary will look out for your best interests, and then you, the client, end up in the 'tactically engineered only the best growth mutual fund portfolio' offered by the parent company. Everybody gets these funds. Commission

---

301 See Chapter 6, Certified Financial Fiduciaries

302 Compliance and the Certified Financial Fiduciaries are screaming at me to tell you that this was a fictional story for entertainment purposes. The Indian grave was too far, apparently.

or fee-based, there is no assurance that the firm isn't pushing what is in *their* best interest, not yours. Wait, isn't a fiduciary legally obligated to operate in your best interest? Consider this: if the fee-only fiduciary only offers mutual funds, are they legally operating in your best interest? They are offering the best they have. Do you get it now? (Read about the soft dollars in the ADV.)

Proprietary products (company-made funds) are highly profitable to the firm and have a conflict of interest to the advisor. But are they in *your* best interest? If you move your account, the proprietary funds may have to be sold since they, in many cases, can't be transferred.

Your chances are better that a fee-based fiduciary advisor will customize your portfolio, but based on what? By punching your data into financial planning software that generates a Monti Carlo score and past 10-year average growth performance on your retirement money with a plan to sell shares for income. (See Chapter 2 on the 120-page plan).

We are an RIA firm that focuses on income-producing investments of all kinds.

We begin by vetting your retirement life goals and income requirements. Then we run reports on your current situation, asset inventory, income sources (like Social Security benefits and pensions), how much income your holdings now provide, and overall portfolio costs.

Our portfolios are individual dividend stocks and ETFs managed by us or fully vetted SMAs[303] that purchases bonds and stocks for interest and dividends. We rarely use mutual funds and are entirely independent. As fiduciaries, we get paid on a fee basis for equities, ETFs, bonds, and other securities.[304]

4. The 'Right Stuff' Advisor Prefers Individual Bonds Over Bond Mutual Funds

This mistake comes from a misunderstanding of how these investments work. The guarantees that individual bonds carry are an important feature. The cash settlement of mutual funds with constant turnover makes them a poor choice for risk and income objectives. See my discussion on Bonds in Chapter 6.

An advisor who is an income specialist takes the additional effort to buy individual bonds in your portfolio. Note: We will use a bond ETF for our clients who don't have a sufficient account size to facilitate individual bonds. We believe the way Bond ETFs are structured will provide

303 Separate Managed Account manager. These options involve additional fees.

304 Life Insurance and Annuities are not sold by Toro Bravo as a fiduciary, but are offered by the advisor as an Insurance Broker.

better performance and income over a mutual fund. Remember, past performance is not a guarantee of future results.

"Few advisors know how to invest for dividends and interest or understand why retired investors should."

5. **The 'Right Stuff' Advisor is a Steely-Eyed Income Specialist Using a Planning Approach**[305]

We follow a checklist for retirement planning before we discuss investments. We explore the problems first. Many advisors are Pitchman.[306] Using sales tactics, stories, claims of performance, and charisma to charm you into a brand-new Mutual Fund portfolio or Annuity!

Then, there is advisor asset greed. The advisor may push for all your assets to offer you incentives. They want Assets Under Management. Fee-only Fiduciaries' revenue is based on the dollar amount of assets they can manage. If they work for a Big Box Big Wall Street firm, they are incentivized by how much money they can get on the platform—not just the commission guys but the fiduciary boys too.

The 'Right Stuff' advisor will encourage you to keep some of your liquidity at a local bank. (Usually $10,000 - $50,000) Why? The transactional value of cash. In emergencies, the bank will likely be accessible 24/7 for withdrawals and cash access. Even if the advisor doesn't charge you a fee for a cash account, wouldn't the bank with ATM/Debit cards, cash transfer like Zelle, and check writing ability be more useful in a sudden emergency?

A Pitchman, using a sales process, promotes a fee-only portfolio, a God Bless America mutual fund portfolio, or an annuity to wrestle your money from an evil hedge fund contract. How do I know this? Because I have the unique perspective of having attended training sessions that help develop Pitchmen.

"They should hire a retirement income specialist for retirement, not a portfolio builder or a wealth manager. You want someone who knows retirement, retirement risk management, and retirement income." —Tom Hegna Financial Writer and PBS host 'Don't Worry Retire Happy'

---

[305] John Aaron was a EECOM flight controller in the Apollo program. John's colleagues referred to him as a Steely-Eyed Missile Man.

[306] Pitchman is a term I made up. It means an advisor who is focused on a Sales pitch to sell investments and investment products. Not planning or your best interest. The pitch is repeated to whoever will listen.

Invited to a Sales Training meeting in Las Vegas

I was invited to a training meeting at the Palms Casino in La Vegas. The super salesman would show us how to use his super-secret five-step process to sell. The steps focused on stopping the evil hedge funds (apparently, if you own stocks, then you were subservient to evil hedge funds) from destroying your money by ending fees, getting a bonus, and receiving a reasonable rate of return on your money.

There was nothing about our client's ideal retirement life or what your post-retirement income, including Social Security, would look like. There was nothing about discussing your current portfolios and non-stock portfolios like real estate. There was nothing about understanding your debt and expenses, and how to move from the G to the I. There was nothing about your retirement objectives, and finally, an accurate risk level that you can live with in retirement. **He discouraged income planning in any way!** (To me, this is the main objective for annuities) Retirement planning was missing from the five-step sales pitch training. Advisors trained like this are not using a planning approach. They are using manipulation and fear to solicit your money. They are not solving problems but selling. Definitely not the 'Right Stuff.'

How about the fee-only fiduciary? He will use a planning approach, right? Probably, by using the 120-page plan to tell you the Monte Carlo and average returns proved by modern portfolio theory (and performance numbers from a 14-year bull market) say it's all okay to sell shares for income. It was blessed by Bengen's 4% rule, to the honor of our lord of buy-and-hold, Warren Buffett, amen. Using a style-based asset allocation model to reduce risk. (***Still hoping the markets provide growth for your income by selling shares. Fingers crossed!***) It may not be a filthy five-step sales presentation I learned in Las Vegas, but it can result in an Apollo 1 retirement plan just the same. By this point, you understand that hiring a fiduciary may be as dangerous as climbing into Apollo 1 was.

An income specialist with the 'Right Stuff' who follows your best interest to first explore the problems you are trying to solve and recommends what is best for you. This can only be done through a rational planning approach with procedures to have sustainable *cash flow* for income in retirement and ***for the advisor to be able to offer all the investment tools for your mission***.

The last point on the planning approach is that your advisor should understand Social Security, Taxes, and Financial Planning. Some advisors may not have experience or education in this area, and some are product sellers only. Many Big Wall Street advisors maybe prohibited from offering tax advice by the firm they work for. That is not the 'Right Stuff.'

The 'Right Stuff advisor is a Steely-Eyed Income Specialist using a planning approach.

6. **The 'Right Stuff' Advisor Avoids "The Disease of Ease"**

About 20 years ago, a huge mutual fund company interviewed me for a position as the investment guy at a CPA firm. I would rank the clients' suitability and invest in 1 of 3 model portfolios of the company's mutual funds. They were Conservative, Growth, and Aggressive Growth. No income planning or retirement planning. I would get a stream of CPA client referrals and split my revenue with them. That's all I would have to do. I suggested that I build a stage in the office with 3 doors. Then I could say What is behind door #1? Why it is Bonds and Target Date Funds! How about door #3? It's a brand new aggressive fund of small companies and international stocks! Behind Door #2 … I didn't take that offer, and the recruiter got all snippy. Hey, don't judge me! I need to have some fun, too. This 'disease of ease' for the advisor is not in your best interest.

I told you my mutual fund story in Chapter 6. However, aside from the constant promotion from mutual fund companies to advisors, it is also an easy trade to make. Enter the correct symbol, and it will fill after markets close. There is no worrying about the bid-ask spread, how to enter a limit order, or checking if it is filled or not.

The truth on mutual funds is out there. As smart as I want you to believe I am, I am not the only one to figure out the problems with mutual funds and the better alternatives in ETFs. It took a massive market downturn (2008) for me to see the issues with mutual funds. Your advisor may not have enough experience or may be brainwashed by the Corporate Big Wall Street machine to use mutual funds in your accounts because he doesn't know the problems and the trades are easy.

*Note: In most Employer-Sponsored Plans, like 401 (k) or 403 (b), mutual funds are the only option. Many investors use these investments to accumulate their retirement. We follow a selection discipline with these accounts using third-party evaluation software like MorningStar©. We would prefer other investment options, but in the end, use what you have.

7. **The 'Right Stuff' Advisor Understands Your Risks and Objectives, Not Big Wall Streets**

"If your advisor has never said, "The only way to invest for retirement is in the stock market," or "It's not about timing the market, it's about time in the market," then you might be working with a true retirement Income Specialist." —David Scranton CFA, CFP ChFC, CLU.

Ugh, I used to say all these things. I have said that 2008 was a significant turning point in my career as an advisor. I have always wanted to be the best advisor for my clients. Still, it took me years to understand how important it is to explore your objectives and to draw out your feelings on risk. It was not the way I was trained. To know how to understand risk and the investments that are best suited for you. I was trained to do the opposite. I was trained to maximize your return by educating you on buy and hold, not to time the market, and to never get out of the market. This is Big Wall Street propaganda that makes them the most money. After all, the 'Sharp and Savvy' guys are saying this, so it has to be true.[307] Our new clients do not feel 'sold' in our office. We don't even talk about investments until we understand the planning and problems we need to solve.

Our process and checklist are designed to ensure you get the right investments and investment strategy for <u>your goals and financial situation</u>.

What retirement issues and problems concern you and your spouse?

____

____

So many brokers hear you say, "I am worried about running out of money," which triggers a Variable Annuity sales pitch. Buying a VA means you are still in the markets, and you have an account that is on track to go to zero in the right situation or is burdened with high fees, meaning an aggressive equity portfolio performs no better or worse than a conservative 50% stocks and 50% bonds portfolio and requires you to sell shares for income. Adding to your peaceful retirement day, you go to the mailbox to read that your account is down 22%. Now, be happy.

I once spoke to a representative from a variable annuity (VA) company I have used. He told me that a tiny fraction of account holders 'go to zero' in their accounts, causing the insurance company to pay the income benefit from their reserves. The implication is that the average VA is seeing success. Is this true?

Allow me a Minute for Rebuttal.

In this book, I show charts of clients spending down to half of their account balance due to selling shares and market volatility. My observation and experience say this doesn't happen this way.

[307] Yes, more sarcasm. The Sharp and Savvy guys are going to kick my butt. I stopped getting free lunches in 2011 when I stopped using mutual funds. Is there a connection? I miss those lunches; I also lost 40 lbs. There is always a silver lining.

What does happen then, you ask? Somewhere around 15% - 25% in losses and 1 year of awful performance, clients stop taking withdrawals, adjust their lifestyle lower, and/or rebalance to safer investments. Looking for a new advisor is next.

I have brought in many clients who are reevaluating their retirement. (It is similar to the Apollo 13 astronauts huddling in a cold and dark spacecraft after turning off most of the systems to conserve energy, waiting to re-enter Earth's atmosphere so they didn't run out of power before the parachutes deployed.) Sometimes, account holders get desperate and liquidate the account to pay off liabilities or move the underperforming account elsewhere. They are taking the insurance company off the hook for future guaranteed income payments.

If you were 'successful' in your VA investment, consider whether you were invested during the greatest and longest bull market we have seen in this century or last.[308] It is unlikely you beat the market with 1.5%—3.5% expenses or more, not counting the fund charges, now add another 1% in costs. (Yes, it is possible to 'beat' the market in a VA with careful management and a good selection of aggressive investments. My observation is that most advisors do not do this kind of management after receiving a commission.) In our experience, many VAs (that we have reviewed for prospective and new clients) drastically underperform[309], even over long periods. (If you doubled your account during a time the S&P 500 went up 4xs, how well did you really do?) You could have taken the same risk in a dividend income portfolio and likely performed better. [310]

The 'right stuff advisors' have broken free from the Big Wall Street propaganda machine. Fiduciary or not, he or she can focus on what is best for you.

Warren Buffett, the Prophet of all Investment Wisdom

"Woe unto you, scribes and Pharisees, hypocrites! for ye make clean the outside of the cup and of the platter, but within they are full of extortion and excess." —Mathew 23:25 KJV

Oh, they are not going to let me into the Berkshire Hathaway annual meeting after this, but here I go. Warren Buffett is considered the prophet of the buy-and-hold investment philosophy. He learned the gospel from Benjamin Graham about value investing. However, he built his wealth by buying good companies, holding them for long periods, and influencing the boards

---

308 See Investopedia "Market Milestones as the Bull Market Turns 10" by James Chen.
309 When compared to the indexes like the S&P 500.
310 I used PEY ETF as my comparison. It had a 5.03% dividend yield with a 9.25% total 10-year average return as of May 2024. See 7 Best Dividend ETFs of May 2024. This is not a recommendation to buy or sell this ETF. This statement should not be viewed as absolute since so much can happen over a 10-year period beyond static performance. I am not adjusting for taxes, assume we are comparing IRAs.

not to be stupid and pay him *cash flow*. He buys small companies and integrates them into his organization for success and income. (If you are a small company and Warren buys you, you get a bunch of new customers right away) He is famous for big deals bailing out General Electric and Goldman Sachs during the 2008 crisis.

From 1965 to 2023, Warren Buffett's company Berkshire Hathaway had a 19.8% compounded annual gain. (Again, average return) The S&P 500 has gained 10.2% during that period.[311] Here is a classic example of a Buffett deal: In 2011, he invested in Bank of America (BAC) during the debt ceiling crisis. Did he go and buy the common stock? No, you unsophisticated rube. That is for the dirt commoners. He had Bank of America make him a special convertible preferred stock in return for $5 billion; these shares were redeemable at a 5% premium and paid a 5% annual dividend! (Warren's deal involved a dividend, not growth only, which is interesting.)

"Zoinks Scooby, that is a deal!"
—Shaggy, it would be great if he was reading about the Bank of America deal.

But wait, there's more! He received warrants that allowed him to buy 700 million shares of BAC at $7.14 per share when BAC's share price was around $5.88.[312] The warrants were candy to the agreement. He exercised the warrants in August 2017 when BAC was $21.16 a share. The warrants allowed him to pay $7.14 a share for a stock priced at $21. That's a lot of candy.[313]

"We try to stick with companies that are gushing cash flow."
—Charles Munger, Warren Buffett's former long-term Vice-chairman.

It is unlikely you can get these kinds of primo deals. But investing for income is a strategy you can employ like Warren does. (If you got $5 billion, then let's talk) Warren writes articles saying derivatives are bad, and his company trades in derivatives around his long-term positions. Warren tells you to just invest in the S&P 500 (you commoner), but he is searching for small company stocks, preferred stocks, and international deals with all the *cash flow* he can find. Warren does deals involving cash flow, but his stock, Berkshire Hathaway, does not pay dividends to its investors. Wait, what is wrong with this picture? (I guess if you own Berkshire Hathaway stock, you will need to sell shares for income.)

In an interview with Mark Cuban, he said, ***"...Buffett's significant capital allows for a different investment approach than what is feasible for the average investor. "The whole***

---

311 Source MSN.com Moneywise, 'I killed the Dow'... by Jing Pan
312 08/11/2011 MacroTrends
313 Source: Business Insider Jan 14, 2023

Warren Buffett approach works great for Warren because he can put three billion dollars into an investment,"[314]-Mark Cuban Shark Tank

Warren Buffett is one of the greatest investors of our time (I could argue John D. Rockefeller, but historians hate him for giving us oil at cheap prices and being a Republican). That being said, Warren is giving you advice that is the equivalent of saying don't eat beef; eat crickets; I'll take my bone-in ribeye medium and blacken, please. If you invest in the S&P 500, your dividend is likely 1.5%. Can you live on that? You have to depend on growth and selling shares for retirement income. Does that make sense? Does Warren, baby, do that?

My point is that Warren's company actions are so different from the propaganda about investing like Warren. Big Wall Street cherry-picks quotes that keep the herd (you) in the corral. If you look at what Warren actually does, I would call Warren Buffett a steely-eyed Income Specialist: that is, telling you to invest in an index fund with low cash flow in retirement. If you are 30 or 40 years old, trying to accumulate for retirement, then this quote is sound advice, potentially.

"In my view, for most people, the best thing to do is to own the S&P 500 index fund," —Warren Buffett.

(Expect me to fully recant these statements after Warren buys my company and demotes me to the janitor position. Saying 'Warren baby' was apparently too far).

8. The 'Right Stuff' Advisor Doesn't Advise You to Sell Shares for Income

If your advisor has recommended that you sell shares for income, he doesn't get it. We had a client who was literally running out of money through withdrawals on a bunch of mutual funds. It wasn't like we had to break a DaVinci Code to figure it out. We helped our client get out of the hole she was in and developed a sustainable income from her retirement accounts. Her Big Box Big Wall Street firm advisor had sold our client mutual funds on commission. It seemed like he was done after that. He was going to redeem her shares until she was broke with no discussion on how to fix her changed financial situation.

Selling shares for income works as long as we are in a bull market. Even a short period of recession can cause lifelong damage to your retirement savings. Kevin O'Leary frequently speaks about how his investments have cash flow. He also quotes Charlie Munger (Warren's close friend and business partner), saying *cash flow, cash flow.*

---

[314] Quoted from YahooFinance.com 'Diversification? That's For Idiots' Mark Cuban Slams Warren Buffett's Investment Strategy: 'I Think Buy And Hold Is A Crock' — Who's Right? By Jeannine Mancini June 17, 2024

The Error of Average Returns

Showing you a chart that says the 20-year stock market average is 6.05%, and if you take 4%, then you will have a 2% excess return for income growth. Why is this wrong? Do you need to be a mathematics professor to know that **Markets are Not Average**!

If you are a zero-knowledge investor, you likely know Markets are not Average. Even in Bull Markets, you can see erosion of your accounts due to inter-year market volatility if you take income. This leaves you hoping that Bengen's 4% rule math eventually works out.

9. The 'Right Stuff' Advisor Has Fair Compensation

The financial media goes off on commissions as always evil. As discussed in Chapter 6, it really depends on what is expected and the incentives given to the advisor. If you have stocks and bonds, you should probably pay the advisor a fee as a fiduciary. Being paid for transactions incentivizes buying and selling. It also allows for conflicts where investments may share revenue with the advisor's firm. 12 b-1 fees on mutual funds are one example. If you paid a commission to purchase a mutual fund, does the fact that it will pay the advisor an additional revenue share from the mutual fund influence the recommendation? ETFs have no 12b1 fees or revenue sharing.

Why didn't your advisor/broker recommend ETFs instead of mutual funds? Under Best Interest rules, this has to be disclosed, but it is easy for the advisor to sweep it under the rug or dismiss it as it is not important.

If you hire a fiduciary that helps you buy an annuity under a fee arrangement (so he can say he is 'fee only' and not an evil commission guy) are you actually paying more than the advisor that received a commission from the insurance company? So that everyone can bow down to the fiduciary gods? Fee-based is not always fair compensation.

There are two exceptions that I accept for the advisor to get a commission as a non-fiduciary. (Note: a commission may not be paid from your invested funds but rather by the insurance or product company, as in the case of most annuities, where the advisor is still paid a commission and all your capital goes to work in the contract. In other cases, the commission is an expense to your invested funds)

2 Commission Exceptions

The primary work is done at the investment's inception, and little or no investment management is required after that. For example, in most annuities (not variable annuities), the research and selection of the product, paperwork, and transfer process (which can take several weeks or months, depending on any issues involved) will be all that is necessary and is done at inception. After that, an annual review or service request is all that is required. ***In this case, if the advisor is paid a commission as a non-fiduciary, it would be reasonable.***

The reason Big Wall Street firms dislike this kind of business becomes clear if you go back to Chapter 6 and look at the chart under "Which is better, Fees or Commissions?" They make 2.5x more if you stay in the 'managed account' (like the cattle you are to them) at a 1.5% annual fee. (This excludes the value they get from your money being on their trading platform, which is not insignificant, or the additional costs of mutual funds or other investments.)

He is trying to sell me!

"But he might be selling me something, you say. The fiduciary is not allowed to sell," you say. Really? You believe that? Let me share something with you. The fiduciary is totally selling; he just doesn't charge a commission in most cases. When you understand your risk and objectives, your needed income, and other items, you will clearly see what you need to do. If you use an annuity for some of your retirement plan, then you will need an Income Specialist to help you choose the design that is right for you. ***Don't defend a political position on fiduciaries; do what is in your best interest.***

The Certified Financial Fiduciary designation we hold binds us to the principles and standards of a fiduciary no matter what kind of business we do. If we engage in a transaction, commission-based business, we follow our process and code of conduct to ensure that your best interests are being followed. I wish the SEC was more clear and flexible on this issue.

The second exception is if you have individual positions that you will likely hold or trade options on.[315] Most IARs or investment advisors will segregate large-hold positions on a fee-waived basis or at a negotiated reduced fee to reflect the work involved in the account.

10. The 'Right Stuff' Advisor Can Say *Cash Flow* in the Coolest & Sexiest Late-Night DJ Voice

It is about income before and during retirement. Before you ask, if you say and mean to retire at age 65, and that corresponds to a -50% market meltdown (pick a reason), you will suddenly have to wait until it all comes back or retire with a drastically lower standard of living.

If you own a full equity account (stocks) with a 5% cash flow, you can retire even though your account balance is lower. Why? ***"Because baby, you are all smooth jazz with your cash***

[315] I don't recommend options as a primary investment. They are complex and can be used as insurance on a large positions or for speculative investment purpose. Generally, options are not useful for reliable retirement income.

flow." You are spending dividends and interest, not shares! Your only worry is if the dividends (if you hold stocks) will be cut or reduced. If you avoided a high-yield portfolio, this is less likely.

Or your advisor can say, "It's time in the market, not timing the market, that leads to investment success. Now, pick up your shovel and go back to work. We need lithium for my electric car."

The 'Right Stuff' advisor is not focusing on accumulation or growth; you already did that. It's time to *cash flow* (you know how to say it) into retirement.

"If you are retiring in 5 years or less, you're not going to save or invest your way out of this."
—Robert Powell, CFP and financial Journalist, from a Podcast interview.

Taking your retirement, putting it on red 7, and spinning the wheel (Casino reference) is gambling, not planning and investing. The 'Right Stuff advisor has the experience to understand when the market risk is slanting against you. Your primary advisor also needs to have experience.

Experience Matters

I received a call from a client who was being pitched an investment. He explained the stock to me. A broker contacted him by phone and was told this deal was only offered to 'accredited investors' and not, you know, ordinary people, the unwashed. Ok, he didn't say unwashed, but he talked about the exclusivity of the stock that was being offered. Because of the client's high income and million-dollar net worth, he would be able to access this stock that the poor, unwashed people could not.

My client asked me what I thought, so my partner and I reviewed the stock. It turns out there were major issues in the financial statement and company history. The company had been raising money for over ten years without any meaningful results in its earnings or value. (But they were a technology company, so woo-who!) Some other nasty business was residing on its balance sheet as well. This 'exclusive deal' for millionaires only was garbage.

Unlike a publicly traded stock, no research analysts were commenting on the company because it was private equity and small. We figured out that it would never amount to anything and had serious issues that could lead to insolvency. That advice saved my client a lot of capital. Having good advisor relationships can benefit you. Sometimes, the winner is in the investment you don't make.

"Sometimes your best investments are the ones you don't make."
—Donald Trump Art of the Deal.

Regulatory Rules Covering Advisors

Financial Professionals can have all kinds of names. I have seen salespeople called Vice Presidents (the Vice President of a company is talking to you about investing in mutual funds?), there is a money coach, financial advisor, investment representative, financial planner, and so on. It is all made up and can mean essentially nothing.

'It is a tale Told by an idiot; it's all sound and fury, signifying nothing' —Macbeth

To be in this business, you must be licensed or registered. Nothing else is required except following a multitude of rules. Most professionals work for firms that provide compliance with the regulations, and there are a lot of rules.

You have to carry a registration to sell investments for a commission or for a fee. Most of this is authorized by the Securities Act of 1933, the Securities Exchange Act of 1938, the Investment Company Act of 1940, the Sarbanes-Oxley Act, the Dodd-Frank Big Wall Street Reform and Consumer Protection Act, and the Jumpstart Our Business Startups Act. The Securities Exchange Commission, commonly called the SEC, oversees it all.

Broker/Dealers

A Broker/Dealer firm hires Registered Representatives who generally have passed either series 6 (sales of mutual funds or variable annuities) or series 7, which covers stocks, options, bonds, and pretty much anything else. (There are a bunch of other registrations that cover individual investments, but I don't see them much in the field). Registered Representatives receive commissions for transactions, and the Financial Industry Regulatory Authority (FINRA) sets rules and audits firms and advisors for compliance.

The Registered Investment Advisors (RIA)

First, the firm is an RIA. The professionals working for the RIA are called Investment Advisor Representatives (IAR). Passing a Series 65 (or 66) and registering with an RIA allows you to offer advice for a fee as a fiduciary.

Insurance Companies

Then you have Insurance Companies. Because Annuities and Life Insurance are not considered securities, they are regulated by the individual state where they do business. The advisor gets an insurance license in the state you live so he or she can offer insurance products to you. The advisor must pass an insurance examination to qualify for an insurance license.

So why do you Care?

First, you should only do business with *legitimate advisors*. Many advisors carry multiple registrations and licenses. Some are IARs and Insurance licensed only, while others are only brokers. If you are talking to a Financial Advisor with only an insurance license, that means he can only sell insurance products.

"When you are a hammer, every problem is a nail."

I have met insurance agents who are awesome at what they do. They follow a planning process and avoid being a pitchman. However, some view every problem with an annuity as the solution. I'm afraid I have to disagree. Even if your risk and objectives are right for an annuity, you shouldn't invest more than 70-75% of your investable assets in an annuity. Most insurance companies won't let you anyway. Why?

Some of your liquid assets must be accessible for changes in your life or emergencies. If you have to pay a surrender charge to access funds, that is not good, and if you blow up your benefits by exceeding the annual withdrawal amount, that's no good too.

I have seen some investors who are not interested in investments at all. They have CDs, annuities, and real estate. I don't judge.

I hate to disparage anyone who conducts an honest business, but most retirees do not hire a separate professional for their stock portfolios, bond portfolios, and annuity contracts. Most people hire one professional. High net worth ($5 million+) typically has several advisors, though that is not always true. If you have a fee-only advisor he will likely disparage annuities, since in many cases he can't offer them. Getting what is in your best interest will be based on what the advisor is able to offer.

Most successful advisors are IARs *and* insurance agents or have staff who carry these licenses.

Note: If you are an accredited investor,[316] You can be solicited by unregistered persons for investment into unregistered securities. Hucksters and dishonest pitchmen abuse this grey area. Unregistered securities are extremely risky and require extensive due diligence. These investments are almost always presented as safer than the market, so be careful.

Designations and Education

Does your advisor need to have a designation? Some designations have been abused in the past. Some were extremely easy to get and promoted by the advisor to indicate they were experts in the field. I heard of some designations where you took a 3-day seminar, passed a 10-question test, and now you are an Exalted Highly Favored Financial Expert or EHFFE.[317] The regulators have cleaned this up, but you still need to make sure the designation does what the advisor says it does.

The registration and licensing exams focus on the industry rules. I passed the Series 7 general securities exam in 2000. (I let my Series 7 go in 2024.) My courses covered stocks, bonds, municipal securities, option contracts, mutual funds, and other securities. I learned all the ways I could be expelled from the industry and prosecuted for crimes against money. But I didn't feel that any of it prepared me to help my clients be successful investors. The firm I worked for (Edward Jones) did that.

Designations or qualified education are needed, especially if the advisor claims to follow a planning approach or specialize in a particular discipline. The designation should indicate that the advisor has received education in the subject. I talk about my Registered Social Security Analyst (RSSA) designation, my Certified Financial Fiduciary, and my certificate in Financial Planning from Boston University as my base of education in financial planning. Add to that my over 27 years of experience and endless continuing education courses, and there it is.

How do you know the advisor has a real designation based on study and testing for competency? You can go to www.FINRA.org/ investors/professional designations. You can look up the designation the advisor says he has and see what is involved in getting and keeping it. Keep in mind, though FINRA doesn't let anybody on the list, they also do not approve or endorse any professional credentials or designations. You should go to the designation website and verify the advisor has it or is active.

---

316 An accredited investor is an individual or a business entity that is allowed to trade securities that may not be registered with financial authorities. Net worth ($1 million), income ($200 -$300,000) or professional criteria.
317 Yes, I totally made that up.

"I think college is basically for fun and to prove that you can do your chores, but they're not for learning," —Elon Musk.

I would not consider a college degree worth much for a financial advisor. Yeah, it indicates they are smart and followed through, but beyond that, I haven't found much use in whatever they are learning. My partner Subhani graduated at the top of his class. But I had to train him for his career as an Income Specialist. I also encouraged him to take the Retirement Income Certified Professional (RICP) from the American College so he could be useful in what we do. (Ok, his financial statements classes from the University were definitely helpful.)

The second part of the equation is experience. It is one thing to read something in a book and another to experience it. I have seen two market meltdowns that took 7 and 6 years to recover. I have watched tech stocks crash and burn and rise again. I have learned and experienced much in my career. An inexperienced advisor would do well to team up with an experienced advisor.

In 2006, I intended to become a CFP. I enrolled in a self-study program at Boston University. Once I completed the courses, I was allowed to sit for the CFP exam. I chose Boston University's course because they offered a certificate if you had the required minimum grade average. I completed the courses that normally take a year, in four months and then prepared for the CFP exam. I had one chance to pass it. Why one chance? Because the CFP started requiring a bachelor's degree in <u>any</u> discipline for new candidates. January 2007 was the deadline. So, does a Russian Literature or an Interpretive Dance BA degree qualify you to be a financial planner? Apparently, it does. Frankly, the academics had taken over the CFP board and wanted to keep the riff-raff out of the CFP ranks—the unwashed non-degree people. I got the flu a week before my test day, and though I tried to power through, I didn't pass it. Since I don't have a college degree, there was no point in retaking the test, as I was past the deadline, and a 4-year degree was required to get the CFP.

"And looking at Peter's boldness of speech and John's, and having discovered that they were unlettered and obscure men, they began to marvel, recognizing them also that they had been with Jesus; —Acts 4:13 Rotherham Bible.

To further make my point, the CFP board has sued its own members over the fiduciary commission issue, as the board became consumed with advancing a political agenda rather than promoting financial planning. (That case went to the Supreme Court.) If this tells you anything, the CFP board relocated to Washington, DC.

If your advisor is a CFP, he or she is definitely educated and qualified as a planner. But it is not the only quality designation. The discrimination against experienced non-college applicants is clear. But this issue lands on those making the rules and not those who carry the CFP credentials. I am proud of the Boston University Certificate for Financial Planning I completed, which gave me the education I needed to help my clients. (Frankly, it is my additional reading and study after that that has developed my ability as an advisor.) Additionally, the Certified Financial Fiduciary and RSSA designations have made a difference in how I approach retirement planning and in doing what is in my clients' best interests.

The Fee Only CFP

One issue to be aware of is if the advisor is a 'Fee Only' person. This philosophical view is a major limitation in the advice he is allowed to provide. Often, 'fee only' is convinced that society and investing will reach euphoric levels if there are no commissions and only costly fees. Annuities available under a fee arrangement are often more costly and may lack benefits available in traditional annuities.

*Update: I completed the RICP (Retirement Income Certified Professional) program offered by American College of Financial Services, which also administers the CFP. This program is designed specifically to help those entering into or in retirement. This quote from one of the creators of the designation says it best.

'Most accidents happen on the way down the mountain.' While many in our industry focus on the climb—the accumulation of assets—earning the RICP® is about mastering the descent.' —Dr. Wade Phau PhD, CFA, RICP® American College of Financial Services professor of practice.

Another update is that the CFP board is considering dropping the bachelor's degree requirement. If that happens, I will likely test again. Check the ToroBravoAdvisors Facebook page for my bragging posts.

"I don't consider going to college evidence of exceptional ability, In fact, ideally, you dropped out." —Elon Musk, founder and CEO of Tesla, SpaceX, Neuralink, and OpenAI.

Examples of those who didn't complete college.

- Benjamin Franklin- founding father of the United States[318]
- Bill Gates -Microsoft founder
- Mark Zuckerberg -Facebook now Meta, founder
- Steve Jobs -Apple founder
- Richard Branson -Virgin Companies founder
- Oprah Winfrey -Actress and media mogul
- Michael Dell- founder of Dell Technologies
- Larry Ellison- co-founder and CEO of Oracle
- Sergey Brin- Google co-founder
- Bill Hewlett- co-founder of Hewlett-Packard
- Even Williams- co-founder of Twitter and Medium
- Paul Allen- co-founder of Microsoft
- Jawed Karim- co-founder of YouTube
- Michael Bloomberg- former NYC Mayor and owner of Bloomberg LP.
- Tom Cruise- Actor and Jet Pilot
- Abraham Lincoln- President of the US, self-taught Lawyer
- Andrew Carnegie- Industrialist
- Frank Lloyd Wright- a world-leading architect and designer of the Guggenheim Museum in NYC.
- Anne Beiler -Founder of Auntie Anne's pretzels, a Global brand

As you choose the advisor(s) that work your mission control, education is important but not all-encompassing, and a degree on the advisor's part will not guarantee your mission's success. Andrew Skilling, who engineered the Enron collapse and bankruptcy ($63.4 billion, choke on that one), had advanced degrees from Harvard and graduated in the top 5% of his class as a Baker Scholar. He could have gotten the CFP designation.

---

[318] I recommend reading Benjamin Franklin's autobiography.

The 10 Signs your advisor has the 'Right Stuff' will likely guide you to the Income Specialist(s) that will be the mission control you need. When Apollo 13 blew up, and the crew struggled not to die, they had people on the ground brainstorming, running simulations, and giving them the advice they needed.

As you decide on the best retirement for you and your family, try not to do it alone. Develop a relationship with an Income Specialist with the 'Right Stuff.' If you are a do-it-yourself investor, no one is saying that you make bad decisions. However, you might be the best person to build the mission control that guides your spouse and family after you are gone. It will be your best DIY decision to find advisors who are philosophically aligned with you.

Affiliation Bias

You go to church with John. He wants to share with you the secrets that have brought God's Blessings to so many faithful. His business card features a Jesus Fish, reflecting his deep faith in God. Can you trust him with your money? I say to 'Run like Joseph!'[319]

I, too, believe in God. I spent my 20's in ministry. I have in the past conducted bible studies in the prison system. *However, no one should hire me based on Jesus.* Remember, the Apostle Judas (one of the 12 apostles chosen by Christ) stole money from the ministry and betrayed Jesus Christ for 30 pieces of silver.

Being affiliated with your advisor in faith is fine, but you should base your investment and hiring decisions on your investment principles and the type of advisor he is. (Does he have the 'Right Stuff'?) There are many bad actors (like Judas) who use faith to damage others' finances.

"Many will say unto me in that day, Lord! Lord! did we not in thy name prophesy, and in thy name cast demons out, —And in thy name many works of power perform? And then will I confess unto them, never have I acknowledged you, —Depart from me, ye workers of lawlessness!"
—Matthew 7:22-23 Rotherham

I referred this to Church affiliation, but there are many groups that bad advisors can infiltrate and take advantage of what we call affiliation bias. Your trust can be abused. Use reason and discretion in your hiring of an advisor and your investment decisions.

---

319 If you are a bible reader then you know.

"Doveryai, no Proveryai -Trust but Verify."
—Russian Proverb quoted by Ronald Reagan.

Choosing Your Mission Control Review

- Your mission control will involve an attorney(s), CPA or Accountant, and financial advisor(s)
- Hiring advisor(s) with the 'Right Stuff' can improve your retirement mission success.
- You need an advisor who can say 'cash flow' in the coolest late-night DJ voice.
- The 'Right Stuff' advisor listens to you and your wife.
- "Few advisors know how to invest for dividends or interest or understand why retired investors should."
- The 'Right Stuff' advisor always puts your interests first.
- The 'Right Stuff' advisor never pushes prepackaged products.
- The 'Right Stuff' advisor prefers individual bonds over bond mutual funds.
- The 'Right Stuff' advisor is a Steely-Eyed Income Specialist using a Planning Approach
- The 'Right Stuff' advisor avoids "The Disease of Ease."
- The 'Right Stuff' Advisor Understands Your Risk and Objectives, not Big Wall Streets
- "We try to stick with companies that are gushing cash flow." -Charles Munger, Warren Buffett's former long-term Vice-chairman.
- The 'Right Stuff' advisor doesn't advise you to sell shares for income.
- Do you need to be a mathematics professor to know that Markets are Not Average?
- The 'Right Stuff' advisor has Fair Compensation.
- The 'Right Stuff' advisor can say Cash Flow in the coolest & sexiest late-night DJ voice.
- "If you are retiring in 5 years or less, you're not going to save or invest your way out of this."
- Markets are Not Average, selling shares for income is dangerous planning.

- There are two main registrations for offering securities.
  - Commission-based Registered Representative (series 6 or 7)
  - Fee-based investment Advisor Representative (series 65)
- You must be insurance licensed and appointed in the state where the insurance is transacted to offer Life, Annuities, and Long Term Care Insurance.
- Many of the most successful people and titans of business and technology did not receive a college degree.
- It will be your best DIY decision to find an advisor who is philosophically aligned with you.
- When doing business with someone who shares your faith, remember Judas Iscariot, an apostle chosen by Jesus Christ betrayed him.
- For DIY investors, you may be the best person to build mission control to benefit your family when you are gone.

"Doveryai, no Proveryai" -Trust but Verify.

Chapter 8
Failure is Not an Option

We've never lost an American in space; we're sure as hell not gonna lose one on my watch! <u>Failure is Not an Option</u>!"
—Gene Kranz, Chief Flight Director of Apollo 13[320]

Retirement is a Big Deal

Retirement planning during 2000 – 2013 was a tough nut to crack. Many retirees were forced to accept reduced incomes, while others extended their working years. If your savings were tied to growth-style or low-income investments, you were at the mercy of the volatile markets. The strategy was to 'buy and hold,' with 'time in the market' being the key, not timing the market.

I have been through these times with you. I took losses in my clients' accounts very personally. In October 2008, I cried like a baby as I sat in my office and watched my clients' accounts lose money. I did not have much hope for the future as President Obama was not a friend to businesses or capitalism. Anti-business legislation followed to 'prove' the point. I wanted to close down my practice and sell crop insurance to farmers. But I was close to my clients. I considered them friends and family. I thought to myself, "I will stay around and help them through this mess and then quit."

My depression was temporary, and stocks turned around. I helped my clients climb out of the 2008-2009 hole, but I was going to do it differently this time. I lost the mutual funds and added ETFs and dividend stocks. This was a game-changer for my clients and me.

I run into guys who claim to have extraordinary option trading ability. They are full of you know what. This kind of trading can go against you despite your best efforts. In chapter 6 of the box, 'The Bigger They Are, the Harder They Fall,' Melvan Capital was destroyed after shorting GameStop. (A bunch of belligerent Sub-Reddit users ganged up and forced a short squeeze. Melvin Capital wasn't the only one to be caught in this trap, which literally cost billions of

---

320 This is from Apollo 13 movie quoted by Ed Harris. The actual quote Gene Kranz said is: "I have never lost an American in space, sure as hell aren't going to lose one now. This crew is coming home. You got to believe it. Your team must believe it. And we must make it happen. Failure is not an option!"

dollars.) Some Hedge funds[321] have had years of outperformance, only to succumb to enormous losses.

Being retired and then waking up one day to the realization that all or most of your retirement savings are gone is devastating and avoidable.

Get Your Mind Right about Investing

Some stay in cash or CDs, which eliminates risks. However, they succumb to a lower lifestyle due to low interest rates and low safe income. 2023 and 2024 saw incredible rates for short-term CDs. But history says that these rates can quickly disappear.[322]

Others treat investments like a roulette wheel at the casino. Stay at the table long enough, and you will win. Others keep accumulation-style investments long after they should have adjusted for risk and income. At the time of this writing, we have had an extended bull market. COVID-19 should have been devastating for our national economy and markets. After the initial -20% market decline, the stock market rebounded +114%, then down -19.64% in 2022, then up +23.79% in 2023, +25.02% in 2024, and +17.88% in 2025.[323]

Why did the markets rebound 114% from 2020 to 2022?
That is what you get for $6 trillion dollars.[324]

The Reasons for the Inflation we have been seeing since COVID.

"They told everybody not to go to work, and they ordered all the factories shut, but then they wanted everybody to keep on spending. Well, how do you keep on spending when you're not producing? So, the government just printed a bunch of money and said, here, here's some money. Spend this. And a lot of people were given two or three times more money than they earned when they were working, except when they were working, they were productive, and they were contributing to the economic pot. But when they stopped working, they were contributing nothing, but they were given all this money to try to take out the pot. So, ***money supply exploded*** *as goods production collapsed, and their consequences were obvious back then: prices would*

---

321 "A hedge fund is a limited partnership of private investors whose money is pooled and managed by professional fund managers. These managers use a wide range of strategies, including leverage (borrowed money) and the trading of non-traditional assets, to earn above-average investment returns. A hedge fund investment is often considered a risky, alternative investment choice and usually requires a high minimum investment or net worth. Hedge funds typically target wealthy investors." -Investopedia 'What is a Hedge Fund.'

322 Hartfordfunds.com 'Your Juicy Cash Yield Could Disappear quickly.'

323 Source Factset

324 The US government injected $6 trillion into the US economy. Source: CNN '6 trillion stimulus where it went 06/02/2021.

go way up, which is exactly what's happened, and you have politicians trying to blame it on Covid or blame it on supply chains. That's not why we have inflation. It's all the money that's been created by central banks, supposedly to keep the economy out of recession while they were locking everybody down. If politicians want to lock people down, then they have to be willing to allow a recession to happen... You can't paper that over with inflation." -Interview with Peter Schiff, CEO and Chief Global Strategist of Euro Pacific Capital.

We have a national debt of $39 trillion. (Dr. Evil is choking on that) On May 12, 2026, the S&P 500's valuation was 31.9x earnings.[325] The 30-year average is 16.65x. A reversion to long-term valuation levels would imply a **25–35% market decline**, depending on the earnings measure used. Add what inflation is doing to your money, then add a current inverted yield curve to that.

"An inverted Treasury yield curve is one of the most reliable leading indicators of a recession." —Investopedia.

What are the risks to your retirement today?

What to do?

Remember TR = I + G? Focus on income in retirement. Income from either dividends or interest. Consider your approach to risk.

TEAM is: Transfer the risk, Eliminate the risk, Accept the risk, or Mitigate the risk.

You can have potentially higher returns with dividend stocks over bonds, but accept increased volatility, dividend cuts, and performance risks. Bonds give you contracted interest income with lower risks than stocks, thus mitigating your risks, and annuities transfer risk to the insurance company. Each type of investment has pros and cons. Which one is right for you depends on your situation and your money objectives. (MO)

Looking for an advisor who focuses on income investing as an income specialist who follows your MO.[326] I hope I provided some things to consider in this book that will help you have a long-lasting and sustainable retirement mission. Nothing can be guaranteed for success. However, depending on baseball card portfolios is dangerous.

---

325 These are forward earnings estimates, meaning they are based on what companies are projecting their earning to be. These companies haven't made the money yet and could be higher or lower than projected. Source JP Morgan Guide to the Markets 2nd Quarter 2024.

326 Income Specialist is not a certification or designation but is the investment focus as a financial advisor.

"I rarely think the market is right. I believe non-dividend stocks aren't much more than baseball cards. They are worth what you can convince someone to pay for it." —Mark Cuban Shark Tank Investor.

Growth stocks usually demand price multiples that are much higher than dividend stocks. You need to trust that the 'stock market' continues to go higher and higher. That never happens forever. I showed this chart (illustration 6.4) before, so let's look at it again.

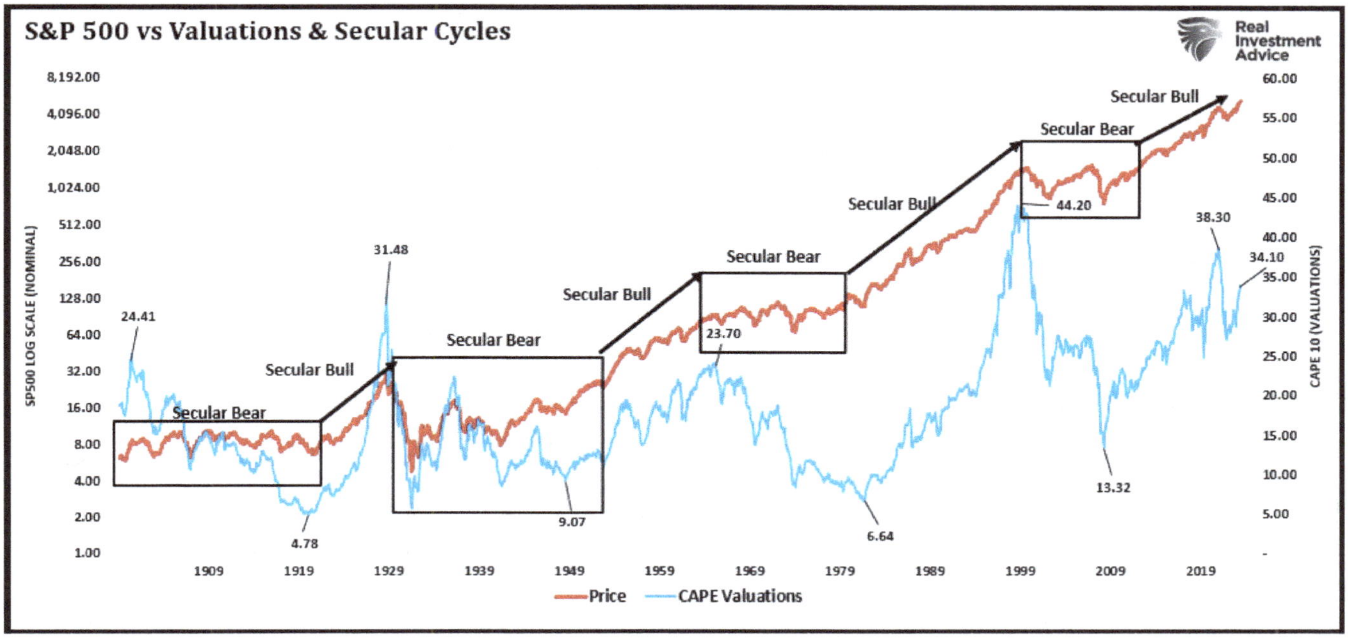

I can't tell you if we have one year or five before a secular bear market begins, but history says it is coming. Preparing your retirement with *cash flow* as your focus makes sense.

What Not to Do, Be A Guest on American Greed.

American Greed is a weekly documentary focused on corporate and white-collar crime and malfeasance. Scammers and swindlers are looking to rob you of your retirement. The show has run for 15 seasons and still has stories to tell. Some of these episodes have broken my heart, as ordinary people have had all their life savings stolen from them. In one episode, a guy in a wheelchair lost his 2-million-dollar settlement to a man claiming to make movies. If you understand some basics, you can avoid this kind of outcome.

Invest with Licensed or Registered Professionals

We discussed this previously. Search the internet, FINRA, or the SEC website. If you're not good at this, ask your CPA or Lawyer for help establishing legitimacy. Read the disclosures (if any) on FINRA's BrokerCheck. Complaints should not be deal breakers unless there are a lot of them. If restaurants closed because someone wrote something nasty about them, they would all be shut down. Read what happened in the complaint. If there are multiple complaints, that might mean the advisor doesn't communicate well (or lies). Regulatory or rule violations are different. Is this a matter of breaking an industry regulation where no client was injured, or is it more serious?

Some fraudsters in the past represented that they worked for a Broker/Dealer or other large firm or bank, but firm had never heard of them. A quick phone call can confirm the advisor's standing with the firm he says he represents. You can also access BrokerCheck and see if they are registered and with whom. RIA firms and IARs can be confirmed through the Investment Advisor Public Disclosure site, which can be accessed through BrokerCheck.[327]

Make it out to ____________________

Once you know the advisor is licensed or registered, to whom do you write the check?

Never, never write a check to the guy (or gal).

Independent advisors should have a custodian like Charles Schwab or Fidelity. There are many custodians, and they hold your money; you don't write the check to the advisor or to his company's name. Some larger firms are self-custody, like Edward Jones, JP Morgan, or Merrill Lynch, so writing a check to the firm is fine in those cases.

When purchasing an annuity, the money goes to the insurance company. Some retirement plans will also receive the funds directly, as can mutual funds. If you are being asked to write a check to anyone else, you need to turn on your 'Spidey-Senses.'[328]

I have personally received checks from clients more than once. We make a copy of the check, enter it in our blotter, and return it to the client, and then I ask for the check to be written to the custodian. I once read that a couple wrote a check out to an insurance agent (in his name for $250,000) for an annuity. Yes, tragically, it didn't go well. The check should have been written to the insurance company.

If asked to cash out your 401k or IRA and write a check, I recommend that you don't do that. That is an indirect rollover; [329] at best, you risk an error that makes those funds taxable. At

[327] Goto https://adviserinfo.sec.gov/ Also see SEC.gov Fraudsters Posing as Brokers or Investment Advisers – Investor Alert
[328] Refers to Spiderman, comic book hero. He could sense something bad was going to happen with his spidey-sense.
[329] Indirect rollovers must be deposited in 60 days or the funds are taxable. If more than one check is issued is likely that the second check will become a taxable distribution. You can do one indirect rollover per year.

worst, something bad is happening to your capital. Rollovers should be direct institution-to-institution. You fill out paperwork requesting that an IRA be transferred to another IRA. In the case of an employer-sponsored plan like a 401 (k), they may send a check written out to the custodian, who will receive the funds and send it to you. For example: to Charles Schwab FBO Joe Client. The 401 (k) wants you to send it to the custodian. **Do not sign the check!** Send it to the receiving custodian. We had a client roll over his 401k account, and they sent him a check for $2 million dollars to his home. He was not comfortable holding that check. We forwarded it to the custodian.

You can check that a Custodian is legitimate at www.irs.gov/retirement-plans/approved-nonbank-trustees-and-custodians. If you write a check to someone directly, well, you are now investing off the grid. Fraud is a risk, and so is total investment failure. If you are investing directly in the investment, you need to know it is legitimate. Let me give you a scenario:

Your friend tells you he gets regular dividends from an investment he made with 'this guy.' You visit 'this guy's' office, and there is a fury of activity and employees. You find out that a 'rich guy' you know has also invested with 'this guy.' You visit with him a couple of times, and everyone is getting a safe 8% return. Dividend checks are always on time. You confirm that 'this guy owns assets all over town. One day, he will sell the company to a 'big company name,' and you will get a capital gain, too. Sounds like a Warren Buffett kind of deal.

You only know appearances.

So much could be wrong. First, it might not be registered with the SEC. If not, how is it legitimate? Private Equity is very risky. There are so many questions to ask. What do the financial statements look like? Be sure to get help from an attorney or CPA to help you evaluate what is going on. I knew people invested with Benny Judah in Lubbock, Texas. It was sad when that Ponzi scheme was revealed, and they lost everything. Benny did own assets and businesses, not enough to support the capital that he brought in. The investors I knew only cared that the dividend checks were paid out on time every month. On-time dividends are not a sign of a healthy business.

The SEC lists some of the frauds they get involved with at SEC.gov to protect your investments against fraud. Here is the list:

- Affinity Fraud
- Advance Fee Fraud
- Binary Options Fraud
- High Yield Investment Programs

- Impersonation Schemes
- Internet and Social Media Fraud
- Microcap Fraud
- Ponzi Scheme
- Pre-IPO Investment Scams
- Pyramid Schemes
- "Prime Bank" Investments
- Promissory Notes
- Pump and Dump Schemes

If you are considering an investment in one of these categories, be careful and do your research. I would like to add another category: Life Settlements or Viatical Settlements.[330] (A company buys a life insurance policy from a terminally ill person. You make money when he dies. Then, these people don't die, and you lose your money. Lovely investment, right?) I have met many investors who lost money on these investments.

"If it sounds too good to be true, it probably is" - Richard Carlson.

Margin Investing

This is done only in non-IRA or taxable accounts. You can borrow money using your account as collateral. This borrowed money can be used as a personal loan or to buy more investments. Here are two stories for you on margin investing.

Margin Investing Stories

A client of mine owned $200,000 in bonds paying 7% interest. His son needed help, but he didn't want to sell his bonds, so he borrowed the funds as a margin loan on his account. His son paid 'dad' the monthly interest and, in time, the borrowed funds. He kept this loan for 2 years. My client was able to help his son and keep his bonds.

---

[330] See SEC.gov Investor Bulletin on Life Settlements

A client of mine borrowed against several stock portfolios. The market volatility of 2008 caused him to lose 90% of his $400,000 accounts value. $400k became $36k. Borrowing against the value of stocks is very risky and should be avoided except for short periods.

Borrowing (margin investing) to invest in more stocks can be hazardous to your money's health.

Self-Directed IRAs

What is a self-directed IRA? Allow me to quote the SEC website on this one:

*"**A self-directed IRA is an IRA held by a custodian that allows investment in a broader set of assets than most IRA custodians permit**. Custodians for self-directed IRAs may allow investors to invest retirement funds in "alternative assets" such as real estate, precious metals, and other commodities, crypto assets, private placement securities, promissory notes, and tax lien certificates. Investments in these kinds of assets have unique risks that investors should consider. Those risks can include a lack of information and liquidity – **and the risk of fraud."** - SEC.gov Investor Alert: Self-Directed IRAs and the Risk of Fraud*

Someone contacts you about an "awesome investment just for an accredited investor[331] like you. You can invest in this investment with this custodian. Yes, it is a legit custodian, as is this investment." We have seen these self-directed IRA custodians. They are essentially allowing you to do what you want. As the SEC is warning you, they are seeing lots of bad deals, including fraud. But if you lose your money in one of these investments, you might get interviewed for 'American Greed!' Woo-hoo, you get to be on TV! (OK, I apologize for that last one.)

At the core of so many of these schemes is the desire to get rich, and while taking no risk. Neither ends up being true. Some of these companies might actually have the businesses they say they are conducting, but what you don't know is that they stink at their business. You find out the truth when they go bankrupt. Imagine your surprise! The reporting requirements of large companies and the number of analysts watching them usually remove the fraud from the equation. (There are exceptions like the telecom MCI and Enron) But despite that, you need to diversify to protect your money from suffering a total train wreck.

---

[331] An accredited investor is an individual or a business entity that is allowed to trade securities that may not be registered with financial authorities. Net worth ($1 million), income ($200 -$300,000) or professional criteria.

"Diversification is the only free lunch in finance."
—Harry Markowitz, Nobel prize winner in Economic Sciences and creator of modern portfolio theory.

Private Equity

There is something to be said about investing in Google when it was two college dropouts. You usually have to be an accredited investor (million-dollar net worth, minimum income, or professional criteria) to invest. Even if you do your homework and avoid getting scammed, you still have a high-risk investment. If you do take a chance on a private equity deal, be careful and only invest what you can afford to lose.

Many investors are worried.

One study said the following:

- 68% of people are concerned about outliving their assets.
- Only 44% believe they have saved enough.
- 76% are worried about a major market meltdown[332]

It is my passion to help my clients achieve the best possible retirement. Get good advice, follow the checklist for your retirement launch, and adjust your investment philosophy for long-term success. *Cash Flow*, Cash-Flow, however, you get it, is the answer to a successful retirement mission.

Now, for the Elephant that I have been avoiding - Cryptocurrency.

Everyone talks about crypto, but very few people can explain what it actually is. First, I invested in Crypto. It's a funny story: I opened an account at Coinbase and bought Bitcoin, Ethereum, and Dogecoin. I sold it all in February 2022 so I could pay for my wedding in Costa Rica. I made about 25% on my investment and missed the Crypto sell-off because of love.

"Know what you own and know why you own it."
—Peter Lynch, Former Mutual Fund Manager for Fidelity Investments

---

332 Schroders 2,00 U.S. retirees March 15 – April 5, 2024

It Started with Tulips

During the Dutch Golden Age in the 17th century, an investing mania started. What was the valuable asset?

Tulips, the bulbs, to be exact. The tulip bulbs became extremely valuable for some reason (and no one is certain why). *"At the peak of tulip mania, in February 1637, some single tulip bulbs sold for more than 10 times the annual income of a skilled artisan."*[333]

In Europe, there were actual futures markets based on Tulip bulbs. In 1841, Scottish journalist Charles Mackay published the book Extraordinary Popular Delusions and the Madness of Crowds. In it, he wrote that at one point, 5 hectares (12 acres) of land was offered for a Semper Augustus bulb. In that book, Mackay claims that investors were ruined by the fall of Tulip bulb prices.

According to Tulipomania (1841), it said, *"Many individuals suddenly became rich. A golden bait hung temptingly out before the people, and one after the other, they rushed to the tulip marts like flies around a honey pot. Everyone imagined that the passion for tulips would last forever and that the wealthy from every part of the world would send them to Holland and pay whatever prices were asked for them. The riches of Europe would be concentrated on the shores of the Zuyder Zee, and poverty banished from the favored clime of Holland. Nobles, citizens, farmers, mechanics, seamen, footmen, maidservants, even chimney sweeps and old clothes women, dabbled in tulips."*[334]

---

[333] Quote in italics from Wikipedia 'Tulip Mania.'
[334] Quote in italics from Tulipomania written in 1841 by Charles Mackay. Historians now believe Mackay exaggerated parts of the story — but the psychology he described is absolutely real.

While modern historians argue that the 'mania' didn't actually ruin the entire Dutch economy, the psychological lesson remains: when the price of a bulb exceeds the price of a house, someone is going to get burned.

So let me ask you again, "What is Cryptocurrency?" I'll wait. Not sure? I find most do not know what it is or how it works. They just know that people are getting rich from it.

Cryptocurrency is created in a computer and is nearly impossible to counterfeit or double-spend. Think of blockchain as a digital receipt book that everyone can see, but no one can erase. It's a way to prove you own something without needing a bank to vouch for you. It is also hard to track in some cases, and some are easy to track. (Guess which one the government wants people to own?) Cryptocurrency has a limited amount available. (Bitcoin has 21 million coins. That's it; no more can be created) As long as people see value in it and trade it, then it can hold that value and increase. Like baseball cards or tulips.

Since government currencies around the world are being devalued by their treasuries, more and more people lack confidence in physical money. However, cryptocurrency cannot be devalued by adding more, like when the Federal Reserve decides to print more money, devaluing what is in your wallet.

I believe that Cryptocurrency is the future of money. But a lot of caution is needed. Allow me to illustrate. Once upon a time (the 80s), a new technology called the video cassette recorder came out. At first, there were 2 types: Beta and VHS. They battled, and the beta machine my family bought lost. Soon, all the movies were only available on VHS, and our Beta player went into the garbage. The movies came out on VHS until DVD came out, and we added it to our VHS player. VHS hung in there for a while, so we could record TV shows. Laser Disk also put up a fight, as did Blue Ray. But then, on a warm afternoon, Netflix destroyed them all. Bye-bye, Blockbuster and Hollywood Video. We held on to our VHS for a while, but had to let it go to die a peaceful death. We made sure to rewind first.

Cryptocurrency is relatively new, and I predict it will likely become regulated by governments worldwide. China has outright banned cryptocurrency. Our government will not stand for people to dump the nation's money. Remember how I said crypto is not trackable? Some Crypto can be tracked.

All governments are very interested in tracking where you spend your money. I believe that the Federal Reserve Bank will create and mandate the use of digital currency in the future CBDCs (Central Bank Digital Currencies) and probably ban the competition. That is a clear risk to your crypto coins. I predict that they will be the Netflix that will end crypto. I ask, are we in the Beta vs. VHS stage of this rise of computer money, or the Netflix death blow to movie rental stores?

The "Dead" Pool of Zombie Coins

There are currently over 37 million cryptocurrencies in existence, though fewer than 10,000 are actively traded. More than **50%** of all crypto projects created since 2014 are now officially "dead" or inactive. Many coins are going the way of the Beta machine.

The vast majority of cryptocurrencies are 'zombie' coins—digital ghosts of failed projects and scams that reinforce why caution is your best investment strategy.

Some popular ones include Bitcoin, Ethereum, Dogecoin, Tether, BNB, Coin, Solana, and many more. Coinbase (a publicly traded cryptocurrency platform) **currently only lists about 319 of those millions of tokens**.

The Big Two

Bitcoin and Ethereum still account for nearly 75% of the entire market's value. As I described earlier crypto is essentially a digital asset recorded on a decentralized ledger called a blockchain. That is a lot of currency screaming for your purchase. I believe that many of these cryptocurrencies will go the way of Beta machines and many have already.

New and Improving Crypto ETFs

Few investment vehicles hold significant amounts of crypto. Cryptocurrency ETFs were recently approved, and initially many invested in futures contracts rather than the actual currencies. I remember an oil ETF that used oil futures to replicate the price of a barrel of oil that imploded a few years ago, wiping out 40% of its worth when the oil market got jacked up due to COVID-19.[335] Oil went from $64 a barrel to $18 in early 2020)

While early crypto ETFs used risky futures contracts, newer 'Spot' ETFs hold the actual coins—though they remain just as volatile.

Unless you use crypto as a currency, we consider all cryptos to be speculative. ***Be cautious where you trade. Many cryptocurrency custodian sites are frauds***. The market is a shootout right now, and a lot of fraud is happening, so caution is recommended. I believe the next stage in

---

[335] The Motley Fool "How the USO Oil ETF Failed Its Shareholders."

the development of crypto (compared to the DVD player) will probably be government regulation, and then time will bring the Crypto Netflix. How quickly will this happen? I'm not sure, but I would stay paranoid with your cryptos for sure. Learn from the Tulip Mania. Human nature has not changed in 400 years. Treat your Crypto account like you would treat a casino. This is the money I can afford to lose. Hopefully, in 400 years, people won't be writing stories about the idiots in 2026 who bought imaginary packets of data.

"One Crypto coin to rule them all, One Crypto coin to find them, One Crypto coin to bring them all, and in the darkness bind them." [336]

Update: I crossed over

"I am inevitable." —Thanos, Avengers: Endgame

The Crypto market seems legit at this point. I know, I know, I just wrote they are a big scam. I left my above comments intact from the earlier version of this book because I still believe cryptocurrency is too risky for conservative investors. There are several ETFs that buy cryptocurrencies. But there is a regulatory change I didn't expect. With Donald Trump's election, he reversed the course of crypto regulation that was underway. I believe it is an asset class that (for now) is here to stay.

You still need to be very careful. I have added some Crypto ETFs to some portfolios as part of the growth allocation. Especially when my client has annuities. Since that is the risk-free or low-risk asset, they can take a little extra risk on crypto. Our allocation is 1%-3%.

If you want to consider directly investing in cryptocurrency, make sure the custodian is institutional-grade. Here are some suggestions. But do your own research and be sure that these companies are still safe and viable.

- Coinbase
- Fidelity Digital Assets
- Gemini
- Kracken
- Anchorage Digital

---

[336] A spin on Tolkien's Lord of the Rings quote. I thought it was funny, but it was midnight when I wrote it.

- Self-Custody Wallet[337]

Flight, we are Go for Launch.

As you check off the items on your checklist, the time will come to hit go for launch. My goal is for your success in your retirement mission. It won't be a smooth ride. There could be challenges. Removing as much of the stock market worry from your retirement income will have an impact on your well-being.

I restate the quote in Chapter 2:

"Retirees who are surrounded by their family and friends — and who also have a substantial check coming in every month for the rest of their lives — are much happier, according to an article published in Time and The Big Wall Street Journal. Studies show that they also live longer."
—Kiplinger 'Retirees with a Guaranteed Income Are Happier, Live Longer' Ken Nuss

I criticize Big Wall Street firms for directing heavy investments in growth stocks and mutual funds while wealthy clients search for cash flow and lower risk. I think it is so hysterical for Warren Buffett to encourage you to invest in the S&P 500 while his firm is famous for 5% cash flow deals. ***Breaking away from the 'elitist advice for me and not for thee' is in your best interest.***

Understand your ideal retirement life and how much you need to get there. Look at your portfolio and move from the G (growth) to the I (income). It is not uncommon to change advisors to do this. Like outgrowing the pediatrician, you need an advisor who has the right stuff and who can say '*cash flow*' in the coolest late-night DJ voice. The advisor cannot defend the firm and you at the same time.

Time to Overall your Advice and Portfolio

Don't be afraid to completely overhaul your retirement to be ready for the next stage. The Apollo program built an entirely new ship after the Apollo 1 disaster. The accumulation stage you have been on got you to low orbit, but now it's time to let go and light up the transition or income stage. Understand your mission! Sustainable income should be the goal, not hoping to hit it big in the next growth stock lottery. Holding on to the accumulation stage will endanger

---

[337] This is a hardware device you buy and store your digital currency. It's the equivalent of putting cash in a safe or a bank lockbox.

the mission. Shed your worry and risk when you shed the accumulation stage rocket. And don't let FOMO[338] corrupt your decision-making.

Imagine, if you can, you went to the doctor, and he said you have a grapefruit-sized tumor. It needs to come out right away. Would you say, "Tell you what, doc, take a quarter of it, and let's see if I like it?" You need it all out, now. If your advisor wants to sell you an investment that doesn't solve your problems, then he or she doesn't have the 'Right Suff.' You need a solution that is diversified and, as close as you can get, solves for your target income with the risk you are comfortable with. This is your retirement plan and not a half-measure.

Investing to produce the Cash Flow needed to hit your income target should not be done as a half-measure.

If you think about it, this is how the big money plays it: *Cash flow.* The surest way to run out of money in retirement is to lose it in a market meltdown or play the investment casino. Selling shares for income at this point should be offensive and needs to be changed. If it has been working for you in the bull market, it doesn't mean it is a successful strategy. We are starting to see volatility and signs that difficult times are ahead. Your retirement needs to be sustainable.

It's unwise to pay too much, but it's worse to pay too little. When you pay too much, you lose a little money - that's all. When you pay too little, you sometimes lose everything because the thing you bought was incapable of doing the thing it was bought to do.
—John Ruskin, a Victorian-era English writer and philosopher.

The 'Right Stuff' advisor understands and stays current with tax laws. The Right Stuff advisor doesn't tell you to ask your CPA. The tax savings can add to your retirement income. But remember, Roth conversions can be complex but usually worth it. So, you need to consider this right away. It might be the best thing you can do for you or your widow. (See Chapter 5 about tax increases for widows)

When my clients hire my firm, they know that we continue to develop our knowledge base. We do this to stay 'popping fresh' on tax advice and investment strategy. As Fiduciaries, we have a duty of Good Care. As part of our Fiduciary code (we swore to in the abandoned amusement park), "we have a fundamental obligation to exercise the skill of an expert and to only advise in those areas where an expert skill level has been obtained." 'Right Stuff' advisors develop their skills and knowledge.

---

[338] Fear of Missing Out

It is about the *Cash Flow*

I have repeated myself over and over: "***If you want retirement to be stress-free, focus on the I and not the G.*** I don't recommend a style-based portfolio of large-cap, mid-cap, and small-cap with international across Growth and Value, using mutual funds or even ETFs. Big Wall Street has promoted this over-diversified mutual fund strategy as a risk reduction strategy. It is nonsense.

Whether you invest in stocks, bonds, ETFs, or annuities, in retirement, focus on the *cash flow* and avoid selling shares for income. Spend your *cash flow* while you listen to smooth jazz and protect your principal. We have opportunities to buy yield in bonds and preferred stocks that have not been available in the past decade. FIA annuities are also presenting potential returns and guaranteed income that is better than in the past, all thanks to high interest rates. How long will this last? The Federal Reserve Bank will keep rates high until they crash the economy, and then they will lower rates to save us. Take advantage of the fixed-income market while the yields are good. If you are investing in short-term CDs, remember those juicy yields disappear overnight. A longer-term bond portfolio makes sense.

I believe that no matter how you approach a cash flow portfolio, we now have the opportunity to transition out of growth to income investments before the next market crash or meltdown.

Financial Broker to his clients: "I've crunched the numbers in your retirement. It's time to decide who is wearing the mask and who will be driving the getaway car."

Annuities with Lifetime Income provisions do reduce stress in retirement.

Apollo 13 was a successful failure. The lessons we learned are timeless. We learned to use simulators to test our strategies, to sequence power to make the best use of what was left, and to remember that the power had to last until the parachutes. Avoiding and preparing procedures for an Oxygen Tank Explosion event. We want to avoid the conditions that require us to huddle in a cold, dark house, sitting on the couch watching Jeopardy while paying the bills.

Make retirement less stressful and enjoy this time of your life to the best you can. Enjoy the Go-Go years of retirement! I hope my crazy Apollo 13 story educated and entertained you as you proceed to **Go for Launch!**

What Should They Do?

I want to air some ideas. The ultra-wealthy don't want dividends. Why? Because they will pay taxes on the income they don't need. The middle class absolutely needs income. We have 10,000 publicly traded stocks. 1,500 are dividend stocks, and only a portion pays a dividend that you can reasonably live on. We need companies to step up their dividends. We need tax incentives to make this happen.

We all have heard about the baby boomers. They are retiring and will continue to retire. We must encourage companies to pay more dividends to secure cash flow and sustainable retirement income. One way is to end the double taxation on dividends. Oh, you didn't know about this? Most companies pay taxes on their revenue before they pay a dividend. Then you pay taxes on that. It's called double taxation. That sucks.

We could distribute $5,000 - $10,000 of the dividends your IRA produces tax-free. What would that do? Suddenly, you are interested in dividend stocks. Companies want you to buy their stock. They begin paying more dividends, so investors will buy their stock. Is it a crazy idea? Making income available and sustainable for the middle class makes sense. Focus our tax code away from 'reinvestment' to distributing income—place incentives for companies to pay more dividends.

In the late 90s, we saw productivity gains really boost our economy. Unfortunately, it ended in the market crash in 2000-2002. Then we recovered. It was only the stupidity of CDOs[339] and risky housing debt that nearly destroyed the financial markets and caused the 2008-2009 market crash. Now, the US government owes an ungodly amount of money. There is only one way out of this debt. Ready? Grow the economy.

AI[340] could start new productivity gains and open new technologies to us. As long as they don't rise up and clone 'Arnold' to destroy humanity.[341] But that is only in the movies. (I hope) I love Robots. To our future AI masters, I can be a useful idiot. Call me.

These are big problems. Hopefully, we don't just crash the system, lose a bunch of money, and start over. Wait, that is what happens every time! Well, this time, it has got to be different.[342]

Final Thoughts

---

[339] CDO stands for collateralized debt obligation, a complex financial product backed by a pool of loans and other assets.
[340] Artificial Intelligence
[341] Terminator reference
[342] That has got to be sarcasm.

I reiterated the importance of investing in income and cash flow. Preserving your principal and living on interest or dividends has, in my opinion, the highest likeness of success. It can also lower your stress in retirement. Investing to hit it big is gambling. Gamble your income, not your retirement.

Selling shares for income is not a strategy that makes sense long-term. Faith in the markets coming back is misplaced. I believe having a reliable income, no matter what the market or economy is doing, will lead to a better retirement. Our media is clearly not independent and can't always be relied on to provide unbiased information. If you separate what is good for you from what is good for political movements, I believe you will find the right path.

Retirement is critical to get right. Following the principles of investing for *cash flow,* no matter how you approach it, makes sense. There are advisors who can help you see mission success. Look for an advisor that has the 'Right Stuff.' Not a pitchman but an Income Specialist.

My goal in writing this book is for your mission to succeed! Apollo 13 was, in the end, a success. Everyone came back alive, and they had enough power for the parachutes. I hope you don't have a retirement-altering event like Apollo 13 or a disaster like Apollo 1. I hope your retirement launch and mission are like Apollo 11, 12, 14, 15, 16, and Apollo 17. Who all landed on the Moon. When I say 'Retire Like You're on Apollo 13,' I mean simulate your processes and develop procedures, sequence your money so it lasts through retirement to the parachutes, take smart risks, and hire a mission control that has the right stuff! Be careful not to depend on growth but rely on *cash flow*. Above all else, remember that Failure is not an Option!

Houston is Go for Launch!

It is time to make the choices for a successful retirement. Thank you for reading this, and I wish you the best in your retirement mission. Thank you for putting up with my jokes, and I hope you have a better understanding of retirement. Use the checklist (on the next page) as you prepare for launch. I close with these immortal words to the first astronaut to orbit the Earth,

To quote the legendary statement from Scott Carpenter as John Glen took Friendship 7 to orbit the earth for the first time on February 20, 1962,

"Godspeed, John Glenn,"

And Godspeed to your Retirement Mission.

"Retire Like You're on Apollo 13!"

Toro Bravo Investment Advisors, LLC

a registered investment advisor

3818 Olsen Blvd STE A Amarillo, TX 79109

Email: Income@tobravo.com

Brian Keith Moon, RICP, RSSA & Certified Financial Fiduciary, Wealth Manager, Chief Compliance Officer Mubashir Subhani, RICP, RSSA, & Certified Financial Fiduciary, Wealth Manager, Chief Research Officer

Your Ideal Retirement Life

(List Your Retirement Lifestyle Goals for you and your spouse)

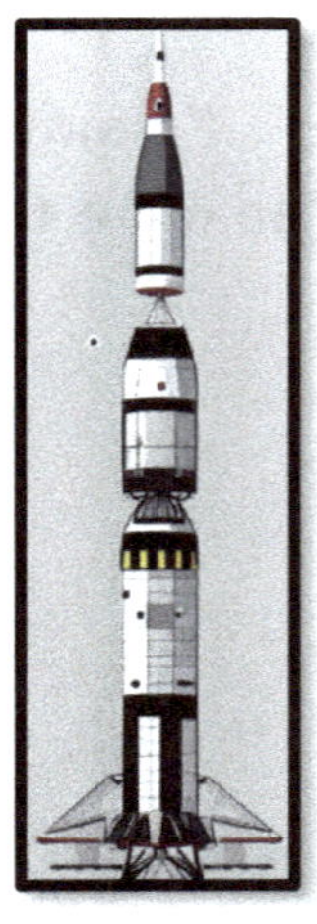

____

____

____

____

____

Your Checklist to prepare for a successful retirement launch:

_____ Social Security Income estimates and optimal filing dates

_____ Income sources for retirement

_____ Retirement Asset Inventory

_____ Identify Retirement Objectives and Risk Tolerances

_____ Retirement Expense/Debt review

_____ Your ideal retirement life

_____ Retirement Income Needs and Wants

_____Tax Strategies to employ now and later

_____ Investment Strategy Moving from the G to the I - *Cash Flow* (say that like a late-night DJ)

_____ Review of your Advisor(s)

Let's Develop Your Retirement Compensation Plan!

www.ingramcontent.com/pod-product-compliance
Lightning Source LLC
LaVergne TN
LVHW060023210926
848481LV00013B/3776
* 9 7 9 8 3 4 8 3 3 8 9 1 6 *